CW01019608

CONTAINING THE COLD WAR IN EAST ASIA

To the memory of my father

CONTAINING THE COLD WAR IN EAST ASIA

British policies towards Japan, China and Korea, 1948–53

PETER LOWE

Manchester University Press
Manchester and New York

distributed exclusively in the USA by St. Martin's Press

Copyright © Peter Lowe 1997

Published by Manchester University Press
Oxford Road, Manchester M13 9NR, UK
and Room 400, 175 Fifth Avenue, New York, NY 10010, USA

Distributed exclusively in the USA
by St. Martin's Press, Inc., 175 Fifth Avenue, New York, NY 10010, USA

British Library Cataloguing-in-Publication Data
A catalogue record for this book is available from the British Library

Library of Congress Cataloging-in-Publication Data applied for

ISBN 0 7190 2508 7 *hardback*

First published 1997

01 00 99 98 97   10 9 8 7 6 5 4 3 2 1

Printed in Great Britain
by Bookcraft (Bath) Ltd

CONTENTS

MAPS

ACKNOWLEDGEMENTS

The research for this volume was assisted generously by the Nuffield Foundation through its Social Sciences Small Grants Scheme and by the British Academy. I am extremely grateful to each body. Research and writing was advanced greatly by the extension of two periods of research leave by the Victoria University of Manchester and I am most grateful to my colleagues for supporting my applications for leave. It is a pleasure for me to thank the staffs of the various libraries and research institutions in which I have worked, in Great Britain: the Public Record Office, Kew; the British Library of Political and Economic Science; the Bodleian Library, Oxford; Churchill College, Cambridge; the John Rylands University Library of Manchester; the Library of University College, Cardiff; the Library of the School of Oriental and African Studies, University of London; and the Institute of Historical Research; and in the United States: the National Archives and the Library of Congress, Washington DC; the Dwight D. Eisenhower Library, Abilene, Kansas; the Hoover Institution on War, Revolution and Peace, Stanford, California; the Harry S. Truman Library, Independence, Missouri; the Seeley G. Mudd Library, Princeton University, New Jersey; and the Douglas MacArthur Memorial, Norfolk, Virginia.

For their encouragement, guidance and occasional diversion from the archives, I am especially appreciative of the help extended by John E. Taylor of the Modern Military Branch, Military Archives Division, National Archives, Washington DC; Erwin Mueller and Herb Pankratz of the Dwight D. Eisenhower Library; Dale Reed, Ronald Bulatoff, Pruda Load, Becky Mead and Kathy Reynolds of the Hoover Institution; Benedict K. Zobrist, Dennis Bilger and Elizabeth Saffary of the Harry S. Truman Library; and Edward J. Boone Jr. of the MacArthur Memorial.

Over the years I have derived encouragement and enlightenment from discussing various aspects of the subjects considered in this volume with the following: Chris Alcock, Roger Buckley, David Clayton, Bruce Cumings, Gordon Daniels, Michael Dockrill, Reinhard Drifte, General Sir Anthony Farrar-Hockley, Richard D. Finn, Jon Halliday, Callum MacDonald, Ian McGibbon, Ian Nish, William W. Stueck, Jr, Ann Trotter and Geoffrey Warner. I would like to thank all those involved in the preparation and production of the Thames Television series examining the origins and character of the Korean war, which was shown on British television originally in the summer of 1988: it was of great value to participate in the seminars accompanying the planning of this series and I am particularly grateful to Phillip Whitehead for his efficient direction of our discussions which led me to consider some features of the international situation in East Asia from a new vantage-point.

Transcripts/translations of Crown copyright in the Public Record Office, Kew, appear by permission of the Controller of HM Stationery Office. I wish to thank the following and, where appropriate, acknowledge permission to quote from collections in their custody: the Library of Congress for the Robert A. Taft, Sr. papers; the Dwight D. Eisenhower Library for the Eisenhower and Dulles papers; the Hoover Institution for the Chennault, Goodfellow, Judd and Lapham papers; the Harry S. Truman Library for the Acheson, Truman and Webb papers; the Seeley G. Mudd Library, Princeton, for the Dulles and Kennan papers; the MacArthur Memorial for the MacArthur papers; Sir George Kenyon and the estate of Sir Raymond Streat for the diaries of Sir Raymond Streat.

The editorial staff of Manchester University Press have shown great patience and have given me discreet promptings from time to time. Latterly I have dealt with Richard Purslow and Vanessa Graham and I am most appreciative of their practical encouragement. I am grateful to Rachel Armstrong and Gemma Marren for their help during the production process.

My father always took a keen interest in my research and writing and it was helpful to review progress with him. I regret that it is not possible for him to see this volume and I have dedicated it to his memory.

Peter Lowe
December 1995

ABBREVIATIONS

ACJ	Allied Council for Japan
Air	Air Ministry papers, Public Record Office, Kew
Cab	Cabinet Office papers, Public Record Office, Kew
CCP	Chinese Communist Party
CIA	Central Intelligence Agency (United States)
COS	Chiefs of Staff (Great Britain)
Defe	Defence papers, Public Record Office, Kew
DMI	Director of Military Intelligence
DNI	Director of Naval Intelligence
DO	Dominions Office papers (Commonwealth Relations Office), Public Record Office, Kew
DPRK	Democratic People's Republic of Korea (North Korea)
ECA	Economic Cooperation Administration
FEC	Far Eastern Commission
FO	Foreign Office papers, Public Record Office, Kew
FRUS	*Foreign Relations of the United States*
JCP	Japan Communist Party
JCS	Joint Chiefs of Staff (United States)
JIC	Joint Intelligence Committee
JPS	Joint Planning Staff (Great Britain)
KMAG	Korean Military Advisory Group
KMT	Kuomintang (party)
MCP	Malayan Communist Party
NATO	North Atlantic Treaty Organisation
NNRC	Neutral Nations Repatriation Commission
NSC	National Security Council
OSS	Office of Strategic Services (United States)
PLA	People's Liberation Army (China)
POWs	Prisoners of war
PRC	People's Republic of China
Prem	Prime Minister's Office papers, Public Record Office, Kew
ROK	Republic of Korea (South Korea)
SCAP	Supreme Commander of the Allied Powers, Japan
UN	United Nations
UNC	United Nations Command (Korea)

UNCOK   United Nations Commission on Korea
UNCURK   United   Nations   Commission   for   the   Unification   and
           Rehabilitation of Korea
UNTCOK   United Nations Temporary Commission on Korea

INTRODUCTION

In 1948 Great Britain occupied a vital role in the formulation of the policies of the Western world in the phase of the real take-off of the Cold War. By 1953 British power had declined markedly; British influence remained significant, as Anthony Eden's contribution to the first Geneva conference demonstrated, but Britain was less central to the definition of Western policies than had been the case in 1948. Ernest Bevin was a great foreign secretary. He helped to shape and determine the basic principles of British power and influence in the period of five-and-three-quarter years that he held office.[1] For some time after the end of the Second World War the prime minister, Clement Attlee, and Bevin hoped it would be possible to achieve cooperation between the United States, Britain and the Soviet Union. Originally Attlee held stronger hopes than Bevin[2]; such hopes collapsed by 1948. The ruthless consolidation of Soviet control of Eastern Europe, extended to Central Europe with the Prague coup early in 1948, was the most important single factor in this process. It was reinforced through awareness of the sheer size of the Soviet army and with the belief that Stalin's legions could sweep inexorably west whenever they chose: the economic weakness of the Soviet Union was not assigned proper recognition as an inhibiting factor, in part because of the economic problems preoccupying Western Europe.[3] Bevin grasped the urgency of establishing a powerful alternative to Soviet power and believed that this must come from the United States. It was uncertain whether the United States would accept this responsibility. In the summer of 1945 it seemed likely that the Americans would depart from Europe within a short period not to return: the customary traditions would assert themselves and entangling commitments would be eschewed. Harry Truman appeared a competent but uninspiring president and was regarded widely as simply serving out the fourth term of his distinguished predecessor until the Republican party returned to office after the 1948 election.[4]

The task of persuading the United States to commit itself to the defence of Western Europe was formidable and Bevin devoted himself vigorously to the challenge. Truman was stanchly anti-communist and moved gradually in the direction of providing political and economic assistance to those threatened by subversion or invasion. The Truman Doctrine and Marshall Aid in 1947 were milestones in the development of American policy but it was unclear how far they would be pursued. The answer emerged eventually through the repercussions of the communist takeover in Czechoslovakia, the Berlin blockade of

1948–49, the signing of the Atlantic treaty, the creation of the North Atlantic Treaty Organisation (NATO) and, above all, through the impact of the Korean war.[5] An American military commitment to the defence of Western Europe did not materialise until General Dwight D. Eisenhower became the first commander of NATO forces in January 1951. As Winston Churchill was to remark subsequently, the Korean war accomplished what Britain desired for so long: an unqualified acceptance by the United States of leadership of the 'free world' and massive rearmament.[6] There was nothing inevitable about this process although matters may assume this character in retrospect. Despite the often acerbic exchanges between Britain and the United States in the course of waging the Korean war Ernie Bevin died, in April 1951, in the knowledge that his strenuous endeavours to foster full American involvement had succeeded. The United States was in the driver's seat but the journey was frequently to be bumpy: the compelling consideration was that the driver had undertaken the responsibility and the vehicle was heading in approximately the correct direction.

By 1951, and far more so by 1954, British aspirations for firm political resolution and commitment by those in Western Europe and in the United States, to the reconstruction and stability of Western Europe were realised. The position in East Asia between 1948 and 1954 was highly confused with considerable doubt over the future direction of American policy. British ministers and officials were distinctly unimpressed with American reactions to the problems existing in Japan, China and Korea. The Truman administration seemed to have no clear idea of where it was going or what it wanted to achieve. The allied occupation of Japan was entering its fourth year in 1948 with a change in direction discernible, away from radical reform towards building up the Japanese economy again; no termination of the occupation was in sight, which was regretted in London. The one consoling feature was the presence of General Douglas MacArthur who was an effective, capable proconsul, more sensitive and balanced in his approach than might have been expected in 1945.[7] The big question-mark in Japan concerned the character of a peace treaty and concomitant security issues.

In China American policy appeared to be in complete disarray. The Kuomintang government of Chiang Kai-shek was disintegrating, although whether the Chinese Communist Party (CCP), led by Mao Tse-tung, would be strong enough to control most or all of mainland China remained a subject for speculation.[8] The pressures within American domestic politics blended or clashed with foreign policy in the case of China. The Republican party was critical of the Truman administration's approach in general and the right wing of the party was outspoken in condemnation of perceived weakness.[9] The China Lobby was not as powerful as it became subsequently but its leading figures were zealous in encouraging shrill protests at the failure to extend more assistance to their hero, Chiang.[10] As British policy-makers viewed matters, American policy in China was drifting dangerously and there was no solid evidence as to how it would evolve or where it would culminate. Perhaps the British were more prone to think in rational terms and to believe that the United States would come to terms with the victors in China as a matter of accepting reality. However, a situation dominated by the rhetoric of Robert A. Taft, Sr, William Knowland, Karl Mundt, Richard Nixon, Walter Judd and (especially from 1950 onwards) Joseph

McCarthy was not one in which acceptance of reality was likely to be the principal consideration. Britain wished to protect its remaining investments in China, develop commerce in the interests of reviving the British economy, and encourage a more moderate response from the CCP, assumig that it did secure control of most of mainland China.[11] Developments regarding Taiwan caused much perturbation in London in 1950. Britain believed that Taiwan should come under the authority of the Peking government and did not subscribe to the American view that Taiwan must be denied to the People's Republic of China (PRC) for strategic purposes.

The position in Korea in 1948 seemed virtually hopeless. The peninsula was divided between bitterly antagonistic regimes. The signs pointed towards a gradual American withdrawal partly concealed by the involvement of the United Nations (UN). The prevailing British view, shared by MacArthur, was that the whole of Korea would probably be communist within a decade. American policy was extremely confused towards Korea: erroneous signals were conveyed to the other side and few people would have forecast that American forces would be committed heavily in the Korean peninsula to prevent Kim Il Sung's regime from conquering the south.[12]

This study examines British policies in East Asia between 1948 and 1953 and does not pursue developments in South-East Asia. Some reference to anxiety regarding the future of this region is necessary. Britain's colonial possessions were still of considerable size, consisting of Malaya, British Borneo, and the treaty relationships with Sarawak and Brunei. Burma became independent in January 1948 and declined membership of the British Commonwealth. Primary British concern centred on Malaya for economic and political reasons. Malaya was the source of much of the world's rubber and tin production and was very significant in British economic objectives. In the political sphere Britain wished to promote reasonably equitable treatment between the three principal communities of Malays, Chinese and Indians. Tension between Malays and Chinese was marked and caused a modification of policy, away from the more radical proposals contained in the concept of 'Malayan Union' towards recognition of Malay interests. A communist insurrection began in 1948 and made additional claims on stretched resources.[13] The rebellion was alarming but less dangerous than it appeared to be since the Malayan Communist Party (MCP) was almost wholly a Chinese movement and was regarded with fervent hostility by most Malays; the majority of Chinese also opposed the MCP. Malcolm MacDonald, the British commissioner-general for South-East Asia, issued trenchant warnings of a threat to Western interests throughout the area if the communist rebellions in Malaya, Burma, Indo-China and Thailand gained more support from within the countries affected or obtained more aid from China or the Soviet Union. MacDonald told the chiefs of staff in June 1949 that:

> Urgent measures were required to increase the powers of resistance of the countries which were now most directly threatened. There was much to be said for concluding some form of South-East Asia Pact on the lines of the Atlantic Pact. It was clear, however, that such a Pact would not be politically possible. The three countries which held the key to the situation were: Indo-China, Siam and Burma ...[14]

Malaya caused deep anxiety but it did not appear that the insurgency could overthrow British rule.

Events in Indo-China were more ominous. The restoration of French rule was not achieved with the necessary skill or realism. Nationalism of anti-communist and pro-communist varieties flourished in Vietnam, Cambodia and Laos but particularly in Vietnam. The fragility of the fourth French republic, with increasingly frequent changes of government in Paris, inspired little confidence. In 1948 the situation caused concern but not, as yet, alarm.[15] MacDonald warned of a chain reaction in South-East Asia, leading to a triumph for communism, unless resolute policies were followed. The United States was far more worried at the stability of South-East Asia by 1949–50, as illustrated in the promise of assistance for France in Indo-China in May 1950 and John Foster Dulles's references to the area in discussions regarding a Japanese peace treaty. Japan was always the priority, as seen in Washington, followed by Taiwan and Korea from the summer of 1950; next came Indo-China, since the United States felt that Britain was capable of handling Malaya.

The British Commonwealth experienced fundamental readjustment after 1945. In essence this was a continuation of trends extending back before the Great War.[16] The old dominions of Canada, Australia, New Zealand and South Africa pursued independent foreign policies, although efforts were made to coordinate decision-making with Whitehall. The Australian Labour governments of the 1940s were more outspoken, if not at times truculent, but this was in part attributable to the ambition and personality of Dr Herbert Evatt, the ambitious minister of external affairs.[17] In 1948 an event of profound significance occurred with the defeat of the United party of Field Marshal Smuts by the National party led by Dr D. F. Malan. Smuts was the greatest statesman produced by the Commonwealth, possibly accentuated by the fact that Smuts fought against the British during the South African war of 1899–1902 and that he always attached great importance to working with Britain in recognition of the liberal outlook which Smuts saw as basic to the evolution of the Commonwealth from the days of the Campbell-Bannerman and Asquith governments.[18] In the short term the radical change in South African politics did not produce an analogous transformation in foreign policy. The National party government feared communism and wished to cooperate with Britain for practical reasons, but the relationship was devoid of the warmth which characterised it under Smuts's leadership. The biggest single development within the Commonwealth was the attainment of independence by India, Pakistan and Ceylon: this dealt a further blow to the old-fashioned concept of the white dominions. India was by far the most significant of the Asian additions. In terms of geographical extent this was hardly surprising, and this was accentuated through Jawaharlal Nehru's determination to assert a distinctive Asian voice and to make clear that the Commonwealth was a forum for a more wide-ranging debate than had been seen previously.[19] Attlee's government was particularly sensitive to Indian representations: Attlee had contemplated the future of India with keen interest since the 1920s and was proud of his government's achievement in granting independence to such an enormous area.

The permanent under-secretary's committee examined the position of the

Commonwealth within the context of the potential creation of a 'Third World Power' in a report completed in May 1949. The committee could see no prospect of the Commonwealth constituting the basis of a body acting with cohesion:

> The Commonwealth is not a unit in the same sense as the United States or the Soviet Union. It has no central authority and is unlikely to create one and its members are increasingly framing their policies on grounds of regional or local interests. The only member of the Commonwealth which might assume a position of leadership within it is the United Kingdom and it seems unlikely that any proposals originating in London for a closer co-ordination of Commonwealth policy would be welcomed at present. It should not be assumed that centrifugal forces are certain to increase and it remains true that concerted action may well be achieved in a crisis. The substantial identity of view among Commonwealth countries is undoubtedly an important influence for world peace. Nevertheless, there is no guarantee that a common policy will be followed ...
>
> Despite the possibility of improved economic consultation, there seems little prospect of the United Kingdom being able to unite the Commonwealth as a single world power. The attraction exerted by the pound sterling and the Royal Navy is now less strong than that of the dollar and the atomic bomb. An attempt to turn the Commonwealth into a Third World Power would only confront its members with a direct choice betwen London and Washington and though sentiment might point one way interest would certainly lead the other.[20]

In defence terms Britain was incapable of providing effective guarantees for the Commonwealth. This was not new or even recent. This had applied before 1914, hence the importance of the Anglo-Japanese alliance in securing the cooperation of Japan in the China Sea and in the Pacific.[21] This was fundamental for Australia and New Zealand. The dramatic Japanese victories in the first phase of the Pacific war were extremely traumatic for the southern dominions. Apprehension existed that Japan could revive and once more pose a grave threat. The report of the permanent under-secretary's committee stated, in effect, that only the United States could give the requisite guarantees. Thus the seeds of ANZUS could be discerned but not the bitter controversy that accompanied the development of American defence leadership in the Pacific when the Churchill government endeavoured to compel admission to ANZUS after 1951.[22] To the student of British policy towards the dominions before 1941, the story of British self-delusion regarding the Commonwealth is a familiar one. For psychological reasons British ministers and officials experienced difficulty in accepting that British power was waning to the extent it was. Labour ministers found it less difficult to accept than Conservatives, although part of the explanation lies in Churchill's robust but dated belief in a concept of Commonwealth which had ceased to exist.

It is fitting to explore further the concept of a 'Third World Power' as assessed by the permanent under-secretary's committee. There were positive arguments in favour of establishing a third force. It would obviate the need to depend excessively upon the United States and would, therefore, attract those who resented the fickleness of American politicians and those who disliked American capitalism. At one time some members of the American State Department considered the merits of such a concept. American isolationists could see a case for it, since it would diminish American involvement in Europe. Some in Europe advocated neutralism because it would permit a third power to exert influence 'out of proportion to its strength, since it could hope to be courted by both sides'.[23] As regards moves towards European unity, current developments, such as Benelux and the Italo-French Customs Union, were essentially economic in nature, if with political implications. It was possible that the new Council of Europe could foster more unity in Europe but this was speculative:

> Whatever the tendencies may be, the fact remains that the military and economic situation of the Western European nations is now such that there can be no immediate prospect of welding them into a prosperous and secure entity without American help; and even with American help it is uncertain whether this can be achieved for some time to come.[24]

Furthermore, the difficulties associated with the future of Germany caused anguish. Should European unity be promoted with Germany contained prominently within it or not? How should the problem of averting a revival in German militarism be tackled? Would 'Germany' connote West Germany or a unified Germany? The committee concluded that no alternative combination was likely to be viable and that Britain and Western Europe must rely on the United States to take the lead in defending the 'free world'. Britain would occupy 'an increasingly important part' and must 'seek to maintain its special relations with the United States'.[25]

British ministers regarded themselves as far more experienced than their American counterparts. Perhaps reading Lord Palmerston's despatches infused Ernie Bevin with a more potent grasp of the traditions of British foreign policy. As he put it on one occasion, the United States was a young and comparatively immature country when it came to devising policy on complex issues and was in need of the distilled essence of experience.[26] Dean Acheson liked Bevin and was prepared to accept Ernie's approach up to a point but he was not disposed to be told too emphatically how to conduct policy, as the sharp reaction of Acheson demonstrated early in the Korean war when Bevin proposed a different course of action to that favoured in the State Department. The 'special relationship' was not as 'special' as the British believed: what counted with the Americans was power in which respect their credit balance was rising and that of Britain falling. Therefore, in the construction of British policy in East Asia between 1948 and 1953 British ministers and officials had to accept that Britain possessed little room for manoeuvre. In only one respect did British policy follow a fundamentally divergent approach from that of the United States – over recognition of communist China in January 1950. Of course, there were marked differences in other cases, notably over certain aspects of waging the Korean war but Britain did not pursue a wholly divergent line during the Korean conflict. The British role in East Asia in the period examined in this study comprised an exercise in playing second fiddle under a conductor of mercurial character and unpredictable mood. As with certain conductors and orchestras, an analysis of developments leads to the conclusion that it is surprising not that conflict arose on occasion but that matters worked out as well as they did.

Notes

1   See Alan Bullock, *The Life and Times of Ernest Bevin*, vol. III, *Foreign Secretary, 1945–1951* (London; Heinemann, 1983), for an excellent account of Bevin's approach to the post and to the numerous challenges facing him.

2   See R. Smith and J. Zametica, 'The Cold Warrior: Clement Attlee Reconsidered', *International Affairs*, 61, no. 2 (1985), pp. 239–52.

3   See J. L. Gaddis, *The Long Peace* (Oxford: Oxford University Press, 1989) and *The United States and the End of the Cold War* (Oxford: Oxford University Press, 1992).

4   See M. J. Lacey (ed.), *The Truman Presidency* (Cambridge, 1989) and Roger Buckley, 'A Particularly Vital Issue?: Harry Truman and Japan, 1945–52', in T. G. Fraser and Peter Lowe (eds), *Conflict and Amity in East Asia: Essays in Honour of Ian Nish* (London: Macmillan, 1992), pp. 110–24.

5   See Nicholas Henderson, *The Birth of NATO* (London: Weidenfeld and Nicolson, 1982).

6   Minute by Churchill, 2 July 1953, FO 371/105508/626.

7   For a lucid, balanced assessment of the occupation, see R. B. Finn, *Winners in Peace: MacArthur, Yoshida, and Postwar Japan* (Oxford: University of California Press, 1992). See also D. Clayton James, *The Years of MacArthur*, vol. III, *Triumph and Disaster, 1945–1964* (Boston, MA: Houghton Mifflin, 1985).

8   See Suzanne Pepper, *Civil War in China, 1945–49* (Berkeley and Los Angeles: University of California Press, 1978).

9   For a detailed examination of arguments within the Republican party in this era with particular reference to the rise of vehement anti-communism, see T. C. Reeves, *The Life and Times of Joe McCarthy: A Biography* (London: Blond & Briggs, 1982).

10   See R. Y. Koen, *The China Lobby in American Politics*, ed. with introduction by R. C. Kagan, paperback edition (London: Harper & Row, 1974) and S. D. Bachrack, *The Committee of One Million: 'China Lobby' Politics, 1953–1971* (New York; Columbia University Press, 1976).

11   See Wenguang Shao, *China, Britain and Businessmen: Political and Commercial Relations, 1949–57* (London and Oxford: Macmillan/St Antony's College, 1991).

12   See Peter Lowe, *The Origins of the Korean War* (London: Longman, 1986), pp. 19–71.

13   For an excellent analysis of developments in Malaya, see Anthony Short, *The Communist Insurrection in Malaya, 1948–1960* (London: Frederick Muller, 1975). The regrettable gap in published documentation relating to post-1945 Malaya has now been filled admirably in A. J. Stockwell (ed.), *British Documents on the End of Empire*, Series B, *Malaya*, 3 parts (London: HMSO, 1995), which pursues developments between 1942 and 1957.

14   For MacDonald's warnings, see chiefs of staff committee, 1 June 1949 COS(49)81(1), Defe 4/22.

15   See D. Lancaster, *The Emancipation of French Indochina* (Oxford: Oxford University Press, 1961), Gabriel Kolko, *Vietnam: Anatomy of a War, 1940–1975* (London: Allen & Unwin, 1986) and Stanley Karnow, *Vietnam: A History*, revised paperback edition (London: Penguin, 1991).

16   See Ritchie Ovendale, *The English-Speaking Alliance: Britain, the United States, the Dominions and the Cold War, 1945–1951* (London: Allen & Unwin, 1985).

17   See R. J. Bell, *Unequal Allies: Australian–American Relations and the Pacific War* (Melbourne: Melbourne University Press, 1977) and Peter Crockett, *Evatt: A Life* (Melbourne: Oxford University Press, 1993).

18   See Keith Hancock, *Smuts*, vol. II *The Fields of Force, 1919–1950* (Cambridge: Cambridge University Press, 1968).

19   See S. Gopal, *Jawaharlal Nehru; A Biography*, 2 vols (London: Jonathan Cape, 1979).

20 Permanent Under-Secretary's Committee, 'A Third World Power or Western Consolidation?', Prem 8/1204.

21 See Peter Lowe, *Great Britain and Japan, 1911–15* (London: Macmillan, 1969), chs 1 and 8.

22 See Percy Spender, *Exercises in Diplomacy: The ANZUS Treaty, and the Colombo Plan* (Sydney: Sydney University Press, 1969), for the views of the Australian minister of external affairs.

23 Permanent Under-Secretary's Committee, 9 May 1949, Prem 8/1204.

24 *Ibid.*

25 *Ibid.*

26 Record of conversation between Bevin and Nehru, 5 January 1951, FO 371/92766/37.

PART I

JAPAN

Map 1   **Japan, East Asia and the western Pacific**

1

BRITAIN, MACARTHUR AND THE OCCUPATION, 1948 TO JUNE 1950

The occupation of Japan was an allied one in a formal sense but in reality it was an American enterprise.[1] Before the end of the Pacific war it was assumed in London that Britain would contribute significantly to the formulation of policy but this proved not to be the case.[2] Ironically Britain and the Soviet Union shared similar feelings of exclusion in 1945–46 before the Cold War developed. President Truman had little interest in Japan and held that American freedom of action should not be hindered by obligations to allies beyond the strict necessities of an allied occupation.[3] Truman wished to see Japanese militarism eliminated and democratic values instilled into the Japanese people. Without particular enthusiasm Truman appointed General Douglas MacArthur to head the occupation.[4] Truman regarded MacArthur as excessively egocentric but MacArthur's lengthy and distinguished military record culminated in the Pacific campaigns and this dictated his appointment as Supreme Commander of the Allied Powers (SCAP). MacArthur believed as firmly as Truman that the United States should direct policy with minimal interference from its allies but with the added feature that he wished to minimise interference from Washington, too. Examining the relationship between MacArthur and the Truman administration brings to mind the observation once made by a member of A. J. Balfour's cabinet in London at the beginning of the twentieth century that a communication from Lord Curzon, the viceroy of India, read as though it came from a foreign government and one not altogether friendly. Up to 1948 MacArthur enjoyed substantial freedom of operation; thereafter his independence diminished but his power remained considerable and greater than has been argued by revisionist historians.[5]

At the start of the occupation in 1945 unduly sanguine objectives were adumbrated – militarism would vanish, true loyalty to democratic values would be inculcated, economy and society would be democratised, women emancipated; in total, American democratic ideals would be transplanted successfully. Exaggerated claims were made at the time for what was being achieved by SCAP but the achievements were appreciable. Emperor Hirohito renounced divinity in 1946, if originally in opaque terms.[6] A new constitution was implemented in 1946–47 through vigorous American insistence: this made clear that Japan was a constitutional monarchy in the Western sense and that responsibility rested firmly with the government, subject to the latter enjoying the support of a majority in the Diet. Under article 9 of the constitution Japan renounced possession of armed forces and was committed to pursuance of a Pacific foreign policy. Measures were taken somewhat belatedly to tackle the problems posed by the zaibatsu (large financial combines) but this proved to be a more intractable challenge than was believed at first. Fundamental reform within the whole of education was applied based on the American model. Women were given the vote and efforts were made to enhance the role of females within society. However, by 1948 deeper questions concerning the evolution of the occupation were surfacing: these resulted from the development of the Cold War, from doubts within certain American circles over the wisdom of the economic and social policies pursued under the occupation, and from a feeling in Washington that MacArthur possessed too much freedom.

From the British viewpoint MacArthur was central to their evaluation of the course of the occupation. In part this reflected the potency of a magnetic personality who inspired profound fascination in all who met him. The impact of the man was no doubt exaggerated: MacArthur did not determine all facets of the occupation and some developments occurred without his knowledge or with his remote approval. However, it would be far more dangerous to underestimate MacArthur's role.[7] The occupation would have assumed a very different character had he not directed it and the outcome might well have been less positive than it was. MacArthur is a difficult person to assess with precision. He possessed great gifts in the scope and breadth of his interests, in his discernment of military challenges, and in appreciation of the kind of reforms Japan required. As has often been remarked, MacArthur espoused policies of sweeping liberal reform in Japan markedly divergent from his attitudes to American politics and society. In Japan he sponsored a 'new deal' whereas in the United States he was forthright in castigating the evils produced by Franklin D. Roosevelt's policies. On the negative side, MacArthur was imbued with excessive faith in his own powers and did not take kindly to criticism of any variety. This was compounded by the fact that he liked to be surrounded by 'yes men', those who comprised his inner circle from the Pacific campaigns and who could be relied on for a sycophantic approach. Foremost among these were Generals Courtney Whitney and Charles Willoughby. Whitney was relatively liberal in his inclinations while Willoughby was reactionary. MacArthur followed a set routine each day and disliked varying it. He displayed no interest in visiting Japan outside Tokyo. He cultivated an air of austere grandeur which fulfilled the role of the proconsul and the shogun combined: he considered this appropriate for impressing Western diplomats or visitors and the Japanese. All Western visitors who met him commented on his theatrical character and stage management of meetings and on his impressive preparation for the topics they wished to pursue with him, be these the experience of the Japanese labour movement, the recovery of the textile industry, or the achievements and failings of Japanese politicians.[8]

The head of the British liaison mission in Tokyo, Alvary Gascoigne, saw MacArthur with considerable frequency, indeed MacArthur met him more often than any other official with the sole exception of his State Department adviser, William Sebald.[9] Before the start of the Korean war their meetings were usually of a cordial nature. Gascoigne proved sympathetic in listening to the general's monologues but was prepared to risk incurring the latter's wrath by speaking more bluntly when the need arose. Their exchanges conformed to the customary character of MacArthur's encounters whereby the bulk of the time was consumed in a lengthy statement by MacArthur, followed by suitable questions and answers. The frequency of their meetings presumably denoted that MacArthur regarded Gascoigne as a sympathetic listener. At the beginning of 1948 Gascoigne assessed the fortunes of the Japanese Communist Party (JCP). Curiously enough the JCP was permitted to operate legally for the first time by MacArthur as an ingredient in his liberalisation when the occupation began: this explains the otherwise improbable scenario of members of the JCP assembling outside the Dai-Ichi building to shout three banzais for the general. Gascoigne reported to Ernest Bevin, the foreign secretary, at the end of January 1948 that support for the JCP was not growing at the rate seen between 1945 and 1947; he estimated membership at 16,200 with approximately 80,000 followers. Communist members of the Diet totalled four compared with six previously. Gascoigne commented, 'No doubt they counted at first upon receiving some support from General MacArthur and they have, I think, been unpleasantly surprised by the obviously anti-communistic attitude of SCAP.'[10] The prospects of the moderate left appeared to strengthen in 1947 when Katayama Tetsu became the first socialist prime minister. MacArthur liked Katayama and regretted his fall, which was attributable to factionalism within his party. MacArthur lamented the disappointing calibre of Japanese politicians to Gascoigne: '... he has endeavoured for the past two years to unearth a first-class politician and statesman' but without succeeding.[11]

The Foreign Office was interested in ascertaining the future prospects for the economy and for the JCP. Gascoigne commented on the obvious connection between the two – communism would be assisted appreciably by an economic collapse:

> It is for this reason that the Supreme Commander has paid such particular attention to the food supplies for Japan. MacArthur is convinced that the only way to keep this country out of the communist maw is to make the people contented and for the moment the only method of doing this is to arrange for substantial imports of foodstuffs and raw materials, as the Japanese economy is very far from having regained its feet. Should America lose interest in Japan and turn off the supplies of foodstuffs and raw materials, then we should undoubtedly see a rapid ascendancy in communist influence throughout the country, coupled with a maximum effort by the Russians to make capital out of the situation ... All the signs that we have had at present are to the effect that America will not allow this country to relapse into a condition such as would make it an easy prey to Soviet plans.[12]

Gascoigne reported that the Soviet mission in Tokyo was large, amounting to around 240 members. It was led by the Soviet representative in the Allied Council for Japan (ACJ), one of the few allied bodies but which possessed little importance, since MacArthur regarded it with open contempt. The Soviet mission had accomplished little in Gascoigne's opinion and this situation was unlikely to change in the foreseeable future.

Considerable speculation surrounded MacArthur's own political ambitions, for 1948 was a presidential election year in the United States and Harry Truman was perceived as vulnerable, if not a loser. Hence the fact that much interest was shown in the contest for the Republican nomination. MacArthur was unquestionably attracted by the prospect of transferring his headquarters from the Dai-Ichi building to the White House: the problem from his viewpoint lay in the fact that he did not relish the battle to secure the nomination in the first place. MacArthur believed that the qualifications afforded by his vast experience constituted the most persuasive argument in his curriculum vitae and that the Republican convention should simply invite him to accept the nomination rather than going through the tedious process of campaigning for it. MacArthur had no intention of leaving Tokyo to participate in American domestic politics until he was certain of receiving his party's support. Congressman Charles A. Eaton, chairman of the House Foreign Affairs Committee, invited MacArthur to return to Washington to put forward his analysis of the situation in China. Clement Attlee's personal representative in Tokyo, General Charles Gairdner, reported on a conversation with MacArthur at the end of February in which MacArthur dismissed the invitation to return 'as part of the political game and not because his views on China were genuinely required'.[13] He added that he was 'too old a bird to be caught in a morass as simply as that'.[14] Instead MacArthur sent a lengthy cable to Eaton, regretting that 'the pressure of my operational duties in the administration of Japan precluded visiting the USA and explaining at some length the necessity for halting the advance of Communism in China'.[15] Gascoigne interpreted MacArthur's willingness to expound his views on China, if by cable rather than in person, as confirming his interest in the Republican nomination. MacArthur felt that the urgency of blocking communist expansion in Asia had not received sufficient emphasis because of the preoccupation with stopping communism in Europe.[16]

MacArthur authorised his name to be entered into certain primary election campaigns but his supporters were not well enough organised and lacked sufficient financial support. Also those supporting MacArthur in Wisconsin were embroiled in factional squabbles within the state Republican party which handicapped MacArthur's bid. This helps in explaining Senator Joseph McCarthy's attack on MacArthur in the Wisconsin primary in the course of which McCarthy drew attention to MacArthur's divorce so as to discredit him in the eyes of Roman Catholic voters.[17] MacArthur emerged disappointingly from his flirtation with the voters in the primaries: his hopes rested on the prospect of a convention unimpressed with the appeal of the other candidates and which might turn to him. On 26 May MacArthur gave Gairdner his assessment of his chances. In reply to an enquiry as to whether he might return to the United States, MacArthur 'replied categorically that unless he received Republican nomination he had no (repeat no) intention of leaving Japan'.[18] He conceded that it was very unlikely that he would be nominated 'but that he did not consider it a complete impossibility and that actually his chances at the present time were, he considered, slightly better than they had been to date'.[19] The leading contenders, Governor Thomas E. Dewey of New York and Senator Robert A. Taft, Sr of Ohio, detested each other and would not compromise. Harold Stassen of Minnesota was too liberal and Senator Arthur H. Vandenberg of Michigan was in poor health. In the circumstances a 'dark horse' candidate might emerge and, clearly, MacArthur saw himself fulfilling this role. MacArthur's hopes evaporated finally when the Republican convention nominated Dewey with Governor Earl Warren of California for vice-president. Discussions between the British and MacArthur focused on Japan once again.

In the course of 1948 MacArthur encountered more criticism from within the United States for the continuing economic weaknesses of Japan which were proving a drain on the American taxpayer and a handicap in organising Western defences amidst the emerging Cold War. Critics within and outside the Truman administration expressed their dissatisfaction: they included Kenneth Royall, General Draper, Averell Harriman and George F. Kennan.[20] Criticism of MacArthur worried British officials because they believed, notwithstanding MacArthur's idiosyncratic qualities, that he was closer to the British government where the future of Japan was concerned than was the Truman administration in Washington. F. S. Tomlinson of the Foreign Office referred to MacArthur's 'remarkable record of achievement' and Esler Dening remarked that, 'The prospect of indefinite American occupation without General MacArthur hardly bears contemplation.'[21] For his part MacArthur described the relationship between SCAP and the British government in warm terms. Gascoigne saw him on 1 July before returning temporarily to Britain:

> I asked the Supreme Commander this morning whether, as I was proceeding to England, he had any special messages which he would like me to give to you. He replied that he wished you to know how very grateful he was for your 'great consideration for and complete understanding of' his international policy here; he also said that he felt that [the] relationship between the United Kingdom Government and his organisation was a 'perfect one'.[22]

British reflection on the future of the Japanese economy was stimulated by George Kennan's visit to Tokyo. Kennan went to Japan to assess the political, economic and strategic situation of Japan.[23] Britain favoured the convening of an early peace conference and Kennan was reported as sharing this view.[24] However, the American government was divided over the issue and there appeared little likelihood of its being resolved within the near future. Discussions had proceeded in the Far Eastern Commission (FEC), the body representing formally the nations responsible for defeating Japan in 1945. The principal British objectives on the economic side were defined by the Foreign Office in March 1948 in the following terms. Japanese industry was functioning at a low level: a realistic assessment of Japanese needs was required. The FEC's view that the appropriate standard of living should be essentially that obtaining in 1930–34 should be endorsed. Reparations should include industrial assets, shipping and shipbuilding capacity beyond Japanese peacetime requirements; Japanese gold deposits and external assets should be available for reparations. Britain agreed that Japan should possess a viable economy; it had not favoured restricting peacetime industries including textiles but was concerned that Japanese competition should not be of an unfair character: 'We want good wages and working conditions in the Japanese factories and the elimination of sharp commercial practices.'[25]

MacArthur responded by agreeing that levels of industry were too low; that the standard of living of 1930–34 could not be achieved within the near future; that little remained of Japanese assets for use as reparations. He did not comment on American economic aid because of the imminence of the Draper mission. MacArthur expressed dissatisfaction at the ponderous deliberations of the FEC.[26] MacArthur's resentment at the growing criticism he was experiencing from big business in the United States was voiced trenchantly on 7 April. Big business opposed the plans for decentralisation which involved breaking up the zaibatsu. These were perceived as undermining Japanese economic recovery and hampering trade. MacArthur expressed bitter remarks about the American 'tycoons' to Gascoigne.[27] He named the 'tycoons' as Forrestal, Royall, Harriman and Draper, who were described as hostile to MacArthur's purge of reactionary elements and as being opposed to economic decentralisation. He believed these critics were motivated by selfish considerations linked with thier own business interests. MacArthur maintained that he was pressing ahead regardless: the purge was virtually completed and anti-trust action was going ahead under Japanese legislation. MacArthur professed to know little of economic plans for Japan possibly being devised in Washington.[28]

MacArthur told Gascoigne on 1 July that he did not envisage fundamental changes in the occupation regime. He was satisfied broadly with the political and social progress achieved: the main challenges lay in the economic sphere. Gascoigne conveyed his 'personal impression' that the Japanese were evincing signs of 'passive resistance' to the occupation. He gave as an example a recent experience of the head of the purchasing and selling section of the British mission who had been treated rudely by officials in the Japanese Trade Ministry. Gascoigne added that the mood of the people was evolving from one of acquiescence to arrogance. Gascoigne welcomed the news that a large military parade would take place on 4 July: this should have a salutary effect. MacArthur commented that he was 'not surprised'.[29] Some of the signs emanating from Washington suggested a far more generous approach to Japan and these perturbed the Foreign Office. Hector McNeil, the minister of state, submitted a minute to Ernest Bevin in June in which he stated his anxiety over American policy. The Americans 'are in grave danger of presenting us with a most nasty political mess through their apparent complete inability to understand the Australian fears about the re-emergence of Japanese aggression'.[30] In addition, McNeil feared that a lenient industrial policy towards the Japanese 'will land us in trouble with our Lancashire members'.[31]

Towards the end of 1948 Gascoigne submitted a balanced, reflective despatch reviewing the situation after three-and-a-half years of the occupation. Gascoigne began by explaining that when he had visited the Foreign Office in London the preceding summer he had been asked how the Japanese people viewed their prospects once a peace treaty had been signed. It was not a simple question to respond to, since the Japanese were unpredictable and to essay an answer involved considering the perspective of the average Japanese citizen. The bulk of the people were not, as yet, thinking too deeply about the future. Gascoigne requested the counsellor for information in the British mission, H. Vere Redman, to investigate since his knowledge of Japan was much more extensive than Gascoigne's. As regards his personal assessment Gascoigne believed that the Japanese desired termination of the occupation and to avoid the application of rigorous controls; to gain as much economic support from the Americans as possible; to exploit rivalries between the allied powers; to secure armed forces again in part because of the advance of communism in China; to reestablish commercial primacy in world markets, especially in Asia; to find *lebensraum* for Japan's expanding population. Gascoigne was sceptical as to how the Japanese outlook had changed since 1941:

> The impact of democracy upon the Japanese mind has, as yet, been almost nil, although great play is, of course, made by the Japanese of going through the 'forms' of democratic practice, because they know that during the occupation they can but obey the dictates of the Supreme Commander and that the more they please him (and through him the United States), the greater will be the bounties which will flow from Washington. It would in any case, to my mind, be folly to expect a nation fundamentally and permanently to accept democracy 'overnight', especially a democracy which has been imposed upon it by the victors during a period of occupation.[32]

The longer-term economic outlook was disturbing and a peace conference would have to devise safeguards against the type of trading practices pursued by Japan before the Pacific war and any move towards totalitarian government, whether of left or right. This was a difficult problem but, Gascoing thought, less challenging than handling the future of Germany. This assumed, however, that the allies would impose real controls upon Japan; if this did not apply then Japan could soon become 'a predatory force' which would threaten allied interests. Developments in China would exert a powerful influence upon Japan. The mutual economic interests of Japan and China, fostered by geography, would bring them together with political consequences hard to evaluate. Gascoigne stated that he had asked MacArthur recently what he felt were the desires of the Japanese in the future. Gascoigne indicated his own doubts regarding Japanese loyalty to democracy in the broader future. MacArthur replied that the Japanese would act eventually in the way that they believed would benefit them most, ignoring ethical or moral factors; he maintained that they would adhere to democratic practices because a 'taste' for democracy had been inculcated successfully during the occupation. The Japanese were conservative basically and would lean towards Western rather than Soviet approaches: the majority of the Japanese admired the United States and Britain (in that order) and Japan would require economic reciprocity from the Western powers. MacArthur added that the Soviet Union had never given anything to anyone and he could not see the Russians offering or the Japanese accepting land in Siberia to meet Japan's population needs.

Gascoigne concluded:

> To sum up, the general felt, therefore, that the great majority of the Japanese were now earnestly looking forward to a democractic future in which they would be closely associated with America and the Anglo-Saxon countries both culturally and for purposes of trade. He did not think that now that they had experienced the benefits of democracy, they would give them up ...

Such is General MacArthur's fervent belief in the lasting effects of his admittedly great work (the drawing up of a democratic 'Blue Print' for Japan), that it would perhaps be too much to expect him to take a sceptical view of the future of this country immediately after the peace. I do not agree with him ... but I can understand the spirit which animates his work – it is that of a 'Crusader' – and this naturally influences his thoughts on the final outcome. He did, however, remark at the close of our conversation that, in his opinion, it would be better if responsible officials would confine themselves to attempting to provide for the contingencies which might arise in the next five or six years instead of trying to gaze into the crystal ball in search of the far distant future, thereby perhaps implying that even he was not convinced that the Japanese might not, in the long run, take a sharp turn, either to the Right or to the left.[33]

In 1948 Yoshida Shigeru succeeded Katayama Tetsu as prime minister and began his era of remarkable dominance in Japanese politics. Arguably, Yoshida had a more profound influence upon the shape of postwar politics than those of his rivals or successors.[34] Yoshida was deeply conservative but was hostile to militarism because of his experiences as a diplomat in the 1920s and 1930s and because he had been placed under house arrest during the final phase of the Pacific war. He was autocratic, an admirer of Britain, often nostalgically recalling the days of the Anglo-Japanese alliance, an advocate of pragmatic cooperation with the United States while exploiting the relationship in Japan's interest as far as was possible. Yoshida was a wily operator whose career was advanced after 1947 through the purge by SCAP of certain potential rivals, notably Hatoyama Ichiro, and by the tenacity displayed increasingly by Yoshida, not least in his handling of labour problems in Japan. He was underestimated frequently by his domestic rivals and by foreign diplomats. MacArthur regarded Yoshida as indolent and preferred Katayama: the fact that the latter was a Christian (Presbyterian) may also have been significant, since MacArthur liked to think that he was advancing Christianity in Japan. Gascoigne recognised the importance of Yoshida but also underestimated him. On 2 February 1949 Gascoigne informed the Foreign Office of a lengthy discussion with the prime minister. Keeping in mind to whom he was responsible, Gascoigne said that he had impressed upon Yoshida the wisdom of dealing skilfully with the vigorous labour movement. Labour unrest could become a major problem if mishandled and Gascoigne referred to the 'methods and machinery' used in Britain to resolve labour disputes, some of which had been pioneered by Ernest Bevin as general secretary of the Transport and General Workers Union or as minister of labour between 1940 and 1945.[35] Yoshida betrayed some unease, perhaps visualising the massive figure of Ernie Bevin waving an admonishing finger. Yoshida proclaimed himself to be a genuine constitutionalist, opposing extremism of left or right.[36] F. S. Tomlinson minuted, 'The truth is that Mr. Yoshida, although able in his own way, does not give the impression of being particularly well-qualified to cope with the intricate political and economic situation in which Japan now finds herself.'[37]

MacArthur favoured a tougher approach to the unions than formerly owing to his concern at the growth of militancy and through his belief that the labour movement should not become too powerful in a period when the Cold

War was looming ever larger. MacArthur and Yoshida were prepared to be ruthless in suppressing labour unrest. At the same time, tenacity should not be taken too far. The American secretary for labor, John W. Gibson, visited Japan in February 1949 and stated in a press conference that MacArthur was proud of his contribution in assisting trade unions after 1945: 'General MacArthur said to me in a very forthright fashion ... that he considered himself the father of the labor movement in Japan and that as long as he was there nothing was going to happen in any way to destroy the labor movement in Japan.'[38] Officials in the Foreign Office regarded Yoshida doubtfully as something of a mischief-maker. In a sense this was justified for the reason explained by Gascoigne earlier on: Japanese leaders wished to restore the independence of their country and would exploit differences between the occupying powers if it suited them. Yoshida was formidable and from the viewpoint of Japan was correct in believing that Japan's future could be advanced best through a combination of cooperating with the United States, eschewing an adventurous foreign policy and concentrating on securing rapid economic progress. Yoshida was too conservative in his inclinations but he may have represented the tendencies of Japanese society reasonably accurately. In 1948–49 American and British officials doubted whether Yoshida would stay in power for long, since Japanese prime ministers succeeded one another briskly. But Yoshida stayed in office until 1954, establishing the foundations for Japan's subsequent development.

In March 1949 MacArthur gave an interview to a prominent British journalist, G. Ward Price, of the *Daily Mail*.[39] MacArthur emphasised his sympathy for Britain. He was of Scottish ancestry and admired British achievements. He defined strategic aims in the Pacific region: it constituted an American line of defence joining with the chain of islands off the Asian coast comprising a barrier against communist expansion. Japan was not intended to be an ally of the United States: rather the wish was for Japan to be neutral but the United States would defend Japan if the latter was the victim of aggression. He did not believe that the Soviet Union would attack Japan: if it made an attempt this would be doomed by Soviet air and naval weakness. MacArthur did not regard communism as possessing serious potential in Japan. He expressed his warm respect for Winston Churchill, thus endearing himself further to the readers of the *Daily Mail*. MacArthur's views regarding Japan's future role were reiterated to Admiral Sir Patrick Brind, C-in-C, China Station, when Brind visited him in July 1949:

> General MacArthur went out of his way to emphasise that [the] United States Government had no intention of converting Japanese into allies against the Soviet Union [or] of re-arming them in any way. They had no reason to trust the Japanese and did not want them as allies. What they did want was a strictly neutral Japan which would become the Switzerland of the Pacific (this is an ideal he has expounded before to Sir A. Gascoigne). General MacArthur added that he did not himself believe the Russians, even if they had the chance, would re-arm [the] Japanese: they knew [the] Japanese hatred of them and they knew they could not trust them. But he did think that the Russians suspected the Americans would re-arm the Japanese since they always attributed the worst possible motives to other people.[40]

MacArthur appeared to envisage the role of Japan in a possible war as comprising a base for American troops with American planes operating from bases in Okinawa, Guam, the Philippines and the Aleutians. Ambiguity concerning MacArthur's concept of Japan as the 'Switzerland' of the Far East (or Pacific) remained. Certainly his thinking was very different from that prevailing in the Pentagon.

Two critics of MacArthur were George Kennan and Robert Taft. Kennan spent three weeks in Japan early in 1948 and conveyed the essence of his views in a lecture to the National War College in Washington on 19 May 1948. Kennan stated that the terms of the Potsdam declaration had been achieved: the challenge was not purging militarism, for that had been accomplished; rather it was a question of deciding the character of Japan once the occupation ended. There was no alternative to keeping American troops in Japan for some years to come. The Japanese economy was very weak and required careful nurturing. Japan needed a government of great sagacity to guide it through the tempestuous world problems. Kennan observed that unfair criticism had been expressed regarding MacArthur's administration: the principal challenges of the early years of the occupation had been handled effectively. But the emphasis should now be switched to the revival of the economy. Kennan felt that the purges had been taken too far and that certain officials within SCAP had become too deeply involved in a personal sense. Kennan was critical of the holding of war trials in Japan and Germany. SCAP and the Truman administration in Washington were out of step with one another and coordination should be strengthened.[41]

MacArthur was censured widely by business circles associated with both the Democratic and Republican parties for his economic policies. The former believed that he was hindering opportunities for the revival of trade and the latter fulminated about MacArthur's pursuing 'socialistic' policies of the kind promoted by Franklin D. Roosevelt. Felix Jager of *Look* magazine wrote to Senator Taft at the end of 1948 drawing his attention to a forthcoming article by Hallett Abend castigating MacArthur's whole postwar programme: MacArthur had been 'highhanded and inept' and had, allegedly, brought Japan to a desperate state in which there was a grave danger of a communist *coup*. Taft read the article and replied to Jager on 7 January 1949 that he had perused it with interest. He was careful in his wording but included oblique criticism of MacArthur: 'I hope that the whole matter of our political and economic policies in Japan, and also in Germany, may be thoroughly investigated by the new Congress. Excellent as our soldiers are, they certainly are not experts in government.'[42] MacArthur reacted irately to the criticism expressed from within and outside the Truman administration: his critics were ignorant or prejudiced and represented the malign influences of vested interests moved by diverse considerations. MacArthur was driven on by a potent commitment to his mission in Japan, as Gascoigne shrewdly reported: while MacArthur was definitely interested in the presidency in 1948 and 1952, his dedication to reforming Japan on democratic lines was entirely genuine. This explains the paradox of a man who was a right-wing Republican (if of idiosyncratic hue) in American domestic politics pursuing liberal policies concerning political reform, women, education, and labour which his right-wing critics, lacking his missionary zeal, condemned as dangerously radical.

British diplomats continued to detect feelings of unrest growing in Japan because of the indefinite prolongation of the occupation. Bevin endeavoured to encourage Dean Acheson to devote more thought to a peace treaty in June 1949 but continued divergence between the State and Defense departments precluded progress being made.[43] Acheson did make encouraging noises and stated, on 17 September 1949, that it was important to proceed with a treaty.[44] Speculation grew regarding the convening of a peace conference. MacArthur told Gascoigne in September 1949 that he remained sceptical as to whether anything would materialise. He did not believe that the Truman administration intended to move in the near future and he had not been consulted. Acheson's professed interest was a 'smokescreen' aimed at placating those countries favouring an early peace treaty.[45] MacArthur told Gascoigne in October that Acheson was worried at the prospect of the British Commonwealth exercising five votes in a peace conference. As regards the future security of Japan, MacArthur felt it unlikely that the American people would support the conclusion of a bilateral treaty. He held that only one venue could be considered for holding a conference – Tokyo. A treaty signed outside Japan would offend the Japanese and should be obviated. MacArthur could think of no one better qualified to chair a conference than himself. He observed mordantly that he would not object to proposals put to Britain by Washington, provided Acheson could induce that 'band of Prima Donnas' located in the competing parts of the Washington bureaucracy to cooperate.[46] There was a certain irony in MacArthur recognising prima donnas but the clash between the State Department and the Pentagon, personified in Dean Acheson and Louis Johnson, was fundamental to the impasse over a peace treaty. Acheson had hoped to make progress but informed Oliver Franks, the British ambassador, in December 1949 that regrettably it was not possible to proceed. He met Franks privately, as he did with some frequency, and said that there was one large and, at present, insurmountable obstacle. Franks deduced correctly that this took the form of opposition from Louis Johnson, the secretary for defense.[47]

Further consideration to strategic implications of a peace treaty occurred in Whitehall towards the end of 1949. The joint planning staff, which advised the chiefs of staff, produced a report in which the basic principles were defined as preventing any country from exploiting Japan's potential in a direction antagonistic to Commonwealth interests, taking steps to avoid a recurrence of Japanese militarism, and permitting the Western powers to use Japan as a base in the event of conflict or the threat of conflict. These aims could be met most satisfactorily through the United States and Japan concluding a bilateral defence treaty under the terms of which the former would be assigned responsibility for fulfilling the naval and air defence of Japan in return for bases and facilities in Japanese territory and which could include the creation of a Japanese army, equipped by the United States. A revival of the shipbuilding industry was not seen as a danger provided that a defence treaty with the United States existed.[48] The chief difficulty for British policy-makers in the domestic context was to secure adequate assurance for the apprehension of Japanese militarism still held powerfully in Australia and New Zealand. Australian leaders and public opinion saw the potential menace of Japan as a greater problem than communist expansion. Eventually John Foster Dulles devised a solution but this was an appreciable distance away at the end of 1949.

In January 1950 Commonwealth leaders assembled for one of their regular conferences. Of symbolic significance on this occasion was the venue. They gathered in Colombo, Ceylon (now Sri Lanka), thus underlining the emergence of the 'New Commonwealth'. Bevin wanted the meeting to take place in Colombo and, despite indifferent health, travelled to the conference and played an active, lively part in its deliberations. Discussions on foreign affairs focused quite prominently on Asia – China, Japan, Malaya and Indo-China. The Japanese aspects were pursued on 11 January: Bevin warned against putting excessive faith upon the conversion of the Japanese to democratic procedures, although substantial progress had been realised. Looking to the future, Japan should be viable economically but not a threat.[49] Percy Spender, the Australian minister of external affairs, emphasised the central concern of the Australian people with a Japanese peace treaty. It was feared that Japanese militarism could revive, perhaps within a generation. There was great bitterness towards Japan in Australia and this could not be dissipated rapidly. At the same time Australia favoured a peace treaty which would facilitate the cooperation of other countries in fostering Japanese recovery and integration within the international community under the leadership of the United States. Spender added that crucial issues in the evolution of Japan must be investigated: he gave as examples the speed and size of Japanese ships, the use of vessels in Antarctica, and possible research in the area of nuclear physics.[50] Doidge of New Zealand advocated an early peace treaty on the grounds that further postponement would strengthen Japanese influence.[51] Sauer, the South African representative, underlined the importance of not treating Japan too severely, with implied allusions to South African experience after the Boer war and Germany's experience in 1919.[52] Nehru of India thought it was high time that the occupation ended for the Japanese people were wearying of it.[53] It was agreed to establish a working party to consider matters relevant to a peace treaty: this comprised the high commissioners in London supported by experts. Acheson had been apprehensive of a possible split between the United States and Britain, on one side, and the Asian members of the Commonwealth on the other side.[54] The working party met almost daily down to May 1950 and was chaired by Esler Dening; the Secretary of State for Commonwealth Relations, Patrick Gordon Walker, appeared at the inaugural meeting and attended only occasionally thereafter.[55]

Nothing could be achieved until Presiden Truman gave approval to the commencement of negotiations leading to a treaty. Truman had not resolved the bickering between the State and Defense departments in 1949 because he did not view the matter as a high priority; in addition, he had personal obligations to Dean Acheson and Louis Johnson, since the former was a personal friend and Johnson had raised finance for Truman's reelection campaign in 1948. The communist victory in China, followed by the conclusion of the various Sino-Soviet treaties in February 1950, rendered the Pentagon reluctant to support a treaty in the belief that it was more important for American forces to remain in Japan and to keep freedom of response unhindered by treaty obligations to the

Japanese. The State Department grasped the diplomatic and political realities pointing towards an early treaty. Truman and Acheson chose an astute Republican lawyer and politician, John Foster Dulles, to conduct the complex negotiations leading to a treaty. At first sight this seemed an odd choice, bearing in mind strident Republican censure of the Truman administration's policies in Asia. There were powerful arguments for Dulles's appointment. He was an authority on international affairs within the Republican party and had attended regularly meetings of the UN General Assembly as a member of the United States delegation. Dulles supported the bipartisan foreign policy for Europe so skilfully pursued by Senator Arthur H. Vandenberg. Dulles was extremely ambitious and hoped to be the secretary of state in the next administration, assuming that the Republicans won the 1952 election. Although a member of the 'eastern establishment' of the party (he was a New York lawyer), Dulles preserved links with the right wing headed by Taft. The pressures upon Dulles were considerable: he was a Republican serving a Democratic administration and was confronted with daunting problems in negotiating a treaty broadly acceptable to diverse interests. The outcome had to be approved by the requisite majority in the Senate in order to secure ratification. Dulles was better placed than most to surmount these challenges, for he was an adept operator, extremely patient and possessed of much guile. Truman had some reservations about appointing Dulles because of criticisms of the administration expressed by Dulles in his campaign to be elected as a senator in New York in 1948 but, as a highly shrewd operator himself, appreciated the cogent political arguments for appointing Dulles. In April 1950 Dulles joined the administration charged with responsibility for negotiating a treaty formally to conclude the Pacific war and the allied occupation of Japan.

MacArthur did not welcome Dulles's appointment. There was room for only one great authority on Japan within the Republican party and it was not Dulles. However, MacArthur had long advocated an early peace treaty, holding that lengthy occupations were counter-productive: in addition, he was looking forward to presiding over a peace conference to approve a treaty. MacArthur assisted Dulles for his own reasons and sought to persuade the right wing of the Republican party to acquiesce in Dulles's negotiations. MacArthur wrote to Taft on 23 March 1950, stating his views on a peace treaty: he rejected the argument that the United States should remain in occupation for strategic reasons as erroneous and dangerous. American interests would be served effectively through having a neutral, free, prosperous and industrious Japan. It was essential to restore American leadership in Asia, tarnished by the communist victory in China: the United States should act boldly in dealing with Japan.[56] MacArthur confirmed to Gascoigne that he was seeking to influence Taft to support an early conclusion of a treaty. MacArthur condemned the views of so-called military specialists in the Pentagon as 'cynical and half baked'.[57] Gascoigne added that MacArthur 'spoke somewhat slighteningly of John Foster Dulles who, he said, knew nothing whatever about the Far East'.[58] In a despatch to Bevin Gascoigne described MacArthur's policy towards the Japanese government as assuming a more liberal character with each passing week.[59] MacArthur defended this trend on the grounds that the extension of the occupation in the absence of a peace treaty compelled him to be magnanimous. He did not intend to interfere in domestic matters in Japan unless the need was imperative. MacArthur expressed ire at British policy: he knew that the British attitude on the political side was different to his but each was entitled to views sincerely held.[60]

On the eve of the outbreak of the Korean war, in June 1950, Gascoigne surveyed the trend of the previous two months. The Japanese were revealing openly their disappointment at the non-materialisation of a peace treaty. From his own experience Gascoigne could confirm the willingness of governors of prefectures, mayors and various officials from ministries, including Imperial Household bureaucrats, to criticise the occupation and the absence of a long-term policy for Japan. The majority of the people wanted a peace settlement as soon as possible and would accept a suitable defensive arrangement protecting Japan. The dilemmas facing the allies resulted from the vacillation characterising the occupation in the previous two years. The JCP had become truculent and abusive and Gascoigne applauded MacArthur's decision to purge the JCP's central committee and the executive staff of its newspaper. MacArthur's action might prove salutary in a wider sense in demonstrating to the people that SCAP was capable of acting decisively.[61]

Events in Korea on 25 June 1950 marked the close of a somewhat slow-moving period of change in Japan during which the likelihood of securing a peace treaty was debated endlessly by British ministers, officials and diplomats. MacArthur's power was at its height between 1945 and 1948 but his authority was still appreciable between 1948 and 1950: it is misleading to see him as a figurehead manipulated by others. MacArthur was never suited to such a role and would not have acquiesced in it. As British officials observed, it was extremely difficult to envisage the occupation without his avuncular and mildly intimidating presence. The radical reforms of the first phase of the occupation disappeared in 1948 to be replaced with emphasis on the gradual revival of the Japanese economy which should be capable of standing on its own feet before too long: this had the dual merit of reducing the pressure on the American taxpayer and of improving Japan's ability to withstand the appeal or threat of communism. MacArthur's crackdown on the JCP provided a further example of the previous trends being reversed sharply. Before the Korean war the prevailing British opinion of MacArthur was distinctly favourable. In British eyes he had been an efficient and successful head of the occupation. On occasions he might be too generous to the Japanese, especially in 1950, but over the peace treaty the attitude of the British and MacArthur was remarkably similar: each advocated an early peace treaty and termination of the occupation. However, there is some doubt as to whether MacArthur was as strongly in favour of a treaty as he stated. A peace conference would mark the end of his role and for a man continuing to eye the White House at a distance it would be wiser to remain in the public vision against an oriental background. Be that as it may, the appointment of Dulles constituted a marked quickening of the pace. Dulles was highly ambitious and determined to produce a treaty, sooner rather than later. The Korean war greatly increased the necessity of concluding a treaty and transformed MacArthur into the head of the UN military campaign in the Korean peninsula. Since Japan had become more important to the United States than before, the probability was that the peace settlement would be distinguished by magnanimity rather than retribution.

Notes

1 For studies of the occupation, see Kazuo Kawai, *Japan's American Interlude* (Chicago: Chicago University Press, 1960), H. B. Schonberger, *Aftermath of War: Americans and the Remaking of Japan, 1945–1952* (London: Kent State University Press, 1989), R. B. Finn, *Winners in Peace: MacArthur, Yoshida and Postwar Japan* (Oxford: University of California Press, 1992).

2 See Roger Buckley, *Occupation Diplomacy: Britain, the United States and Japan, 1945–1952* (Cambridge: Cambridge University Press, 1982).

3 See Roger Buckley, 'A Particularly Vital Issue? Harry Truman and Japan, 1945–52', in T. G. Fraser and Peter Lowe (eds), *Conflict and Amity in East Asia: Essays in Honour of Ian Nish* (London: Macmillan, 1992), pp. 110–24.

4 For a comprehensive account of MacArthur's career, se D. Clayton James, *The Years of MacArthur*, 3 vols (Boston MA: Houghton Mifflin, 1970–85). The final volume provides a thorough assessment of MacArthur's role in Japan and Korea between 1945 and 1951.

5 See Michael Schaller, *The American Occupation of Japan: The Origins of the Cold War in Asia* (New York: Oxford University Press, 1985) and *Douglas MacArthur: The Far Eastern General* (New York: Oxford University Press, 1989).

6 For the text of the emperor's renunciation, see *FRUS 1946*, vol. VIII, pp. 134–5, imperial rescript, 1 January 1946. For a clear statement of the emperor's commitment to a new constitution guaranteeing respect for human rights, see *ibid.*, p. 174, imperial rescript, 6 March 1946, contained in press release issued 6 March 1946.

7 The most detailed account of MacArthur's role in the functioning of SCAP is provided in D. Clayton James, *The Years of MacArthur*, vol. III, *Triumph and Disaster, 1945–1964*.

8 See 'Sir William Strang's Tour in South-East Asia and the Far East', note by Bevin, 17 March 1949, CP(49)67, Cab 129/33, part 2. Upon the character of his meeting with MacArthur, Strang wrote: 'Like most great public men, General MacArthur has a strong sense of the theatre, and he has it in supreme degree. He is also an indefatigable and unsparing talker. But the idiosyncracies should not blind one to his really massive, if somewhat unsubtle abilities. He is undoubtedly a great figure …' Strang thought that MacArthur entertained genuine admiration for Britain: he had treated British interests with 'scrupulous fairness'. MacArthur appeared confident that his democratisation of Japan would survive but Strang encountered few others in Tokyo who shared this opinion.

9 Clayton James, *The Years of MacArthur*, vol. III, p. 695.

10 Despatch from Gascoigne to Bevin, 29 January 1948, FO 371/69819/2626.

11 Despatch from Gascoigne to Bevin, 13 February 1948, FO 371/69819/3508.

12 Letter from Gascoigne to C. F. A. Warner, 14 February 1948, FO 371/69819/3838.

13 Memorandum by Gairdner, 26 February 1948, enclosed in letter from Gascoigne to Dening, 28 February 1948, FO 371/69819/3978.

14 *Ibid.*

15 *Nippon Times*, 5 March 1948, enclosed in letter from Gascoigne to Dening, 6 March 1948, FO 371/69820/5021.

16 Letter from Gascoigne to Dening, 6 March 1948, *ibid.*

17 For a discussion of the campaign for the Republican nomination in 1948, see Clayton James, *The Years of MacArthur*, vol. III, pp. 216–19 and T. C. Reeves, *The Life and Times of Joe McCarthy: A Biography* (London: Blond and Briggs, 1982), p. 146.

18 Tokyo to FO, 27 May 1948, FO 371/69911/7609.

19 *Ibid.*

20 See letter from Gascoigne to Dening, 10 January 1948, FO 371/69885/1287, for observations on the opinions of Royall, secretary for the army, and Draper, under-secretary for the army. Royall was reported as having advocated the building-up of Japan against 'totalitarian threats' in a speech delivered in San Francisco on 7 January 1948. Royall

and Draper were regarded as spokesmen for big business in the United States. For a wider discussion of the 'Japan Lobby', see H. B. Schonberger, 'The Japan Lobby in American Diplomacy, 1947–1952', *Pacific Historical Review*, 46 (1977), pp. 327–59.

21 Minute by F. S. Tomlinson, 28 January 1948, with minute by Dening, 29 January 1948, FO 371/69885/1368.

22 Tokyo to FO, 1 July 1948, FO 371/69911/9266.

23 See G. F. Kennan, *Memoirs, 1925–1950* (London: Hutchinson, 1968), pp. 381–91.

24 Tokyo to FO, 11 March 1948, FO 371/69885/4043, with minute by F. S. Tomlinson, 17 March 1948.

25 FO to Tokyo, 18 March 1948, *ibid.* Lew Douglas, the American ambassador in London, reported British interest in securing an early peace treaty, see *FRUS 1948*, vol. VI, pp. 664–5, Douglas to Acheson, 20 February 1948.

26 Tokyo to FO, 20 March 1948, FO 317/69885/4362.

27 Tokyo to FO, 7 April 1948, FO 371/69886/5237.

28 *Ibid.*

29 Tokyo to FO, 1 July 1948, FO 371/69911/9266. See also *FRUS 1948*, vol,. VI, pp. 719–21, Sebald to Acheson, 29 March 1948, and letter from Dickover (London) to Butterworth, 2 April 1948.

30 Minute by McNeil, 3 June 1948, FO 371/69927/8332.

31 *Ibid.*

32 Despatch from Gascoigne to Bevin, 18 December 1948, FO 371/76178/7527.

33 *Ibid.*

34 See Roger Buckley, *US–Japan Alliance Diplomacy, 1945–1990* (Cambridge: Cambridge University Press, 1992). For a valuable examination of Yoshida's career, see J. W. Dower, *Empire and Aftermath: Yoshida Shigeru and the Japanese Experience, 1878–1954* (Cambridge, MA: Harvard University Press, 1979).

35 For Bevin's earlier as well as later career, see the magisterial biography by Alan Bullock, *The Life and Times of Ernest Bevin*, 3 vols (London: Heinemann, 1960–83).

36 Despatch from Gascoigne to Bevin, 2 February 1949, FO 371/76179/2420.

37 Minute by Tomlinson, 17 February 1949, *ibid.*

38 *New York Times*, 17 February 1949, FO 371/76180/2938.

39 *Daily Mail*, 2 March 1949, FO 371/76210/3323.

40 Tokyo to FO, 13 July 1949, FO 371/76210/10430.

41 Lecture by Kennan, 'The Present Situation in Japan', National War College, Washington, DC, 19 May 1948, folder, May–September 1948, box 17, Kennan papers, Seeley G. Mudd Library, Princeton. See also *FRUS 1948*, vol. VI, pp. 691–712, report by Kennan, 25 March 1948, for a full account of his discussions with MacArthur in Tokyo.

42 Letter from Jager to Taft, 31 December 1948, enclosing article by Hallett Abend to appear in the next issue of *Look*, and letter from Taft to Jager, 7 January 1949, box 907, Robert A. Taft, Sr papers, Library of Congress, Washington D.C.

43 Council of Foreign Ministers (Paris) to FO, 15 June 1949, FO 371/76211/8775. During the meeting of the Council of Foreign Ministers, Bevin spoke to Acheson, observing that there were a number of aspects upon which the British and American governments diverged over Japan, citing issues involving reparations, gold holdings and trade. Britain desired a clearer understanding on these matters. Acheson expressed willingness to talk to Sir Oliver Franks.

44 Record of meeting in State Department, 17 September 1949, FO 371/76212/14555.

45 Letter from Gascoigne to Dening, 19 September 1949, FO 371/76213/14735.

46 Despatch from Gascoigne to Bevin, 21 October 1949, FO 371/76213/16818.

47 Washington to FO, 9 December 1949, FO 371/76214/18486.

48 Report by joint planning staff, 20 December 1949, JP(49)163 (Final), Defe 6/11. Note also reports on defence cooperation with Australia and New Zealand, 3 and 5 November 1948, Defe 6/7. See, too, *FRUS 1949*, vol. VII, part 2, pp. 901–2, memorandum by Butterworth, 18 November 1949.

49 Meeting of Commonwealth leaders in Colombo, January 1950, FMM(50)5, 11 January 1950, Cab. 133/78. See also memorandum by UK delegation, 9 January 1950, FMM(50)2, *ibid.*

50 *Ibid.*
51 *Ibid.*
52 *Ibid.*
53 *Ibid.*
54 Colombo to FO, 13 January 1950, FO 371/83828/7.
55 For the deliberations of the Commonwealth Working Party on Japanese Peace Treaty, 1950, see Cab 133/28.
56 Letter from MacArthur to Taft, 23 March 1950, box 628, Taft papers.
57 Letter from Gascoigne to Dening, 17 April 1950, FO 371/83830/67G.
58 *Ibid.*
59 Despatch from Gascoigne to Bevin, 16 April 1950, FO 371/83814/19. See also *FRUS 1950*, vol. VI, pp. 1114–16, Jessup to Acheson, 10 January 1950. MacArthur told Jessup that in the context of the peace treaty he had received excellent cooperation from the State Department and that the difficulties were created by the Defense Department.
60 Despatch from Gascoigne to Bevin, 16 April 1950, *ibid.*
61 Despatch from Gascoigne to Younger, 12 June 1950, FO 371/83831/93.

2

THE ROAD TO A JAPANESE PEACE TREATY, JUNE 1950 TO MAY 1951

Britain attached considerable importance to working closely with the Commonwealth during the prolonged exchanges with the United States concerning a peace treaty with Japan. Ironically, in the course of pursuing a settlement with Japan significant gaps opened up and cohesion within the Commonwealth was not as great when the peace conference ultimately assembled in San Francisco, in September 1951, as had been hoped in the summer of 1950. These developments were not unexpected when examined in a wider perspective and, if surprise is occasioned, it is that the Labour government under Attlee, and its Conservative successor under Churchill, was not better prepared for the outcome. As regards the old dominions Canada had no deep interest in issues affecting Japan and was preoccupied more with the repercussions on relations with the United States. Lester Pearson, the Canadian minister of external affairs, was active in the UN during much of this period and could prove a persuasive spokesman for the Commonwealth when Canada wished to make its voice heard.[1]

Australia was undoubtedly most seriously affected by a peace treaty. This resulted primarily from the traumatic effects of the Pacific war. Many Australians feared a Japanese invasion in 1942 and 1943 and their vulnerability, when faced with a ruthless adversary, shaped profoundly their subsequent reactions and behaviour.[2] Australia continued to worry that Japanese militarism would revive and it was this menace that determined Australian policy more than anything else. Associated with this point was the growth of Australian nationalism. This predated Japanese aggression but the latter stimulated the assertion of Australian interest. The Australian Labour Party was clearly identified with this trend, as illustrated in the pronouncements of the prime minister, John Curtin, and the minister for external affairs, Dr Herbert Evatt, during the first half of the Pacific war. The emphasis upon closer relations with the United States was modified in 1944 and 1945 as Curtin and Evatt became more suspicious at the flexing of American political and economic muscles. Evatt was widely perceived as ardently desiring the pursuance of a far more independent foreign policy.[3] Evatt wanted desperately to be leader of the Labour party and prime minister but his naked ambition, and capacity for becoming involved in acrimony, frustrated his aims and he served as minister for external affairs for most of the 1940s under Curtin and his successor, Ben Chifley.

The Labour government in Canberra was defeated narrowly in the general election held in December 1949 and was replaced by a conservative coalition comprising the Liberal and Country parties, headed by Robert Menzies. Menzies was a rather old-fashioned politician in one sense in that he adhered to the loyalties of 'kith and kin' and to the monarchy: these loyalties were coming to be viewed with diminishing enthusiasm by some Australians. Beneath his bluff exterior Menzies concealed a highly astute political grasp which explained why he dominated politics for a decade and a half.[4] The minister of external affairs down to 1951 was Percy Spender who was more critical in his approach to Britain than was Menzies. As Spender made clear in his subsequent reflections, he had felt since the 1930s that Britain was incapable of defending Australia and that Australian security should be located in a blend of its own efforts and with reliance upon the United States.[5] New Zealand clung to its ties with Britain, although here, too, faith in the old loyalties had been shaken by the wartime experiences and New Zealand leaders felt that the United States was better placed to defend New Zealand than was Britain.[6] South Africa was the least affected and leaned towards the American preference for a generous treaty with Japan, influenced by its own experience after the South African war and the experience of Germany with the Versailles treaty in 1919.

As regards the new Commonwealth, India adopted a more pronounced role of leadership in Asia under Nehru.[7] He was critical of the simplistic assumptions guiding the direction of American foreign policy. He advocated an early peace treaty of liberal character. India's attitude towards Japan was ambivalent but Nehru did not wish to be associated with retribution. Pakistan and Ceylon were less involved and sympathised with a reasonably magnanimous treaty. Burma had decided against accepting membership of the Commonwealth upon gaining independence in 1948 and was not concerned directly in the exchanges.

In May 1950 the Commonwealth working party on a Japanese peace treaty agreed that all countries represented in the FEC should be invited to help in drafting a treaty; in addition, Ceylon and, possibly, Indonesia should be asked to take part. Chinese participation was seen, correctly, as presenting numerous problems.[8] However, the Soviet Union and China should be invited to assist, at least until it became clear that they wanted to proceed in a direction contrary to that favoured by the democracies. In the context of strategic aspects, the British delegation defined the fundamental aims of a settlement as comprising the comprehensive demilitarisation of Japan (which had been achieved), implementation of suitable protection against the contingency of renewed Japanese militarism, and fostering a Japan committed to a peaceful policy in future. Japanese economic potential must be denied to the Soviet Union yet Japan must be capable of attaining economic viability. Japan would require adequate protection from attack and this could be provided by the application of a multilateral guarantee by those countries attending a peace conference. Clearly the Soviet Union and China would not form part of such a guarantee. A multilateral pact should be concluded including the preparation of a concerted defence plan. As an alternative a bilateral defence pact between Japan and the United States could be signed but this would involve the possibility of Japanese defence forces being raised to cooperate with the American forces: such a possibility 'would be very unwelcome to some Commonwealth countries'.[9] The role of internal security forces in Japan required careful consideration because the latter could be converted rapidly into military forces: it might be feasible to stipulate the type of arms allowed to such forces. The menace resulting from the reappearance of secret police must be avoided. The British government tended to think that the danger of a recurrence of Japanese aggression could be obviated by 'long range economic controls, which would be operated under an international agreement negotiated outside the Treaty'.[10] Where shipbuilding was concerned, Commonwealth delegations doubted the wisdom or, perhaps, desirability of determining limits on the size and speed of ships constructed in Japan. However, Japan's merchant shipbuilding capacity was substantially greater than peacetime requirements: accordingly, surplus capacity could be cut.

On the economic side the working party thought that Japan might be instructed to observe 'internationally recognised general principles of commercial policy' but it was decided that this should be examined further.[11] Reparations appeared largely a futile matter to pursue because it was held that reparations could not be obtained from industrial assets or from current production. Japanese assets abroad would have to be investigated further: Britain believed it had a prior claim on assets in Switzerland, since they were based very substantially upon remittances made by Britain for utilisation by the Red Cross for helping British prisoners of war (POWs). It was agreed generally that Japanese gold deposits should be available for reparations. Concern was expressed over the reemergence of the zaibatsu, despite MacArthur's endeavours to secure the removal of this threat.[12] On territorial features, sovereignty should be confined to the principal home islands as would be stipulated in the peace conference. Australia, New Zealand and South Africa were each interested in the renunciation of Japanese political and territorial claims in the Antarctic continent and adjacent islands. The working party favoured an admission that 'the Japanese militarist regime' had been responsible for provoking the Pacific war: this was analogous to the policy followed for the Italian peace treaty.[13] Divergent views were expressed within the working party over the need for establishing control machinery for the period following the application of the peace treaty. New Zealand was sceptical as to whether remote controls would be sufficient and believed that controls supervised by the United States would be required. Britain was becoming more hostile to the use of physical controls in Japan: if such controls were contemplated, it would be necessary to consider how far force could be applied or economic sanctions used. Canada felt that the threat of Japanese military revival could be contained most successfully via a defence agreement between the United States and Japan but that ways of enforcing the ban on militarism should be considered together with long-range economic controls. South Africa viewed enforcement as the essence of the problem but felt that the United States must handle this side. India, Pakistan and Ceylon favoured a multilateral structure for security: the dangers inherent in intervention in Japanese internal affairs had to be kept in mind.[14]

John Foster Dulles departed for East Asia in the middle of June 1950 to fulfil exchanges with MacArthur, Yoshida and others regarding the form of a peace treaty. He visited South Korea just before the outbreak of the Korean war and Dulles was in Tokyo when news of the North Korean advance arrived. This development accentuated Dulles's determination to negotiate a treaty as soon as practicable: the international situation was too dangerous to extend any longer uncertainties over the future of Japan. In addition to this, the success of his efforts bore a direct relationship to the future of Dulles's career. Alvary Gascoigne, the shrewd head of the British liaison mission, reported to Ernest Bevin on 9 July regarding Dulles's visit. The Korean conflict dominated everything and it was impossible to see MacArthur or his senior advisers other than William Sebald. MacArthur appeared to have shifted his opinion from a previously stated preference for American military bases existing only in islands close to Japan (Okinawa and the Ryukyus) to maintaining bases in the home islands of Japan. Dulles wished to advance fairly swiftly and, in the short term, with a drastic 'loosening' in the occupation regime, although it was not yet possible to assess Dulles's views in detail.[15] In September President Truman dismissed Louis Johnson, the secretary for defense, and appointed General George Marshall as his successor. This assisted considerably with the negotiation of a treaty, for Johnson's feud with Dean Acheson had delayed progress. Dulles told Esler Dening (who was then in New York) that the administration would proceed rapidly with a treaty. It was imperative to elicit the full support of the Japanese people in the midst of the Korean struggle. The American government believed that a treaty should be of a very liberal character. It would be dangerous to allow a power vacuum to obtain and he envisaged that American troops should stay in Japan for an undefined period.[16]

Understandably the Soviet Union regarded American aims with deep suspicion. Dulles believed in talking to a wide spectrum of opinion including Soviet representatives. He had a surprisingly candid discussion with Jacob Malik, the Soviet delegate to the UN, in October. Dulles explained that he wished to achieve a stable Japan dedicated to peace and without bitterness towards the countries identified with the occupation. Malik interestingly did not refer to the Council of Foreign Ministers (which could facilitate greater intervention by the Soviet Union) or the involvement of communist China in the conclusion of a treaty. Gladwyn Jebb, the British delegate to the UN, asked John M. Allison, Dulles's chief official in the State Department, whether a report that Dulles had conferred with Wellington Koo connoted an intention to involve Chiang Kai-shek's regime in negotiating a treaty: Allison responded evasively and this confirmed the speculation. Dulles told Malik that he desired Soviet involvement in negotiating a treaty. Malik replied that proposals over security suggested a further extension of American military occupation:

> Dulles frankly agreed that from the Soviet point of view there was some justification for this interpretation. He stressed, however, the present defenceless position of Japan; and he emphasised that the United States had neither the desire nor the capacity to maintain troops in Japan in such quantities that they could conceivably be regarded as a potential threat to the Soviet Union or any other power ...
>
> The conversation, which was very friendly throughout, then became general and ended with an exposition by Malik on the theory and practice of Communism. Malik particularly stressed that Communism is not an export

article and the Soviet Union has no desire to turn the Japanese or anyone else into Communists.[17]

Although the Soviet Union indulged in predictable ritualistic denunciation of American imperialism in Asia, its reactions throughout the treaty negotiations were less of a problem than might have been anticipated: the explanation is probably to be found in Stalin's customary caution in the international sphere and he had no desire to exacerbate the dangerous situation in East Asia.

Bevin asked Gascoigne to keep him informed on trends in Japan and Gascoigne sent the first of the letters requested on 18 November. Gascoigne focused particularly on MacArthur who was almost totally preoccupied with the war in Korea. MacArthur appeared confident of final victory in Korea notwithstanding the grave threat of huge Chinese action:

> He certainly remains the complete Dictator and he is enjoying some strong Republican backing in the States. President Truman would probably like to see him eased out of his job here, and there are some who think that one of Truman's main reasons for wanting an early Japanese peace is that it would bring with it MacArthur's exit from Japan.[18]

Gascoigne's feelings towards MacArthur were much more critical than they had been before the Korean conflict and he remarked on the deep resentment felt by the British at MacArthur's failure to consult them over aspects of occupation policy. The Japanese people were gaining from the effects of the 'Korean boom' in the economy. There was a mood of reasonable contentment in Japan but there was concern over possible escalation of the war in Korea. Gascoigne thought that Britain's position in Japan had improved in recent months.[19]

Esler Dening visited Japan in December and conveyed his assessment to Sir William Strang, the permanent under-secretary. Dening met many people and saw something of life outside Tokyo. The standard of living was still poor. Dening commented:

> But I gained the impression that the Japanese have not really changed and I should expect all their characteristics to become evident as soon as they are free. This may not be entirely agreeable to us but I think it is inevitable, and I came away more convinced than ever that it is high time that the dead hand of occupation should be removed. We have, in short, to allow Japan to find her own level in the world as soon as possible. The Japanese themselves probably have a good deal to learn as to what that level will be. We for our part must accept that a full sovereign Japan will do what she likes and we may not always like what she does. But I think there are sufficient safeguards in the hard facts of the present and the probability of the future to justify our accepting this risk. The alternative of keeping Japan in quarantine presents to my mind far greater dangers.[20]

MacArthur was so generous to the Japanese that he might have handed everything of significance to them unless a peace treaty was negotiated soon. It would be in Britain's interest to secure the ability to deal with Japan directly instead of being hampered by having to observe the role of SCAP. The problem of Chinese participation in a treaty was extremely intractable but Chinese and Soviet actions would be governed by perceptions of their interests whatever transpired. Dening felt that the Americans were unlikely to emerge very favourably from the occupation: the Japanese would not show appreciation once they secured their independence again. Japan might attempt to force Britain away from the United States and this must be averted. Another danger was that Japan and China might collaborate economically and this would include political perils in that the JCP could gain from the support of its Chinese comrades.[21] Dening's views were essentially gloomy and reflected quite accurately prevailing opinions in the Foreign Office: the positive achievements of the occupation and the sagacity shown by MacArthur in Japan (in contrast to Korea) were not recognised.

The extremely alarming developments in Korea following Chinese intervention depressed Dulles, although he may have exaggerated the sombreness for his own purposes. He spoke to Hubert Graves of the British embassy in Washington on 19 December. One of the most important challenges facing him was to ensure that Japan remained within the democratic camp. Dulles believed that the Soviet Union was focusing on Germany and Japan. In terms reminiscent of Halford Mackinder, Dulles saw Soviet ambitions embracing the land mass lying between the Atlantic and Pacific Oceans. The Japanese might be weighing up where their future loyalties should be placed. The Western powers must concentrate on offering Japan attractive terms. Graves interpreted Dulles's pessimism as designed to convince Britain of the necessity for achieving a very generous settlement. It was essential to keep Japan in the Western zone of defence in the Pacific: he conceded that pressures might build up within the United States rendering it difficult to conclude a treaty if the Soviet Union turned the screw on Japan, possibly by occupying Hokkaido.[22]

From the beginning of 1951 the momentum increased as Dulles became immersed in the full intricacies of negotiations. Within the British constitutional system issues were referred to the cabinet and it is important to appreciate the different emphases between the politicians in cabinet and the civil servants. The latter were well aware of the trend towards more magnanimous treatment of Japan, which had become a conspicuous feature of American policy and of SCAP's attitude since 1949. Officials in the Foreign Office were not very sympathetic towards Japan and believed that problems would emerge soon after the occupation ended. However, the United States was the dominant influence and Britain had to adjust accordingly. Members of the cabinet, with the exception of the foreign secretary, were not conversant with the finer points and felt that Britain possessed more freedom of action than was the case. The impression derived from reading cabinet minutes is that members were affected considerably by memories of the Pacific war and of atrocities committed by Japanese forces; this was fuelled by the campaigns of POW organisations. In addition, the Labour cabinet was highly conscious of its pledge to maintain full employment and to regalvanising the British economy: this, in turn, required an effective export drive. Recollections of Japanese competition resulted from 'unfair' practices connoting sweated labour and low wage rates. Therefore, the cabinet felt little inclination to be unduly generous towards Japan; it took some time to grasp that Britain would have to acquiesce in American decision-making or risk an exacerbation in relations with Washington, already rocked by friction caused by the Korean war. Bevin was in fast-declining health at the beginning of 1951 and could not provide a sustained grip on cabinet deliberations. Bevin resigned reluctantly in March 1951 and was succeeded by Herbert Morrison. He was largely ignorant of issues when he assumed office, took time to find his bearings, and was driven on by his wish to have noticeable impact as foreign secretary so as to advance his claim to be the next leader of the Labour Party and, hopefully, prime minister. Thus at cabinet level fluctuations in policy-making could be discerned.

On 2 January Bevin spoke to papers circulated, addressing the broad scope of a peace treaty and claims for compensation by individuals; a memorandum was distributed by the minister of defence dealing with security aspects. In discussion particular attention was drawn to the position of China; to fears entertained in Australia and New Zealand regarding possible Japanese aggression; and to difficulties over controlling Japanese shipbuilding capacity. Bevin observed that a report from the chiefs of staff recommended that Japanese rearmament should commence soon after a peace treaty had been signed: 'It now appeared, however, from a recent statement by General MacArthur (about which we had not been consulted) that the United States Government might be prepared to allow some degree of rearmament in advance of the conclusion of the Treaty'.[23] Commonwealth prime ministers met in London in January to review policies. Significant points conveyed by Bevin included reiterated emphasis on the desirability of a treaty being concluded soon; and that Britain must keep the right to discriminate against Japan economically if necessary, as notified to Commonwealth prime ministers at their meeting in September 1950, for which reason Britain would oppose extension of most favoured nation terms to Japan unless each country wished to do so.[24] The peace treaty should be accompanied by the signing of a bilateral defence treaty between the United States and Japan providing for American resources to be made available for the defence of Japan; Japan would agree to create armed forces of a designated size embracing land, air and naval elements. Britain intended to urge utilisation of Japanese gold deposits for reparations but accepted that payment of other forms of reparations would not be feasible on a large scale. It was envisaged that Britain would press for destruction of excessive Japanese shipping tonnage beyond a stipulated figure but this would very likely be opposed by other countries, particularly the United States.[25]

In discussion among Commonwealth leaders on 9 January, Harrison of Australia expressed concern that too liberal a treaty might emerge: Australia was apprehensive of a renewed Japanese military threat just as France feared a future German threat. No evidence had been adduced to advance the argument for a genuine Japanese conversion to democracy and a peaceful policy. It was accepted that Japan's friendship must be secured because of the expansion of the Cold War but Harrison doubted whether Japan could be relied upon in the longer term. Australia would accept limited Japanese rearmament to cope with internal order but did not desire extensive rearmament and the growth of heavy industries. It followed that a peace treaty should include sufficient protection against revived Japanese military power. An American guarantee of military support would satisfy Australia and Harrison enquired whether Britain would endorse Australia's request for a guarantee. Australia accepted that the Japanese economy must grow but preferred this to comprise emphasis on light rather than heavy industries. Japan should accept reasonable trading practices:

> Australia's standpoint could be summed up as follows. She objected to the military resurgence of Japan; she could not agree to unlimited Japanese re-armament; and she was not prepared to rely on keeping Japan as an ally of the democracies. Australia needed security against any future aggression by Japan.[26]

Liaquat Ali Khan of Pakistan supported conclusion of a peace treaty as soon as possible, in part because of the emergence of communist China. Japan possessed important potential economically and 'Asia must turn increasingly to Japan for supplies of manufactured goods'.[27] Sidney Holland of New Zealand stated that his country's situation resembled that of Australia: limited Japanese rearmament was inevitable but it should be confined to necessary land forces with severe restrictions being imposed for naval and air forces.[28] Nehru argued against further procrastination: the longer this continued the more exasperation would grow in Japan. It was not practicable to contemplate returning sovereignty to Japan while erecting restrictions. Half-measures were not feasible. It might be possible to control the supply of raw materials to Japan: indirect restriction was better than direct limits on armed forces. Nehru did not think it would be wise to change article 9 of the constitution. Such a step might provoke the Soviet Union or China to attack and this could cause a world war. Nehru hoped that Japan would opt not to maintain armed forces, since this would remove it from the centre of conflict.[29]

Louis St Laurent of Canada agreed broadly with Britain's position. He preferred dealing with Japanese shipbuilding through control of raw materials: '... such a course would be psychologically preferable to destroying a potential source of prosperity'.[30] Dr Dönges, the South African finance minister, reflected a more detached attitude for geographical reasons. The chief aim was to prevent Japan from falling into the Soviet orbit. This meant that conclusion of a peace treaty soon was essential. It was obvious that the Japanese people were becom-ing restless and attainment of a fair treaty would obviate the kind of predicament feared by Australia and New Zealand.[31] Dudley Senanayake of Ceylon argued for a treaty which would allow Japan to resume sovereignty without restrictions: the alternative could be a Japan moving towards communism.[32] Attlee commented that Japanese military strength had rested on access to raw materi-als in Korea and Manchuria. Since these sources were no longer available, it was less likely that Japan would prove a military menace. The apprehension voiced by Australia and New Zealand was understandable but a realistic approach must be adopted: this meant accepting that the occupation could not continue for much longer.[33]

In subsequent discussion that day Commonwealth representatives observed that control of imported raw materials would not give satisfactory protection against Japanese rearmament. Arrangements for security in the Pacific region could assume the form of a Pacific pact but, given prevailing atti-tudes within Australia, it was difficult to envisage inclusion of Japan within such a pact. One argument against imposing limits on Japanese rearmament was that

Japan would be in a favourable commercial situation which could rebound on other countries. Equally the danger of Soviet or Chinese aggression against Japan had to be remembered. Reparations was a divisive issue: Nehru waived possible Indian claims but Harrison referred to vigorous views expressed by POW organisations in Australia. Summing up, Bevin emphasised the importance of arriving at a treaty rapidly. He favoured a single treaty to be signed between Japan and those who had fought against it. If the Soviet Union and China refused to take part, he would support the signing of a more limited settlement as soon as feasible.[34] While there were appreciable differences of emphasis, it was agreed generally that a peace settlement soon was imperative.

Defence problems caused much anxiety. Dulles recognised how important it was to mollify Australia and New Zealand, which would necessitate offering a guarantee against renewed Japanese aggression. However, he did not wish to include Britain within a defence agreement for three reasons: firstly, because France would then press for admission, as would the Netherlands and Portugal; secondly, because Dulles wished to avoid undue criticism from the right wing of the Republican party; and thirdly, because he believed that American leadership should be asserted and that British influence in the Pacific was waning unavoidably. There was considerable cogency in these views but it could be anticipated that omission of Britain would be resented, especially in the Conservative Party. Dulles invited Oliver Franks to see him on 12 January, so that he could bring the ambassador up to date on his plans. He intended departing for Japan in about ten days time, the principal objective being to determine whether general strategy in the Pacific area could be pursued on a basis of cooperation with Japan. This involved an assessment of the extent to which Japan was capable of fulfilling its own defence; the mood of the people; and the relevance of the constitution. Dulles said that after a peace treaty came into operation the United States could provide air and sea power with Japan meeting the demands of its land defence. The future of the economy was linked with events in South-East Asia and the aim of linking industrial production to the rice and other resources in South-East Asia could be jeopardised. Economic problems could be offset through inviting Japan to join what Dulles defined as a 'white Anglo-Saxon club'.[35] This would make the Japanese feel more secure and enhance their prestige. It followed that the Japanese must be coaxed rather than coerced. He contemplated the future character of defence in the Pacific as being based on an 'island chain' comprising Australia, New Zealand, Indonesia (if willing), the Philippines, Japan and the United States. In response to a question from Franks, Dulles said that he regarded Britain's role as that of a 'valued consultant' but not as a direct participant. He thought that his scheme would satisfy Australia and New Zealand, which was a fundamental aspect.[36]

The British chiefs of staff preferred a defence pact distinct from a peace treaty and held that the American proposal to include security arrangements within a treaty would indicate that these provisions had been *imposed* with undesirable consequences. They doubted whether it would be sensible to set up a Pacific Defence Council: it could be regarded as too elaborate and it might encourage others to demand membership. As regards Britain itself, exclusion could be seen as suggesting a retreat from British responsibilities, which in turn

could affect adversely the position in Hong Kong and Malaya. Dulles's proposals were regarded as unacceptable as conveyed.[37] The cabinet discussed the issue
of Pacific defence on 12 February; Dulles's 'island chain' was criticised as
unsound in strategic and political terms. If too much emphasis was placed on
islands, then Taiwan could be put forward for inclusion, which could mean that
Australia and New Zealand would have to support the Kuomintang regime. The
first sea lord believed that the most effective way of removing apprehension in
Australia and New Zealand might be to guarantee their security via a tripartite
pact. The cabinet decided that its objections should be transmitted to Dulles.[38]
In the light of British representations and of further reflection, Dulles moved
away from the concept of an 'island chain' towards an agreement between the
United States, Australia and New Zealand only. The cabinet resumed discussion
on 1 March when Attlee described Dulles's modified ideas as a great improvement. However, the cabinet was divided, some members seeing a treaty as
desirable because it would afford adequate protection to Australia and New
Zealand and British exclusion as realistic because Britain could not continue to
accept more commitments, given the pressure on its resources. Other members
considered a comprehensive Pacific pact analogous to NATO as necessary; in
addition, British exclusion would be demeaning to British prestige. The cabinet
decided to defer further discussion.[39]

Meanwhile, in Tokyo General MacArthur's lengthy term as SCAP was
drawing to a close, rather more rapidly than MacArthur realised. Sir George
Sansom, a former diplomat and distinguished Japanologist, visited the general
on 17 January. Sansom was a shrewd observer and captured the positive as well
as the negative characteristics of MacArthur. The general was certainly impressive and was unquestionably 'a great man, whatever his shortcomings'.[40] While
not conveying anything of profound character, he 'put on one of his perfor-
mances', which was difficult to surpass in terms of virtuosity. Sansom added:

> He describes his own views and actions in such language that they appear to
> have a kind of absolute validity, an almost superhuman rightness. He emboi-
> ders all his themes and is not always strictly truthful. If facts do not fit with
> the ideal picture he wishes to draw, he alters them.
>
> All the same, he is not merely fantastic. His political and military views have
> a logical coherence and he thinks things out very carefully. He may base
> himself upon some mistaken premises, but it would be dangerous to dismiss
> his opinions as only irrational or prejudiced. He has often proved right and I
> think his average is fairly high. His trouble is vanity.[41]

MacArthur repeated his disapproval of protracted occupations and denied that
the Japanese had been converted fully to democracy. The occupation had
devised the means whereby the Japanese could become true democrats if they
wished. He praised the people for their hard work and achievement. He also
praised the *genro* of the Meiji era and, by implication, saw himself as fulfilling a
similar task – 'great men, great patriots, who were above party, "unaffected by
the cross-currents of day-to-day politics"'.[42]

Alvary Gascoigne had served as head of the British liaison mission in
Tokyo since July 1946. He was an able, hard-working diplomat and represented
British interests capably. He gained MacArthur's trust and this in part explains

the frequency of their meetings before the outbreak of the Korean war: an additional reason was that MacArthur needed British support at times against undesirable interference from Washington. Bevin decided towards the end of 1950 that Gascoigne had served in Tokyo for long enough and that he should proceed shortly to Moscow as ambassador. Gascoigne sent a personal letter to MacArthur on 27 December 1950 informing him of his impending departure: Gascoigne described his four-and-a-half years in Tokyo as the most memorable in his career. He thanked MacArthur for his kindness in the past.[43] MacArthur later described Gascoigne as 'sharp' and more capable than Esler Dening, Britain's first ambassador in Tokyo after Japan regained sovereignty.[44]

As was customary at the end of a tour, Gascoigne produced a lengthy, reflective despatch covering the period between July 1946 and his departure in February 1951.[45] Before going to Japan in 1946 he had been warned that MacArthur might be awkward, since he enjoyed the reputation of being an Anglophobe. However, MacArthur greeted him most cordially, at that time being at the zenith of his career. MacArthur tackled the principal challenges inherent in the occupation with vigour and panache. In the main he directed the occupation with perception and skill. Japanese domestic politics had always been corrupt and did not show a significant improvement after 1945. The occupation was most successful in the commercial and economic spheres and the level of economic recovery in the latter period was most encouraging. Much of the credit for this belonged to those who came from Washington on special missions to tackle particular economic dilemmas, most obviously inflation in 1949 when the Dodge mission remedied the problem through emphasising a balanced budget, termination of export subsidies, diminution in import subsidies, and channelling American economic aid into works of capital reconstruction. Japan benefited enormously from the large demand for goods and services engendered by the Korean war: by the close of 1950 the goods and services supplied by Japan to UN forces in Korea aggregated just over 182 million US dollars.[46] Japan's basic economic position was uncertain, however, since the stimulus resulting from the Korean struggle created 'a somewhat deceptive appearance of prosperity'.[47] It was essential to secure a peace treaty soon: extension of the status quo would antagonise large numbers of Japanese. It was impossible to impose a restrictive treaty: the Western powers would have to limit importation of badly needed raw materials. Rearmament was inevitably contentious but was bound to occur. During a period of world crisis Japan must contribute to the defence of the West. If a peace treaty came into force within eighteen months Gascoigne was not pessimistic of the immediate future. The longer term would be shaped by the trend of international politics in East Asia and by the inclinations of the people. Japan was more likely to move towards the right than to the left. Communism would only appeal to the Japanese if they felt they were faced with no alternative. Gascoigne's view was similar to that prevailing in the Foreign Office but he was, arguably, slightly less gloomy than his colleagues in Whitehall.

A short time before drafting his farewell despatch Gascoigne visited the prime minister, Yoshida Shigeru, who was largely satisfied with Japan's progress. Yoshida described the progress in developing the national police reserve, comprising 75,000 men, as positive: the men were enthusiastic and should prove very efficient. They were being trained by American officers and were using American equipment. As regards rearmament Yoshida did not discern significant support among the people for economic reasons. Gascoigne thought Yoshida's personal attitude had changed from an unwillingness to contemplate rearmament to a recognition that it was unavoidable. Yoshida seemed worried at a potential growth in communist support and blamed Koreans for acting as communist agents in Japan: this was not untypical of his harsh approach towards the Korean community. Yoshida professed optimism concerning his survival as prime minister. Gascoigne ended by stating his liking for Yoshida. He identified the latter's positive characteristics, often ignored in the Foreign Office. Yoshida was lively and shrewd and at the age of 76 'had no particular axe to grind'.[48] Yoshida was basically an Anglophile but was not happy with Britain at present because of the delay in accepting a Japanese 'overseas agency' in London and because of criticism of his government sometimes expressed by *The Times* correspondent in Tokyo:

> In reality Yoshida feels hurt. I think that we are not at present actively wooing Japan to the same extent as the United States. Moreover, he does not, or will not, appreciate that some time must pass before the British colonial subjects in the United Kingdom territories of South-East Asia overcome their hatred of the Japanese for the barbarous manner in which the latter behaved in Hong Kong and Malaya, as well as in North Borneo and Sarawak during the second world war.[49]

Gascoigne endeavoured to reassure Yoshida of Britain's desire for cordial relations.

Gascoigne's successor, George Clutton, continued his predecessor's policy of visiting Yoshida once a month. Yoshida indicated, when they met on 14 March, that he did not wish to sign a peace treaty because of his recollections of the German experience with the treaty of Versailles in 1919.[50] The developing acrimony between MacArthur and the Truman administration over the Korean war probably explained Clutton's assessment on 19 March that MacArthur and his circle now wished to postpone a peace treaty because MacArthur did not want to relinquish his role as SCAP as long as the Korean war continued. It was virtually impossible to see MacArthur and there were rumours that he might be replaced by General Mark Clark.[51]

Dulles returned from his visit to Tokyo in February feeling that significant progress had been achieved. He described the existing differences between Britain and the United States as involving Japanese shipbuilding capacity, restoration of allied property in Japan and a war guilt clause. Two of these aspects were difficult to surmount because Dulles held strong opinions on them. He was firmly opposed to a reduction in shipbuilding capacity: assenting to this would doom any Japanese government in office at the time. He had no firm opinions regarding restoration of allied property in Japan; however, if property owners inside Japan were awarded compensation, those outside Japan, receiving nothing, would be aggrieved. Dulles stated that MacArthur was wholly opposed to compensating owners of property. He disapproved strongly of a war guilt clause because of his experience as a young member of the American delegation at the Paris peace conference in 1919.

Franks, the ambassador in Washington, did not see this as a serious problem. Progress was being made towards a tripartite agreement between the United States, Australia and New Zealand: after his visits to Australia and New Zealand, Dulles accepted that his previous proposal, linked with an 'island chain', had been unsatisfactory. However, the subjects of a peace treaty and of Pacific security had become prominent topics for debate in Australia. He had tried to see Dr Evatt without success and suspected that the latter was avoiding him.[52] Dulles said he had not pursued Chinese aspects in Tokyo.

The Foreign Office and the State Department proceeded discretely with the preparation of distinct drafts of a treaty. The provisional amended draft extended to 37 pages and was communicated to Washington on 23 March. The British draft was completed early in April. Robert Scott minuted that warm congratulations should be conveyed to Charles Johnston, Gerald Fitzmaurice, and the members of the Japan and Pacific department for their industry and thoroughness.[53] Roger Makins minuted his regret that the Americans had produced their draft first, which could engender confusion.[54] Sir William Strang observed, with the disdainful air of a mandarin, that: 'The Americans will probably not take kindly to this accurate draft of ours. May prefer their own rather slapdash productions. But we must try it on, even though we are rather late with it.'[55] Herbert Morrison was still in the early stages of adjusting to the pressure of business falling on the foreign secretary, having succeeded Bevin in March. He rather crossly minuted that he had been unable to study the draft properly, since it had reached him at a function he was attending the previous night:

> it is now part 11 pm & I must get my week-end sleep to make up for the 3 ams of the week. Mr. Barclay [private secretary] asks for return am tomorrow. Well, I don't propose to lose my sleep & my health because of that. So here are the pp. I have 'looked' at & as he suggested – in view of its length this is all that is poss[ible] – if Office is to get things away tomorrow as asked for.
>
> So I accept assurances that the great bulk has Cab[inet] authority & I note that HMG & the Commonwealth not committed. On this basis transmission can proceed. But don't forget Cab. at right time.[56]

Dulles moved to explain his policy to the American public in a speech delivered in Los Angeles on 31 March. He gave a careful, judicious and informative address. He remarked, on consultation with the Soviet Union, that the Russians had participated in talks for a period of three months but now that a treaty was fast materialising had taken fright. The Soviet Union had announced publicly that it would not extend the discussions over a treaty. Dulles hoped that the Soviet Union would think again.[57] Anglo-American exchanges became more difficult in March and April 1951 because of a more assertive line being adopted by the Labour cabinet. Morrison chaired a cabinet meeting on 22 March when Attlee was ill. Morrison told his colleagues that the United States wanted to make swifter progress but that two important aspects affecting China had to be clear: communist China should be involved in negotiations for a treaty with Japan and Japanese soverignty over Taiwan should be renounced with Taiwan being ceded to 'China': this should be on the understanding that it would not prejudice an ultimate decision as to which Chinese regime should be permitted sovereignty over Taiwan. In discussion some members urged delaying negotiations on a Japanese treaty if possible. Otherwise the United States might press for the Kuomintang regime to participate as the *de jure* administration, which would alienate some members of the Commonwealth and the Chinese population in Malaya. It was somewhat difficult to discuss a treaty while the war in Korea went on. Also final agreement had not been arrived at among Commonwealth countries. The cabinet, 'Invited the Foreign Secretary to seek means of delaying further proceedings for the discussion of a Japanese Peace Treaty'.[58] This was the sole occasion when the British government departed from its long-held opinion that a peace treaty should be concluded quickly. The decision was mistaken and arose partly because of Morrison's lack of experience in the Foreign Office: Bevin would have grasped the likely effects immediately. The United States was offended and Japanese leaders blamed Britain for the failure to advance rapidly. Morrison soon realised his error and told the cabinet on 2 April that it would be foolish to persevere in an attitude that would deprive Britain of just recognition for the policy followed until ten days before; the cabinet agreed to approve a resumption of the policy of completing a treaty quickly.[59]

Dulles was upset at the vacillation of Britain, and disliked the emphasis placed on the participation of the Peking government. He saw Oliver Franks on 6 April and said bluntly:

> We had suddenly placed two very large rocks on the road of progress. In fact he had been led to wonder whether it might be impossible to reach agreement with us and in that case whether the United States might not have to make a unilateral arrangement with Japan, a thought which caused him the deepest concern.[60]

He could not comprehend the way British policy was evolving. Dean Rusk was present during the discussion and pointed out, in all fairness, that it was the British who had advocated a treaty for a long time while the United States vacillated. Franks explained the position as he saw it as comprising divergences over shipbuilding and a war guilt clause; issues of procedure such as Chinese participation; the British wish to produce a draft of a treaty did not result from a desire to be difficult but rather to secure as satisfactory a treaty as possible. Dulles responded that he was not trying to diminish Britain's role in East Asia, as was apparently feared by Gascoigne: Britain must continue to play a prominent role in East Asian affairs. Over China Dulles focused, not on the invitation to the Chinese government, but on the problem of how to deal with it so as to ensure that the Peking regime did not block progress through resort to negative tactics.[61] According to the American record of this discussion, Franks attributed vacillation in London recently to drift within the Foreign Office caused by Bevin's declining health and Morrison's inexperience.[62]

Dulles was irate for two reasons and he stated these in a letter to an old friend, Ferdinand Lathrop Mayer, sent on 10 April. He was handling extremely delicate matters exacerbated by problems within the American government and the negative attitude shown by Herbert Morrison.[63] The former referred to the climax to the acrimonious dispute between President Truman and General MacArthur, now coming to a head, and which accentuated the political challenges facing Dulles because of the rage bound to be voiced by the Republican right wing when MacArthur involuntarily surrendered his posts in Japan and Korea. Carping from the British, uttered by a foreign secretary who was essentially ignorant of the matters he was addressing, was simply too much. If the domestic uproar over MacArthur's removal became too great, Dulles might have to resign but he would not quit if this could be avoided.

Just as Dulles was concentrating more upon convincing the wider public, so Morrison prepared to influence the media. Charles Johnston drafted notes in readiness for Morrison's encounter with diplomatic correspondents. Johnston focused on reparations, textiles and shipping. With reparations the problem arose from the huge divergence between total claims against Japan and Japan's ability to pay. The American taxpayer had paid around two billion US dollars to sustain the Japanese economy since 1945: Britain wished to see the economy maintaining itself. In the case of textiles it was neither wise nor possible to incorporate restrictions within a treaty. Apart from the need for the economy to be effective, large areas, notably parts of South-East Asia, required textiles urgently and the British industry could not meet the demand. A typical argument of the Labour government was then inserted by Johnston into the briefing: '... we hope that the young and vigorous trades union movement in Japan, by securing a more reasonable wage rate, will reduce the risk of unfair Japanese industrial competition such as we had to face before the war'.[64] With shipping Britain did not contemplate restrictions of a direct nature but rather tackling shipbuilding capacity, which reached inflated proportions during the war: as 'off the record' information, Morrison could indicate that consideration was being given to including action over shipbuilding capacity in a peace treaty. However, the American government was firmly opposed for practical and political reasons.[65]

On 5 April Robert Scott, together with Johnston and C. P. Scott, met representatives of the Japan Association: the latter embraced British firms pursuing business in Japan. The meeting was chaired by J. S. Scott of John Swire and Sons Limited, chairman of the Japan Association. He stated the principal interest of the Japan Association as comprising, 'whether it would succeed in securing non-discriminatory treatment in Japan for British commercial interests'.[66] Before the Pacific war the Japanese made strenuous endeavours to force British business out by creating problems over leases, by implementing financial restrictions, and so on. It was hoped further that the treaty could deal positively with validation of postwar purchases of property by foreigners in Japan and that non-discriminatory treatment should be obtained for British shipping. It was held strongly that payments of corporation tax by British companies since the war should be refunded.[67] The briefing for this meeting pointed out that the situation in Japan had changed substantially in the previous two years: British policy towards Japan became more liberal because of the repercussions of the Cold War. The Foreign Office would urge compensation, restoration of British property in Japan, and payment of compensation for damage (probably in yen). It was hoped that prewar claims against Japan would be revived; compensation would not be pursued for damage to property outside Japan or for personal prejudice claims.[68]

The dismissal of MacArthur contained dangerous implications for the fate of a peace treaty. From the viewpoint of treaty negotiations and so far as Britain was concerned, it was fortunate that Dulles was handling matters. Right-wing Republicans were deeply suspicious of British motives at the best of times, let alone in a situation in which a great American hero, and a prominent right-wing Republican himself, had been removed in circumstances in which the 'smoking gun' pointed and fired at MacArthur had been primed in London. MacArthur was understandably vindictive after his removal: it was again fortunate for the British that he did not possess more political guile. Dulles had to juggle the various challenges facing him with fine judgement and he could not expose himself too obviously to the accusation of being manipulated by the Machiavellian British . Charles Johnston assessed the position on 18 April and concentrated on specific features.[69] One of the most serious was clearly the dispute over China and Taiwan and how this should be addressed in a treaty. Johnston felt it would not be sensible to approach the Peking government at this time but it should be feasible subsequently:

> With the removal of the General we can in fact expect that in time it will become easier for us to influence United States policy in the Far East in the way we want: it would seem a pity to run any risk of prejudicing this process by a move which would be impossible to keep secret and would be bound to influence and exaggerate our present differences.[70]

The vital consideration was to exclude the Kuomintang regime from involvement rather than to secure Chinese communist participation. British tactics must conform with the cabinet's decision on 22 March not to advance compromise proposals to the Americans: the aim should be to induce the Americans to suggest a compromise. Possibly Britain should move towards a previous American sugges- tion that a peace treaty should require renunciation of sovereignty by Japan without defining 'China' and with a suspensory device to facilitate further reflec- tion. Britain and the United States were in agreement that the fate of Taiwan must be deferred pending a wider East Asian settlement. Sir William Strang and Herbert Morrison were convinced by Johnston's arguments but Morrison empha- sised that he must act in conformity with cabinet decisions.[71]

George Clutton, acting head of the British mission in Tokyo, met Dulles on 20 April. Dulles said that Japanese leaders feared that differences between the Americans and the British could delay the conclusion of a treaty. Dulles described these apprehensions as unjustified but it appears that he had encour- aged the Japanese to react in this way earlier in April as a means of bringing pressure to bear on the British. Clutton enquired as to how the Kuomintang regime was viewed in the context of obtaining signatures: after initial hesitation Dulles commented that without Kuomintang signature it might be impossible to obtain the necessary support for ratification in the Senate.[72] In Washington amiable discussions between the Foreign Office and the State Department proceeded in which the American and British drafts of a treaty were compared. The British draft was longer and more explicit than the American draft. Franks reported that the American delegation had accepted British arguments on several points, including the preamble and arrangements for the end of the occu- pation. The thorny issues of China and Taiwan were put on one side as too complex to pursue for the present. The British representatives reserved the British position over the Antarctic and disposal of gold. Apart from China and Taiwan, the principal problems concerned the Congo Basin treaties and general economic relations. The British wished to obtain Japanese renunciation of rights under the Congo Basin treaties which would render it much more difficult for the Japanese to compete in Africa. The Americans were willing to look further at the overall economic situation. Other awkward aspects, including claims, he disposal of Japanese property in neutral and ex-enemy countries, and debts, had not yet been discussed.[73] When Dulles left Tokyo on 23 April, he struck Clutton as having a positive approach and as desiring Chinese cooperation between the United States and Britain in order to secure as much identification of common interest as possible. Dulles seemed to view the British draft favourably but Clutton added that this did not apply to certain of his staff who disliked the British proposals. Clutton conceded that Dulles might be masking his real opinions.[74] In fact, it seems clear that Dulles was genuine in wanting to work with Britain and secure one agreed draft but that he was determined that the outcome should fulfil American rather than British intentions.

The talks in Washington ended early in May. The British position was reserved over Taiwan, the Antarctic, the Ryukyu islands, the fate of war criminals, fisheries, UN property, Japanese gold deposits, assets in neutral and former enemy countries, and disputes. The British position was also reserved over general economic relations, although the American delegation moved some way towards Britain with reference to Japanese renunciation of rights in renounced territories, and international agreements, but with American reservations regarding the Congo Basin treaties, debts, war claims, and disposal of German property in Japan. Therefore, the discussions in Washington, reported Franks, reduced but did not liquidate areas of divergence. Franks was encouraged in the main by the progress achieved: while there was a considerable way to go each side understood the other's position better.[75] Clutton spoke to Yoshida on 30 April when the prime minister returned from an electioneering trip. Yoshida was pleased with the British attitude concerning a peace treaty and said that the Japanese people looked forward to the peace settlement and were appreciative for the magnanimous approach shown by the United States and Britain.[76] Clutton also saw the new SCAP, General Matthew B. Ridgway, and was impressed with the latter's friendly, straightforward approach: this was very different from the theatrical atmosphere inseparable from meetings with MacArthur. Ridgway praised the calibre of British troops in Korea.[77]

The Foreign Office assessed where matters stood in minutes drafted by C. P. Scott and Charles Johnston on 11 and 15 May. Scott identified the remaining difficulties as comprising Chinese participation and Taiwan; whether the Republic of Korea should be involved; restitution and restoration of allied property in Japan; disposal of Japanese assets in neutral and former enemy countries; reparations with reference to Japanese gold; and the Congo Basin treaties.[78] It would be necessary to decide on appropriate procedure. Johnston wrote of how helpful John M. Allison had been, 'a mixture of friendliness and effectiveness which seems rare among State Department officials, and he set the tone of the talks, which though business-like, was completely friendly and informal'.[79]

Dulles was conscious of the volatile state of American opinion, meaning that the joint Senate hearings into the reasons for MacArthur's dismissal were proceeding in Washington in May. Dulles would pursue the contentious problems concerning China and Taiwan once emotionalism in the United States subsided. A solution might be reached on the basis that neither Chinese regime should sign a peace treaty, thus deferring a decision. Allison indicated confidentially that a compromise on lines proposed separately by Canada and Britain was being examined.[80]

In the middle of May 1951 the prospects for securing an agreed Anglo-American draft treaty were encouraging. Significant differences still remained and these would require full discussion during Dulles's forthcoming visit to London when he would meet leading cabinet ministers. The two governments agreed that a treaty should be of liberal character, although the United States was more inclined towards generosity than Britain. Civil servants in Britain leaned more towards the American view as a matter of realism; their political masters were less inclined towards magnanimity and there were to be a few awkward exchanges during Dulles's visit in June. On the defence side the Attlee government acquiesced in American strategy for the Pacific region, resting upon close collaboration between the United States, Australia and New Zealand with the formal exclusion of Britain. Doubts over the reactions in the American Senate remained and would depend in part on the outcome of the MacArthur hearings. The most positive aspect was that Dulles was the central personality in determining tactics and not Dean Acheson. Dulles was uniquely placed to handle Republican critics: there was no love lost between MacArthur and himself and Dulles was far more skilful, and devious in navigating treacherous waters, at least in this stage of his career.

Notes

1 For Pearson's views on international developments in this period, see J. A. Munro and A. I. Ingles (eds), *Mike: The Memoirs of the Right Honourable Lester B. Pearson*, vol. II, *1948–1957* (Toronto: University of Toronto Press, 1973).
2 See Geoffrey Bolton, *The Oxford History of Australia*, vol. V (Oxford: Oxford University Press, 1990), pp. 3–40.
3 See R. J. Bell, *Unequal Allies: Australian–American Relations and the Pacific War* (Melbourne: Melbourne University Press, 1977) and David Day, *Reluctant Nation: Australia and the Allied Defeat of Japan, 1942–45* (Melbourne: Oxford University Press, 1992).
4 For Menzies's earlier career, see A. W. Martin with Patsy Hardy, *Robert Menzies: A Life*, vol. I, *1894–1943* (Melbourne: Melbourne University Press, 1993). For a discussion of the 'Menzies era' in the 1950s and 1960s, see Bolton, *Oxford History of Australia*, vol. V, pp. 89–162.
5 Percy Spender, *Exercises in Diplomacy* (Sydney: Sydney University Press, 1969), pp. 21, 24.
6 See Ann Trotter, *New Zealand and Japan, 1945–1952: The Occupation and the Peace Treaty* (London: Athlone Press, 1990) for a valuable survey: note especially pp. 92–172 for discussion of New Zealand responses to the negotiations over a peace treaty.
7 See Sarvepalli Gopal, *Jawaharlal Nehru: A Biography*, vol. II, *1947–1956* (London: Jonathan Cape, 1979), which includes considerable discussion of Nehru's views relating to foreign issues.
8 Commonwealth working party on Japanese peace treaty, 1–17 May 1950, FO 371/83832/105.

9 *Ibid.*
10 *Ibid.*
11 *Ibid.*
12 *Ibid.*
13 *Ibid.*
14 *Ibid.*
15 Despatch from Gascoigne to Bevin, 9 July 1950, FO 371/83832/103. See also *FRUS 1950*, vol. VI, pp. 1230–7, summary report from Dulles to Acheson, 3 July 1950.
16 Letter from Dening to R. H. Scott, 23 September 1950, FO 371/83833/128.
17 New York (Jebb) to FO, 27 October 1950, FO 371/83834/162.
18 Letter from Gascoigne to Bevin, 18 November 1950, FO 371/83816/63/G. See *FRUS 1950*, vol. VI, pp. 1349–52, letter from Dulles to MacArthur, 15 November 1950, in which Dulles wrote of the need to promote bipartisan cooperation over the peace treaty. Dulles censured the activities of a 'rather noisy newspaper group which supported the Republicans and which is beating the drums for reckless action which would involve us deeply in war on the mainland of Asia' (p. 1351).
19 Letter from Gascoigne to Bevin, 18 November 1950, FO 371/83816/63/G.
20 Letter from Dening to Strang, 8 December 1950, FO 371/83837/217.
21 *Ibid.*
22 Washington to FO, 20 December 1950, FO 371/83839/232/G.
23 Cabinet minutes, 1(51)4, 2 January 1951, Cab 128/19.
24 'Japan: Japanese Peace Treaty', memorandum by Bevin, PMM(51)5, 2 January 1951, Cab 133/90.
25 *Ibid.*
26 Minutes of Commonwealth ministers meeting, PMM(51)6, 9 January 1951, Cab 133/90.
27 *Ibid.*
28 *Ibid.*
29 *Ibid.*
30 *Ibid.*
31 *Ibid.*
32 *Ibid.*
33 *Ibid.*
34 *Ibid.*
35 Washington to FO, 12 January 1951, FO 371/92529/116/G.
36 *Ibid.*
37 FO to Tokyo, 30 January 1951, FO 371/92529/24/G.
38 Cabinet minutes, CM13(51)1, 12 February 1951, Cab 128/19.
39 Cabinet minutes, CM16(51)3, 1 March 1951, Cab 128/19.
40 Record of interview between Sansom and MacArthur, 17 January 1951, FO 371/92521/3.
41 *Ibid.*
42 *Ibid.*
43 Letter from Gascoigne to MacArthur, 27 December 1950, folder British mission correspondence, Japan, box 108, MacArthur papers, MacArthur Memorial, Norfolk, Virginia.
44 Memorandum by Murphy, 30 April 1952, folder, MacArthur testimony, box 63, Acheson papers, Harry S. Truman Library, Independence, Missouri. Robert Murphy recorded a frank discussion with MacArthur in which the general revealed his continued bitterness over his dismissal a year earlier. MacArthur described Dening as not being 'as bright' as Gascoigne.
45 Despatch from Gascoigne to Bevin, 6 February 1951, FO 371/92521/5.
46 *Ibid.*
47 *Ibid.*
48 Conversation between Gascoigne and Yoshida, 22 January 1951, FO 371/92521/4.
49 *Ibid.*
50 Letter from Clutton to R. H. Scott, 16 March 1951, FO 371/92536/186.
51 Letter from Clutton to R. H. Scott, 19 March 1951, FO 371/92537/211/G.

52 Washington to FO, 28 February 1951, FO 371/92532/100.
53 Minute by R. H. Scott, 5 April 1951, FO 371/92538/222.
54 Minute by Roger Makins, 5 April 1951, *ibid.*
55 Minute by Strang, 5 April 1951, *ibid.*
56 Minute by Morrison, 6 April 1951, *ibid.*
57 Letter from F. S. Tomlinson to Charles Johnston, 31 March 1951, FO 371/92539/225.
58 Cabinet minutes, 22(51)3, 22 March 1951, Cab 128/19.
59 Cabinet minutes, 23(51)7, 2 April 1951, *ibid.*
60 Washington to FO, 6 April 1951, FO 371/92538/227.
61 *Ibid.*
62 *FRUS 1951*, vol. VI, part 1, memorandum by Allison, 5 April 1951. Note also, *ibid.*, p. 931, letter from Dulles to MacArthur, 18 March 1951, in which he described the British attitude as worrying, particularly in relation to Australia, where he suspected the Attlee government of wishing to assist the 'rather anti-American' Labour Party at the forthcoming general election. Dulles remained suspicious of British motives. He wrote to Acheson on 25 April summarising discussions at the Pentagon with General Marshall and the joint chiefs of staff: 'I said that it was not yet apparent whether the British really wanted to go along with us or whether they wanted to split with us on Japan as they had on China. I said this would probably not be developed for a few weeks, during which time I might have to go to England. I said that if there was going to be a definite split on policy with Japan that might introduce new elements which would make it desirable to review the situation.' See *FRUS 1951*, vol. VI, part 1, p. 1020, memorandum from Dulles to Acheson, 25 April 1951.
63 Letter from Dulles to F. L. Mayer, 10 April 1951, folder, Japanese peace treaty, box 53, Dulles papers, Seeley G. Mudd Library, Princeton University.
64 Notes by Johnston for Morrison, 6 April 1951, FO 371/92539/234.
65 *Ibid.*
66 Record of meeting held in Foreign Office, 5 April 1951, FO 371/92535/177.
67 *Ibid.*
68 Brief for meeting with representatives of Japan Association, no signature, 5 April 1951, *ibid.*
69 Minute by Johnston, 18 April 1951, FO 371/92544/312. See *FRUS 1951*, vol. VI, part 1, pp. 972–6, memorandum by Dulles, 12 April 1951, in which Dulles recorded his reactions to the news of MacArthur's removal (upon which he had not been consulted) and his discussions with leading figures in the Republican party. See also Stephen Ambrose, *Nixon*, vol. I, *The Education of a Politician, 1913–1962* (London: Simon and Schuster, 1987), pp. 222, 239. Nixon used the Korean war skilfully to advance his career: he supported MacArthur vociferously and condemned the Truman administration's subservience to British pressure (p. 239). For the views of McCarthy, see T. C. Reeves, *The Life and Times of Joe McCarthy: A Biography* (London: Blond & Briggs, 1982), p. 370.
70 Minute by Johnston, 18 April 1951, FO 371/92544/312.
71 Minutes by Strang, 18 April and Morrison, 18 April 1951, *ibid.*
72 Tokyo to FO, 21 April 1951, FO 371/92542/294.
73 Washington to FO, 26 April 1951, FO 371/92544/320.
74 Letter from Clutton to Johnston, 24 April 1951, FO 371/92544/330.
75 Washington to FO, 4 May 1951, FO 371/92547/366. Note draft of treaty as agreed in Washington talks, FO 371/92547/373.
76 Tokyo to FO, 1 May 1951, FO 371/92547/383.
77 Letters from Clutton to Morrison, 1 May, and to R. H. Scott, 7 May 1951, FO 371/92655/10, 12.
78 Minute by C. P. Scott, 11 May 1951, FO 371/92548/395.
79 Minute by Johnston, 15 May 1951, FO 371/92549/405.
80 *Ibid.*

3

DULLES VISITS LONDON: THE CLIMAX TO ANGLO-AMERICAN NEGOTIATIONS, MAY TO AUGUST 1951

The crucial stage in determining British policy towards a Japanese peace treaty occurred at the end of May and in June 1951. The climax to the years of preparation and exploration at last arrived. The shape of a treaty would be finalised during a visit to London by John Foster Dulles. The Labour cabinet sought to establish British preferences and, to some extent, in a direction contrary to that pursued in Anglo-American exchanges in the last few months. Herbert Morrison told his colleagues in cabinet on 28 May that:

> the initial question for the Cabinet to consider was whether they should seek to impose a harsh treaty upon Japan or whether it would be wiser to seek a peace settlement which the Japanese would regard as reasonable. It was important to avoid driving the Japanese into the arms of Russia, and on this account he favoured the relatively mild proposals which had emerged from the discussions with the United States Government.[1]

In the ensuing debate the points made included the policy followed within the Commonwealth with special reference to Australia and New Zealand: they would support the United States because of the promise of a Pacific pact for defence. Australia wanted Japanese gold used for reparations; India favoured a more generous approach to that so far envisaged and would probably urge that the Peking government should be involved in discussion of a draft treaty. Some members of the cabinet advocated placing limitations on Japanese rearmament; it was thought undesirable that a vanquished foe should regain so rapidly freedom to expand its military and naval power. This was linked with the suspicion that Japan's former imperialist and militarist past might not have been buried as successfully as some maintained. Furthermore Germany would seize upon the Japanese precedent for demanding analogous freedom. Other cabinet members observed that Japan should assist in countering the Soviet menace in East Asia and that this objective could be attained only if Japan possessed effective means of defending itself. In addition, the United States held that the degree of Japanese rearmament should be decided in defensive pacts outside the formal peace treaty.[2]

In a memorandum circulated beforehand Morrison summarised the nature of exchanges between the British and American governments during the previous month.[3] Morrison deemed the talks in Washington to have resulted in suitable compromise on both sides. The revised draft of a treaty was the product of positive proposals by each and were 'fairly evenly balanced and in length the document is somewhere between the original United Kingdom and United States drafts', as regards initiatives taken by the American and British representatives.[4] The talks clarified certain of the suspicions starting to develop on the American side that 'despite our protestations to the contrary, we might in fact be trying either to delay the Peace Treaty or to give it a restrictive and illiberal character'.[5] Dulles had indicated that he personally favoured the circulation of a joint Anglo-American draft to all interested governments: this was not yet the official position of the American government but would no doubt assume this character shortly. Morrison was attracted by the suggestion because he discerned an opportunity for emphasising the significant British contribution and, as a logical deduction, the important part played by Herbert Morrison in reaching this point: '... there seems to be no reason why we should hide our light under a bushel or to try to conceal the very considerable influence which we have had on the shape of the peace settlement as it is beginning to emerge'.[6]

Other arguments for working very closely to secure an agreed final draft included the credit which would accrue to Britain in global terms; the fact that Britain and the United States could cooperate thoroughly and in detail would remedy erroneous judgement over Britain's role connected with Britain's exclusion from the Pacific defence pact and would counterbalance the unfortunate effects engendered by the arguments concerning the Korean war and relations with China; if it were objected that Britain was merely 'hanging on the Americans' coat-tails', it could be pointed out that a joint peace treaty would reflect more fully British influence than would a draft produced solely by the United States; another possible objection was that the Japanese government might blame Britain for features of a joint treaty which it disliked but this was of dubious validity; a more substantial criticism centred on Commonwealth views and the kind of criticisms from contrasting standpoints, which could emanate from Australia (over the fate of Japanese gold) and India (over procedural aspects) but this dimension had to be faced up to if British leadership was to count for anything. Morrison outlined a timetable including detailed discussion with Dulles in London early in June; circulation of a joint draft; further exchanges over the ultimate text, probably to be pursued in Washington; reference back to each government for approval; signature of the treaty; and, lastly, ratification. The Commonwealth should be kept fully informed. The position concerning China was delicate: Morrison was persuaded of the merits of a Canadian proposal that a treaty should include an arrangement for China to sign but that signature should be deferred until appropriate. Morrison recommended that he be authorised to talk to Dulles and to secure agreement that Chiang Kai-shek's government should be excluded from a treaty but that 'an accession clause' should be inserted for China to utilise when necessary conditions, to be approved by the signatories 'on Chinese and Far Eastern questions generally', had been met.[7] The problem of Taiwan was best handled through pursuing further the existing agreement between the United States and Britain that because China was preventing fulfilment of the Cairo declaration as regards Korea, China could not gain from the declaration where Taiwan was concerned.[8]

The cabinet met again on 29 May. Discussion focused particularly on the extent to which Japanese rearmament should be encouraged or controlled. Morrison opened the discussion by recalling that safeguards should be realised through the conclusion of a discrete defence pact between the United States and Japan, to be concurrent with a peace treaty. Japan would depend upon the Western powers for supplying submarines, larger naval vessels and bombers. Allied forces would remain on Japanese soil and economic interaction would act as a restraining influence over Japanese ambitions of a prewar (or wartime) character. This method of dealing with Japan had been approved by Commonwealth governments. Morrison said that he recognised, nevertheless, the merits mentioned in cabinet the previous day of the argument for defining in a treaty how far Japan should rearm rather than leaving this unclear.[9] Accordingly, he would propose to Dulles that the relevant paragraph should be omitted from a draft treaty because of the objections that would be voiced. This would not entail changing the aim of pursuing security aspects outside a treaty via a discrete defence pact. The chief of the imperial general staff, Field Marshal Sir William Slim, commented that Japan should assist in containing communism in Asia and rearmament could not be avoided. But it was wholly reasonable to establish restrictions on the nature of rearmament. The chiefs of staff did not wish, however, to state whether limitations were best achieved through putting restrictions in a treaty or through having a separate defence arrangement. The following debate showed that the majority in cabinet believed in modifying the previous cabinet decision, reached on 2 January 1951, and of making another attempt 'to persuade the United States Government that the Peace Treaty should include some reference to the limitations which were to be placed upon Japanese rearmament'.[10] Those adopting this position emphasised that an absence of such explicit limitations would offend many people in Britain and in other countries which had experienced Japanese aggression. Such an omission would be peculiar because all peace treaties in recent history included restrictions on the ability of the defeated country to rearm. Inclusion of limitations within a peace treaty would possess more cogency than the alternative of depending on Japan's voluntary acceptance via a bilateral defence pact with the United States. It seemed to be the case that other Commonwealth members were tilting towards applying tougher requirements upon Japan: this was illustrated in a telegram sent by Robert Menzies advocating the adoption of necessary protection against a Japanese military revival and a prohibition on the construction of a strong navy.[11]

However, others in cabinet underlined the Asian dimension, namely that Asian members of the Commonwealth might hold different views and a split on racial lines within the Commonwealth must be avoided, especially on matters so crucial for the future of Asia. Another argument hinged on the threat from communism and the fact that the Western powers could not accept the entire burden of preventing communist expansion without the help of Asian states. The cabinet agreed that Japan should be permitted partial rearmament: 'They considered, however, that the Foreign Secretary, in his forthcoming discussions with Mr. Dulles, should make every effort to secure agreement that these limitations of Japan's right to rearm should be specified in the Peace Treaty.'[12] If this proved unattainable, Dulles should be informed that a peace treaty should not refer to a sovereign right to rearm as indicated in article 6(b) of the provisional draft. With regard to shipping Morrison said that the Truman administration generally concurred with the British view that Japan should restrict shipbuilding capacity voluntarily: this would be pursued in his discussions with Dulles. Some cabinet ministers wanted to limit shipbuilding capacity within a treaty. The repercussions for the British shipbuilding industry could be serious unless action was taken: such limits had been incorporated within the treaty with Italy and shipbuilding in Germany had been controlled. The majority preferred action outside the framework of a treaty: this was more likely to secure acceptance by the Japanese. It was pointed out that American pressure compelled a modification of the restrictions imposed on German shipbuilding. In any event, Japanese resentment should not be incurred, since it would lead to more friction in the long run. In the case of the Ryukyu islands, the cabinet desired a renunciation of Japanese sovereignty over the islands to be included within a treaty. Hugh Gaitskell, the chancellor of the exchequer, criticised a premature concession to the United States over the question of Japanese gold holdings. He commented that West Germany had given up all gold deposits as well as making much bigger payments as reparations. The United States might claim the gold if Japan surrendered it but Britain should press the argument further: this would conform to statements made in parliament.[13] Morrison responded, perhaps ironically, 'that he would gladly arrange for the Chancellor of the Exchequer to put this point of view to Mr. Dulles'.[14]

Sir Hartley Shawcross, the president of the Board of Trade, spoke of the importance of the issues involved in the Congo Basin treaties and allied property in Japan. It was highly desirable to secure formal termination of the most favoured nation rights enjoyed by Japan through the Congo Basin treaties. Otherwise Japan 'would be able to flood the markets in the Treaty area with low-priced textiles and to inflict serious damage on our own textile industry'.[15] Shawcross also referred to the need to consider payment of compensation to allied owners of property in Japan. Patrick Gordon Walker, the Secretary of State for Commonwealth Relations, drew attention to the views of India regarding China's position: the Indian government might recommend communicating the draft treaty to the Peking government. Morrison had confirmed already that he would pursue the Canadian proposal for preventing either Chinese regime from signing a treaty.[16] Therefore, from the cabinet exchanges it is clear that a number of problems remained which would necessitate a suitable spirit of compromise on both sides to surmount.

Dulles threw himself energetically into a hectic series of meetings with British ministers in the first fortnight of June. He demonstrated that he possessed a thorough grasp of the diverse topics he was handling: the full range of his skills in negotiations was revealed. Morrison met Dulles on 4 June and summarised British views over rearmament. He reminded Dulles of the strong opinions held in Britain arising from Japanese maltreatment of civilians and POWs: the cabinet held that the present draft of a treaty gave Japan excessive freedom to rearm. In addition, the issue of Chinese participation was complex: the cabinet would not deal with Chiang Kai-shek's regime. Other topics to be pursued included gold holdings and the question of sovereignty over the

Ryukyu, Bonin and other island groups (the United States was not now proposing that Japan should surrender sovereignty). Dulles defended fluently the
argument for being very liberal in framing a treaty and again referred, as he was
prone to do, to his experience at the Paris peace conference and the disaster of
the Versailles treaty. He compared the bitterness often encountered in Britain
towards Japan with the American perspective: in the latter case, hatred of Japan
diminished swiftly after Japanese surrender. With reference to Chinese signature,
it might be feasible for each Chinese regime to sign on behalf of the territory
occupied by it.[17] A technical sub-committee consisting of Gerald Fitzmaurice,
C. P. Scott (Foreign Office), Miss M. Dennehy (Board of Trade), Robert Fearey
and Stanley D. Metzger (State Department) met during Dulles's visit to advise
the principals and to assist in required redrafting.[18]

On 5 June Kenneth Younger, the minister of state in the Foreign Office,
Dulles and officials from each government introduced a discussion of the problems associated with China. Younger referred to a Canadian proposal that
neither Chinese regime should sign and a treaty should state that 'China' should
accede subsequently when a larger degree of unity existed as to which Chinese
regime should be regarded as representing China. Younger indicated that the
necessary majority should be two-thirds including the occupying powers.
Dulles's suggestion that each regime should sign caused serious difficulties: the
Labour government would not wish to sign a treaty also signed by the
Kuomintang regime. It would be invidious to commit the Japanese government
to a treaty signed by Chiang Kai-shek's administration which could affect
adversely future relations with mainland China. Dulles observed that the aim
should be to maximise possible adherence to a treaty; from the American angle,
it was essential to produce a treaty acceptable for ratification in the Senate. He
denied a report in *The Times* of 5 June that his purpose in London was to secure
acceptance of Kuomintang adherence to a treaty: he believed this rumour was
the work of someone in Washington wishing to embarrass him on his return. He
elaborated on his idea that both the Peking and Taiwan regimes should sign: he
was fully conscious of the political atmosphere in the United States which would
render it awkward to pursue. The various possibilities as he saw them were that
there should be no Chinese signature; that a series of bilateral peace treaties
should be signed instead of a multilateral one; or that it might be feasible for
governments other than the principal parties to adhere to a multilateral agreement before or after its ratification – the Japanese government could then decide
with which Chinese regime peace would be signed. Dulles understood Britain's
particular position and stated that he was not trying to force Britain into recognising Chiang Kai-shek's regime: 'He was above all anxious to keep the Japanese
Peace Treaty free from entanglement with the Chinese problem because the
Japanese Peace Treaty was in itself a most important matter.'[19] He said candidly
that what worried him was the emotional state of American public opinion and
he did not wish to jeopardise ratification in the Senate. Sir Esler Dening thought
that the Japanese would act pragmatically and pursue commercial relations with
both Chinese regimes. As regards Taiwan Dulles wished to keep the status of the
island unchanged other than removing Japanese rights. Charles Johnston
referred to India's recommendation that Taiwan should be ceded to China: he

floated a suggestion that Taiwan should be ceded to 'China' but to stipulate that this should not be implemented until a substantial measure of agreement had been attained as to which government should be accepted; Dulles rejected it because it would render a UN contribution to a settlement more difficult.[20]

On 6 June Dulles saw Younger and officials from the Foreign Office again but he also enjoyed a lively exchange in a separate meeting with Hugh Gaitskell. On the former occasion Dulles handed Younger a memorandum dealing with Chinese participation, proposing the exclusion of the Peking government from involvement in a treaty. Dulles also supplied a memorandum addressing Japanese rearmament. To allay Australian fears, Dulles said he would state in a speech on 7 June that the United States would provide the air and sea forces for Japanese defence. On the Chinese issue, he explained that he did not object to indicating future Chinese accession but there were objections to a number of the principal parties because this would limit Japanese sovereignty after a peace treaty took effect: Japan should have the right to conclude bilateral treaties with China, the Soviet Union, and Italy if she chose, on the basis that benefits associated with the treaties would apply automatically to allied powers signing a peace treaty with Japan.[21]

In the meeting between Gaitskell and Dulles on 6 June the chancellor advanced robustly the argument for not being unduly generous to Japan – indeed, the argument for engaging further in retribution. Gaitskell emphasised the strength of anti-Japanese attitudes in Britain, explicable because of the savage treatment of POWs during the Pacific war. British public opinion would resent Japan receiving particularly lenient treatment and, for example, escaping with fewer reparations than Germany. Dulles replied with equal vigour, pointing out that the United States had covered the deficit in the Japanese balance of payments throughout the occupation but had refrained from utilising Japanese gold because it should be regarded as a reserve at the termination of the occupation when the economy must become self-sustaining. However, if the gold was available, then the United States should have the chief claim on it so as to return some of the sum of 2,000 million US dollars expended by the American government. Dulles remarked that, in considering the comparison with Germany, the loss of Japanese colonial possessions and investments must be given proper acknowledgement: 'He claimed that no nation had ever paid such a severe penalty for a war of aggression.'[22] Gaitskell responded that account had to be taken of what was forfeited by a vanquished country and what was gained by the victor. The existence of East Germany rendered comparison more awkward but, nevertheless, the divergent experiences with reparations was remarkable. To return Japanese gold might be unwise when the subject of repaying postwar advances to Britain and the United States was discussed. Gaitskell's hostility to Japan was manifest in his concluding observation that the United States should take all of the gold instead of returning it to Japan. Dulles concluded by commenting that the Japanese standard of living had to be preserved at a certain level so as to minimise the appeal of communism.[23]

A further meeting took place on 6 June in the Foreign Office. Morrison stated that he could make no commitment without consulting the cabinet. He had been urged by both sides in the House of Commons that day to keep in mind the inhumane treatment of POWs and the necessity of ensuring that justice was done. Morrison thought that a peace treaty could refer to the rights and obligations of the UN charter: he would like an assurance in writing concerning rearmament but he appreciated the reluctance of the Japanese government to comply – the substance of an assurance would suffice. Dulles replied that there was only one way of avoiding the possibility of a renewed Japanese military threat:

> The United States Government wanted to continue with the substance of the occupation but not the form. They wanted to maintain United States armed forces in Japan with the consent of the Japanese.[24]

The United States was endeavouring to reconcile security with sovereignty: if a peace treaty included drastic restrictions of Japanese rearmament, the Japanese would hardly consent to American forces remaining on Japanese soil. This was a cogent argument and expressed directly. Morrison reverted to compensation for POWs, stating that it should not be pursued directly by the state: it would be preferable for it to be handled via the Red Cross or an analogous body. Over China disagreement persisted, since Morrison rejected Dulles's suggestion that each Chinese regime should sign because of the fierce reactions that would occur if Chiang Kai-shek's regime was invited to sign. With regard to Japan's former island possessions, meaning Taiwan, south Sakhalin, and the Kuril islands, Japan should renounce interest in each; the UN would have to determine the fate of Taiwan. Morrison conveyed British unhappiness regarding shipping in the sense of a future naval threat and of what was deemed 'unfair' competition. John M. Allison of the State Department said that American shipowners were also concerned over competition. Morrison undertook to report to his cabinet colleagues with the aim of securing reasonable compromise.[25]

The cabinet reviewed progress on 7 June and received a memorandum from Morrison. The foreign secretary stated in cabinet that Younger was handling the detailed deliberations and that Dulles had met Attlee, Gaitskell and himself. In the main he regarded Dulles's approach as encouraging and it was hoped, on both sides, that full agreement could be reached before Dulles departed at the end of the following week. Morrison reminded colleagues that if agreement could not be reached, then the United States might proceed without Britain: 'This would have most damaging effects on our future relations with Japan and on our prestige in the Far East.'[26] Regarding rearmament, Dulles was willing to make minor modifications in wording in the relevant article to meet British objections but he was not prepared to go beyond this slight concession. The cabinet agreed to accept the American view and not to press further for a restriction on rearmament within a treaty: at the same time, the United States should be urged to make a public statement regarding the nature of the American–Japanese defence understanding to be made no later than publication of the text of the treaty and preferably sooner.[27] As ever the issue of Chinese participation was intractable. Of the three possibilities floated by Dulles – an invitation to each Chinese regime to sign, the treaty to comprise a series of bilateral pacts with Japan having the freedom to sign an agreement with either China, or the treaty to be a multilateral pact to be signed by either Chinese regime and with no accession clause or reference to China in the treaty – the third could be accepted, although it was not as satisfactory as the British proposed.[28] The cabinet decided that neither the first nor the second was acceptable and it was sceptical of the third. In an accurate assessment of future developments, 'it was pointed out that if Japan were left nominally free to make her own arrangements with China, she would be more likely, while under United States tutelage, to enter into relations with the Chinese Nationalist Government'.[29] This would mean that Britain had facilitated recognition of the Kuomintang regime and admitted the latter, after all, to participation in the treaty. As against this view, it was argued that any treaty signed by Japan with either Chinese government would be wholly separate from the multilateral peace treaty and that once Japanese sovereignty was restored, Japan could conclude agreements as it wished. The cabinet decided that renewed endeavours should be made to persuade Dulles that neither Chinese regime should sign.[30]

As regards Taiwan, Morrison stated that Dulles was unwilling to contemplate the British desire for Taiwan to be ceded to 'China' with the identity of the latter postponed for ultimate resolution. Dulles wanted provision made merely for Japanese renunciation of sovereignty over the island. This was not particularly satisfactory but would connote no sacrifice of principle: if the United States agreed to the British proposal for Chinese participation in the treaty, Britain's aim would, in essence, have been secured so that the fate of Taiwan would have been deferred for resolution when wider agreement could be reached. The cabinet noted the position of India that it could not sign a treaty failing to stipulate return of Taiwan to China. The cabinet agreed, however, that if the United States accepted Britain's proposal for Chinese involvement, Britain would meet the United States over Taiwan on the understanding that a final decision regarding Taiwan would be left until more general concurrence had been obtained.[31] On other aspects, it was agreed that the revised draft treaty should require Japanese renunciation of sovereignty over the Kurils and south Sakhalin; that Britain would not oppose maintenance of Japanese sovereignty over the Ryukyu islands because the United States would maintain military occupation; that a decision over how to limit Japanese shipbuilding should be deferred until more information was available; that a further attempt should be made to convince the American government that Japan should not keep the gold reserves but that if this did not meet with success, Britain would submit to the American preference; and that further discussions should take place with Dulles concerning the Congo Basin treaties.[32]

The arcane question of the Congo Basin treaties was pressed vigorously by Sir Hartley Shawcross, the president of the Board of Trade, when he met Dulles on 8 June. The substance of the matter resulted from Japanese rights arising from a treaty signed in 1885 and under the peace treaties signed in Paris in 1919, which conferred a privileged status upon Japan. According to the current American ideas this status would be reiterated in a peace treaty. In turn this would allow Japan to export large quantities of cheap textiles at the expense of the Lancashire cotton industry. The British contention was that Japan's right should be liquidated because it arose from Japan's having supported the allies in the Great War. The British aim was not to exclude Japan totally from this African market but to prevent an overwhelming flood of Japanese textiles. Shawcross underlined the delicacy of Britain's balance of payments position: in order to help the rearmament drive in Britain, the intention was to stimulate textile exports by 40 per cent over the previous year in order to remedy the deficiency of other exports. Apprehension regarding Japanese competition was significant politically in Britain.[33] Dulles replied that a comparison should be made with Italy: in the latter instance, it had been decided not to disallow Italian rights as a signatory of the Saint-Germain convention, although in a modified form. The United States was prepared to apply the same formula with Japan. It had to be remembered that Japan had lost its colonial empire and had been promised access to raw materials and ultimate participation in world trade relations. Dulles did not want to hand propaganda to the JCP (a point he made in other contexts, too) and that the American government was unhappy about considering action divergent from broad commercial policy.[34] Shawcross rejected the comparison with Italy because the latter had controlled colonies in Africa and did not experience the particularly low labour standards found in Japan. There was no British fear concerning Italian competition in Africa but there was strong anxiety over future Japanese competition.

Morrison and Dulles met also for further discussions on 8 June. Morrison confirmed Shawcross's emphasis upon textile problems relating to the Congo Basin treaties. Morrison explained the cabinet's attitude over China. Britain would accept one of Dulles's suggestions that neither Chinese administration should be acceptable in the context of the peace treaty without the consent of, perhaps, two-thirds of the principal parties. Dulles spoke of the importance of restoring Japanese sovereignty so that the Japanese government could decide how it wished to proceed; he thought it out of the question for Japan to conclude an arrangement with Taiwan as though the Kuomintang regime controlled the whole of China. He said personally that he would be pleased if Japan could also arrive at certain arrangements with the Peking government: it is very doubtful whether this was really his opinion. Dulles once more referred, skilfully, to the political difficulties facing him in the United States: he had accepted with reluctance the British proposal which went, at least, to the limit and possibly beyond the limit of what was politically possible in the United States. If this proposal did succeed, it would be attributable to Dulles's personal role in the Republican party: such was the state of American domestic politics he could give no assurance that it would be accepted. He would be open to attack from critical Republicans on the grounds that he had not obtained Kuomintang admittance to signing the treaty and that he acquiesced in British appeasement. Of course, it suited Dulles to make such utterances but the malign role of 'old guard' Republicans plus McCarthy was such that Dulles's statement was entirely plausible.[35]

The cabinet met again on 11 June. Morrison reported failure to convince Dulles over Chinese participation.[36] Morrison was influenced to some extent by Dulles's worries about the criticism he would encounter from the 'MacArthur wing' of the Republican party.[37] Two-thirds ratification for a treaty was required in the Senate: Dulles reasoned that even if all Democrats voted in favour (which was uncertain), it would still be essential to secure the positive support of approximately half of the Republican senators: 'Mr. Dulles, as a Republican himself, could assure us that in the present state of United States politics this would not be feasible.'[38] Morrison could foresee the danger of a 'most difficult and embarrassing situation arising if the Senate denied ratification'.[39] Morrison proposed that Britain should proceed through neither Chinese regime signing the treaty, that no accession clause would be included, and that Japan could determine its future relations with China after securing full restoration of sovereignty and independence. Morrison believed that, as a reciprocal gesture, Dulles should then accept the British argument for depriving Japan of its rights under the Congo Basin treaties. Some members of the cabinet expressed dismay at the suggested arrangement regarding China. American troops would be present in Japan 'and in many respects Japan would be in the position of an American satellite'.[40] It followed logically that Japan would see the wisdom of recognising the Kuomintang administration in Taiwan. It would be invidious to support a peace settlement moving in this direction. Other cabinet members remarked that it was preferable to have Japan under American than Soviet influence. Japan would need raw materials from other countries and several of the signatories to the peace treaty could exercise influence in consequence. Less realistically some argued that it did not follow that Japan was bound to recognise Chiang Kai-shek's regime: longer-term Japanese economic interests would push Japan towards an accommodation with the Peking government. The defect with this logic was that it ignored the potent pressures which the United States was capable of exerting (and did exert). A further possibility in the opinion of some was that Japan could recognise one Chinese administration as controlling Taiwan and another as controlling mainland China.

Some dissatisfaction was voiced regarding the trend of talks over Taiwan. It would not be accurate to refer to the wishes of the people of Taiwan, since Chiang Kai-shek would make up their minds for them. It was also held that reference to the role of the UN had to be expressed carefully: it might be best to state that the future of Taiwan would be discussed 'in the light of the Charter of the United Nations'.[41] The cabinet was not happy with the position concerning gold holdings. It would not be easy to explain to British public opinion why the Japanese should retain gold deposits: it would be better for the United States to keep the gold 'in trust' for the present.[42] The cabinet, therefore, wanted Morrison to discuss it further with Dulles but, if he did not make progress, then British objection would be withdrawn. Shipbuilding was again deferred while the topic was pursued in Tokyo.

On 14 June Kenneth Younger told the cabinet that Dulles had agreed that Japan should relinquish its rights under the Congo Basin treaties. Other minor aspects had been resolved or were under consideration. Renewed efforts had been made to persuade Dules to accept the British case over gold holdings but Dulles would not agree: he had emphasised again that the Japanese economy required the gold to assist in its initial economic endeavours. Morrison and Gaitskell each stated that Britain should compromise and accept the American position.[43] The cabinet authorised publication of a draft peace treaty, which would be considered in conjunction with other interested powers. Morrison told his colleagues that a joint draft should be published within the next few weeks: the cabinet could assess the draft when it was completed.

Morrison and Younger met Dulles for the final session during Dulles's strenuous visit on 14 June. Morrison thanked Dulles for his constructive approach: the talks had gone encouragingly in the main, contrary to press speculation. Morrison summarised the opinions of the cabinet regarding gold holdings and shipping. Over the former, British objections would not be pressed further, so that Dulles had triumphed over this aspect. However, shipping remained a contentious issue. Britain was an important maritime power with a vocal shipping lobby consisting of shipowners and trade unions. Anxiety was accentuated through awareness of Japan's previous record. John Allison was about to visit Tokyo again and Morrison proposed that Allison should secure a voluntary declaration from the Japanese agreeing to fair terms for the British interests involved. Dulles commented that the immediate problem was for Japan to increase its shipping because it was carrying only between 17 and 18 per cent of requirements. American experts believed that it would be another ten years before Japan could carry 50 per cent of requirements. Concern over shipping was a long-term matter. Dulles reflected on the broad philosophy behind the treaty. Like MacArthur he did not see the Japanese as having changed because of the occupation:

> It was, however, part of their character that they could not be compelled to do things. They were people who liked conforming and doing what was correct. He thought we should capitalise on this quality by inviting them into their club but explaining the rules which they must keep, and that they would then keep them on a voluntary basis.[44]

In response to an enquiry from Morrison regarding the possible appeal of communism in Japan, Dulles repeated his professed opinion that communism could easily develop because of the Japanese liking for conformity. So far communism had not advanced because it was identified with the Soviet Union. Dulles closed by stating his satisfaction with the achievements of his mission to London.[45]

Dulles broadcast to the British people at the end of his visit. He presented a skilfully argued review of his mission when he spoke on the BBC Home Service on 14 June. He said that it was impossible to guarantee that a liberal peace treaty would succeed but he could state with certainty that any other kind of treaty would fail. Dulles added that he and the British people were equally aware that Japan's past record was bad: the memories of the horrors inflicted by the Japanese military in Singapore and Burma and of the dreadful sufferings of POWs were all too vivid. But it was necessary to look ahead and secure stability in the future.[46] Dulles returned to the United States confident in the knowledge that he had handled the complex exchanges in London with great dexterity and perception.

Morrison reported to the cabinet on 18 June. He had been unable to reach agreement over Taiwan: Dulles would not accept the wording favoured by the cabinet describing a role for the UN. It had been agreed that the American and British governments should each make a separate statement of its attitude. The cabinet feared that this would imply greater divergence than was the case and preferred a joint statement that 'the future of the island had still be discussed'.[47] On the following day Morrison circulated a memorandum explaining procedure for the next stage of handling the peace treaty. The agreed draft treaty resulted from the draft devised during the talks in Washington in April and May. Changes in the new draft had been forwarded to the cabinet for consideration. Since Dulles departed, relevant government departments had exchanged views and reached agreement. The only outstanding problem concerned shipping. The draft treaty would be submitted to the American and British governments for approval within the next week. An outline would be sent to Commonwealth governments. Following approval by the American and British governments, other governments including Commonwealth ones and the Soviet Union would be approached officially and their reactions solicited. The draft treaty would be published when appropriate. The American government aimed to convene a peace conference for the purpose of signing the treaty formally in the middle of August, the venue being San Francisco. The American and British governments were in agreement that the Soviet Union must be treated in the same way as other powers and given the opportunity to take part in the peace settlement. But the Soviet argument that preparation of the peace treaty must be pursued in the Council of Foreign Ministers (Britain, the United States, the Soviet Union and China) could not be entertained. The British view consistently had been that the treaty must be prepared through extensive consultation among the powers concerned and that Britain could not accept exclusion of the Commonwealth and France, which would be a consequence of following the Soviet proposal. If the Truman administration accepted Dulles's recommendation that the United States should not press further the suggestion that the Kuomintang regime should sign the treaty, this would be a major gain for British policy. Morrison added that the United States had made important concessions during the Washington and London talks and that the present draft, when compared with the original American draft of March, constituted 'an improvement beyond all recognition, and roughly half of it has in fact been contributed by the United Kingdom'.[48] Given the problems created by, and bequeathed by, General MacArthur, the progress made was most salutary. Morrison paid a generous and well-merited tribute to Dulles: 'That it had been possible is largely due to the constructive and open-minded attitude of Mr. Dulles himself and in particular to his realisation of the importance of our connections with the Common-wealth.'[49]

Esler Dening produced a thoughtful assessment of possible remaining problems. The most fundamental involved American public opinion and the challenges facing Dulles in navigating the treaty through the treacherous waters of congressional criticism; a close watch should be kept on the shifting political scene in Washington. The Soviet Union and China would be hostile and could deter some countries from signing the treaty. Asian opinion might be influenced by references to the danger of conflict if the bilaterial defence pact between the United States and Japan activated the Sino-Soviet treaty; France could react adversely to such propaganda. The Commonwealth was divided in that India disliked the continuance of American bases in Japan and the bilateral defence pact. Australia and New Zealand were obsessed with security, supported the pact and felt that it should be given maximum publicity. British public opinion might respond critically when the treaty was published.[50] Dening added that Japan should be impressed with the magnanimity of the treaty and there should be no criticism from this quarter.[51] Confirmation of Nehru's unhappiness with the treaty came at the beginning of July. The high commissioner in New Delhi reported that Nehru feared that the treaty might have a destabilising impact on propsects for peace in East Asia.[52]

The reactions of British industry and public opinion became somewhat clearer in the course of July. Textiles, shipping and the Staffordshire potteries represented the principal areas of concern, as had been the case for several years. C. P. Scott of the Foreign Office attended a dinner party given by the Board of Trade for the Textile Fibres Advisory Committee on 3 July. Scott summarised their views as anticipating that Japanese competition would assume a formidable character; expressing concern that the treaty could not prevent competition becoming more dangerous; frequent contact with Japanese manufacturers after the implementation of the treaty might discourage the Japanese from engaging in cut-throat competition; the textile interests favoured the transmission of a warning to Japan, at a suitable point, emphasising the undesirability of reverting to prewar practices.[53] The difficulties besetting the Lancashire textile industry represented a familiar list of the reasons for the decline of a once great industry: the drawbacks of being the first in the field in terms of industrialisation and of not modernising, of an uneconomic structure with too many firms, of trade unions pursuing old-fashioned approaches, and inadequate investment. Raymond Streat devoted considerable time and effort, as chairman of the Cotton Board, to endeavouring to achieve rationalisation, efficiency and the adoption of progressive practices.[54] It was an uphill struggle and the brave attempt to regalvanise the Lancashire textile industry failed. Lancashire MPs and trade unionists were vociferous in stating their opinions and in seeking to defend the industry. The whole subject area required careful handling by a Labour government pledged to full employment.

The government was more deeply preoccupied with shipping for economic and strategic reasons. Indeed arguments over shipping temporarily overtook the aspect of Chinese involvement as a matter for concern and speculation. Morrison circulated a memorandum to the cabinet at the end of July discussing developments since Dulles left London. John Allison, Dulles's chief adviser, travelled to Tokyo after the London meetings to investigate Japanese voluntary arrangements for a diminution in shipbuilding capacity. On 3 July Allison submitted a memorandum drafted by Japanese officials arguing that existing shipbuilding capacity was not excessive. Present capacity was stated as 676,000 gross tons a year rather than the figure of 810,000 cited by the British: the divergence in statistics was explicable because of the exclusion, or inclusion, of disused yards. The yards in use were said to be functioning at between 70 and 80 per cent with output at between 400,000 and 500,000 tons a year. It was thought that Japan would have 1,549,000 tons of ocean-going ships by the end of 1952. In order to meet the needs of commerce with the United States and other areas, Japan would require 2,236,000 tons of ocean-going ships in 1953.

An additional 700,000 tons would be needed by 1953, mainly from new construction. According to projections of Japanese trade down to 1956, it was believed that the existing capacity of Japanese shipyards could be fully utilised, at least to 1956. Morrison commented that there were appreciable difficulties in determining Japanese requirements and there was room for more divergence. British officials did not accept a number of assumptions made by Japanese officials. It appeared, even accepting Japanese estimates, that Japanese capacity would be excessive after 1956. Therefore, the Japanese fleet could go on expanding after 1956 or Japanese competition to obtain shipbuilding contracts would grow. The British believed that Japan's capacity need not be more than approximately 400,000 tons a year. The cabinet had accepted that limits could not be inserted for security reasons and British criticism would have to be based on the argument that present capacity was uneconomic from Japan's viewpoint. The United States disagreed, as did India, Pakistan and Ceylon; Australia and New Zealand agreed with Britain. It was not desirable to accentuate divisions of opinion within the Commonwealth but it was held that Britain must adhere to its firmly argued beliefs. Morrison advocated notifying the United States that Britain regarded capacity as excessive and that it should be diminished outside the terms of the peace treaty. Because of apprehension for security reasons in Australia and New Zealand, they should be informed and could support representations being made to Washington.[55]

The cabinet considered Morrison's memorandum on 1 August. The minister of transport endorsed Morrison's statement: trenchant opinions were held in the ministry and it was considered that Britain's case should be advanced vigorously. Japan undoubtedly possessed the potential of proving a dangerous competitor. During the ensuing cabinet debate, attention was drawn to fears in Britain regarding Japan as a competitor in general. It was not simply the shipping industry which felt alarm:

> At the same time, it was widely recognised that it would be unprofitable to seek to reduce this competition by including restrictive provisions in the Peace Treaty. Japan's population was expanding rapidly, and, unless a democratic regime was allowed to find some economic means of supporting this population, the country would fall into economic distress which would be exploited by communism.[56]

Continued British concern was conveyed to the United States on 14 August.[57] The issue rankled but the United States adhered to its stance that the Japanese economy must be self-sustaining.

The Staffordshire potteries were the least important from the government's outlook, since this comprised a limited area of competition. However, the two Labour MPs for Stoke-on-Trent, Ellis Smith and A. Edward Davies, were zealous in asking parliamentary questions and in urging Staffordshire's case by all methods available.[58] More broadly, a considerable range of parliamentary questions was put forward in July before and after publication of the draft treaty. In a debate on 26 July concern was voiced over a number of matters by several MPs, including Ralph Assheton (Conservative, Blackburn West), Sydney Silverman (Labour, Nelson and Colne) and Emrys Roberts (Liberal, Merioneth). Questions focused on textile competition, and labour standards in Japan. Shawcross responded that he had visited Manchester during the previous week and had met both sides of the cotton industry to discuss the peace treaty.[59] Dening wrote to George Clutton in Tokyo that the peace treaty had emerged relatively unscathed from the foreign affairs debate. The only real target for attack centred on reparations in the context of compensating POWs. The criticism amounted to a request for additional money to be provided for distribution but it was of a vague character. It appeared unlikely to the Foreign Office that more than minor amendments would prove necesssary; shipbuilding was rather awkward to pursue and was being investigated. Dening was struck by the absence of criticism in the House of Commons over China's non-participation or over Taiwan. The British compromise over China appeared to have won respect. Dening was somewhat naive in assessing Dulles's attitude concerning China:

> You have our full authority, when suitable opportunities arise, in informal conversation with influential Japanese to represent to them the advantages from their own point of view of pursuing a *via media* over the Chinese problem after the Treaty comes into force. We believe that Dulles and the State Department are sincere when they told us that they are opposed to Japan recognising Chiang Kai Shek [sic] when she is free to do so.[60]

A. F. Maddocks minuted on 26 July that letters were arriving from bodies and individuals containing observations on the peace treaty; the focal points for criticism were limited and concerned absence of restrictions on rearmament and failure to invite the Peking government to participate. This offset partially the muted critical comment in the House of Commons.[61]

Japanese reactions to publication of the draft treaty on 12 July were largely as expected. It was seen as no worse than could be anticipated. Most Japanese expressed only one valid criticism: that in several respects, for example reparations, and the participation of China, the treaty indicated problems but did not solve them. The Yoshida government had given no real lead to the public. A good deal of comment from political parties centred on the Kurils, south Sakhalin, the Ryukyus, Bonins, and other island groups and the merits of returning them to Japan; however, such statements had a ritualistic stamp on them. Clutton and the Foreign Office devoted some attention to the desirability of securing Emperor Hirohito's personal endorsement of the treaty. This was felt to be sensible in order to give further recognition of the treaty as in Japan's best interests. This was ironical because the new constitution of 1947 confirmed the transformation of the emperor into a Western-style constitutional monarch and it was not appropriate for the emperor to play a part other than the ultimate formalities of acceptance. Morrison was in favour of the emperor's indicating support and the topic was pursued in discussions between the Foreign Office and the State Department. Clutton pursued the possibility of obtaining publication of an imperial rescript but he was informed by William Sebald that the government section of General Headquarters, SCAP, was very unenthusiastic on constitutional grounds and thought that powerful objections would be made in the Diet.[62] A telegram was sent to Tokyo on 2 August, explaining British interest in using the emperor to lend greater authority to acceptance of the treaty:

I still attach great importance to securing the Emperor's public endorsement of the Treaty. It had certainly not been my intention to suggest that the Emperor should issue anything except on the advice and with the consent of his Government in accordance with the constitution. An Imperial rescript would no doubt carry the most weight in view of its traditional prestige in Japan. An alternative method would be for the Emperor to broadcast on the analogy of the broadcast in which he denied his divine origin. I can see no reason why some such means could not be found by democratic and constitutional channels for him to exhort his prople to carry out the provisions of the Treaty. This could and would have an important effect, particularly in the more traditionally minded circles.[63]

The State Department was not in favour of the British suggestion. This provoked a British complaint that the Americans were being unduly solicitous in dealing with the emperor's role. The Yoshida government decided against involving the emperor or the Imperial Household in what was regarded as a political matter.[64] Yoshida visited Clutton on 30 August and conveyed the emperor's gratitude for British assistance in arriving at a treaty of a 'non-punitive character' which was 'unique in history'.[65] The attempt of Morrison and the Foreign Office to encourage a more direct role by the emperor is peculiar but is linked probably to the more pessimistic attitude among British diplomats to the future development of Japan and of a gradual undermining of the achievement of the occupation. The American attitude was wiser than the British: the emperor's role should remain strictly as redefined in the constitution adopted and implemented in 1946–47.

Notes

1 Cabinet minutes, 37(51)7, 28 May 1951, Cab 128/19.
2 *Ibid.*
3 Memorandum by Morrison, CP(51)137, 23 May 1951, Cab 129/45.
4 *Ibid.*
5 *Ibid.*
6 *Ibid.*
7 *Ibid.*
8 *Ibid.*
9 Cabinet minutes, 38(51)2, 29 May 1951, Cab 128/19.
10 *Ibid.*
11 *Ibid.*
12 *Ibid.*
13 *Ibid.*
14 *ibid.*
15 *Ibid.*
16 *Ibid.*
17 Record of meeting between Morrison and Dulles, 4 June 1951, FO 371/92553/498. See also brief for ministerial discussions with Dulles, n.d., FO 371/92553/479. For the American records of Dulles's discussions in London, see *FRUS 1951*, vol. VI, part 1, pp. 1106–34 including the text of the revised Anglo-American draft of a peace treaty, 14 June 1951 (pp. 1119–33).
18 Summary record of first meeting of the technical sub-committee, 5 June 1951, FO 371/92554/507 and second meeting, 6 June 1951, FO 371/92554/509. A. F. Maddocks attended the second meeting.

19 Record of meeting held in House of Commons, 5 June 1951, FO 371/92554/513.

20 *Ibid.*

21 Record of meeting, 6 June 1951, FO 371/92554/514.

22 Treasury memorandum by A. J. Phelps, 6 June 1951, FO 371/92557/564A.

23 *Ibid.*

24 Record of meeting in Foreign Office, 6 June 1951, FO 371/92554/515.

25 *Ibid.*

26 Cabinet minutes, 41(51)1, 7 June 1951, Cab 128/19. See also memorandum by Morrison, CP(51)155, 7 June 1951, Cab 129/46.

27 *Ibid.*

28 Memorandum by Morrison, *ibid.*

29 Cabinet minutes, *ibid.*

30 *Ibid.*

31 *Ibid.*

32 *Ibid.*

33 Record of meeting in House of Commons, 8 June 1951, FO 371/92552/516.

34 *Ibid.*

35 Record of meeting held in Foreign Office, 8 June 1951, FO 371/92556/547.

36 Cabinet minutes, 42(51)1, 11 June 1951, Cab 128/19.

37 See memorandum by Morrison, CP(51)158, 9 June 1951, Cab 129/46.

38 *Ibid.*

39 *Ibid.*

40 Cabinet minutes, 42(51)1, 11 June 1951, Cab 128/19.

41 *Ibid.*

42 *Ibid.*

43 Cabinet minutes, 43(51)3, 14 June 1951, Cab 128/19.

44 Record of meeting in House of Commons, 14 June 1951, FO 371/92556/563.

45 *Ibid.*

46 Radio address by Dulles, BBC Home Service, 14 June 1951, folder, Japanese peace treaty and security, box 53, Dulles papers, Seeley G. Mudd Library, Princeton University.

47 Cabinet minutes, 44(51)5, 18 June 1951, Cab 128/19.

48 Memorandum by Morrison, CP(51)166, 19 June 1951, Cab 129/46.

49 *Ibid.*

50 Minute by Dening, 18 June 1951, FO 371/92561/653.

51 Minute by Dening, 19 June 1951, *ibid.*

52 New Delhi to Commonwealth Relations Office, 3 July 1951, *ibid.*

53 Minute by C. P. Scott, 8 July 1951, FO 371/92562/670.

54 For the wide range of Streat's activities, see Marguerite Dupree (ed.), *Lancashire and Whitehall: The Diary of Sir Raymond Streat*, 2 vols (Manchester: Manchester University Press, 1987), vol. II, pp. 423–615. This is a valuable source for the problems of the Lancashire cotton trade and for the relationship between government, industry and trade unions. Streat was chairman of the Cotton Board from 1940 to 1957 and revealed great patience, skill and dedication. I am most grateful to Sir George Kenyon for kindly allowing me to consult the diary before publication.

55 Memorandum by Morrison, CP(51)234, 30 July 1951, Cab 129/47.

56 Cabinet minutes, 57(51)5, 1 August 1951, Cab 128/20.

57 Minute by C. H. Johnston, 28 August 1951, FO 371/92592/1309/G.

58 For examples of parliamentary questions, see extracts from *Parliamentary Debates, Commons*, 11 June and 4 July 1951, as reproduced in FO 371/92556/554 and FO 371/92562/671.

59 Extract from *Parliamentary Debates, Commons*, 26 July 1951, as reproduced in FO 371/92576/895.

60 Letter from Dening to Clutton, 27 July 1951, FO 371/92573/864.

61 Minute by Maddocks, 26 July 1951, FO 371/92573/869.

62 Tokyo to FO, 31 July 1951, FO 371/92575/905.

63 FO to Tokyo, 2 August 1951, *ibid.*

64 Washington to FO, 13 August and FO to Washington, 11 August 1951, FO 371/92582/1039.

65 Tokyo to FO, 30 August 1951, FO 371/92590/1274. For a discussion of Japanese views towards a treaty, see M. M. Yoshitsu, *Japan and the San Francisco Peace Settlement* (New York: Columbia University Press, 1983) and R. B. Finn, *Winners in Peace: MacArthur, Yoshida and Postwar Japan* (Oxford: University of California Press, 1992), pp. 245–312. The final text of the treaty, with two declarations by the Japanese government and a protocol, dated 13 August 1951, was released simultaneously by its joint sponsors, the United States and Great Britain, at 4 p.m. on 15 August 1951, the sixth anniversary of Japan's surrender at the end of the Pacific war.

4

THE SAN FRANCISCO CONFERENCE AND THE END OF THE OCCUPATION, AUGUST 1951 TO APRIL 1952

The preparations for British representation at the peace conference to be held in San Francisco, contain some unintentionally humorous aspects. Herbert Morrison was ambitious, although at a comparatively late stage in his career, to reach the top and secure the leadership of the Labour Party when Clement Attlee retired. At the same time, Morrison was conscious of the need to protect his health and not to capitulate to the pressures that had killed his predecessor. A minor theme of Morrison's minutes is a consistent protest at the quantity of business he was expected to handle: Morrison resented the arrival of the ubiquitous red boxes in the evenings or at weekends when he was entitled to relax. He was, therefore, torn between a wish to keep a high profile and a determination not to exert himself excessively. Originally he did not intend going to the San Francisco conference: this showed an insensitivity to the importance of the occasion. However, his officials also assumed that the signing of the peace treaty would be a formality, not requiring the attendance of a minister from the Foreign Office; it was anticipated that the lord chancellor would head the British delegation.[1] Robert Scott admitted the error on 19 July, following the arrival of a telegram from Sir Oliver Franks, conveying the strong wish of Dean Acheson and John Foster Dulles that Morrison should participate in the conference: the Truman administration wanted the conference to be a major occasion and the countries taking part should be represented at the highest level. In addition, Acheson wanted to discuss other matters with Morrison including a European army, a German defence contribution, and strengthening NATO; their talks could begin in San Francisco and conclude in Washington. Acheson pointed out that Morrison's presence would underline the closeness of Anglo-American cooperation and assist future collaboration. Dulles added that developments in Korea, perhaps connected with the signing of an armistice, could cause unexpected problems upon which it would be essential to confer.[2] Morrison reluctantly consented to attend if he could but stated that the dates of the conference caused personal inconvenience because he was aiming to take a short holiday in Norway late in August: he could arrive in San Francisco for the climax to the conference but someone else would have to lead the British delegation for the opening sessions. Morrison suggested that signature of the treaty be deferred until 10 September which would probably suit other foreign ministers remaining in the United States for the Atlantic Council meeting on 17 September.[3] Franks contacted Acheson and Dulles who responded that they could not change conference arrangements for Morrison's convenience: a number of other American conventions had been forced out of hotel accommodation to allow the conference to assemble and to exclude more would create much acrimony. The plan was to begin on 4 September and for the peace treaty to be signed on 7 September, with the concluding plenary session taking place on 8 September. It might be feasible to alter the date for signature from Friday 7 September to Saturday 8 September and this could be explored further.[4] Morrison accepted this suggestion, confirming that he would reach San Francisco on the evening of 7 September, which would mean that signature would occur on the 8th.[5]

Having rather grumpily agreed to attend, Morrison began to focus on the necessity of emphasising the British contribution – and, of course, the contribution of Herbert Morrison – to the negotiation of the peace treaty. He drafted a minute instructing that a telegram be sent to Washington requesting more prominent acknowledgement of the British role.[6] This read in part:

> We do not wish to advertise the influence we have exerted behind the scenes but in the circumstances ... we think that excessive modesty about our contribution would be against the interests of His Majesty's Government and of Anglo-United States cooperation generally. It seems to us that it would also be to the United States Government's own advantage in their relations with the other Governments concerned to avoid letting the draft Treaty appear as a purely single-handed American achievement.[7]

Franks duly spoke to Dulles who maintained that acknowledgement had been made to British assistance: the problem, according to Dulles, was that the press sometimes failed to report fully enough. He had striven to preserve bipartisan cooperation to secure eventual ratification: such suggestions appeared in the press occasionally, indicating that the British were only acquiescing reluctantly to help in convincing right-wing Republicans. Franks added that the embassy suspected the devious Dulles of inspiring certain reports. The Soviet decision to participate would probably lead to more emphasis on Britain's role.[8] During the conference Acheson was reasonably generous in his references to British assistance.

The attitudes of other interested parties became clear in late July and August. Yoshida Shigeru was unwilling to lead the Japanese delegation, fearing the odium that might be incurred in consequence. Discontent had been voiced by some, including the young Nakasone Yasuhiro who had written to Senator Taft in January and February criticising the 'disgraceful' concessions made by Yoshida.[9] Nakasone commented that Americans were well intentioned but maladroit in dealing with Asians. He sent Taft a copy of a paper he had forwarded to Dulles: this advocated greater freedom for Japan including rearmament, full support against communist aggression, and an undertaking that Japanese should be allowed to emigrate to particular countries: in addition, those previously purged in Japan should be depurged. Nakasone observed that new, dynamic leaders were required in order to defeat communism and this would not be accomplished by decrepit survivors of bygone days such as Chiang Kai-shek, Syngman Rhee or Bao Dai.[10] However, in July Yoshida changed his view: the revised treaty appeared to be the best Japan could hope for and it was clearly the responsibility of the prime minister to attend. It was announced in Tokyo on 8 July that Yoshida would go to San Francisco and this was confirmed at the end of July. The precise composition of the delegation remained to be resolved: the other three principal political parties (apart from Yoshida's Liberal Party) had not submitted names thus far. The government decided that it would not be appropriate for an imperial prince or a member of the Imperial Household to attend. It was possible that the chief justice of the Supreme Court would go but it was decided subsequently that the judiciary must be kept distinct from the executive and the chief justice remained in Tokyo.[11]

Nehru was critical of the treaty and, to the dismay of the British, decided that India would almost certainly not attend the conference and would oppose the treaty: the attempt to preserve unity within the Commonwealth on this question failed. Nehru believed that the current Yoshida government came largely from the 'old military clique' and he feared that Japan would rearm rapidly. Nehru considered younger people in Japan to hold different opinions and the situation could change when the younger generation took power. He believed that Yoshida might want Chiang Kai-shek to be a signatory. Nehru's anxiety was influenced by his unhappiness with American policy towards the Korean war. The British high commissioner in Delhi commented that underpinning Nehru's observations was a 'deep distrust, if not of American intentions certainly of their policy'.[12] Nehru felt that the United States was proceeding on the assumption that another world war was likely, 'and that they were subordinating to military factors every other consideration, political, psychological and economic'.[13] On 24 August it was announced definitely that India would play no part in the San Francisco conference. India objected to Japan being compelled to accept a defence agreement with the United States and held that Japan should decide such matters after sovereignty was restored.[14] Profound British regret was communicated immediately to Nehru.[15]

The motives of the Soviet Union in attending the conference stimulated endless speculation. Dulles believed that the Soviet approach might be linked with events in Korea and that the Russians might propose postponement of signing the treaty as a prerequisite for arriving at an armistice in Korea.[16] The Foreign Office discerned the Soviet motive as wishing to appear reasonable and in line with the Potsdam agreement. Soviet influence would be exerted with those Asian countries which were undecided in their policies concerning the peace treaty. It was likely that the Russians would urge postponement of a peace treaty until a conference was convened to address overall far eastern issues, including Taiwan, Japanese rearmament and Chinese representation in the UN. The basis of Soviet policy probably rested upon using tactical manoeuvres to ensure that the peace conference became preoccupied with other issues involving Korea and China: this would mean that the conference would be protracted and unproductive. Appropriate Anglo-American tactics should be deployed in San Francisco to defeat Soviet recalcitrance.[17] However, it would not be wise to give the impression that the treaty was being railroaded through the conference. Chou En-lai issued a statement on 16 August in which he condemned the way in which the peace treaty was being prepared: Chou recalled the lengthy war

China had been forced to wage against Japan so recently. The proposed treaty would perpetuate American control of Japan and Taiwan. The San Francisco conference could be seen only as illegitimate in the eyes of the Chinese people.[18]

The State Department and the Foreign Office exchanged opinions regarding the organisation and personnel for the conference. Dulles told Franks that while Acheson would act as president of the conference, it would not be sensible for him to fulfil too dominent a role. What was required was a reliable deputy for Acheson and he wondered whether Sir Carl Berendsen of New Zealand might be a suitable person.[19] Franks doubted the desirability of this choice and considered either Lester Pearson of Canada or Paul-Henri Spaak of Belgium as preferable. Dulles added the unwelcome news that General MacArthur would most probably address the conference at an early stage. MacArthur would confine his remarks to an exposition of his work as SCAP and would not pursue other issues.[20] The Foreign Office agreed that Berendsen would not be an appropriate choice and his nomination could provoke a jealous reaction from Spender. Spaak would also be unsuitable and was currently out of office in Belgium. Pearson was regarded as the best choice. The thought of MacArthur making a speech did not evoke enthusiasm.[21] MacArthur did not take part subsequently: he spurned angrily an invitation to speak, since he could not accept the limitations indicated.[22]

Clutton forwarded a further assessment of Japanese attitudes towards the treaty on 23 August. The predominant reaction was that the treaty was the best attainable in the circumstances. There was a similar acceptance of a bilateral defence treaty with the United States but there was anxiety over the continuance of American military bases in Japan, which could invite aggression. Clutton remarked that it would be naive to expect the Japanese to rejoice over the treaty, since it confirmed formally Japan's vanquishment in war.[23] Undignified arguments should be avoided in Britain's view where Soviet participation in the conference was concerned. The State Department reviewed the situation. A renewed Chinese offensive in Korea was possible, according to Dean Rusk. In general the State Department believed that the Soviet Union was not in a position to fight a world war but Rusk warned that undue emphasis should not be put on this aspect. Rusk deemed Japan to be of continued primary importance in Soviet planning.[24] The Foreign Office prepared a briefing paper dealing with the peace treaty and the Soviet problem: it was recommended that the United States and Britain confine responses to statements made by Soviet delegates to 'a lofty and forbearing tone'.[25] This followed on from a meeting held on 27 August, attended by Sir Pierson Dixon, P. Mason, Frank Roberts, Robert Scott and S. Y. Dawbarn. The Soviet delegates could start by assailing the conference as illegal and urging that a different conference of the five most interested powers be summoned. As an alternative a Soviet draft could be proposed to replace the Anglo-American draft. Neither of these tactics would stop signature of the treaty. Another contingency was that the Soviet Union could declare willingness to sign the treaty on condition that a four- or five-power conference be held to examine important far eastern issues. The latter might comprise Japanese rearmament, Taiwan and Korea in this order. While such a development would be embarrassing, it could not halt signature. Yet another contingency was that the Soviet Union might propose a general conference to consider the East Asian or world situation. Those present agreed that the Soviet Union lacked the ability to prevent a treaty being signed. The United States and Britain could act in combating Soviet tactics through issuing a tripartite statement conveying views of Soviet propaganda. It would be feasible to put forward disarmament proposals in the UN General Assembly or to issue a statement following the Washington talks, to be held after the San Francisco conference.[26] On balance it was considered best not to issue statements in a bid to head off Soviet criticism but to act calmly and not to be rattled. Acheson and Dulles thought that trouble could occur with the Soviet Union over procedural rules: this could delay matters and it might be necessary for the conference to designate a firm date for signature of the treaty.[27]

Kenneth Younger led the British delegation at the start of the San Francisco conference, pending Morrison's arrival. Soon after Younger arrived he was visited by Yoshida who stated how appreciative he was of Britain's assistance in producing a treaty which was 'more generous than I expected'.[28] Yoshida was satisfied with the broad approach. Younger welcomed his remarks and underlined Britain's wish to rebuild relations amicably. Younger recorded Yoshida's emotional comments:

> Yoshida referred with some emotion to the long standing tradition of friendship between our two countries, a tradition unhappily broken by the war. The Japanese leaders before the war, he said, had gone 'crazy and lost common sense and he hoped this would never recur'.[29]

The conference assembled formally on the afternoon of 4 September and was called to order by Acheson. He spoke effectively in a dignified and constructure manner: he could not forget Japan's past record but he looked to a happier future. The British delegates emphasised the necessity of Acheson's presiding over the adoption of rules of procedure in case the Soviet delegates created difficulty. Oliver Franks spoke to Andrei Gromyko who led the Soviet delegation: they exchanged opinions politely on the likely duration of the conference.[30] Adoption of rules of procedure was moved jointly by the United States and Britain and was completed quickly and without amendment: the earlier apprehension proved unfounded. Gromyko spoke on the subject of Chinese representation. Acheson, who was in the chair, acted resolutely, if in a manner described by Younger as 'irregular'.[31] Proposals advanced by Gromyko and his Polish supporters were defeated swiftly. Acheson was elected formally to the chair with Sir Percy Spender of Australia as vice-chairman. Sponsoring speeches were made by Dulles and Younger in the afternoon. Younger commented: 'I thought that Dulles's references to China were moderately phrased; listening to him, I could not help reflecting that the distance American thinking must move in regard to China was much less than the distance it had moved in the last six years in regard to Japan.'[32]

Gromyko spoke very rapidly and provided a long, clear and carefully argued attack on the treaty and the thinking behind it. It was a predictable speech, delivered lucidly. American policy towards Japan was depicted as resulting from ulterior reasoning intended to satisfy American imperialism.

The treaty did not include adequate guarantees against future Japanese aggression: indeed, it had no solution to the limits of rearmament in Japan and violated seriously the rights of the Chinese people. The treaty did not fulfil the responsibilities undertaken by the United States and Britain and a peaceful, stable Japan was not going to result from the treaty. Gromyko put forward what he described as a 'declaration' including amendments to the proposed treaty and inserting new articles based on the relevant clauses in peace treaties concluded with the European satellite states. Gromyko's bearing was restrained and he delivered his address without passion. However, the Soviet contribution was a vigorous rebuttal of the treaty and there could be no compromise between the two positions.[33]

Yoshida's speech struck Younger as failing to meet the demands of the occasion and to be rather inappropriate; on the other hand, Yoshida was thinking of the audience in Japan instead of the one he was addressing in San Francisco. Gromyko, backed by his Polish allies, protested at Acheson's failure to circulate the Russian amendments. Dulles made a concise, balanced speech. When Younger spoke he regretted the absence of China and criticised some of Gromyko's remarks.[34] Morrison duly arrived in time for the concluding session and formal signature. In his speech, on 8 September, Morrison apologised for not having been present throughout and welcomed warmly the terms of the treaty. He recalled Britain's lengthy relationship with Japan, terminated regrettably by war in 1941 and now restored. He congratulated the American government for its strenuous work in arriving at the treaty and in arranging the conference. The absence of China was unfortunate but, as Morrison put it, all present understood the reasons. He believed that the foundations of effective democracy had been laid as a result of the achievements of the occupation.[35] Acheson paid tribute to Morrison and to the British contribution. Robert Scott reflected on the character of the conference in a letter to Sir William Strang. The principal enigma concerned the behaviour of the Soviet delegation: why had Gromyko not exerted more impact? Scott acknowledged that Gromyko conveyed his points of substance capably but he had not pursued procedural opportunities to be obstructive and had, in short, not acted in the accustomed Soviet manner. Scott's impression was that the Soviet foreign minister had been talking simply for the record rather than with the intention of achieving concrete aims. It was possible that Gromyko wanted to demonstrate Soviet support for China, in the wider interests of Sino-Soviet relations, but knew he could not prevent the conference from approving the treaty. Scott pondered the state of Sino-Soviet relations: if his analysis was accurate, did it not indicate that relations between the two leading communist powers must be more delicate than had been thought? Acheson enjoyed 'a great personal triumph', especially in the effect on American public opinion. As an example of technological progress, Acheson's chairmanship was witnessed by an enormous number of Americans, perhaps 45 million, in consequence of the first nationwide television programme from west to east coast.[36] As regards the Commonwealth, the conference was successful. Junius Jayawadene of Ceylon made a fine impression. The delegates from New Zealand and Pakistan made decisive speeches. The Canadian contribution was sound and Sir Percy Spender of Australia was less outspoken than usual. Scott's only harsh words were applied to the 'parrot-like inanities' emanating from Latin American delegates.[37]

Immediately preceding the signing ceremony, Morrison saw Yoshida. After initial pleasantries, Morrison emphasised that the Japanese government must adopt a positive approach to social and economic issues in Japan:

> It was essential that the people should know and understand these problems and that the habit of cooperation with the government should be developed. In particular, I attached great importance to educating the trade unions and employers organisations in economic facts so as to encourage them to take a responsible attitude. There was anxiety in Great Britain lest pre-war conditions of sweated labour and competition were revived. In the interests of the people of Japan and of relations between Japan and Britain it was essential that this should not happen. Indeed, I felt that my signing of the Treaty would be justi-fied only if the Japanese Government took steps to see that there was no recurrence of these conditions.[38]

Yoshida proclaimed his own view to be exactly the same. His aim was to deepen understanding of, and support for, democracy in Japan, since it was in the best interests of the country and was the only means of retaining positive relations with the United States and Britain. Yoshida then referred to China, which was badly in need of democratisation: the future of Japan was bound to be linked with that of China. Morrison responded:

> I mentioned recognition of China, emphasising that we were not seeking to interfere. It was a decision to be taken by the Government and people of Japan for themselves. I thought, however, that he would be well advised to ponder very carefully and to take no precipitate action. Though the Treaty was signed, it was not yet in force; and it would be unwise of Japan by some hasty action in this important matter to stir up controversy in the various legislative bodies in the countries which had to ratify the Treaty. He took the point and was non-committal.[39]

Morrison went on to refer to British anxiety regarding the allied property compensation law and hoped that an acceptable, amended law would be applied as soon as possible. Morrison thanked Yoshida for his support with the negoti-ations for the Anglo-Japanese payments agreement: Yoshida commented that issues should not be viewed too narrowly. Morrison and Yoshida ended their discussion with a few curious remarks by Morrison concerning ambassadors. He spoke warmly of Sir Esler Dening who had been appointed as British ambas-sador and hoped that a suitably qualified Japanese representative with brains and energy would be appointed.[40]

On his return to London, Morrison described the course and outcome of the conference in favourable terms when he addressed the cabinet: 'The Conference at San Francisco for the signature of the Peace Treaty with Japan had, in his view, proceeded very satisfactorily and there had been no feeling among the Western nations that Russia had been treated unfairly in this matter.'[41] He regarded his meeting with Yoshida as encouraging and members of the Commonwealth had performed positively – with the exception of India, presumably. It is fair to say that while there were some thorny issues at times in the prolonged exchanges over the terms of the treaty, Anglo-American relations were generally good in the context of determining the character of the treaty: certainly there was far less friction over Japan than was the case with either China or Korea. Naturally there were varying assessments over how liberal the treaty should be and the Americans were always more generous in this respect than the British. Similarly the Americans were noticeably more sanguine concerning the future of Japan than the British. British officials contributed effectively to the actual drafting of the treaty: the confidence of Sir William Strang in the superior drafting skills of his officials was borne out. Dulles sent a cordial expression of gratitude for the assistance of Gerald Fitzmaurice, in particular, during the concluding stages of redrafting in August.[42] However, it would be erroneous to focus too heavily on British help in drafting because the vital consideration was that drafting took place within parameters defined by the United States. Without the strong guidelines laid down by the Truman administration and particularly by Dulles, a treaty prepared by the British would have been less liberal. The conference itself proceeded happily in the congenial surroundings of San Francisco. It was an excellent venue, preferable to the alternatives hazarded. Perhaps the operatic choruses in the productions in the San Francisco Opera House, where the conference met, served, figuratively, to cheer on the prospects for a more stable Japan built on the foundation offered by the peace treaty.

In October 1951 the Labour government of Attlee succumbed to defeat and Winston Churchill returned to office for the last time. Churchill was elderly, in declining health, but showing his usual shrewdness in weighing up political challenges.[43] He hoped to secure improved relations with the United States following the arguments caused by disagreements over China and Korea, but he soon discovered that this was more difficult than he had thought. Anthony Eden returned to the Foreign Office, an office he had first occupied almost 16 years earlier. Eden was the restless heir-apparent to Churchill, keen to inherit the party leadership and premiership but compelled to exercise patience until the old statesman finally retired. Eden's own health was poor, as revealed in Evelyn Shuckburgh's diaries, which include numerous examples of the strain Eden experienced.[44] Eden was prone to throw tantrums when matters did not go as he wished and he could be extremely unpleasant, although the storms departed as suddenly as they arose. Eden did not like Dean Acheson or John Foster Dulles, the two secretaries of state with whom he conducted business while foreign secretary. Eden and Acheson were both prima donnas of an arrogant outlook and Dulles was seized with a growing sense of mission in combating communism. This was not an encouraging recipe for harmony at the top in Anglo-American relations: it is not surprising, at a personal level, that friction occurred.

Predictably the first serious controversy resulting from the Japanese treaty resulted from the uneasy compromise over Japan's future relations with China. The course of events should have occasioned little surprise in Whitehall, for the pressures within American politics pointing towards a tough stand against communist China were manifest and, encouraged by Senator McCarthy in particular, were growing. Dulles had made it clear that he would take no risks with ratification in the Senate. Therefore, a logical inference was that Dulles would apply pressure to Yoshida to provide reassurance that Japan would not recognise the Peking government. Dulles drafted a letter for Yoshida to send to him (Dulles), which was forwarded on 24 December: this stated that the Japanese government would recognise Chiang Kai-shek's regime in Taiwan. It was a devious act on Dulles's part but understandable, given the mood in the United States and keeping in mind Dulles's ambition to be the next secretary of state. On the flight from San Francisco to Washington Morrison told Acheson and Dulles that Japan should not take a decision rapidly as to which Chinese government to recognise: he had understood Dulles to concur, previously, that Japan should decide only when free to do so, that is, *after* the peace treaty had been ratified. Acheson and Dulles appeared receptive to Morrison's opinion. Dulles stated that the Japanese government would require an understanding with the Kuomintang authorities in Taiwan but this need not assume the form of actual recognition.[45] Difficulties in Anglo-American relations over this matter developed in November 1951. Presentation of the treaty in the Senate was handled by Senators H. Alexander Smith (Republican, New Jersey) and John D. Sparkman (Democrat, Alabama). Dulles wished to take no risks and notified the Foreign Office on 12 November that he would like British policy to be modified. Meetings were held in the Foreign Office on 13 and 14 November, attended by Livingston Merchant and Arthur Ringwalt on behalf of the American embassy and by Robert Scott, John Shattock, Charles Johnston and C. P. Scott, on behalf of the Foreign Office. Merchant indicated that while the American government wanted to honour the agreement reached between Dulles and Morrison in June, it desired British acceptance of 'reasonable relations' between Japan and Taiwan. Robert Scott reiterated the British view that Japan was not free to negotiate an agreement with Chiang Kai-shek's administration before the peace treaty came into operation. The British government was unwilling to assist in undermining the agreement reached in June.[46] Robert Scott believed that Britain would have to make some concessions towards Dulles's preoccupation with ratification and favoured an amended formula whereby any agreement reached between the Yoshida government and Chiang's regime would not be concluded until after the multilateral peace treaty had come into operation.[47]

At this point one of Anthony Eden's critical moods arose. Eden had not been consulted fully by his officials on this question amidst the pressure of other business Eden was conducting. Eden became irate over officials usurping decision making and was annoyed by American pressure to change policy. Scott sought to defend himself by reminding Eden that Morrison had told Yoshida at San Francisco that Britain was not trying to interfere with Japanese recognition of China, since the government and people of Japan had to decide at the appropriate moment what the decision should be. The British government would respect this decision, provided that it was, in Morrison's words, determined by a 'free Japan'.[48] Eden minuted 'unwise' in the margin of Scott's minute.[49] Scott explained to Eden that Dulles was confronted with difficulties over ratification owing to pressure from the MacArthur section of the Republican party. Eden inserted critical remarks in the margins at various points in Scott's explanation, adding that he was *not* willing to accept the formula recommended by Scott and would have preferred to have spoken to Livingston Merchant himself. The argument became acrimonious. Sir William Strang minuted, classically, that a genuine misunderstanding had occurred.[50] However, Eden was not committed in consequence of Scott's discussion with Merchant: the manner in which Scott had acted was in conformity with past practice. However, whether the formula should be approved was arguable and he (Strang) entertained doubts, unless it was proposed to change British policy; Eden commented here, 'It is not.' Strang continued that Britain did not recognise the Kuomintang government in Taiwan: the British consul in Tamsui met only with local authorities. Strang thought it would be wise for Britain to keep out of disputes in American domestic politics. Was Britain bound to assist Dulles in appeasing MacArthur and his supporters? Eden could not resist responding to this rhetorical question and added, 'I think not' in the margin.[51] If Britain accepted the proposed formula, it could become contentious in American politics, British politics and in dealings with Japan. Strang proposed that Britain should not oppose Japanese contacts with Chiang Kai-shek's regime, provided these comprised preliminary exchanges but a formal agreement with the United States should not be entered into by the British government.[52]

Eden repeated his criticism of his officials in a minute written on 19 November:

> I am far from happy about this. I simply cannot understand how events could have run so far and fast without any kind of authorisation from me.
>
> Decisions of policy must not take place in the dep[artment] without reference to me or to Sir W. Strang. I am always ready to put my initials to a policy or decision I agree & take the responsibility. I am not prepared for policy to be initiated in this way without my knowledge & agreed with State Dep[artmen]t without even knowing the F.O. view.[53]

Acheson must be told that Eden could not consent to what was proposed. Eden was about to depart for discussions with the Americans and French in Paris; Scott was about to leave for a visit to East Asia. Eden stated that he must see Scott's instructions before he left for Japan, adding in a concluding crack at his officials, 'I must know where we are being led.'[54]

A telegram was sent to Paris, for communication to Acheson, stating that while Britain wished to cooperate as closely as possible with the United States, it was not possible to accept the formula discussed by Scott and Merchant. It would be permissible for the Japanese government to conduct preliminary discussions with Chiang Kai-shek's government but it would not be acceptable for the Japanese government to grant formal recognition. Sir Esler Dening had advised Yoshida accordingly and Eden endorsed this guidance.[55] Eden then met Acheson in Paris to pursue the issue directly. Acheson argued that Japan must commence discussions with the authorities in Taiwan in order to assist trade but that a formal agreement should be deferred until the peace treaty applied. The Japanese government must decide of its own volition eventually: the American preference would be to support an agreement with the Kuomintang authorities. Eden said that he understood the need for initial contacts but, 'I thought that any question of their recognising Chiang Kai-shek or getting tied up with his regime would create great difficulties for us and for them in the future.'[56] Acheson responded that a treaty made between the Japanese government and the Kuomintang should be arrived at on the understanding that Chiang's regime was the *de facto* power in Taiwan. Eden warned of the danger of giving the impression that Japan was pursuing a claim to Taiwan and Acheson agreed that this required consideration. It was agreed that Dulles should examine the issue with Dening when in Tokyo.

Dulles believed it was imperative to secure clear Japanese recognition of Chiang's regime and he conveyed this to Esler Dening when they met on 14 December. Dening outlined British arguments and said Chiang Kai-shek had no future: Dulles concurred personally but alluded to a sizeable volume of American opinion which believed otherwise. Dulles added that Taiwan must be denied to the Chinese communists. He said he would not 'fudge' on the agreement he had concluded with Morrison in June. He sought to argue that his current actions would not preclude Japan from determining longer-term relations with mainland China. Dening expressed scepticism and enjoyed the better of the ensuing brief debate with Dulles. The latter still professed to be able to find a solution that would satisfy the immediate situation.[57] Dening deduced correctly that Dulles was adamant at proceeding regardless of British reservations: he warned Dulles against giving the Japanese people the impression that their prime minister could be bullied into doing whatever they wished. Such an interpretation would not help in promoting the kind of Japan that Britain and the United States wished to see in the future.

Eden reacted vigorously: Franks was instructed to see Acheson and emphasise British anxiety. If Japan signed a treaty with the Kuomintang regime, this could be construed only as recognition of that regime. There were signs in Japan of irritation at American heavy-handed tactics and it was contrary to past assurances from Acheson that Japan would not be browbeaten. Eden stated, and underlined, the word 'not' personally, that Acheson should not push the Japanese into acting over Taiwan before the peace treaty came into force. Eden added, in a private addendum for the ambassador, that distinct from his disapproval of Dulles's ideas, the tactics pursued were unwise because they constituted a further example of domestic convenience (the perceived necessity of mollifying Republican senators) taking precedence over the longer-term repercussions of the course of action recommended.[58] Franks saw Acheson who stressed the dilemma facing him in ensuring ratification in the Senate.[59] The *Manchester Guardian* aptly described the stupidity of the American refusal to accept that the communists controlled China:

> The Peking Government is in many respects a dreadful thing but its control of China is a fact. Dr. Johnson said that he did not believe in the Lisbon earthquake: it was too terrible. That is really the attitude of the Americans who will not recognise Mao Tse-tung. If Japan recognised Chiang Kai-shek its act would have to be interpreted either as an absurdity or as a signal that it would direct its policy to supporting Chiang in his quite hopeless ambition to recapture mainland China.[60]

Articles in a similar vein appeared in the *News Chronicle* and *Daily Herald*.[61]

Acheson told Franks on 10 January 1952 that the senators active in the 'China lobby' might be able to secure sufficient support to achieve the required one-third blocking mechanism in the Senate to obviate ratification.[62] Dening reflected on events during the preceding month in a telegram sent to London on 16 January. It was hard to escape the conclusion that Dulles's behaviour was duplicitous: at a time when Eden was pursuing discussions with Acheson and Dulles the latter had already forced Yoshida in the desired direction to the point where he was committed or was a long way towards this objective. Yoshida's letter was clearly worded by the State Department: this was obvious from the degree to which Japan was committed and China provoked thereby.[63] Eden reacted with ire after perusing the text of Yoshida's letter. He deplored the phraseology and underlying message:

> If I had understood that a document of this kind was going to be published at this time and in this way I would have spoken even more emphatically at our meeting. I am surprised that we had no advance notice at all from the American side of the intention to publish and that they left it to the Japanese to inform us.[64]

Franks contacted Acheson and the latter conveyed his deep regret for the unpleasantness and failure to consult fully: this was (allegedly) attributable to the State Department not having investigated congressional timetables carefully.[65] Eden felt he should obtain his predecessor's opinion to ensure that their reactions were the same:

> Mr. Herbert Morrison tells me that he regards the letter as inconsistent with the views Dulles expressed to him in London and in the United States. You may, if you think fit, let Mr. Acheson know this.[66]

Churchill visited Washington in January and addressed Congress. In an effort to placate Britain Dulles wrote to Churchill on 17 January applauding his 'magnificent address to Congress' and adding his warm appreciation for Churchill's reference to the Japanese peace treaty and to Dulles's work in negotiating it. Dulles apologised for the 'misunderstandings' which had occurred in the previous few days.[67] The latter comment infuriated Eden who described Dulles's communication as extremely dishonest.[68] Dulles's tactics were highly devious but, if the ends justified the means, he was vindicated when the Senate approved the peace treaty in March with only a small number of senators (mainly old guard Republicans) voting against. Dulles's demanding assignment was at an end: he had triumphed notwithstanding Eden's chagrin at certain of the methods employed. Dulles at once wrote to Acheson in cordial terms announcing his impending resignation from the Truman administration.[69] Presidential politics were dominating the scene in the United States where an acrid contest was raging for the Republican nomination involving principally General Eisenhower and Senator Taft. Dulles had to advance nimbly to the next phase of his strategy to become secretary of state as from January 1953. This objective could not be furthered through continued membership of a Democratic administration. Dulles defended his tactics in dealing with the peace treaty in an exchange of correspondence with David Astor, editor of *The*

Observer. Dulles wrote to Astor on 24 March that the Senate would not have ratified the treaty without assurances concerning the recognition of 'China' by Japan. He pointed out that an attempt was made to move an amendment to the treaty, making it clear that China connoted the Kuomintang government, and this was defeated by 48 votes to 29 with several senators sympathetic to the amendment absent including Taft. As a result of Dulles's influence, Alexander Smith and William Knowland took the lead in defeating the amendment, although they were both strong supporters of Chiang Kai-shek (Knowland was referred to as 'the Senator for Formosa').[70] It was unfortunate that the story of the negotiation of the peace treaty closed on a somewhat sour note in Anglo-American relations. Dulles's achievement was a very substantial one and it is unlikely that another American politician would have surpassed or equalled his efforts – rather the reverse. Nelson Rockefeller, a prominent younger Republican, wrote to Dulles on 27 March congratulating him warmly on his strenuous labours with the peace treaty which could prove decisive in the future: Dulles could now speak with great authority on the Far East. Rockefeller welcomed Dulles's decision to assist in the presidential campaign.[71] The final episode in the unfolding of the nature of the relationship between the Yoshida government and Chiang Kai-shek's administration came with the signing of a treaty between the two parties on 28 April, which was described by the chief legal authority in the Foreign Office, Gerald Fitzmaurice, as denoting recognition of the Kuomintang regime as the *de jure* government of China.[72]

On the economic side Dening, still accredited to SCAP until the formal termination of the occupation, assessed the problems in fostering closer co-operation. He wrote that the Board of Trade was not sympathetic to Japan and that Japan was evidently not going to receive most favoured nation treatment in the matter of goods. Dening regarded certain British industries as particularly vulnerable, for example, rayon, textiles, toys, electrical accessories and appliances, hardware, cameras, pottery and enamelware. If Britain pursued an exceptionally liberal policy, then serious unemployment could ensue in these industries. It was necessary for firm decisions to be taken in London regarding the nature of commercial relations with Japan: it would be futile to consider a new commercial treaty unless Japan was granted most favoured nation status.[73] In February Yoshida told Clutton that he would try to ameliorate the position regarding Japanese competition with the Staffordshire potteries, which had given rise to vocal protests in England.[74]

The allied occupation drew quietly to a close in March and April 1952. Ratification of the peace treaty rendered an end imminent. Mutual expressions of respect and goodwill were exchanged between General Matthew B. Ridgway and the allied missions in Tokyo. Ridgway was the guest at a lunch given in his honour on 7 April: he acknowledged the tributes he received and modestly but correctly pointed out that MacArthur should be the recipient of tributes rather than himself.[75] The occupation ended on 28 April and Dening sent Eden an appropriate concluding despatch in terms of his accreditation to SCAP before assuming his new role as Britain's first postwar ambassador to an independent Japan. Dening compared the evolving character of the occupation from the missionary zeal of 1945–47 to the current concern with Japanese rearmament:

If one were asked to characterise the Occupation and its effect upon the Japanese people over the last two years, one could say with truth that its most noticeable effect has been the mental confusion induced in the Japanese by the change in the American attitude from an almost missionary and visionary zeal to make Japan into a completely pacifist state to an equally missionary zeal to encourage her rearmament. Much of the good which the Occupation has undoubtedly brought to Japan is vitiated by this. Until two years ago complete pacifism was the badge and sign of progress and international respectability: today it is evidence of susceptibility to Communist indoctrination. Doubt has thus come to be cast on democracy, parliamentary institutions and all the other new wonders which the Occupation brought in its train.[76]

The Japanese were weary of the occupation: 'the Japanese people are now heartily sick of the presence of their American benefactors and continue to tolerate them only because they realise that they are necessary to their security'.[77] Dening ended that it was fitting in its way that the campaign to create a memorial to General MacArthur had so far accumulated the equivalent of approximately 200 US dollars.

Dening was unduly negative in his assessment. Naturally the Japanese wanted the occupation to terminate: after almost seven years this was scarcely surprising. The political reforms of the occupation, while certainly not fulfilling the original radical aspirations, created an effective constitutional monarchy. Japanese rearmament assumed appreciable proportions but without resulting in the kind of renewed military and naval menace feared in the early 1950s. British policy towards Japan was negative in a number of ways resulting from the trauma of the blows administered so devastatingly in 1941–42, together with the vivid recollections of atrocities committed. The British preoccupation with opposing communism did not extend so far as to favour markedly generous treatment of Japan in 1951. American policy towards Japan was more far-sighted and well-founded than British politicians and officials thought. It was easily the most successful feature of American policy in East Asia after 1945. To close on a further note of irony, the praise for this outcome should be lavished, not on President Truman's Democratic administration but rather on those two contrasting, idiosyncratic Republicans, Douglas MacArthur and John Foster Dulles.

Notes

1 Minute by R. H. Scott, 19 July 1951, FO 371/92573/852.
2 Washington to FO, 18 July 1951, FO 371/92568/781.
3 FO to Washington, 19 July 1951, *ibid.*
4 Washington To FO, 20 July 1951, FO 371/92569/810. See also *FRUS 1951*, vol. VI, part 1, pp. 1216–17, Acheson to Sebald, 20 July 1951.
5 FO to Washington, 24 July 1951, *ibid.*
6 A minute by C. H. Johnston, 3 August 1951, noted that Morrison had drafted a minute calling for action in approaching Washington, FO 371/92585/1144.
7 FO to Washington, 7 August 1951, *ibid.*
8 Washington to FO, 21 August 1951, FO 371/92586/1168.
9 Letters from Nakasone to Taft, 30 January and 27 February 1951, with enclosure, folder, Japan, 1947–51, box 667, Robert A. Taft, Sr papers, Library of Congress, Washington D.C.
10 *Ibid.*

11 Tokyo to FO, 31 July 1951, FO 371/92576/907.

12 New Delhi to Commonwealth Relations Office (CRO), 14 August 1951, FO 371/92583/1065.

13 *Ibid.*

14 New Delhi to CRO, 24 August 1951, FO 371/92585/1138.

15 CRO to New Delhi, 25 August 1951, *ibid.* See also *FRUS 1951*, vol. VI, part 1, pp. 1288–91, letter from M. K. Kirpalani to Dulles, 23 August 1951.

16 Washington to FO, 14 August 1951, FO 371/92582/1050.

17 FO to Washington, 15 and 16 August 1951, *ibid.*

18 Peking to FO, 16 August 1951, FO 371/92583/1087.

19 See Ann Trotter, 'Sir Carl Berendsen and Japan', in Ian Nish (ed.), *Aspects of the Allied Occupation of Japan, International Studies*, 1986/4 (London: ICERD, London School of Economics, 1986), for a helpful and entertaining assessment of Berendsen.

20 Washington to FO, 7 August 1951, FO 371/92579/960.

21 FO to Washington, 9 August 1951, *ibid.*

22 See D. Clayton James, *The Years of MacArthur*, 3 vols. (Boston, MA: Houghton Mifflin, 1970–85), vol. III pp. 353–4.

23 Tokyo to FO, 23 August 1951, FO 371/92581/1186.

24 Washington to FO, 28 August 1951, FO 371/92589/1259.

25 Briefing paper dealing with Japanese peace treaty, 29 August 1951, FO 371/92590/1276. Note also *FRUS 1951*, vol. VI, part 1, pp. 1300–2, memorandum by Acheson for Truman, 29 August 1951.

26 Minute by Dawbarn, 29 August 1951, referring to a meeting held on 27 August, FO 371/92591/1282.

27 San Francisco to FO, 3 September 1951, FO 371/92593/1332.

28 San Francisco to FO, 4 September 1951, FO 371/92594/1334.

29 San Francisco to FO, 5 September 1951, FO 371/92594/1348.

30 San Francisco to FO, 6 September 1951, FO 371/92595/1354.

31 *Ibid.*

32 *Ibid.*

33 *Ibid.* See also *FRUS 1951*, vol. VI, part 1, pp. 1334–5, Acheson to Webb, 6 September 1951.

34 San Francisco to FO, 8 September 1951, FO 371/92595/1367.

35 Speech by Morrison, 8 September 1951, FO 371/92598/1403.

36 Letter from R. H. Scott to Strang, 10 September 1951, FO 371/92598/1404.

37 *Ibid.*

38 San Francisco to FO, 12 September 1951, FO 371/92616/5.

39 *Ibid.*

40 *Ibid.*

41 Cabinet minutes, 60(51)3, 27 September 1951, Cab 128/20.

42 Minute by R. H. Scott, 13 August 1951, FO 371/92583/1062.

43 For Churchill's final phase in office, see Martin Gilbert, *Winston S. Churchill*, vol. VIII, '*Never Despair*' (London: Heinemann, 1988), pp. 653 ff., and J. W. Young (ed.), *The Foreign Policy of Churchill's Peacetime Administration, 1951–1955* (Leicester: Leicester University Press, 1988).

44 See Evelyn Shuckburgh. *Descent to Suez: Diaries, 1951–56*, selected by John Charmley (London: Weidenfeld and Nicolson, 1986). See also Robert Rhodes James, *Anthony Eden* (London: Weidenfeld and Nicolson, 1986).

45 Washington to FO, 14 September 1951, FO 371/92603/6.

46 Record of meetings in FO, 13–14 November 1951, FO 371/92603/16.

47 Minute by R. H. Scott, 17 November 1951, FO 371/92605/23. See also *FRUS 1951*, vol. VI, part 1, pp. 1393–4, Webb to embassy (Paris), 7 November 1951, enclosing message from Dulles to Acheson. Dulles suggested that the recent change of government in Britain might constitute a suitable opportunity for achieving progress in obtaining at least a limited treaty between the Yoshida government and the Kuomintang regime. Clearly Dulles did not anticipate Eden's acerbic reaction. See also pp. 1406–7, Gifford to Acheson, 17 November 1951, recording a conversation with Robert Scott: the

latter indicated that the problem in securing progress lay in Eden's hostile attitude. Eden told Scott he did not realise that relations between Japan and the Kuomintang regime were subject to review.

48 *Ibid.*
49 Comments by Eden, 17 November 1951, *ibid.*
50 Minute by Strang, 17 November 1951, *ibid.*
51 Comments by Eden, 17 November 1951, *ibid.*
52 Minute by Strang, 17 November 1951, *ibid.*
53 Minute by Eden, 19 November 1951, *ibid.*
54 *Ibid.*
55 FO to Paris, 19 November 1951, *ibid.*
56 Paris to FO, 22 November 1951, FO 371/92605/25.
57 Tokyo to FO, 14 December 1951, FO 371/92605/37.
58 FO to Washington, 16 December 1951, FO 371/92605/38.
59 Washington to FO, 18 December 1951, FO 371/92605/43.
60 *Manchester Guardian*, 19 December 1951, FO 371/99403/2.
61 *News Chronicle* and *Daily Herald*, 19 December 1951, *ibid.*
62 Washington to FO, 10 January 1952, FO 371/99403/4.
63 Tokyo to FO, 16 January 1952, FO 371/99403/8.
64 FO to Washington, 16 January 1952, *ibid.*
65 Washington to FO, 16 January 1952, FO 371/99403/10.
66 FO to Washington, 22 January 1952, *ibid.*
67 Letter from Dulles to Churchill, 17 January 1952, FO 371/99404/33.
68 Minute by C. H. Johnston, 23 January 1952, summarising Eden's reaction, *ibid.*
69 Letter from Dulles to Acheson, 21 March 1952, folder, Japanese peace treaty, box 61, Dulles papers, Seeley G. Mudd Library, Princeton University.
70 Letter from Dulles to David Astor, 24 March 1952, *ibid.*
71 Letter from Rockefeller to Dulles, 27 March 1952, *ibid.*
72 Minute by G. G. Fitzmaurice, 9 May 1952, FO 371/99405/77.
73 Letter from Dening to R. H. Scott, 21 January 1952, FO 371/99441/1.
74 Letter from Clutton to R. H. Scott, 21 February 1952, FO 371/99411/10.
75 Letter from Dening to R. H. Scott, 7 April 1952, FO 371/99472/1.
76 Despatch from Dening to Eden, 28 April 1952, FO 371/99472/4.
77 *Ibid.* For a discussion of the aftermath of the San Francisco conference, see Roger Buckley, 'From San Francisco to Suez and Beyond: Anglo-Japanese Relations', in W. I. Cohen and Akira Iriye (eds), *The Great Powers in East Asia, 1953–1960* (New York: Columbia University Press, 1990), pp. 169–86.

PART II

CHINA

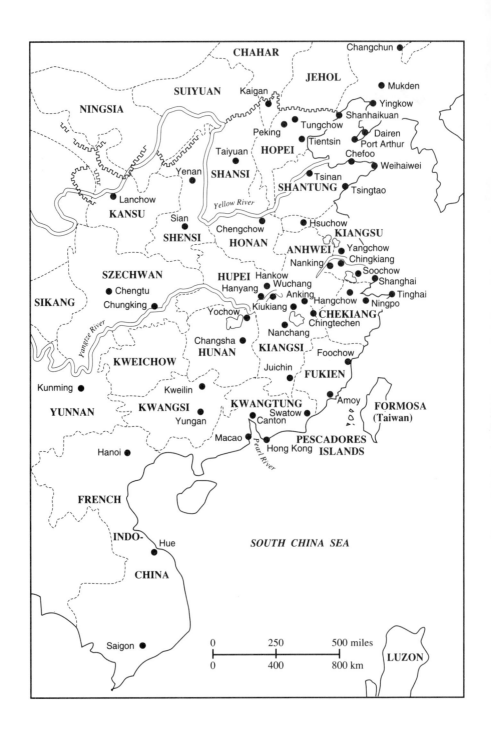

Map 2 **China**

5

THE FALL OF THE KUOMINTANG

The greatest single development in East Asia after 1945 was the Chinese communist victory in the civil war, culminating in the proclamation of the People's Republic on 1 October 1949. The struggle between the Kuomintang and the communists was so protracted – it dated at least from 1927 – that foreign observers were shaken by the speed of the denouement. The fall of the Kuomintang (KMT) occurred with astonishing speed in 1948–49.[1] However, this was not as surprising as it appeared at first sight: the KMT was an amorphous organisation throughout its history and during the lengthy ascendancy of Chiang Kai-shek (from 1927) reactionary forces inexorably tightened their grip on the party and government. Military influence grew rapidly, although the military was factionalised and included some who were jealous or resentful of Chiang: warlords like Yen Hsi-shan who had clambered aboard the KMT bandwagon when Chiang claimed to have unified China in order to protect their regional powerbases;[2] landowners and some of the powerful businessmen of the treaty ports; and the assorted cronies and hangers-on of the leader derisively termed 'Peanut' by General 'Vinegar Joe' Stilwell.[3] Few foreign observers had faith in the capacity of the KMT to transform itself into a progressive movement but they had not believed that it would be so speedily relegated to the 'dustbin of history'. The British government felt little affection for Chiang Kai-shek, understanding his xenophobia and old-fashioned approach to running China. Britain wanted stability in China for political and economic reasons. Britain's formal empire in South-East Asia and its interests in the Pacific region made it extremely desirous of avoiding serious difficulties in China, which could produce problems in Hong Kong and accentuate tensions in Malaya. In the economic sphere the aim was to see trade flourish so as to contribute to restoring the British economy and Britain's international status.

At the beginning of 1948 KMT troops in Manchuria were endeavouring to fulfil Chiang's aim of restoring the authority of the Nanking government in an area that had not experienced effective intervention from the central government since the closing years of the Ch'ing dynasty. While understandable politically, Chiang's action was unwise because it diverted the KMT from its principal region of strength in southern China to an abortive attempt in the north to outmanoeuvre the communists. The challenges confronting the communists in Manchuria were formidable and have often been underestimated, as shown by Steve Levine.[4] They had been excluded from Manchuria by the Japanese creation of Manchukuo and it took considerable effort to build up their resources. The British ambassador to Nanking, Sir Ralph Stevenson, reported on 20 January 1948 that the military situation in the north was deteriorating fast; his American colleague, John Leighton Stuart, had confirmed that Changchun and Kirin were to be abandoned, although an attempt would be made to retain Mukden. Stuart believed that for American economic aid to be effective, Chiang's government must be assisted in maintaining a foothold in Manchuria.[5] The Foreign Office wanted information on the intentions of American policy: little had been heard for a lengthy period.[6] On 12 February Stevenson sent a despatch to Bevin enclosing a report by Lionel (Leo) Lamb on a visit he had made to the north in the second half of January. Lamb indicated that a communist victory in Manchuria was expected and this was likely to apply elsewhere in north China; the local people were so weary of the KMT that the communists were seen as far preferable. Lamb was fairly optimistic regarding the communist attitude to foreign interests and deduced that the communists would proceed carefuly in consolidating their position.[7]

In a further despatch sent two months later, Stevenson reported on the latest developments. He remarked that despite the inherent differences between the approaches of the Russian and Chinese communist movements, 'It would, however, be a mistake to imagine that in the long run this would not result in subservience to Moscow and the growth of evil and oppression which is the natural concomitant of Communism wherever it occurs.'[8] Stevenson enclosed assessments by two colleagues, Burdett and Franklin. Burdett observed that from what he had seen in Tsingtao and Mukden in the previous two years the Chinese would judge communism by its results; he anticipated significant difficulty in the communists attaining effective control of the whole of north China and that the communist ideology might differ markedly from that seen in Europe.[9] Franklin's appreciation was dated 19 March. He identified the growth of defeatism as the key factor. KMT control was restricted to little more than the Peking–Tientsin corridor, rail communications and certain garrison towns. It was likely that KMT authority would collapse, although the timing was uncertain. It was hard to avoid the conclusion that the eclipse of the KMT was imminent. The KMT had never been popular and cynics would argue that the KMT functioned as its own fifth column. The United States might decide to extend considerable economic and military assistance but it was doubtful what would be achieved thereby and American action could be resented as denoting intervention in the civil war. Direct American armed action, if it occurred, would be very significant but the practical difficulties would be enormous. American public opinion would be dubious; the Chinese communists would react fiercely in their propaganda; and, in strategic terms, American troops could be vulnerable in the Peking–Tientsin corridor. The most convincing conclusion was that the communists would take over north China before long. They might try to establish a federation of autonomous political entities such as North Korea, Manchuria, north China, Inner and Outer Mongolia. Franklin thought that a communist regime in north China would focus on agrarian reform with land distribution as its chief aim. Foreigners would probably be permitted to continue their activities for the present but long-term prospects were not encouraging.

Developments in the Soviet zone of Germany perhaps constituted a viable basis of comparison.[10]

Speculation persisted as to the real nature of American policy towards China. The secretary of state, General George Marshall, possessed unusual recent experience of China through his extended efforts to achieve a compromise between the KMT and the communists in 1946. His presence in China was a disillusioning experience and led him to express strong criticism of the corruption and imcompetence of the Nanking regime. The Truman administration's handling of China became a focus for vehement Republican criticism of the failure to halt the advance of communism. Even Senator Arthur H. Vandenberg (Michigan), the Republican chairman of the Senate Foreign Relations Committee, who was a firm advocate of a bipartisan policy towards Europe, censured policy in China.[11] An acrimonious debate took place within Congress over aid to China. The journalist, Alistair Cooke, reported in the *Manchester Guardian* on 23 February on exchanges between Marshall and the House Foreign Affairs Committee on 20 February. Cooke wryly remarked that the Republicans wanted to assist China not because of their affection for China but because of their dislike for Europe (this applied particularly to old guard Republicans rather than those of Vandenberg's persuasion). Marshall was pessimistic in his remarks to the House committee concerning the KMT's ability to survive.[12] At a press conference on 10 March Marshall stated that the American government still supported inclusion of the communists within a coalition government. While he condemned the communist rebellion, it was clear that he assigned a certain legitimacy to the Chinese communist movement.[13] Marshall conceded that recent events in Czechoslovakia caused added tension. President Truman removed ambiguity by stating categorically that the United States did not wish to see communists participating in government anywhere in the world. A difference in approach was obvious between Truman and Marshall and the latter's reactions were detemined by his experience in China.[14]

The British ambassador in Washington, Lord Inverchapel, observed that agitation over the China Aid Bill was stirred up by Walter Judd, a Republican from Minnesota who had served in China as a medical missionary before the Pacific war.[15] Judd became one of the central figures in the 'China lobby', the group comprising some members of Congress, businessmen and figures prominent in the media, which pursued a vigorous campaign for increased aid to China.[16] Judd's voluminous private papers include extensive correspondence over a lengthy period demonstrating his intense interest in matters involving China and his commitment to the cause of Chiang Kai-shek. In August 1948 Judd wrote to Dr Lucius Porter at Yenching University in Peking:

> After months and months of work, it has at last been possible to break the bottle neck and obstructionism, approaching sabotage, in our own State Department. At last some supplies should begin to flow towards China in sizeable quantities. Whether it is still in time to save the situation is of course very dubious. It was questionable even last fall when I was there. How much worse after ten months of what can properly be called studied neglect on the part of our Executive Department. Nothing has been done here except reluctantly and only after the most importunate pressures from a few of us in Congress ... [17]

In a later letter, in December 1948, Judd wrote that it was not too late to send military help to China. A first-class military adviser supported by adequate staff was required. The Truman administration had made no real attempt to defeat communism in China: instead it connived at KMT destruction.[18]

A Republican with very different views from those of Judd was Roger D. Lapham who headed the Economic Cooperation Administration (ECA) programme in China. Lapham was a shrewd, amiable businessman who had served as mayor of San Francisco. While staunchly anti-communist, Lapham appreciated the magnitude of the social and economic problems in China and the failure of the KMT to deal with these problems. Lapham visited Washington in October 1948 and met the president and other members of the government in the White House and the Pentagon. Lapham summarised his views in a letter to a colleague in China as they had been communicated in discussion with General Wedemeyer. Lapham saw American aims as identical in foreign and military policy. The ECA was part of the implementation of the policy; resources for ECA should be increased so that the Cold War could be waged more efficiently; no aid should be extended without control connoting the ability to veto or to designate; in China it must be understood that the communists were winning and the possibility of the collapse of the KMT had to be grasped; assistance should be extended to leaders or groups capable of resisting the spread of communism; land reforms and other progressive measures were required in order to defeat communism; it was inconceivable to give aid to a communist government or to a coalition including communist members.[19] In a separate memorandum Lapham criticised the muddle prevailing in American policy in China which assisted the communists. American assessments should be revised so as to concentrate on more attainable aims, for example securing a coordinated approach to north China, Manchuria, Korea and Japan: 'The strategic and economic relationship of North China and Manchuria with Korea and Japan is especially clear.'[20] Lapham was more realistic than Judd and, while disliking the communists, realised why they had been successful. Lapham diverged more markedly from Judd in 1949, as will be seen in the next chapter. As a prominent Republican in California, Lapham met Governor Earl Warren, the Republican vice-presidential candidate, and Senator William F. Knowland, in October and November 1948 on the eve of the presidential election.[21]

American economic aid to China continued but with no real prospect of reversing the declining fortunes of the KMT. At the end of October 1948 the embassy in Nanking reported that from the military perspective the dilemma of the KMT government could only be described as desperate. Morale was deteriorating and criticism of Chiang Kai-shek was expressed openly. Some leading Chinese castigated Chiang personally:

> and were even expressing the hope that the Communists would soon take over control of this area as life under their administration could not be worse than it was now. There is no doubt that the President has forfeited entirely the respect and loyalty of the masses in the North where he has failed to make any public appearance or other gesture of encouragement to the common people.[22]

As usual Chiang was preoccupied in watching his rivals within the KMT and preventing Yen Hsi-shan and Fu Tso-yi from reaching a compromise with the communists.

In November the governor of Hong Kong, Sir Alexander Grantham, visited Tokyo and met MacArthur. The general was the preferred choice of some Republicans for 'rescuing' the alarming situation in China but MacArthur wisely preferred to stay in Tokyo. MacArthur did not regard the communist successes in Manchuria and north China as likely to cause problems in Japan. He doubted whether Mao would allow the Soviet Union to take over airfields in north China. If he was wrong, then the consequences would be serious in that he would be surrounded by Soviet planes from Vladivostok to the Yangtze. As regards the military advance of the Chinese communists, MacArthur felt it was unlikely that they would advance beyond the Yangtze at present.[23] In the middle of November Leo Lamb speculated on the fate of the Nanking regime. The precise moment when the communist occupation reached the north bank of the Yangtze opposite Nanking depended on the result of the current battle at Hsuchow. The best the KMT could hope for was to block the communist advance temporarily. Communist occupation of the whole region north of the Yangtze could stimulate either the departure of Chiang Kai-shek with a takeover by Li Tsung-jen, the vice-preisdent, who would try to achieve a compromise with the communists, or Chiang might retire to Canton or Taiwan with his loyal followers in a final bid to delay a communist triumph. Chiang's leadership was bankrupt and he could survive only with American support. Lamb added that the communists had acted with restraint towards foreign interests in the hope of being rewarded with recognition of a communist government.[24]

Lamb met T. V. Soong, Chiang's brother-in-law and a former foreign minister. Soong professed confidence but Lamb remarked that he seemed ill at ease. From the conversation Lamb deduced that Soong believed that a 'third world war is inevitable and that ultimately this is the only road to the solution of China's problems.'[25] The American assessment was as bleak as the British. Sir Oliver Franks informed London on 17 November of a discussion with Robert Lovett; he told Lovett that Britain's responsibilities in other areas meant that it was not feasible for Britain to follow a positive policy in China but that the British government wished to lend what support it could to the United States. Lovett said that Chiang could retire from office or use either Kwangtung or Taiwan as a base for a last stand. Chiang's prestige had disintegrated. The Truman administration would watch matters closely including the possible emergence of Li Tsung-jen.[26] On 18 November Lamb stated the sobering fact that the KMT army had lost approximately half a million men with equipment since the start of the communist campaigns in October. A communist victory was unavoidable; he assumed that the Americans would wish to hold Taiwan at all costs.[27] Lamb thought that when the communists formed a government, the latter could suffer from internal strains which could allow the Western powers to exploit matters to their advantage. Peter Scarlett minuted scepticism and referred to the impact of events in Yugoslavia which suggested that regardless of whether communist movements were orthodox or heterodox, they were equally antagonistic to non-communist powers.[28] Esler Dening commented that it would be futile to bolster Chiang's regime, since it had proved hopelessly inept:

the size of China meant that it was bound to take longer for the communists to establish themselves than had been the case in Poland or Yugoslavia.[29]

From Singapore Malcolm MacDonald conveyed the assessment arrived at by the Bukit Serene conference which had looked at the Chinese communist successes in the light of the difficulties facing the colonial powers in South-East Asia. The effects of a total communist victory throughout mainland China would affect all territories in South-East Asia. The military threat to Malaya and Indo-China would be intensified. Communist ability to infiltrate trade unions would be facilitated. Britain and the United States should try to hold Mao's armies to the north of the Yangtze with the purpose of keeping a moderate and sympathetic Chinese government in office. The local defence chiefs held that Hong Kong must be defended in all eventualities and it was also important to retain a presence in Taiwan. MacDonald urged that the undesirable repercussions of frustrating national ambitions should be emphasised to the Dutch and the French with reference to their respective approaches in Indonesia and Indo-China. A positive political and economic policy towards Thailand was most desirable.[30] MacDonald's report confirmed the apprehensions that were all too real in Singapore but were not especially realistic as regards political prospects in China.

On 24 November Stevenson notified the Foreign Office of a lengthy discussion with Leighton Stuart. The American ambassador said that he was under powerful pressure to persuade Chiang Kai-shek to retire. However, Chiang was adamant that it was his duty to remain in office. Stuart summed up the choices facing his government as procrastination or deciding on full-scale military aid to the KMT; a further possibility was to promote the establishment of a coalition government and the fourth was to withdraw totally from China. Stuart added that much depended on whether Marshall remained secretary of state; Stevenson responded that it was already too late and the KMT was defeated.[31] Scarlett sardonically minuted that the American government was likely to procrastinate further.[32] The economic situation continued to worsen at an accelerating rate as inflation reached catastrophic proportions. Urquhart, the consul-general in Shanghai, wrote to Leo Lamb observing appropriately that while he had been in church on Sunday the price of rice was ascending skywards even more rapidly than his prayers.[33] Hubert Graves wrote to Scarlett on 22 November describing a meeting with Walton Butterworth, head of the China division in the State Department. Graves explained:

> The fact of the matter is that the State Department is ham-strung in its policy towards China. There is the over-riding direction – said to be firmly held by the Secretary of State – that the State Department is not to take any action which would involve the United States in China's civil war. Until the President, the Secretary of State, and the new Congressional leaders have had an opportunity to review the situation it looks as though the Administration will adopt a 'wait and see' attitude, except to the extent that they will speed up their withdrawal of the multitude of Service dependants and others who wish to take advantage of transport facilities ...[34]

Graves believed the administration would not be influenced by demands from Chiang for direct American action.

At the end of November Stevenson reported indications that the KMT regime was considering transferring its capital from Nanking to Canton. Stevenson was sceptical as to its feasibility. If such a move occurred, help would not be forthcoming in providing transport to, or accommodation in, Canton. He recommended that the British embassy should remain in Nanking, adding that the same view was taken by his American, French, Dutch and Belgian colleagues. If Chiang Kai-shek and his chief followers departed, Britain could, if necessary, send a senior diplomat to accompany them. If the embassy left Nanking and had to return at a future date, then the British position would be invidious and possibly undignified; it would definitely entail a decision concerning formal recognition of an alternative Chinese government.[35] In Shanghai considerable anxiety arose at the danger of a breakdown in law and order if the communists captured Nanking and resumed their advance. The mayor of Shanghai communicated his fears to foreign representatives at the beginning of December. It was clear that the mayor aimed to involve the United States and Britain if he could.[36] In Washington Walter Judd, Senator Styles Bridges (Republican, New Hampshire) and General Claire Chennault were doing their best to stir up as much debate as possible over communist success in China; controversy was accentuated by the visit of Madame Chiang Kai-shek whose presence engendered emotional reactions.[37] The Foreign Office advised that if the situation in Shanghai worsened, then the choice appeared to be between evacuation or assisting the Chinese forces of law and order. The former would constitute a military operation and might cause friction with the communists; in addition, British property could be destroyed. Perhaps the British government should not disclaim all responsibility for helping to preserve law and order, although the perils in becoming involved were obvious.[38]

Officials in the Foreign Office reflected on the nature of Chinese communism in November and December 1948. Guy Burgess was the principal author of memoranda assessing ideological developments. Burgess was, of course, an even greater and more intimate authority on Marxism than his colleagues in Whitehall believed. A telegram, approved by Ernest Bevin, was sent to various British representatives abroad on 22 November stating that the internal manifestations of communism in China and the eventual impact on communist doctrine resulting from the effects of the Chinese national character could not be foreseen. However, evidence was sufficient to disprove the contention of *The Times*, in a leading article published on 8 November, that Mao's movement was wholly independent of Moscow. It must be anticipated that the Chinese communists would follow the same path as their comrades in Europe: they would encourage coalitions with left democratic parties and then take them over. The final result would be that 'the Communist cuckoo pushed the other birds out of the nest'.[39] Bevin's aim was to align British policy with that of the United States if possible; the telegram concluded with a sombre warning that those who had endeavoured to work with the communists in Europe had failed.

P. D. Coates minuted on 22 December that the chief aim of British policy was to protect its interests and this indicated the undesirability of being provocative. However, it had to be kept in mind that Mao and his colleagues did not confine their activities to China: intelligence obtained in Malaya showed that links existed between the Chinese and Malayan parties; similarly, links operated between the Chinese communists and the communist movements within Indo-China. The growth of bellicose communism in South-East Asia and India developed from the Calcutta conference which met at the beginning of 1948. Coates noted that it was widely held that the Calcutta conference functioned under orders from Moscow. He concluded that it was not the British but the Chinese communists who were provocative.[40] Scarlett felt that a suitable balance must be struck in formulating policy and that it would be erroneous to reveal excessive caution in dealing with the communists. Some might think that the communists resembled 'a cuddly kitten' when viewed at a distance but it could turn out to be a creature of far less amiable character.[41] Dening judiciously opted for giving Stevenson freedom to respond as he saw fit: the Soviet Union might be waiting for Britain to err. Dening doubted whether overt propaganda against the communists accomplished much.[42]

Kenneth Royall, the American secretary of the army, visited London in December and when at lunch with the chief of the imperial general staff, observed that the best plan for defence policy in the Far East would be to abandon Japan and defend a line much further south. William Hayter felt Royall's remarks need not be taken too seriously.[43] Dening was less dismissive and was prompted to reflect on current dilemmas in China and Japan in a letter to Graves. The Chinese communists were likely to establish a coalition government in 1949 and this would render it more feasible to contemplate recognition. Dening underlined his reservations concerning American policy:

> We … feel that unless there is a *concerted* Far Eastern policy soon, the future can only develop to our common detriment. American policy failed in China because they failed to appreciate Chinese intransigence; it has virtually failed in Korea because they failed to appreciate Korean intransigence; and it is my personal view that it will eventually fail in Japan because they fail to appreciate Japanese intransigence. Where we shall all be then I shudder to think. Mr. Royall, in conversation with the CIGS, expressed the view the other day that the best defence in the Far East would be to abandon Japan and defend a line much further south. I wonder how long it will be before this defeatist outlook finds more general expression. I have an uneasy feeling that, having burnt their fingers, the Americans are adducing reasons to themselves why they should abandon the Far East. This is, of course, what Australia and New Zealand in particular have always feared.[44]

Dening added that in 1949 it would be necessary to make a determined effort to emphasise the realities and to see a coherent far eastern policy devised in Washington. The most appropriate time could be when the Atlantic Pact had been disposed of, assuming that pressures in East Asia would permit waiting this long. Dening's anxiety over Royall's attitude was not borne out because Royall was disavowed by Truman and MacArthur.[45]

The consul-general in Tientsin considered the main characteristics of Chinese communism in a telegram sent on 24 December. He described their approach as combining agrarian reform, toleration of private industries, welcoming foreign capital within communist guidelines, promotion of greater efficiency in existing industries, fair treatment of workers, and the fostering of closer cooperation between capital and labour.[46] Burgess minuted that the programme was predictable:

> We must expect the Chinese N.E.P. outlined here and in Mao Tse Tung's speech to last while a firm social basis for Communist political power is achieved through agrarian reform and some form of Trade Union development and to be followed until sufficient Communist administrators and technicians plus an assurance of necessary imports both of raw materials and machinery have been secured. Then, expropriation and dictatorship will be attempted – cf. the liquidation of Russia's N.E.P.[47]

Urquhart reflected on prospects for British business in a despatch to Stevenson forwarded on 17 December. It was a matter for speculation as to how far the Chinese communists would adhere to the Moscow line but there was reason to hope that the Chinese spirit of individualism would encourage a more independent policy. Divergent attitudes might develop among Chinese leaders and it was difficult to envisage one Chinese leader possessing the power to compel the party to move in one direction: 'I suggest that the Russians may be nearly as worried about the difficulties of controlling the Chinese communists as the Americans are of checking them.'[48] Urquhart suggested that Western commerce should be maintained and Western assistance provided. To ensure effectiveness an understanding with other interested governments was necessary; his American colleague had indicated that there were various aspects upon which American policy had not yet cohered and that it could take time for policy to crystallise. Urquhart's despatch was sent to the Foreign Office and Scarlett wrote to him in January 1949 that a paper prepared for the cabinet concluded that the weakness of a communist-dominated China might not afford an opportunity to obtain reasonable treatment for British interests. The Foreign Office was hampered by inadequate information on the nature of communist intentions. It appeared that they were orthodox Marxist-Leninists: it was sanguine to think that they could be induced to desert communism to become 'middle of the road socialists'.[49] Scarlett agreed with Urquhart that British firms should remain in China and endeavour to transact business with the communists. This became a familiar refrain in the construction of British policy towards China – the aim should be to conduct 'business as usual' in the belief that economic realities in China and the onerous responsibilities of conducting government would engender a spirit of tolerance in Peking.

In the course of 1949 the cabinet was more directly involved in consideration of policy, given the combination of the inexorable decline of the KMT towards Taiwan or oblivion, the necessity to discuss the defence of Hong Kong, and the issues inherent in coming to terms with the communists. On 12 January Ernest Bevin informed his colleagues that Chiang Kai-shek had enquired whether the British, American and French governments would be willing to mediate between the KMT and the communists. Bevin stated that the Truman administration was unwilling to entertain the proposal, although he favoured ascertaining the reactions of the Soviet Union and France. The colonial secretary and the secretary for commonwealth relations each drew attention to the delicate implications for Britain's relations with the Asian members of the

Commonwealth; they might resent interference in the internal affairs of China. Bevin commented that from his own viewpoint he would prefer not to intervene. The cabinet decided that Chiang should be told that Britain was not willing to mediate at this juncture.[50] On 8 March the cabinet discussed memoranda circulated by the foreign and colonial secretaries dealing with Malaya and Hong Kong. During the discussion Bevin said bluntly that China was in chaos. Trade was effectively halted but there were indications that the communists would be prepared to reach barter deals with British firms. Bevin stated that other countries must be consulted and that suitable economic measures to defend British interests must be investigated. Liaison between the different police and intelligence organisations in South-East Asia must be improved.[51] The colonial secretary reviewed the position in Hong Kong: care must be shown so as to hold the balance between the contending political groups. Some members of the cabinet expressed doubts over ignoring communist activities in Hong Kong but others pointed out that it was sensible not to take action which would render it more difficult to establish positive relations with the communists.[52] It was pointed out that if action were taken against local communists in Hong Kong, the consequences for British nationals in mainland China would have to be evaluated. Thus a balance was required between suppression of the communist insurgency in Malaya and a realistic response to the triumph of communism in China.

On 17 March Bevin circulated a memorandum to his colleagues containing a report by the permanent under-secretary in the Foreign Office, Sir William Strang, in which Strang assessed the outcome of a tour he had made in East and South-East Asia. Strang stated he had spent four days in Hong Kong and had reviewed problems in the Crown colony with the governor, Sir Alexander Grantham. Strang added that the turmoil in China was paradoxically not without its encouraging features: 'The chief danger to Hong Kong would be a united China whether Kuomintang or Communist.'[53] Approximately 11,000 refugees had entered Hong Kong since November 1948. It looked as though the communists would act with moderation after formally establishing a government:

> It was not certain that they would depart from this policy, but it would be prudent to asume that they would. Most people who knew China were reluctant to believe that the Chinese people would be communised on the Soviet Russian model. This did not mean that Mao Tse-tung and his associates were not Kremlin indoctrinated and directed.[54]

Strang visited Shanghai between 9 and 11 February. He was struck by the brooding air of menace as the city awaited its fate. It was the third most populous city in the world with an estimated population of approximately six million. It was separated from most of its hinterland. The energetic KMT mayor, K. C. Wu, realised that he was waging a losing battle but indicated that he would fulfil his responsibilities. Strang met representatives of the principal British companies – the Hongkong and Shanghai Bank, the British-American Tobacco Company, Unilevers and other concerns. Sir Ralph Stevenson spoke at the meetings:

> He could not foresee how a Communist regime would behave to foreign interests. The Kuomintang had behaved scandalously in this respect. For

this reason the British community had not definitively made up their minds what to do in the event of the transfer of Shanghai to the Communists. He thought they would stay and rely on their experience and skill to pull them through.[55]

One leading businessman present, Keswick, concurred 'and even spoke of the British Community as a kind of fifth column which might apply its skill, good name and contacts to develop and encourage the ineradicable Chinese passion for trade, even if the Communists came in'.[56] Stevenson believed that the KMT was finished and that its leaders would try to negotiate local settlements in their home provinces. He did not believe that the Chinese would tolerate Soviet domination of Manchuria. Stevenson interestingly commented that the Soviet Union still maintained diplomatic relations with the KMT government which might suggest doubt as to its ability to achieve a satisfactory arrangement with a new regime. He defined the Soviet view towards Mao, probably correctly, as follows: 'It should not be assumed that the Soviet Government wanted Mao Tse-tung to sweep the country. They might prefer him to concentrate on North China for the present.'[57] Strang met the Indian ambassador to China, K. M. Panikkar, who was later to play a controversial role in reporting Chinese views. On this occasion Panikkar commended the British policy of non-intervention and 'watchful waiting'. Panikkar deemed it essential to avoid hostility to the new order: the best approach comprised mutual respect for each other's interests. It should prove possible to conduct trade and perhaps to place diplomatic relations on a positive basis.[58] Thus the conclusion drawn from Strang's visit to China was that a pragmatic policy was advisable and that with a measure of luck it should be possible to arrive at an accommodation with the new rulers in Peking.

The advance of the communists rendered it necessary to consider the defence of Hong Kong. The cabinet met on 5 May to discuss a defence appraisal. Attlee circulated a paper discussing political factors involved in containing a threat to the security of Hong Kong, including the possibility of inviting assistance from the Commonwealth and the United States. In cabinet debate it was noted that Hong Kong could not be defended against an onslaught by a major power advancing from the mainland: this had, of course, been made brutally clear by the Japanese in 1941. The intention of the chiefs of staff was to strengthen British forces in Hong Kong so as to cope with limited internal unrest or sporadic guerrilla attacks. It was not thought likely that Chinese communist forces would constitute the kind of threat that would be seen if a state such as the Soviet Union attacked Hong Kong. The cabinet approved proposals to strengthen the garrison in Hong Kong.[59] On 23 May the colonial secretary informed his colleagues that KMT influence in Hong Kong had declined steadily and the more prominent communists living in the colony had departed for the mainland. The governor had ordered all parties to register with the authorities. One difficulty was to foster sufficient confidence in Britain's future role: out of a total population of almost two million not more than 10,000 people, including the police, could be fully relied on to maintain order in the event of a grave threat materialising.[60]

The process of considering Britain's relations with the communists was disturbed briefly by the episode involving HMS *Amethyst*. In its way this was a fittingly symbolic indication of the final end of Western naval activity on China's great river. The *Amethyst* represented a token of support for British interests redolent of a bygone era. The frigate was trapped in part of the Yangtze by the advance of communist forces. After being detained the *Amethyst* made a dramatic escape from communist gunfire. Nor surprisingly this caught the imagination of the British press and lively accounts of the glorious defiance of the communist army appeared.[61] The commander and crew were fêted in various ports on the return journey and were given a boisterous reception when marching through London. Politically it was embarrassing for the government which was slowly moving towards recognition of the communists. As regards the impact on the communists, it is likely that it strengthened their already potent detestation of Western imperialism and it intensified the inclination to drive home the lesson to Western governments and nationals that the old days of Western arrogance and superiority were at an end.[62]

Notes

1 For the development of Chinese communism in the period down to the assumption of power, see J. K. Fairbank and A. Feuerwerker (eds), *The Cambridge History of China*, vol. XIII, part 2 (Cambridge: Cambridge University Press, 1986), pp. 609–870. See also Suzanne Pepper, *Civil War in China, 1945–49* (Berkeley and Los Angeles: University of California Press, 1978).

2 For a revealing study of Yen, see D. G. Gillin, *Warlord: Yen Hsi-shan in Shansi Province, 1911–1949* (Princeton: Princeton University Press, 1967).

3 For Stilwell's mordant observations on Chiang, see T. H. White (ed.), *The Stilwell Papers* (New York: Sloane, 1948) and Barbara Tuchman, *Stilwell and the American Experience in China, 1911–45* (New York: Macmillan, 1970).

4 See S. Levine, 'A New Look at American Mediation in the Chinese Civil War: The Marshall Mission and Manchuria', *Diplomatic History*, 3 (1979), pp. 349–76.

5 Nanking to FO, 20 January 1948, FO 371/692527/1120. For an account of Sino-British relations after 1945, see Zhong-ping Feng, *The British Government's China Policy, 1945–1950* (Keele: Keele University Press, 1994).

6 FO to Washington, 27 January 1948, FO 371/692527/1120.

7 Despatch, Stevenson to Bevin, 12 February 1948, FO 371/692528/3295.

8 Despatch, Stevenson to Bevin, 7 April 1948, FO 371/69531/6117.

9 Letter from S. L. Burdett to Leo Lamb, 19 March 1948, *ibid.*

10 Appreciation by Franklin, 19 March 1948, *ibid.*

11 See A. H. Vandenberg, Jr (ed.), *The Private Papers of Senator Vandenberg* (London: Victor Gollancz, 1953), pp. 335, 351, 450–2.

12 *Manchester Guardian*, 23 February 1948.

13 Washington to FO, 12 March 1948, FO 371/69584/4026.

14 Washington to FO, 12 March 1948, FO 371/69584/4034.

15 Washington to FO, 12 March 1948, FO 371/69584/4026.

16 For broad discussion of the China lobby, see R. Y. Koen, *The China Lobby in American Politics* (London: Harper & Row, 1974) and S. D. Bachrack, *The Committee of One Million: 'China Lobby' Politics, 1953–1971* (New York: Columbia University Press, 1976). Some valuable information is to be found in Bruce Cumings, *The Origins of the Korean War*, 2 vols, vol. II, *The Roaring of the Cataract, 1947–1950* (Princeton: Princeton University Press, 1990), pp. 102–60. T. V. Soong, Chiang Kai-shek's brother-in-law, was immensely wealthy and actively supported leading figures in the China lobby (see Cumings, *The Roaring of the Cataract*, p. 153). Louis Johnson, the eccentric secretary for defense in the Truman administration, leaked highly confidential information to the KMT embassy in Washington (see *ibid.*, p. 159).

17 Letter from Judd to Porter, 14 August 1948, Judd papers, box 149, folder, China 1948, Hoover Institution, Stanford, California.
18 Letter from Judd to Dr Alma L. Cooke, 27 December 1948, *ibid.*
19 Letter from Lapham to Allen Griffin, 25 October 1948, Lapham papers, box 1, folder 3, Hoover Institution.
20 Memorandum, 'United States Policy in China', marked 'Dave Gordon', 15 October 1948, Lapham papers, *ibid.*
21 Earl Warren was a shrewd political operator and was three times elected governor of California. He was a leading figure in the liberal wing of the Republican party. Thomas Dewey chose Warren as his running mate in the 1948 election but, as Warren later recalled, Dewey did not coordinate his campaign with Warren's; it is probable that Warren would have been a more effective candidate than Dewey and he might have defeated Truman. See Oral History, Earl Warren, interview conducted by Jerry N. Hess, May 1972, pp. 21–3, copy in the Harry S. Truman Library, Independence, Missouri.
22 Nanking to FO, 28 October 1948, FO 371/69541/5167.
23 Tokyo to FO, 13 November 1948, FO 371/69542/15991.
24 Nanking to FO, 16 November 1948, FO 371/69542/16138.
25 Nanking to FO, 15 November 1948, FO 371/69542/16143.
26 Washington to FO, 17 November, 1948, FO 371/69542/16203.
27 Nanking to FO, 18 November 1948, *ibid.*
28 Minute by Scarlett, 23 November 1948, *ibid.*
29 Minute by Dening, 23 November 1948, *ibid.*
30 Singapore to FO, 23 November 1948, FO 371/69542/16438.
31 Nanking to FO, 24 November 1948, FO 371/69543/16577.
32 Minute by Scarlett, 26 November 1948, *ibid.*
33 Letter from Urquhart to Lamb, 9 November 1948, FO 371/69543/16615.
34 Letter from Graves to Scarlett, 22 November 1948, FO 371/69543/16781.
35 Nanking to FO, 30 November 1948, FO 371/69543/16821.
36 Shanghai to FO, 3 December 1948, FO 371/69545/17092.
37 Washington to FO, 30 November 1948, FO 371/69545/17094.
38 FO to Nanking, 10 December 1948, FO 371/69545/17336.
39 FO to HM's representatives in various capitals, 22 November 1948, FO 371/69545/17436.
40 Minute by Coates, 22 December 1948, FO 371/69548/17966.
41 Minute by Scarlett, 23 December 1948, *ibid.*
42 minute by Dening, 3 January 1949, *ibid.*
43 Minute by Hayter, 15 December 1948, FO 371/69550/18545/G.
44 Letter from Dening to Graves, 29 December 1948, *ibid.*
45 See the discussion of British and American policies towards Japan in chapter 1.
46 Tientsin to FO, 24 December 1948, FO 371/69550/18506.
47 Minute by Burgess, 4 January 1949 (wrongly dated 1948), *ibid.*
48 Despatch from Urquhart to Stevenson, 17 December 1948, FO 371/69550/18520.
49 Letter from Scarlett to Urquhart, 17 January 1949, *ibid.*
50 Cabinet conclusions, 12 January 1949, CM2(49)3, Cab 128/15.
51 *Ibid.*, 8 March 1949, CM18(49)2.
52 *Ibid.*
53 Note by Bevin, 17 March 1949, enclosing report by Strang, CP(49)67, Cab 129/33, part 2.
54 *Ibid.*
55 *Ibid.*
56 *Ibid.*
57 *Ibid.*
58 *Ibid.*
59 Cabinet conclusions, 5 May 1949, CM32(49)2, Cab 128/15.
60 Memorandum by colonial secretary, 23 May 1949, CP(49)120, Cab 129/35.
61 For a lively account of the *Amethyst* crisis, see M. H. Murfett, *Hostage on the Yangtze: Britain, China and the Amethyst Crisis of 1949* (Annapolis: Naval Institute Press, 1991).

62 For the views of the foreign secretary and first lord of the Admiralty, see joint memo-
    randum circulated to the cabinet, 25 April 1949, CP(49)93, Cab 129/34. For the views
    of the Chinese communists, see Qiang Zhai, *The Dragon, the Lion and the Eagle:
    Chinese–British–American Relations, 1949–1958* (London: Kent State University Press,
    1994), ch. 1 and Weiguang Shao, *China, Britain and Businessmen: Political and Commercial
    Relations, 1949–57* (London and Oxford: Macmillan/St Antony's College, 1991), pp.
    1–29.

6

RECOGNITION OF THE COMMUNIST GOVERNMENT AND THE FATE OF TAIWAN

British policy in 1949–50 centred around the associated issues of recognition of the Chinese communist government, proclaimed formally on 1 October 1949, and the future of Taiwan. A serious divergence in approach between the British and American governments developed between the autumn of 1949 and the summer of 1950 over both problems; this might have assumed gravity but for the outbreak of the Korean war which compelled the Attlee government to accept that differences should not be carried too far. American policy was determined by a mixture of developing phobia over communism, domestic acrimony over the 'loss' of China, and the traditional American attitude that recognition was an act of moral approval. British policy was governed by a combination of appreciation of Britain's historic role in China, the wish to promote trade and defend Hong Kong, and the traditional British attitude that a government in control of most or all of a country should be recognised.[1]

In January 1949 Chiang Kai-shek supposedly 'retired' and the vice-president of the KMT government, Li Tsung-jen, temporarily assumed a more prominent position. Chiang and Li had long been rivals: Chiang bitterly opposed Li's election as vice-president and the fact that he was elected by the usually subservient KMT deputies may be taken as underlining the extent to which faith in Chiang had declined. Li was perceived as a leader who would try to reach a compromise with the communists. Chiang had no intention of transferring power and retained his grip via the network of loyalties to him within the party and army. American representatives in China quickly lost confidence in any possibility of the KMT retaining power in the mainland. The chief of the ECA mission in China, Roger D. Lapham, was appalled at the corruption and ineptitude of the regime and argued for the adoption of a more realistic American policy. The head of ECA, Paul Hoffman, visited Shanghai in January 1949 and made statements implying that he and Lapham favoured continuing economic aid to a coalition government including communist members on the understanding that such a government preserved essential freedoms. The State Department held that this went too far, somewhat ironically since Hoffman and Lapham were both businessmen and both Republicans.[2] Lapham sent a memorandum to Hoffman on 9 March stating flatly that the KMT regime was beyond salvation. Nothing could halt this inexorable process and the American government should not attempt any form of military action in China. Lapham felt that the United States should seek to influence a Chinese communist government through commercial channels. No restrictions on the American export trade to China should be applied other than military or strategic material. The principal aim was to avoid domination of China by a government actively or potentially antagonistic towards the United States: the 'open door' should remain open. Lapham emphasised a point made vigorously by Attlee and Bevin – American policy should work to prevent a satellite relationship developing between the Soviet Union and China. Lapham observed that one feature of the Sino-American relationship was unchallengeable: American influence was much less than had been the case in 1945. The United States was involved in a civil war and the Truman administration backed the losing side, not simply with economic aid but with arms and ammunition. It would be wise to eschew thought of extending further military assistance either to the KMT or to any other anti-communist group that might appear. The aim should be to assist the poverty-stricken peasants who constituted most of the population: American personnel should be deployed in rural China with no motive apart from improving living standards.[3]

At the end of June Lapham produced a final report on his twelve months in China, following his recall. He summarised the work of his mission and the considerable obstacles he had faced. Of these currency inflation proved the most serious. When he arrived, in June 1948, one American dollar could buy 1,400,000 Chinese dollars. Some months later one American dollar could purchase nearly twelve million Chinese dollars. Approximately 70 per cent of KMT government income went to pay for the armed forces. The so-called currency reform, introduced by the KMT in August 1948, was a fiasco: Chinese were coerced into surrendering gold, silver or foreign exchange to receive a worthless new currency. Lapham ended his report on a sensible, flexible note which could profitably have been observed by many of his fellow citizens in the future: 'One thing the year has taught me – you cannot afford to hold to fixed ideas. You must keep fluid, face things as they are and not as you would like to have them.'[4] Lapham spoke publicly on 8 September 1949 when he addressed the Commonwealth Club of California in San Francisco. In a note attached to the published version Lapham stated that his views were arrived at entirely independently of the China White Paper, published by the State Department on 5 August; indeed he used much of the material from his final report to Hoffman.[5] Lapham bluntly described Chiang Kai-shek as extremely incompetent to the chagrin of right-wing Republicans who regarded Chiang as a hero. He acknowledged Chiang's courage in resisting the Japanese and in opposing communism:

> But the good work a man did yesterday cannot offset his failures of today, and the fact remains that the Generalissimo is a stubborn, obstinate man, who refused to delegate authority, who relied on incompetent favourites for many of his subordinates and who put on the shelf competent military men who could have helped him. Not only is he responsible for the defeat of the military front ... he can largely be blamed for the failure on the economic front. Lacking first-hand knowledge in this field, he did little or nothing to establish civil reforms, or to take effective steps to offset the well-planned operations and propaganda of the Communists.[6]

Lapham acknowledged the efforts of KMT officials who tried to operate effectively, notably K. C. Wu, the mayor of Shanghai with whom he had exchanged views on the problems of governing a great city in the light of his own experience when mayor of San Francisco. It would be a mistake to support Chiang again for he was wholly discredited. It was reported that Chiang was sustained by the hope that war would occur between the United States and the Soviet Union in which eventually he was bound to receive American support: 'If war with Russia should develop and we need China's aid – let us not back a Chinese leader who has lost the confidence of his people.'[7] Lapham condemned Congress for having made an appropriation of 125 million US dollars to China for military aid to the KMT: 'This $125,000,000 can be considered as thrown down the rat-hole.'[8] If aid was sent in future, then the American government should accept responsibility for ensuring efficient use of it.

Lapham emphasised his own detestation of communism and he supported the European initiatives of the Truman administration. He believed it would be futile for the United States to contemplate sending an army or air force to China to intervene in the civil war. He referred to economic aspects including British interests in trade and Hong Kong. It seemed clear that Britain wished to preserve opportunities for trade. 'It seems obvious that Britain and the United States should make every effort to agree on a policy towards the Chinese Communists. It is to our mutual advantage to do so.'[9] He opposed implementation of an economic blockade. The best way to outmanoeuvre the Russians in China was to maintain contacts with the new government with the purpose of reducing suspicion and preventing the Soviet Union from exploiting the situation. Lapham grasped the nettle of recognition and revealed that he had reached the same conclusions as Attlee and Bevin: 'The only practical way to keep the door open, as well as to listen and observe what goes on behind the bamboo curtain, is to accept the fact that we may soon have to recognize in such areas as they control, the Communist Government, as the de facto government, and be prepared to recognize it whether or not we like it.'[10] He ended his address by commending the wisdom of achieving a bipartisan policy towards China and maintained that in making the speech he was contributing to public debate just as he had done as mayor of San Francisco: 'I always tried to call my shots as I saw them.'[11]

Lapham's analysis was wise and persuasive. Not surprisingly it offended members of the China lobby and Walter Judd wrote to Lapham in December condemning recognition of the communist government in China: he placed blame for the demise of the KMT on the shoulders of the Truman administration and inept American officials in China. Judd wrote:

> It seems incredible but doubtless will come to pass that our government should recognise and start building up the Communists in China with such moral and material supplies. It will tell the undecided millions in Asia that there is more to gain by going over to the Communists. They then get Russian assistance and American too ...[12]

Lapham responded by acknowledging Judd's superior knowledge of China but reiterated the crucial arguments advanced in his address in San Francisco. He enclosed a further memorandum of 29 December 1949 crisply restating his views.[13] Unfortunately the views expressed by Senator Robert A. Taft, Walter Judd, Claire Chennault and Alfred Kohlberg were more typical of American reactions to events in China.[14]

Dean Acheson succeeded General Marshall as secretary of state in January 1949. He was a man of great tenacity, strength of character and arrogance. He was interested in the future of Japan and Korea but showed no particular concern over China: here his approach was to play for time while 'the dust settled'. He was exasperated at the record of the KMT and decided that the best method of exposing the corruption and ineptitude of Chiang's regime was to publish a record of the American government's dealings with the KMT. It was understandable but unwise. It is rarely sensible for a government to publish a detailed record when handling an on-going situation which is still controversial. The China White Paper was published in August 1949, but instead of calming the waters it exacerbated criticism of the Truman administration and of Acheson himself.[15] In private Acheson tended towards the views of Roger Lapham but political necessity dictated caution. Truman had lost all confidence in the KMT but he was vehemently anti-communist and was not inclined to consider recognition of the communist government. General MacArthur was in tune with other right-wing Republicans and expounded the case for American intervention. He met the Huber congressional committee on its far eastern tour in September 1949. His remarks illustrated his penchant for sweeping generalisations together with the powerful prejudices which affected his assessments of China:

> Relatively little effort will be required now to turn the tide in China but the longer we wait we will find difficulties mounting in geometric rather than arithmetic proportions. The Communist forces are grossly overrated. Evidences of their weakness are slowness of their advances, the administrative and logistic difficulties which are inherent in their situation.[16]

MacArthur continued that Chiang was surrounded by corrupt officials: he was intelligent but ignorant of the art of war. Chiang possessed, however, the resolution and character to make him a national leader. MacArthur did not reflect on the curious fact that Chiang had already been a national leader for 22 years and that most of these years had been devoted to fighting his internal or external foes. The correct strategy, in MacArthur's opinion, was to assail 'the Reds' where it would hurt them most which meant in the air and at sea. He recommended a wide-ranging declaration condemning communism; putting 500 fighter planes under the command of someone like Chennault; facilitating the creation of a volunteer force to support Chennault; and implementing an economic blockade of China including the destruction of coastal cities. As regards the Soviet Union, he conceded that there was a danger of Soviet involvement but he did not deem it to be serious.[17]

Acheson discussed China with Bevin when they met on 13 September. Acheson said there would be no hasty action over recognition. The United States would insist that a communist government must accept fully its international obligations and recognition need not be accorded until Mao's government controlled the whole of mainland China. 'Bevin said the British were not in a hurry to recognize but they have big commercial interests in and trade with

China and were not in same position as we were relatively or absolutely.' Bevin underlined his concern over Hong Kong and warned of the dangers of obduracy in forcing the Chinese into the arms of the Soviet Union. Acheson remarked that he doubted whether recognition would be significant in keeping China out of the Soviet orbit.[19]

Within Whitehall considerable discussion occurred over the complexities of recognition in the summer of 1949. The Far Eastern (Official) Committee existed to coordinate the responses of the various government departments involved in East and South-East Asia. The Foreign Office circulated a memorandum to the committee on 8 August dealing with issues raised by the American ambassador in a letter sent to Bevin a fortnight before. There was no prospect that the KMT government could maintain its position in the mainland. The Chinese communist leaders were orthodox Marxist-Leninists and their existing policy 'constitutes a serious threat to Western political and economic interests not only in China but also in South East Asia'.[20] A clear distinction was drawn between dealing with the threats posed by communism in South-East Asia and in China. The aim should be to construct a viable front capable of containing communism in South-East Asia. In China an attempt to intervene in the dying stages of the civil war would be counter-productive and would push the Chinese people towards, rather than away from, the communist government:

> It is therefore considered that the only hope of encouraging the emergence in China of a less anti-Western tendency is to give the new regime time to realise both the necessity of Western help in overcoming its economic difficulties, and the natural incompatibility of Soviet imperialism with Chinese national interests (e.g. in Manchuria).[21]

British policy should avoid direct confrontation and equally eschew appeasement. Western firms should try to stay in China for as long as possible so as to facilitate commercial contact which, in turn, could encourage political contact:

> Although there can be no doubt about the fundamental hostility of Chinese Communism to foreign mercantile communities, it nevertheless remains possible that experience may induce a more realistic attitude in the Communist authorities, who are at present themselves to some extent prisoners of their own propaganda. There are few grounds for optimism as to the future; but British trading communities abroad have weathered many storms in the past, and we are by no means convinced that we should be wise to abandon what remains of our position in China until it becomes abundantly clear that it is untenable. It is, of course, practically certain that long-established and deep-rooted commercial establishments and connections, once abandoned, could never be restored.[22]

The Foreign Office rejected what was understood to be the view of the American government that Western capitalists who remained in China 'have put themselves in the position of hostages in their search for private gain and are therefore deserving of little sympathy.'[23] This did not connote that British firms should stay if conditions became unduly humiliating. Evacuation of British nationals was not favoured: it was believed that the prevailing mood was in favour of remaining, although there had recently been an increase in those preferring evacuation.

As regards recognition, the UN charter, under articles 23 and 27(3) appeared to mean that without a Chinese representative the UN Security Council could take decisions only on procedural matters. Accordingly, *de jure* recognition should not be terminated until it could be extended to the new government. The issue of determining recognition was not urgent but would arise when the communist armies had conquered additional territory in southern China. It looked as though a communist government could be established in mid-autumn 1949. The Commonwealth and the North Atlantic powers should aim to achieve a relationship with the new China analogous to that existing with Yugoslavia. The timing of recognition was important: it would be unwise to do so prematurely but equally foolish to delay for too long.[24] Since the KMT government was fast declining, the timing of withdrawing recognition should be decided for practical reasons. The crucial aspect was that of UN representation. It was likely that the KMT regime would still represent China during the new session of the General Assembly. Close consultation with the Commonwealth and North Atlantic powers was essential.

Part of the memorandum was incorporated within a cabinet paper circulated by Bevin on 23 August. The main cause for immediate concern resulted from the KMT blockade of Shanghai and Tientsin. The blockade of the latter would probably cease to be effective because of communist occupation of certain islands at the entrance to the Gulf of Pechili. However, the blockade of Shanghai was effective in stopping the entrance or departure of merchant ships. British firms in Shanghai were in dire straits and were currently subsidised from their head offices in London. Some would have to close if the blockade continued for much longer. A suggestion had been made to the American government for parallel representations to be conveyed to the KMT authorities to allow ships to dock for relief purposes. Initially the United States was negative in response but it was subsequently agreed that a parallel approach could be made on the basis that the priority would be evacuation of nationals instead of relief. Because ships carrying supplies could be used for evacuation, the American view was accepted and representations made to the Canton government on 15 August. The KMT authorities were willing in principle for a vessel to dock in Shanghai: they would not permit cargo to be carried which could assist the communists directly. In general the position in Shanghai was worsening: the point was approaching where it might be necessary to consider escorting ships through the blockade on the assumption that the KMT government adhered to its existing policy.[25]

Bevin was focused on Anglo-American relations. Consultations had periodically occurred but the direction of American policy had been unclear. It had been thought that the Truman administration was sympathetic to the British preference for keeping 'a foot in the door' but thinking in Washington had apparently changed and American nationals would probably be evacuated from China. American consulates in Canton, Kunming, Chungking and Tihwa were to be closed and their staffs in Nanking and Shanghai reduced. Bevin had agreed that Britain would look after American interests. It was difficult to interpret the contrasting evidence of American intentions as shown in the China White Paper and in withdrawal of consuls.[26] Bevin envisaged withdrawing the British ambas-

sador, Sir Ralph Stevenson, for consultations when it appeared that a communist government would be proclaimed. The cabinet discussed Bevin's paper on
29 August and approved his proposals. Bevin and Creech Jones, the colonial
secretary, submitted a paper assessing the position of Hong Kong. They felt that
the government should be prepared, in principle, to consider the future of Hong
Kong with a friendly, stable and democratic Chinese government, but in the
absence of such an administration Britain would remain in Hong Kong. Some
ministers held that the only way of preserving Hong Kong was to place it under
an international regime. It would be best for Britain to take the initiative in this
matter. It was noted that the Labour government in Australia had raised doubts
about delay. Other cabinet members argued that such action would convey
weakness and there were inherent problems in proposing an international regime
for Hong Kong: did Britain have the right to vary the terms of a leased territory? Furthermore this could be a means whereby the Soviet Union would seek
a voice in the fate of Hong Kong. The predominant feeling in cabinet was to
approve the views of Bevin and Creech Jones that Britain could discuss the
future of Hong Kong only with a well-disposed and democratic government in
China. Bevin was authorised to discuss Hong Kong with Dean Acheson.[27]

Stevenson submitted further reflections to Bevin on 1 September from
Nanking. His views could be summarised in one word – 'trade'.[28] By adhering
to a policy based on commercial priorities he felt that various complexities could
be avoided while simultaneously securing tangible advantages. In the political
sphere a continued British presence would encourage non-communist elements
to persist in opposing communism without making this too overt as Acheson
had done in his public communication explaining the China White Paper.
Placing such emphasis on trade did not denote an abandonment of cultural and
educational objectives: Stevenson recommended that the British Council should
'redouble its efforts'.[29] Continued British presence would involve unpalatable
features such as dwelling under Chinese communist concepts of justice and
security; suitable protests should be made when necessary to emphasise civilised
standards. Stevenson advocated a pragmatic policy devoid of the shrill rhetoric
which underlined American representations:

> we should not (repeat not) make up our minds in advance about how things
> are going to turn out here, particularly in regard to the subservience of the
> new regime to Moscow, but should follow our usual empirical methods in
> dealing with it.
> ... in general, we should judge the new regime by what it does and not
> (repeat not) by what it says and we should act accordingly. This does not mean
> that we should ignore abuse after we have established relations. We will then
> have grounds for reacting and can raise as much trouble as seems desirable.[30]

Stevenson described Hong Kong as 'our thorniest problem': the best way was
to persuade the communist government to tolerate British rule in the colony
through ensuring that the communists gained as much from this situation as did
Britain itself. Sabre-rattling should be avoided and reinforcements of forces sent
to Hong Kong should be withdrawn quietly once stability returned to the areas
of southern China occupied by the communists. Stevenson was concerned at

American attitudes: he feared that American strategists did not perceive Hong Kong as 'the perimeter of Pacific defence against Communism'.[31] He intended to follow the example set by his Australian and Canadian colleagues in meeting the local communist head of the Foreign Nationals Bureau.[32]

In the main Stevenson's reasoning was sensible but he tended to assume that appropriate representations in favour of civilised standards would prove salutary and beneficial. As later events showed, the communist government had no intention of deferring to the protests of Western imperialism and believed that it was time that the imperialist powers learned that they must adjust to Chinese communist standards instead. However, Stevenson was right to state that current American policy contained no hint of positive solution. On 1 October Mao Tse-tung proudly proclaimed the establishment of the People's Republic of China. Mao saw it as a magnificent occasion for China and for world socialism. The humiliating century of exploitation by Western and Japanese imperialism was at an end. For world socialism the second great revolution of the twentieth century reached its climax. For Mao himself it was eloquent testimony to his outstanding gifts as a leader. A sobering note, however, is that Mao's greatest achievements lay in the past: in power Mao developed into a despotic and ultimately disastrous leader.[33]

On 1 October Stevenson assessed the probable consequences, in a procedural sense, of the emergence of the new regime. Two decisions had been announced: firstly, that the new government 'may negotiate establishment of diplomatic relations on a basis of equality, mutual interest and mutual respect of territorial sovereignty with those foreign Governments which sever relations with the Kuomintang reactionaries and adopt a substantive attitude towards the People's Republic of China'; secondly, that following the proclamation of the new government a telegram would be sent to the UN General Assembly informing the latter of the proclamation and emphasising that the Peking administration 'is the only Government capable of representing the Chinese people and denying the representative status of all delegates appointed by the bogus reactionary remnant of the Government at Canton'.[34] Stevenson commented that he was not aware of the outcome of discussions between Bevin and Acheson regarding recognition. He felt that so long as the KMT government functioned in Canton, it would be awkward to contemplate withdrawal of recognition. Therefore, unless the issue was resolved by the UN Security Council and General Assembly (which was improbable), a curious period would intervene in which a new Chinese government operated over most of China recognised by some states. In the short term the new government would most likely accept the anomalous concomitants but if a lengthy delay occurred, a harsher response could be anticipated. Stevenson proposed that in order to diminish inconvenience, the British consul-general in Peking should be told, within the near future, to convey an official message to the Ministry of Foreign Affairs essentially as follows:

> His Majesty's Government in the United Kingdom are carefully studying the situation resulting from formation of the Central People's Government. Friendly and mutually profitable relations both commercial and political had existed between Britain and China for many generations. It is hoped that these

will continue in the future. His Majesty's Government ... therefore suggest that pending completion of their study of the situation, informal relations should be established between His Majesty's Consular Officers and the appropriate authorities in the territory under the control of the Central People's Government for greater convenience of both Governments and promotion of trade between the two countries.[35]

Stevenson did not regard the proposal as connoting *de facto* recognition as this would involve delay and would most probably be rejected by the new government. His proposal might be rejected by the Chinese communists but it was worth pursuing: if it succeeded, it would improve matters, and if it failed the position would be worse. He added that his telegram was prepared in consultation with his Indian and Australian colleagues who concurred generally in it. It is particularly relevant to note the reference to India and Australia. Nehru believed in following a distinctive, independent foreign policy in which the dimension of Indian leadership in Asia would emerge strongly. Nehru disliked communists, since he fought them in India, but he appreciated the fundamental importance of the new China and was determined to seize the opportunity to act positively. The Australian Labour government of Ben Chifley, while harbouring no love of communism either, felt similarly that realities must be faced; however, a general election took place in Australia at the end of 1949 and this resulted in the return of a Liberal–Country coalition led by Robert Menzies which was not inclined to contemplate early recognition. The Foreign Office accepted the cogency of Stevenson's recommendation and instructed the consul-general in Peking to approach the communist authorities informally.[36]

For once the normal careful observation of correct procedures within the Foreign Office was absent. The French government pointed out that the form of the communication amounted to *de facto* recognition, despite Stevenson's advice to the contrary. Belatedly, officials sought legal guidance and discovered that, inadvertently, Britain had extended what could be regarded as *de facto* recognition.[37] The Foreign Office consoled itself with the reflection that the Chinese communists had shown no interest in *de facto* recognition but the damage had been done. Public debate within Britain and the United States increased. A parliamentary motion was brought forward on 20 October by a group of left-wing Labour MPs – D. N. Pritt, Lester Hutchison, John Platts-Mills, Leslie Solley and Konni Zilliacus – urging recognition; they were described in the Foreign Office file jacket as 'Communist MPs'.[38] The *Washington Post* advocated recognition in a leader published on 18 October and the *New York Times* urged caution in its leader on the following day.[39] James Reston wrote a lengthy article in the *New York Times* on 23 October setting the dilemma in the context of American decisions on recognition extending back to the similar preoccupations of the Taft and Wilson administrations over China in 1912–13.[40] Reston saw Truman as facing far more pressure than had been the case with his predecessors in 1912 and 1913. Britain, India, Australia and the Netherlands wanted to recognise the communist government. From the American viewpoint the vital question was whether recognition would assist or hinder world communism: would the new China work very closely with the Soviet Union or could it be persuaded to follow the path established by Marshal

Tito in Yugoslavia? Reston explored the political complications in Washington: past practice indicated that a decision in favour of recognition should be taken by the president but Acheson had given an undertaking to consult Congress. Firm support for the KMT regime still prevailed in Congress as illustrated in the attitudes of two Massachusetts congressmen of contrasting views within the Republican party. The House minority leader, Joseph W. Martin (a supporter of General MacArthur) and Christian A. Herter (later to succeed Dulles as Eisenhower's secretary of state) each opposed recognition. Reston pointed out that since the time of Woodrow Wilson the moral component in recognition assumed more significance: 'The pro-Nationalist bloc on Capitol Hill not only opposes recognition of the Chinese Communists now but tends to insist that recognition should not be granted at any time to a regime that did not come to power by constitutional means.'[41] The growing acrimony within Congress rendered it most unlikely that support for recognition would be forthcoming.

At the end of October the Foreign Office advanced the case for recognition in telegrams to Washington along the lines advocated by Stevenson on 1 October: unless the Western powers adopted a positive attitude, it would not be feasible to influence Mao's government in the desired direction. The KMT regime represented the past and not the future. The Soviet Union and the satellite states had now recognised the Peking government and a number of Russian technicians had arrived in north China. For political and practical reasons Bevin favoured *de jure* recognition: he was advised that this was legally justifiable. The implications for British interests would be assessed at a conference of British representatives in the Far East which would meet from 2–4 November.[42] Butterworth of the State Department reacted with predictable lack of enthusiasm. He said that he would like to know what the representatives gathering in Singapore thought of *de jure* recognition. According to his information the commissioner-general, Malcolm MacDonald, felt that recognition could cause difficulty. Furthermore, was there reason to think that Britain would gain from recognition?[43] Butterworth asked whether Bevin was diverging from the understanding reached at the meeting of the three foreign ministers (American, British and French) in September. When he read the telegram Bevin appreciated the need to watch matters meticulously: 'The Office must be careful not to do anything without my knowledge & approval.'[44] The British government understood that the communist regime controlled 70 per cent of China comprising 75 per cent of the total population, thus leaving the KMT in nominal control of about 30 per cent of the area with 25 per cent of the population.[45] On 5 November Bevin indicated that he did not wish to act on recognition before the Commonwealth conference assembled in Colombo at the beginning of January 1950: 'Hold this recognition up. It will come up at meeting with Acheson. I do not anticipate action while Assembly is sitting or until we have met at Colombo unless we are forced.'[46]

The British representatives from East and South-East Asia met at Bukit Serene at the start of November and approved the views of the ambassador to China, Sir Ralph Stevenson, and of the governor of Hong Kong, Sir Alexander Grantham, that *de jure* recognition should be accorded in order to assist British interests in China and Hong Kong. The conference held that no formal restrictions should be included but that Britain should issue a unilateral statement of their understanding that the new Chinese government accepted its international obligations.[47] The secretary of state for Commonwealth relations, Philip Noel-Baker, saw Nehru on 13 November and the Indian prime minister said that the ambassador in Nanking, Panikkar, advocated recognition as soon as possible. Nehru expressed understanding for the problems facing the Attlee government.[48] Additional Indian pressure was applied on 21 November when the Indian high commissioner communicated a memorandum pointing out that the communist forces were continuing to advance in western China and were within 90 miles of Chungking, the wartime capital of China. In India's view it would be dangerous to postpone recognition for long.[49] Stevenson had left Nanking by the last ten days of November and John Hutchison, the chargé d'affaires, reported on 22 November that the visit of the Soviet cultural mission, ostensibly to celebrate the 32nd anniversary of the October revolution, was being used sedulously to spread Russian propaganda. He added, interestingly and ominously, that there was little indication that the Peking government would welcome recognition from other powers.[50]

American policy was complicated by the detention of the consul-general in Mukden, Angus Ward: the *Washington Post* pointed out that this made it more difficult to contemplate American recognition within the near future.[51] The United States produced a resolution for the General Assembly which was deemed dangerous by the Foreign Office because it could be applied against British and American interests including Hong Kong. It seemed unwise to express criticism of the Peking government when *de jure* recognition was under discussion. Attempts were being made to dissuade the United States from pursuing it.[52] Senator William F. Knowland (Republican, California), a prominent right-winger and member of the Armed Services Committee, visited Japan in November as part of a far eastern tour. Knowland met MacArthur and Chennault in Tokyo. The latter advocated an immediate grant of 1,200 million US dollars to the KMT government so as to prevent the whole of China from going communist. Knowland did not endorse the figure demanded by Chennault but spoke strongly on recognition. Knowland urged the British not to grant recognition: 'I believe the British will make a very grave mistake if they recognize Communist China. Locking the front door in Europe and leaving open the back door in Asia seems hardly the way to make friends and influence people.'[53] It came as no surprise in Whitehall to hear that MacArthur was vehemently opposed to recognition. Gascoigne, the head of the British mission, talked to General Almond, MacArthur's chief of staff, on 25 November and listened to a vigorous denunciation of the evils that would ensue from recognising 'Red China'. Gascoigne responded that if recognition was not given, still greater damage would be done.[54]

The crunch at last arrived in the middle of December and the cabinet took the crucial decision in favour of recognition. Bevin circulated a memorandum to his colleagues on 12 December in which he commented on the unfortunate difference of opinion with the United States. Acheson considered recognition to be premature and wanted assurances that the communist government would observe China's international obligations. Bevin was convinced by the arguments for granting recognition in the near future.[55] In cabinet he stated that he had done his best over a prolonged period to ensure full coordination among the Western powers and he regretted that the attitude of the United States made this impossible to achieve. Noel-Baker indicated that the Commonwealth was in agreement, although South Africa did not want to grant recognition in the near future. India, on the other hand, would probably extend recognition before the end of December.[56] The cabinet approved the recommendation to grant recognition.

The Foreign Office then focused on making the necessary arrangements and explaining these to its representatives in Nanking and Washington. John Hutchison in Nanking urged that the crucial points in the official note should state the desire for normal relations with China; should say that pending the appointment of an ambassador, it was hoped that Hutchison would be accepted as chargé d'affaires *ad interim* and that the transfer of Hutchison, his staff and archives to Peking should be facilitated; and that the British representative in Taiwan, E. T. Biggs, should notify the *provincial authorities*, not the central KMT authorities, of intended recognition.[57] The text of the proposed British note was sent to Hutchison on 23 December. This acknowledged the fact that the greater part of China was controlled by forces loyal to the new government in Peking:

> In these circumstances His Majesty's Government in response to Chairman Mao Tse-tung's proclamation of October 1st, 1949 are ready to establish diplomatic relations on the basis of equality, mutual benefit and mutual respect for territory and sovereignty and are prepared to exchange diplomatic representations with the Central People's Government.[58]

On 3 January 1950 Biggs was instructed to inform the provincial authorities in Taiwan.[59]

The ambassador in Washington was instructed to see Dean Acheson and deliver a personal message from Bevin. This stated that the cabinet had decided to recognise the Peking government; the actual date of recognition had not been finalised but might be 2 January. Bevin emphasised that Britain had deferred acting for as long as was practicable. A range of considerations affecting not only British interests in China but Hong Kong, Malaya and Singapore made recognition necessary. To delay further would assist the aims of the Soviet Union. Bevin closed by reiterating that the Attlee government did not approve of the Chinese communist government but it was necessary to face unpalatable features. Bevin reminded Acheson that the United States and Britain recognised the Soviet Union and the satellite states. Thus Bevin reached the same conclusion as that advanced by Acheson's fellow countryman, Roger D. Lapham in September – recognition was sensible and unavoidable.[60]

On 30 December 1949 India formally recognised the Peking government. Nehru's note to Chou En-lai referred to the 'immemorial friendship' between India and China. A. A. E. Franklin, now serving in the Foreign Office in London, minuted sardonically that this 'friendship' was greatly strengthened by the existence of the Himalayan barrier: as late as 1942 India and China knew little about each other.[61] Sir Oliver Franks informed London on 3 January that the atmosphere in Washington concerning China was less favourable than a month earlier 'and we shall probably be in for a sticky patch immediately after our recognition of Communist China'.[62] Franks commented that the Truman administration was partly responsible for the deteriorating situation because of its inability to construct a unified policy on far eastern issues. The bipartisan concept had not applied to Asia and some Republican leaders utilised China in order to castigate the administration. He believed that Truman and Acheson would adhere to their existing approach which could be summarised as regretting the British decision on recognition but eschewing recriminations while extending limited support to the KMT in Taiwan. Closing with advice for the Foreign Office news department, Franks suggested that the British press should concentrate on the theme that if the KMT could not sustain itself in Nanking, then it stood little chance of restoring its fortunes from the island of Taiwan. He added that care was required in handling the issue given the attitudes of such prominent Republicans as former president Herbert Hoover, Senators Taft and Knowland, and Congressman Judd. The British press should argue that a positive American approach was needed to encourage Asian countries striving to resist communism. Franks said that the distinguished journalist, Walter Lippman, had told a member of the embassy staff that the British should continue revealing the stupidity of the China lobby. Franks thought this was the view of the State Department.

The text of the British note formally recognising communist China was communicated to the Peking authorities on 6 January 1950. It read:

> I have the honour to inform Your Excellency that His Majesty's Government in the United Kingdom of Great Britain and Northern Ireland, having completed their study of the situation resulting from the formation of Central People's Government of the People's Republic of China and observing that it is now in effective control of by far the greater part of the territory of China have this day recognised that Government as the *de jure* Government of China. In these circumstances His Majesty's Government in response to Chairman Mao Tse-tung's proclamation of October 1st, 1949 are ready to establish diplomatic relations on the basis of equality, mutual benefit and mutual respect for territory and sovereignty and are prepared to exchange diplomatic representatives with the Central People's Government.
>
> Pending the appointment of an Ambassador, Mr. J. C. Hutchison has been nominated as His Majesty's Chargé d'Affaires *ad interim*. Accordingly I have the honour to request that you will receive him and transact official business with him in that capacity and further that he may be granted all necessary facilities for the transfer of himself, his staff and the archives of His Majesty's Embassy from Nanking to Peking.[63]

The Peking government responded coolly and showed no enthusiasm for entering into full diplomatic relations with Britain. The legacy of Western imperialism, the close identification of Britain with the United States in the Cold War, and the isolationism of the Chinese leadership converged to convince Mao that he could afford to wait. Bevin and his cabinet colleagues were disappointed at the negative Chinese reaction.[64] When Bevin met representatives of the China Association on 16 March he indicated his disappointment with the fruits of recognition:

He now had some doubts of the Government's decision to recognise the Central People's Government. One particular reason why he had advocated recognition in early January was the presence of Mao Tse-tung in Moscow and the need to show him that Russia was not the only country which was prepared to treat with him. The situation might by now have been even worse if we had not recognised then. In any event, it had not been a popular move.[65]

Bevin's reference to Mao's visit to Moscow drew attention to the whole question of the Sino-Soviet relationship. This was central to the debates as to whether world communism was a monolithic movement or not. Attlee and Bevin detested Chinese communism and regarded it as a menace but they maintained that, given skilful tactics, it should be possible to separate China from the Soviet Union or, at any rate, prevent them from working very closely together. The challenge lay in persuading the Truman administration to accept this reasoning. Acheson was attracted by the concept if sceptical of the chances of achieving it.[66]

Mao arrived in Moscow on 16 December 1949 for his first foreign visit: he remained there for over seven weeks and was joined by Chou En-lai for the latter part of the discussions. Good relations with the Soviet Union were axiomatic to the consolidation of the PRC in 1949–50. Mao harboured no great affection for the Soviet role in China, which had proved inept and dictated by Soviet interests rather than the advancement of the CCP. But Mao respected the historic achievements of the Bolshevik revolution and he favoured tough, brutal leadership, under which criterion Stalin certainly qualified. In 1945–46 Mao hoped for a reasonable relationship with the United States: by 1948 such hopes were patently unrealistic and Mao looked to Moscow for economic assistance and for political alignment. Mao wished to meet Stalin early in 1949, a message to this effect having been sent to Moscow on 30 December 1948.[67] Stalin responded on 14 January 1949 that this was not convenient.[68] Subsequently Stalin met Liu Shao-ch'i and apologised for not having done more to assist the CCP during its war against the KMT. Later Stalin sent 200 Soviet advisers to China.[69] Stalin appreciated fully the importance of following developments in China closely and influencing the establishment of the PRC. Goncharov, Lewis and Xue Litai state that in the first months of 1948 Stalin deduced that in future China would be a partner for the Soviet Union and would not fall into the category of the satellite states in Central and Eastern Europe.[70] Diplomatic recognition was granted to the PRC by the Soviet Union on 2 October 1949, the day following the formal creation of the PRC.

Mao travelled to Moscow by train in December 1949. A fascinating assessment of Mao's mission is to be found in the monograph by Goncharov, Lewis and Xue, based on Chinese and Soviet sources. The length of Mao's stay confirmed the complexity of the negotiations. Stalin and Mao eyed one another warily, as befitted prima donnas of their characters and attainments. Stalin was, of course, the more experienced of the two and pursued tactics aimed at conveying that he was the senior communist leader. The likelihood that the talks would not be distinguished by marked cordiality was established during Mao's journey to Moscow via the Trans-Siberian railway. The Chinese offered hospitality to Soviet representatives joining them on the train but this was declined.[71] When

Mao reached Moscow he was welcomed formally but for much of the period he spent in Moscow was left to his own devices. Stalin stated that he understood the extent of Mao's achievements: what mattered in politics was winning and Mao was certainly a 'winner'.[72] However, Stalin criticised the calibre of Mao's theoretical writings and deprecated the tendency of the CCP to be too nationalistic.[73] Earlier in 1949 Mao was impressed by Stalin's admission to Liu Shao-ch'i that Soviet policy had erred in China and he looked forward to receiving a personal apology from Stalin.[74] It was not forthcoming. This was arguably another way in which Stalin reminded Mao of his inferiority: Stalin gave a more explicit apology to Mao's deputy than he produced for Mao during the far more important talks in Moscow. It was not surprising that Mao sulked for part of his visit.[75] His first journey outside China was not a happy one.

As regards the substantive issues, Stalin was determined to maintain the Soviet position in Manchuria, which was offensive to Mao. Goncharov, Lewis and Xue state that a number of secret agreements were concluded during the meetings, some of which have not yet become available in the Soviet archives or have been located.[76] In February 1950 an Additional Agreement was signed representing Soviet rather than Chinese aspirations. China agreed not to permit nationals of third countries to live in, or to pursue, industrial, financial or commercial interests in Manchuria and Sinkiang; the Soviet Union undertook to apply analogous limitations in Soviet territory in East Asia and in the Central Asian republics.[77] Mao regarded Chinese acceptance as extremely humiliating and told Molotov six years afterwards that the Soviet Union acted as an imperialistic state.[78] The issue was rendered more delicate because Dean Acheson, in his famous National Press Club address in January 1950, mocked China's ability to act independently through emphasising Soviet imperialism in Manchuria, Mongolia and Sinkiang. Salt was rubbed into the wound as Mao was compelled to acquiesce in the continuation of Soviet imperialism.[79] Mao wanted to secure as strong a promise of Soviet support as possible, given American provocation (as he saw it) including the rebuilding of Japan and ambiguous American intentions concerning Taiwan. Stalin shared Mao's anxiety but was prepared to go only so far in a defence agreement. He was unwilling to promise total support incorporating nuclear weapons, despite the successful Soviet testing of an atomic bomb in 1949.[80] Stalin urged China to invade Taiwan, which marked a reversal of the advice proffered from Moscow earlier in 1949.[81] Mao felt strongly over Taiwan and was irate at the failure of the People's Liberation Army (PLA) to capture three small KMT-held islands in October–November 1949. It was difficult to see how Taiwan could be taken in the near future, although Mao pressed ahead with preparations for an invasion.

Now we shall return to considering the British assessment of the talks. The British ambassador in Moscow, Sir David Kelly, reported on 31 January 1950 that, although it was hard to obtain accurate information, it seemed clear that the talks were very contentious.[82] Mao seemed to have adopted a tough line and was disinclined to be browbeaten by Stalin. Esler Dening drafted a lengthy minute on 2 February giving his assessment. He believed that Mao wanted tangible economic help to rebuild the Chinese economy. The Russian priority was probably political and very likely took the form of desiring a treaty of alliance with China. An alliance could compromise a defensive agreement under which China would grant military facilities, possibly including bases, for the use of Soviet forces if war occurred or was threatened. The length of Mao's stay was probably related to attaining agreements which he could represent as fair and acceptable. The Soviet Union would not wish to see full diplomatic relations established between Britain and China.[83]

Hutchison reported on 6 February from Peking that he understood, from information received, that Mao's discussions were going badly as regards economic issues and perhaps from the political viewpoint.[84] The Sino-Soviet treaty and agreements were announced on 14 February. The agreements consisted of a treaty of friendship, alliance and mutual assistance; an agreement concerning the Chinese Changchun railway, Port Arthur and Dalny under which the Changchun railway would revert to China following the signing of a peace treaty with Japan and Soviet forces would be withdrawn from Port Arthur; and an agreement on the granting by the Soviet Union to China of long-term economic credits so as to pay for supplies of industrial and railway equipment from the Soviet Union. The treaties were signed by Andrei Vyshinsky and Chou En-lai on behalf of the two governments. The far eastern department produced an analysis of the agreements.[85] The 1950 treaty resembled the 1945 treaty in being valid for a period of 30 years, subject to extension. It was designed to combat a renewed military threat from Japan or a threat from states allied with Japan. The character of the treaty resembled those concluded between the Soviet Union and the satellite states of Eastern Europe. Under the agreement relating to railway issues, Port Arthur and Dairen the far eastern department noted that the 1950 agreement contained the consent of the Soviet Union to the transfer to China of Soviet rights in the property and administration of the railway. The Soviet Union was prepared to waive its rights as soon as a peace treaty with Japan was signed but reserved the right to resume use of the base in the event of war with Japan. On the financial side the Soviet Union agreed to extend a credit of 300 million US dollars over a five-year period for acquiring Soviet equipment and materials, including those suitable for power stations, metallurgical plants, mining and railway equipment. Interest was fixed at 1 per cent with repayment to be completed by the end of 1964 and this would be supplied in raw materials, tea, gold or in US dollars.

Looking more broadly at the outcome of the Moscow talks, the far eastern department stated that on the surface the Soviet Union appeared to have made concessions with little in return. Soviet propaganda could depict the outcome as a magnanimous policy towards a friendly state. China could emphasise in its propaganda that Chinese interests had been defended firmly and that it was necessary to work with Russia because of external threats and Soviet magnanimity assisted this objective. Stalin seemed to have drawn the right deduction from his mishandling of Yugoslavia and was handling China carefully. Closer examination indicated that Soviet concessions were less generous than they appeared to be. It was unlikely that the United States and Japan would provoke a war and the Soviet promise of support was less significant than it appeared. In addition, the Soviet Union might find a pretext for not withdrawing from Manchuria, for example because a peace treaty with Japan had not been concluded and because detailed arrangements would have been made. The financial settlement was not very generous given China's needs. There could well be secret agreements, especially for military aspects.[86]

The most contentious issue in Anglo-American relations concerning China, apart from recognition, centred around Taiwan. The island was governed as an integral part of the Japanese empire between 1895 and 1945. The Japanese ruled Taiwan rigorously but without alienating the inhabitants to the degree seen in Korea: the resources of the island were exploited in Japan's interests.[87] The allies agreed at the Cairo conference of November–December 1943 that Japan should be stripped of its colonial possessions; Taiwan would revert to China but this would not take formal effect until the conclusion of a peace treaty with Japan. In reality the allies acquiesced in the return of Chinese authority at the end of the Pacific war when KMT forces occupied the island. The native populace did not wish to experience Chinese rule and there was significant support for the Taiwanese autonomy movement. Chiang Kai-shek felt no sympathy for the native inhabitants and approved of the drastic suppression of a native rebellion in February 1947. E. T. Biggs, the British consul in Tamsui, reported to Sir Ralph Stevenson in March 1948 that there were rumours of another insurrection, although foreign representatives did not deem this likely. Biggs explained that thorough censorship was enforced by the KMT authorities and all native Taiwanese newspapers were suppressed. Chinese carpetbaggers dominated important positions and flaunted their wealth 'which they are extracting from Formosa with an ostentation unknown in Japanese days'.[88] Their standard of living had been higher under the Japanese and the Japanese administration was more effective and honest. Discontent at Chinese corruption and injustice was substantial.

The swift decline of the KMT raised urgent questions for American policy-makers. Was Taiwan important enough for the United States to become directly involved in denying the island to the communists? The State Department doubted the wisdom of being committed in this way while the Pentagon was influenced increasingly by strategic debate on the geopolitical importance of Taiwan. In January 1949 Hubert Graves, a member of the British embassy's staff in Washington discussed Taiwan with Walton Butterworth who placed emphasis on the strategic argument. Butterworth said that the United States did not want communist forces to take Taiwan because it would bring communist airfields close to the American garrisons in the Philippines. He thought that the United States army advisory group was likely to remain for the time being. He acknowledged that discussions might have occurred between the Chinese and MacArthur but, if so, he had not heard of them. Graves put the final question directly to Butterworth: 'I asked Butterworth what the United States Government's attitude would be to a Chinese Communist Government's demand for Formosa under the terms of the Cairo statement but could get nothing more than the answer "We will cross that bridge when we come to it".'[89]

In July 1949 Chiang Kai-shek visited Manila and fostered contacts with President Quirino of the Philippines: this encouraged speculation that he might be contemplating retreating to the Philippines with a government-in-exile if he could not hold Taiwan.[90] Chiang also developed contacts with Syngman Rhee and public debate focused on the possibility of a Pacific anti-communist front. Interest in the Foreign Office focused in part on the relationship between Japan and Taiwan with the question of how deeply MacArthur might seek to involve himself in the murky issues surrounding the decline of the KMT and the future roles of Taiwan. Alvary Gascoigne summarised the position for the Foreign Office in September:

> Some seven months ago MacArthur pointed out to me that Formosa was obviously a vital strategic point in the 'Island Line' and must be kept at all costs within the Allied sphere of influence [Gascoigne was referring to a telegram sent on 9 February 1949]. He certainly, therefore, holds the view that its domination by the Communists would be a grave threat, not only to communications between Japan/Philippines, but also to the United States 'front line' in the Pacific/Philippines/Okinawa/Japan.[91]

During a briefing held on 8 September for Malcolm MacDonald, who was visiting Tokyo, the G-2, General Willoughby, stated that he personally included Taiwan within the American line of defence (that is, Philippines/Okinawa/Japan). As Gascoigne remarked, Willoughby would not have said this without knowing that it was MacArthur's opinion. There had recently been press discussion regarding Japanese nationals being 'smuggled' from Japan to Taiwan. It appeared that General Nemoto and 'an insignificant number of senior Japanese officers plus some junior officers' had been smuggled to Taiwan since the end of June 1949.[92] This suggested that MacArthur was not unwilling to see the Japanese assisting in the defence of Taiwan four years after their expulsion from the island. A report from the consul in Tamsui in December confirmed that Japanese military personnel were advising the KMT forces, according to remarks made by the American military attaché in Tamsui.[93]

Chiang's emissary, Wu Te-chen, visited Tokyo in late August as part of the flurry of activity including Chiang's visit to the Philippines in July and his visit to South Korea early in August. Wu was reported to have told MacArthur that the KMT was capable of retaining Taiwan indefinitely and to have repelled any suggestion of establishing an international trusteeship for Taiwan.[94] Biggs reported in September 1949 that indignation was expressed by KMT provincial papers at rumours that Taiwan might be taken over by the United States and placed under MacArthur's jurisdiction.[95] Whatever the truth of these reports Biggs stated that American interest was growing and that American consular staff had been doubled within the past few weeks; he detected appreciable nervousness over the problems of defending Taiwan despite claims to the contrary. The Foreign Office was puzzled at conflicting evidence of American intentions. Butterworth had told Dening that Taiwan was bound to fall to the communists eventually and the United States could not prevent this occurring. On the other hand, Biggs indicated that American involvement was growing rapidly. Dening minuted on 20 October: 'The State Dep[artmen]t may not have been telling the truth – I do not trust Mr. Butterworth – but he did say that they saw no means of preventing Formosa from falling under Communist domination.'[96] The time had come to clarify American intentions when a suitable opportunity arose. On 8 December Sir Oliver Franks summarised a discussion with Dean Acheson. Chiang Kai-shek had been told that sufficient aid remained from the past to defend Taiwan and the United States could not provide military assistance:

> Mr. Acheson shares your opinion that the island will eventually fall into Communist hands – probably before the end of 1950. Butterworth thinks Chiang may hold the position a little longer and feels that even a year's respite is very useful. Butterworth also regards the military provisioning of the Nationalist forces as a method of buying time and he is anxious that nothing should be done which will induce Chiang to throw in the sponge before he is forced by defection or other causes to do so.
>
> Mr. Acheson also said that the United States Administration does not consider that the loss of Formosa to the Communists would necessarily have a serious influence on the United States military position in the Far East. Neither in its relationship to Japan nor in its proximity to the Philippines is the island likely to be an important menace for some time.[97]

A week later Gascoigne visited MacArthur and asked him for his opinion. MacArthur replied that he was speaking purely personally. He believed that Taiwan had been assigned to the trusteeship of KMT China on the understanding that peace and prosperity would obtain in the island; unfortunately the Chinese civil war prevented this from coming to fruition. He continued:

> Therefore he would, if he were the United States Government make a unilateral declaration to the effect that the United States would not permit Formosa to be used either as a springboard for Chiang Kai-shek to attack Red China or as a goal of Red ambitions. He felt that this would stop Mao from making any efforts to seize the island.[98]

This was a temporary expedient: in the longer term he had not decided what solution would be fitting but he seemed to be leaning towards placing Taiwan under a UN mandate. MacArthur added that he had in mind a unilateral declaration by the United States because it would be too difficult to involve Britain owing to the impending recognition of the Peking government; furthermore, as the United States controlled Japan it was logical for Taiwan to be viewed as an American responsibility.[99] It is particularly interesting to note that MacArthur's definition of the temporary expedient anticipated precisely the line adopted by President Truman in his public statement of 27 June 1950.

The American joint chiefs of staff held that strategic factors concerning Taiwan assumed greater importance and that the forces of world communism would be strengthened to an undesirable degree by the acquisition of Taiwan. The debate in Washington gathered momentum in the spring of 1950 and Acheson encountered growing pressure in his preference for avoiding intervention in Taiwan. On 5 June Franks dined with Acheson for one of their regular private meetings: Acheson said that he and his staff were considering the future of Taiwan. Was it feasible to avert a communist takeover of Taiwan short of implementing military action? There was no intention of assuming responsibility for the defence of Taiwan but the prospect of Taiwan being captured by the communists was not congenial; the State Department was examining how to maintain its present status. Acheson added that the consequences for South-East

Asia if Taiwan fell would be considerable. Franks thought that Acheson was uncertain as to what should be done; he did not ask Franks to pursue it with Bevin. Franks held that funds might be made available for military purposes in Taiwan. Since the discussion was informal, Franks communicated its essence in a letter to Dening.[100] Robert Scott minuted that it was a disturbing report and the chiefs of staff should be invited to comment. Sir William Strang, the permanent under-secretary, minuted 'There are seeds of trouble here'.[101]

At the end of May MacArthur sent a strongly worded memorandum to Washington emphasising the strategic necessity of denying Taiwan to the communists, which included his famous reference to the danger of Taiwan becoming a floating aircraft carrier aimed at American defences in East Asia and the western Pacific.[102] On 22 June Hubert Graves wrote to John Shattock of the far eastern department commenting on signs that more problems would occur over Taiwan. He recalled Truman's statement on 5 January 1950 that the United States would not involve itself in determining the fate of Taiwan. It was now clear that policy was changing at a high level:

> Curiously enough no one in the State Department, junior to Dean Rusk, knows of this reconsideration, nor have they heard that Acheson had spoken to the Ambassador about Formosa. In recent conversations with us and the Australians, members of the Far Eastern Bureau maintain that they have no knowledge of any impending change and they hold the view that MacArthur's recent insistence on a review of the Formosan problem is not likely to cause the National Security Council to go back on its previous decision.
>
> For what it is worth we would add that we are not as sanguine as the Far Eastern Bureau. The Army Department is again developing arguments in favour of placing the island under MacArthur and the White House is said to be considering a declaration after the manner of the Monroe doctrine.[103]

The decision had been reached by Truman, Acheson and the joint chiefs that Taiwan must be denied to the communists. This did not mean reversing policy towards the KMT and embracing them, as urged by the China lobby. Taiwan would not be allowed to go communist: what would happen ultimately remained to be seen. Dean Rusk, then an assistant secretary of state, has referred to consideration being given in Washington to implementing a coup to remove Chiang Kai-shek and perhaps to replace him with an American-educated general, Sun Li-jen.[104] Sun was a capable soldier but it was unclear what political qualifications he possessed. Franks summarised the alternatives on 30 June. Truman's statement of 27 June, addressed primarily to the war in Korea, emphasised that Taiwan would not be taken by the communists but beyond that no one knew what would happen. Franks defined the possibilities as switching policy to support Chiang but this was improbable; conferring autonomy on Taiwan but there was little sign of an effective indigenous nationalist movement; placing Taiwan under a UN trusteeship operated by the United States; accepting transfer to the Peking government but this was manifestly impossible. Franks thought that trusteeship was most likely to be pursued.[105] Franks pointed out that the whole situation as regards Korea and Taiwan was potentially calamitous:

The possibility of reaching some form of *modus vivendi* with the new China in which the United States might participate now appears increasingly remote and, on the contrary, it has to be reckoned with that the Korean war might, at the worst, through the Formosan issue, be broadened into an open breach between the Western democracies and the Communist powers over the whole of the Far East.[106]

For the Attlee government the linking of the discrete issues of Korea and Taiwan was alarming. It followed logically from British recognition of the Peking government that the latter should, at some point, complete its victory by taking over the various islands off the Chinese coast of which Taiwan was the most important. However, it was obvious that this would not occur in the near future. The most practicable line for Britain to follow was to discourage the United States from action which could exacerbate matters. Truman, Acheson and Dulles (who was handling the Japanese peace treaty) hoped to reach a solution which would not mean supporting Chiang Kai-shek for years to come and which would, to some extent, meet the aspirations of the indigenous inhabitants of Taiwan. The concept of a UN trusteeship offered the most encouraging way forward. Such hopes were doomed by China's full-scale intervention in Korea in October–November 1950. Taiwan would be dominated by those who had abandoned the mainland in 1948–49 for at least 40 years and Chiang Kai-shek would survive almost as long as Mao Tse-tung, even though Chiang's China was confined to certain islands off the Chinese coast.[107] Chiang enjoyed the consolation of proving an economic Phoenix: having presided over the incredible shambles to which the Chinese economy was reduced in the later 1940s, Chiang presided over the early stages of the process whereby Taiwan emerged as a major economic force and a state far wealthier than the state run by those who had inherited the 'mandate of heaven' in 1949. Such are the ironies of history.

Notes

1 For discussion of American policy, see N. B. Tucker, *Patterns in the Dust: Chinese–American Relations and the Recognition Controversy 1949–1950* (New York: Columbia University Press, 1983) and Qiang Zhai, *The Dragon, the Lion, and the Eagle: Chinese–British–American Relations, 1949–1958* (London: Kent State University Press, 1994). For consideration of British policy regarding recognition, see also R. Ovendale, 'Britain, the United States, and the Recognition of Communist China', *Historical Journal*, 26 (1983), pp. 139–58.

2 *FRUS 1949*, vol. IX, p. 616, memorandum prepared in the Office of Far Eastern Affairs, 25 January 1949. Note also Bruce to Cabot, 26 January 1949, stating that the policy of the Truman administration clearly precluded aid being extended to areas falling under communist control.

3 *FRUS 1949*, vol. IX, pp. 626–30, memorandum from Lapham to Hoffman, 9 March 1949.

4 *Ibid.*, pp. 666–7, report from Lapham to Hoffman, 30 June 1949.

5 'The Chinese Situation as I Saw It', address by Lapham, 8 September with prefacatory note, 13 September 1949, folder, China, 1949, box 149, Judd papers, Hoover Institution, Stanford, California.

6 *Ibid.*, p. 3.

7 *Ibid.*, p. 7.

8 *Ibid.*

9 *Ibid.*, p. 11.

10 *Ibid.*, pp. 11–12.

11 *Ibid.*, p. 12.

12 Letter from Judd to Lapham, 10 December 1949, folder, China, 1950, box 250, Judd papers, Hoover Institution.

13 Letter from Lapham to Judd, 4 January 1950, with enclosed memorandum, 28 December 1949, folder, China, 1950, box 250, Judd papers.

14 For discussion of Kohlberg, see Bruce Cumings, *The Origins of the Korean War*, 2 vols, *The Roaring of the Cataract, 1947–1950* (Princeton: Princeton University Press, 1990), vol. II, pp. 108, 153. For Kohlberg's dealings with Joseph McCarthy, see T. C. Reeves, *The Life and Times of Joe McCarthy: A Biography* (London: Blond and Briggs, 1982), pp. 220–1, 248.

15 For Acheson's reflections on China, see Dean Acheson, *Present at the Creation: My Years in the State Department* (London: Hamish Hamilton, 1970), pp. 302–70.

16 *FRUS 1949*, vol. IX, p. 545, memorandum by Moreland, 5 September 1949.

17 *Ibid.*

18 *Ibid.*, p. 82, memorandum by Acheson, 13 September 1949.

19 *Ibid.*, p. 83.

20 Memorandum by Foreign Office, 8 August, 1949, FO 371/75813/11653.

21 *Ibid.*

22 *Ibid.*

23 *Ibid.*

24 *Ibid.*

25 Memorandum by Bevin, 23 August 1949, CP(49)180, Cab 129/36, part 2.

26 *Ibid.*

27 Cabinet conclusions, 29 August 1949, CM54(49)1, 2, Cab 128/16.

28 Nanking to FO, 1 September 1949, FP 371/75813/13102.

29 *Ibid.*

30 *Ibid.*

31 *Ibid.*

32 *Ibid.*

33 For a stimulating discussion of Mao, see Stuart Schram, *Mao Zedong: A Preliminary Reassessment* (Hong Kong: Chinese University Press, 1983).

34 Nanking to FO, 1 October 1949, FO 371/75816/14782.

35 *Ibid.*

36 FO to Paris (and other capitals), 5 October 1949, *ibid.*

37 FO to Paris, 10 October 1949, FO 371/75816/14878.

38 Parliamentary motion, copy, 20 October 1949, FO 371/75818/16027.

39 *New York Times*, 17 October 1949, and *Washington Post*, 18 October 1949.

40 *New York Times*, 23 October 1949.

41 *Ibid.*

42 FO to Washington, two telegrams, 29 October 1949, FO 371/75818/16370.

43 Washington to FO, 1 November 1949, FO 371/75818/16417.

44 Minute by Bevin, no date, *ibid.*

45 Minute by F. S. Tomlinson, 26 October 1949, FO 371/75819/16459.

46 Minute by Bevin, 5 November 1949, no date, FO 371/75819/16531.

47 Singapore to FO, 4 November 1949, FO 371/75819/16589.

48 Record of conversation between Noel-Baker and Nehru, 13 November 1949, FO 371/75823/17462.

49 Minute by Bevin, 21 November 1949, enclosing memorandum from Indian high commissioner, no date, FO 371/75823/17477.

50 Nanking to FO, 22 November 1949, FO 371/95823/17484.

51 *Washington Post*, 16 November 1949.

52 Commonwealth Relations Office to New Delhi, 24 November 1949, FO 371/75824/17812.

53 Despatch from Gascoigne to Bevin, 19 November 1949, FO 371/75824/17854.

54 Letter from Gascoigne to Scarlett, 26 November 1949, FO 371/75826/18369.

55 Memorandum by Bevin, 12 December 1949, CP(49)248, Cab 129/37, part 2.
56 Cabinet conclusions, 15 December 1949, CM72(49)3, Cab 128/16.
57 Nanking to FO, 16 December 1949, FO 371/75827/18896.
58 FO to Nanking, 23 December 1949, *ibid.*
59 FO to Tamsui, 3 January 1950, *ibid.*
60 FO to Washington, 16 December 1949, FO 371/75828/19057.
61 Minute by Franklin, 3 January 1950, on Nanking to FO, 31 December 1949, FO 371/83279/1.
62 Washington to FO, 3 January 1950, FO 371/83279/26.
63 FO to numerous embassies, 5 January 1950, FO 371/83280/37.
64 FO to Tokyo, 12 February 1950, FO 371/83279/30.
65 Record of Bevin's meeting with representatives of the China Association, 16 March 1950, FO 371/83344/30.
66 For debates within the administration, see Tucker, *Patterns in the Dust*, pp. 140–91.
67 Chen Jian, *China's Road to the Korean War: The Making of the Sino-American Confrontation* (New York: Columbia University Press, 1994), pp. 68–9.
68 *Ibid.*
69 *Ibid.*, pp. 72–3.
70 S. N. Goncharov, J. W. Lewis and Xue Litai, *Uncertain Partners: Stalin, Mao and the Korean War* (Stanford, CA: Stanford University Press, 1994), p. 25.
71 *Ibid.*, p. 85.
72 Chen Jian, *China's Road to the Korean War*, p. 81.
73 Goncharov, Lewis and Xue, *Uncertain Partners*, p. 104.
74 Chen Jian, *China's Road to the Korean War*, p. 81.
75 Goncharov, Lewis and Xue, *Uncertain Partners*, p. 104.
76 *Ibid.*, p. 125.
77 *Ibid*, pp. 121–2.
78 *Ibid.*
79 *Ibid.*, p. 123.
80 *Ibid.*, p. 118.
81 Chen Jian, *China's Road to the Korean War*, pp. 89–90, 99–102; Goncharov, Lewis and Xue, *Uncertain Partners*, pp. 148–51.
82 Moscow to FO, 31 January 1950, FO 371/83313/29A.
83 Minute by Dening, 2 February 1950, FO 371/83313/29A.
84 Nanking to FO, 6 February 1950, FO 371/83314/33.
85 Memorandum, 'The Sino-Soviet Treaty and Agreements of 14th February, 1950', no date, FO 371/83315/88.
86 *Ibid.*
87 See R. H. Myers and M. R. Peattie (eds), *The Japanese Colonial Empire, 1895–1945* (Guildford: Princeton University Press, 1984).
88 Report from Biggs to Stevenson, 10 March 1948, FO 371/69621/4966.
89 Letter from Graves to Scarlett, 16 January 1949, FO 371/75738/1397.
90 See Manila to FO, 16 July 1949, with minute by Tomlinson, 19 July 1949, FO 371/75763/10599.
91 Tokyo to FO, 17 September 1949, FO 371/75770/14000.
92 *Ibid.*
93 Tamsui to FO, 9 December 1949, FO 371/75778/8488.
94 Tamsui to FO, 22 August 1949, FO 371/75802/12505.
95 Tamsui to FO, 4 September 1949, FO 371/75802/13215.
96 Minute by Dening, 20 October 1949, on despatch from Biggs to Bevin, 27 September 1949, FO 371/75804/15291. According to Biggs, American personnel in Taiwan in October totalled 71, including 26 consular staff and 17 service attachés, see Tamsui to FO, 16 October 1949, FO 371/75804/15500.
97 Washington to FO, 8 December 1949, FO 371/75805/18448.
98 Tokyo to FO, 16 December 1949, FO 371/75805/18891.
99 *Ibid.*
100 Letter from Franks to Dening, 7 June 1950, FO 371/83320/9.

101 Minutes by R. H. Scott, 10 and 13 June and Strang, 10 June, *ibid.*

102 MacArthur to Department of Army, 29 May 1950, RG6, box 8, Formosa file, MacArthur papers, MacArthur Memorial, Norfolk, Virginia.

103 Letter from Graves to Shattock, 22 June 1950, FO 371/83320/12.

104 See Peter Lowe, *The Origins of the Korean War* (London: Longman, 1986), pp. 111–13.

105 Despatch from Franks to Younger, 30 June 1950, FO 371/83320/13.

106 *Ibid.*

107 Chiang Kai-shek died in 1975 and Mao Tse-tung died in 1976.

7

ECONOMIC SANCTIONS AND TRADE

The huge Chinese military intervention in Korea brought closer the danger of full-scale war against China. In December 1950 Attlee and Bevin urged the United States to cooperate in attempting to reach a settlement of crucial areas of dispute between China and the West comprising recognition, Chinese membership of the UN and Taiwan. Truman and Acheson were, in essence, hostile to such a course, since they doubted its efficacy and it exposed them to intensified criticism from domestic opponents. Nevertheless they acquiesced in UN attempts to negotiate an agreement with Chinese communist emissaries in New York in December 1950: acquiescence rested on the cynical but accurate assumption that the talks would founder over Chinese demands for greater concessions than the United States could contemplate.[1] At the beginning of 1951 Commonwealth prime ministers assembled in London to review world problems. In his welcoming speech Attlee stated his pleasure at meeting colleagues soon after his visit to Washington. Full-scale war against China must be avoided. While the United States did not want all-out war, it was prepared to accept a 'limited war': Attlee regarded this as worrying because it could escalate. Britain and the United States diverged most obviously over recognition and Taiwan. The Truman administration was prone to consider China as under the control of the Kremlin: Attlee did not believe that China would accept the status of a Soviet satellite indefinitely.[2] Nehru, the Indian prime minister, largely concurred. Realism was essential in dealing with international problems. India had consistently followed a positive policy towards China with the aim of reducing Chinese dependence on the Soviet Union. India regarded American policy as inherently dangerous where China was concerned. Nehru agreed with Bevin's philosophy that the most effective way of combating communism in Asia was to improve living standards. He did not think that the Soviet Union would provoke war.[3] In the subsequent meeting Robert Menzies advanced the case for the United States in the light of the American lead in defending the 'free world'. The problem with China was that the UN, in effect, was already at war.[4]

On 5 January Bevin spoke in more reflective mood. If asked whether China was an aggressor in Korea, he would reply in the affirmative; if invited formally to declare China an aggressor, he would answer negatively. There were considerable dangers in formally condemning China and these must be kept in mind. Bevin pointed out, in response to Nehru's observations, that China had done itself a disservice through pursuing negative policies, for example following

British recognition of Mao's government and its support for the insurgency in Malaya. Chinese policy towards Indo-China was a further example.[5] Nehru emphasised the necessity for caution and for not being rushed into dangerous courses: he agreed with Bevin that conciliation should be pursued in New York.[6] On 8 January Bevin stated that the United States wished to see China condemned formally for aggression and that the Truman administration intended to implement a limited war against China. Nehru commented that China could not accept the principles advocated by the Cease-Fire group on 4 January.[7] On 9 January Bevin reported an American desire for an initiative to be taken by the Commonwealth prime ministers: the principal objectives were to induce the United States and China to attend a conference on far eastern problems and to obviate further divergence in policy between Britain and the United States.[8] The prime ministers agreed on their proposals but the omens were not good for the United States and China agreeing to compromise.[9] The supporting documentation included an assessment by the joint intelligence sub-committee of China's vulnerability to application of economic sanctions by the UN: this concluded that China could probably withstand economic pressures in the event of the UN taking action.[10] Menzies was the most sympathetic to the United States: his approach was influenced by important issues relating to the Japanese peace treaty and Pacific security in which American support for Australia and New Zealand was crucial. The same consideration affected Sidney Holland, the New Zealand prime minister. Nehru was the most sympathetic to China as part of his determination to develop Indian leadership in Asia. Liaquit Ali Khan of Pakistan broadly agreed with the aim of achieving compromise between the United States and China. Dr Dönges, the South African minister of finance representing his prime minister, Dr D. F. Malan, wished to avert a greater war, since there was no wish in South Africa to expand the strictly limited commitment in Korea.

Conciliation failed, primarily because of Chinese recalcitrance but American policy was also unyielding. Truman and Acheson aimed to restore the tarnished authority of the administration through securing passage of a resolution in the UN General Assembly condemning Chinese aggression: this would open the way for application of economic measures against China. This led, in the second half of January 1951, to the most dangerous phase in Anglo-American relations during the Korean war.[11] On 1 February 1951 Britain voted for the American motion condemning China. The Attlee cabinet was very divided over whether to abstain, vote against the American proposal, or vote to support it. Attlee and Gaitskell emphasised how important it was to support the United States and the cabinet complied. Britain was then faced with the delicate issue as to how far Britain could go in enforcing economic sanctions against China. Several considerations merged to influence British policy. On the political side there was still hope that China might adjust its policy and desire a measure of understanding with the West which could assist diplomatic relations. Hong Kong always must be kept in mind. In the economic sphere lingering hopes for developing trade influenced thinking. There was also the vital question as to how responsive China would be to economic pressure.

Analysis of the political, economic and strategic repercussions of applying sanctions were produced in various government departments early in 1951. An assessment of implications for British shipping, prepared in January 1951, stated that trade between Britain and China had improved during 1950 following the end of the civil war in the mainland and the slackening of the KMT blockade.[12] Imports into Britain in eleven months of 1950, down to December, comprised approximately 14,000 tons (£2.6 million) compared with 12,000 tons (£1.5 million) during the same period in 1949: in 1947 the figures were 30,000 tons (£7 million). Export figures were more favourable. In 1950 British exports were estimated at a minimum of 19,000 tons (£3 million) compared with 6,000 tons in 1949 (£2 million) and 25,000 tons (£8 million) in 1948. The intensification of a ban on certain strategic exports to China was already cutting available cargo; the current volume of exports for liner cargo was not very significant with the partial exception of one item, 100,000 tons of soya beans. British shipping firms were apprehensive that their vessels could be seized and accepted that trade would diminish. Since January 1950, when Britain extended recognition, active commerce between Hong Kong and the principal Chinese ports had developed, initially through the KMT blockade and then more flexibly after Truman's decision to neutralise Taiwan. Trade with Shanghai was handicapped by navigational difficulties. Shipping operated over a considerable geographical area embracing Malaya, Indo-China, Japan and the China coast. Localised regional trade was possibly greater than ocean traffic given the character of the Chinese economy and that the number of suitable vessels in communist hands was small. However, China was heavily reliant on ships flying foreign flags. The value of Chinese imports from Hong Kong in the first nine months of 1950 was three and a half times that of 1949.[13] Ocean trade was not likely to suffer too seriously in the short term but locally based trade would be gravely affected. In a broader perspective the consequences would be appreciable; shipping companies would forfeit their extensive properties in China and the prospects for British trade subsequently would be diminished. It had to be remembered that on the eve of the development of the Sino-Japanese war, in 1936, Britain was at the top of the list of ocean shipping entrances and clearances. It was essential, if restrictions were enforced, that appropriate notice was given so that tonnage would not enter Chinese ports or be given enough time to escape. It was believed that a minimum of five days notice was required from the initial warning; ten days to a fortnight would be preferable. Legal aspects required clarification, since ambiguity surrounded the precise position of British ships trading with China if measures were introduced. Shipping companies should be persuaded to cooperate; if necessary resort could be made to defence regulations.[14]

The Additional Measures Committee was established in February 1951 to supervise adoption of sanctions. Sir Gladwyn Jebb, the chief British delegate to the UN, was deeply involved in the work of the committee. Jebb reported on 16 February that he had exchanged views with the United States delegation and that there did not seem to be serious differences regarding timing and procedures. It was agreed that decisions must be reached carefully and without excessive haste. A bureau comprising Sarper (Turkey) as chairman, Nisot (Belgium) as vice-chairman and Shann (Australia) as rapporteur would be created. The Americans accepted that there should be a close relationship between the Additional Measures Committee and the Good Offices Committee.[15] On the following day the Foreign Office informed Jebb that a preliminary analysis of the political and economic repercussions of applying sanctions had been completed. This confirmed the statement made by Jebb in the General Assembly on 1 February that, 'My Government has the gravest doubt: whether any punitive measures can be discovered which are not dangerous, double-edged or merely useless.'[16] Enforcement of sanctions would diminish Western contacts with China and would be opposed by India and other Asian members of the Commonwealth. In the economic sphere the government could not accept drastic sanctions because they would not affect China as a whole, would accentuate tension in East Asia, would increase the problems experienced in Hong Kong and Indo-China, would be opposed by some members of the UN and would divide the Commonwealth between its older and more recent members. The UN could adopt a selective embargo of strategic materials with the aim of restricting China's military potential but even this would engender tension and divide the Commonwealth.[17] The danger of forcing China further towards the Soviet Union had to be understood. For these reasons Britain believed that conciliation rather than coercion should be the aim, which connoted emphasising the contribution of the Good Offices Committee rather than the Study Group on additional measures. A full, meticulous exchange of views between the two governments was imperative.

In detailed comment sent to Washington on 17 February it was stated that China was not particularly dependent on seaborne imports; sanctions would achieve little more than cause difficulties for movement and supply of the Chinese armed forces in the field. Divisions would develop within the UN in which the Asian and Arab group might coalesce to oppose measures affecting the civilian economy in China. For Britain a total embargo on exports to China might be disastrous for Hong Kong, since approximately 45 per cent of the colony's exports went to China. Unemployment and hardship could ensue with possible consequences for security. A selective embargo might have to be considered which would not create difficulties in Hong Kong and which would meet with more support in the UN. This would denote an embargo based on strategic criteria. It would affect metals and ores, machinery and tools, vehicles, chemicals and oil. China could probably evade shipping controls through making alternative arrangements. Britain would be resolutely opposed to a rigorous naval blockade: to try to enforce it would produce strong opposition and could lead to a much larger war.[18]

The chiefs of staff considered the consequences of applying comprehensive sanctions and concluded that they would diminish prospects of the Asian Commonwealth countries cooperating militarily against communism. Differences between Britain and the United States over implementation of sanctions could undermine defence cooperation. In a worst-case scenario Chinese retaliation could lead to growing pressure on resources in Hong Kong, Indo-China, Burma, Thailand and Malaya.[19] On 17 February Robert Scott sent Jebb an assessment of the Office's views towards communist China. British policy still aimed at achieving a 'moderating' influence and demonstrating British sincerity for good relations. The objective should be to follow an approach blending patience, caution and restraint while responding vigorously where necessary. It would be unwise, as Jebb had remarked, to seek to ingratiate ourselves: Chinese tenacity should be respected. Basic British sympathy for the Chinese people should be conveyed. The Chinese people desired stability and economic reconstruction; they must be worried that Mao's government might be willing to go too far in subordinating Chinese interests to those of the Soviet Union. British policy-makers wanted to see a more independent Chinese policy developing which would be less dependent on the Russians. On the positive side the communist government had eliminated corruption and introduced more efficiency. But this was offset by the growth of a police state. The free press had vanished and with it had gone freedom of expression. If China's aims were peaceful, then this should be demonstrated through the fostering of diplomatic relations with the West. Scott closed with a reiteration of the value of a balanced approach, combining firmness with flexibility.[20] Scott's assessment was a mixture of the accurate with the misleading. He underestimated the reasons for Chinese cooperation with the Soviet Union at this time which arose from the state of international relations during the Korean war and the challenges of developing the Chinese economy. It was characterised by a somewhat patronising tone.

On 23 February Jebb reported the views of the State Department for a draft programme of measures. The Additional Measures Committee should begin by considering economic measures which could be brought to the General Assembly for recommendation. The committee should consider possible restrictions on trade with China; enforcement or supervision of economic measures; a drafting resolution possibly stating that Chinese representation in UN bodies would not be granted so long as China pursued aggression in Korea; non-recognition of the fruits of aggression; and possible termination of diplomatic relations with Peking.[21] On the same day Oliver Franks assessed State Department reactions to British views on economic and political sanctions. On the economic side the State Department was receptive but this did not apply over political aspects. The United States acknowledged that a total embargo was not feasible and should not be pursued. The State Department sympathised over shipping controls and they had at no time contemplated a naval blockade. They thought of a resolution which would introduce an embargo on exports to China of petrol, oil and lubricants; atomic energy materials; arms and ammunition; and implements of war and associated items. Individual members of the UN should decide which commodities fell within these categories. The State Department stressed the domestic pressures in the United States; if the present ideas failed, then American public opinion would demand tougher action.[22]

British diplomatic representation in Peking changed in February 1951. Sir John Hutchison, who had moved to Peking amidst high hopes of a new era dawning in Anglo-Chinese relations, retired. As was customary, Hutchison drafted a final report in which he reflected upon his mission and contemplated the future.[23] He began by explaining that his despatch in part followed past communications with Sir John Sterndale Bennett and Sir Esler Dening; he acknowledged the help of his staff in the embassy, especially Addis and Bryan. Throughout its history China had been a country of immense contrasts, not least between refined culture and grinding poverty. China was ripe for revolution when the communist movement appeared because of the legacy bequeathed by the Ch'ing dynasty, exacerbated by civil war and foreign imperialism. Hutchison remarked on the distinction between Soviet and Chinese communism. The Chinese movement was truly indigenous and nationalist. It was heavily influenced by Russia in the 1920s but evolved through its own efforts. He rightly observed that the Chinese succeeded because they discarded the Stalinist path to power. The initial achievement of Mao's government in combating the challenges faced was considerable. Currency and prices had been stabilised; communications had been restored and internal trade promoted. The flagrant injustice of maldistribution of wealth had been tackled to the ire of those deprived of assets. The most impressive feature was 'the integrity of purpose and the personal incorruptibility of the officials of all ranks serving under the People's Government both central and local'.[24] There was no viable alternative to the communists: the discredited KMT regime could not return to the mainland unless this occurred as part of an American occupation. Although the CCP had moved away from the Stalinist domination under Mao's leadership, the CCP was following a policy which could broadly be described as 'Stalinist'. The Soviet Union was regarded as a model in many spheres and Mao's regime possessed some – but not all – of the deplorable characteristics of communist regimes elsewhere.

As regards the relationship between China and the Soviet Union:

> There is no evidence that the association of China with the Soviet Union (whatever the extent and nature of that association may be) is not wholly voluntary and certainly none whatever that the Chinese Communist Party takes orders from Moscow: nor is there evidence to show Soviet control in any department of the Chinese Government above a purely technical level.[25]

Since Chinese intervention in Korea had occurred, it appeared that the influence of Soviet military advisers had grown.

Hutchison saw the Chinese attitude towards foreign firms as negative and likely to continue as such. The Chinese aim would be to restrict trade as far as possible to Chinese channels. Future international trade would comprise trade with China, omitting trade in China. The foreign policy of China would probably resemble that of the Soviet Union but this did not mean that Chinese policy was dominated by the Kremlin.[26] The alliance between China and the Soviet Union appeared bizarre to those who knew China well and was a transient feature. The United States was regarded as deeply antagonistic because of American actions before and during the Korean war. Britain was perceived as endorsing American policy and as having followed a negative policy. Recognition had not been depicted in London as a positive move, in Chinese eyes, but rather as a step taken grudgingly. However, Chinese leaders understood the force of American pressure on Britain 'and the moderating influence which His Majesty's Government have exercised on immediate American Far Eastern policies'.[27] Hutchison did not anticipate really cordial relations because of Britain's identification with the United States. His report illustrated his natural feelings of regret that more had not been achieved in developing Anglo-Chinese relations during the previous 18 months.

Officials in the Foreign Office felt that Hutchison had been rather too conciliatory in his attitude to the communist authorities. Hope still existed that some progress might be made. Hutchison's successor was Lionel ('Leo') Lamb who had served in China previously. Instructions were sent to Lamb on 2 March in which he was advised to put forward a candid statement of his 'personal opinions'. He should indicate that as regards diplomatic relations, nothing had been achieved and no reply had been received to the British communication of 17 June. At the same time Lamb should not press the point too strongly. He should allude to the definite advantages for China of entering into positive relations with the West. Britain wished to reduce tension in East Asia rather than exacerbate it. Lamb should deprecate Chinese criticism of alleged 'insincerity' in statements referring to Britain. The lack of wisdom of two Chinese communists who had visited Britain recently was remarked upon in that they had 'restricted their contacts while in the United Kingdom almost exclusively to the British Communist Party which gained no seats at the last election and is in no way representative of the British people'.[28] If Lamb was asked about Malaya, overseas Chinese communities or the Hong Kong aircraft case (this will be discussed later in this chapter), then he should respond that he would have to consult the Foreign Office.

Lamb duly called on the vice-minister for foreign affairs on 8 March. He followed the instructions sent from London. The vice-minister said that Lamb enjoyed the position of 'negotiations representative'. Lamb spoke of the need to strengthen the Chinese economy which could be attained by promoting sound trade relations with Britain. The vice-minister observed that British merchants were engaged in commerce, notably John Keswick. This comment was repeated. The meeting was amiable but inconclusive.[29] Little likelihood of improving relations appeared to exist; on the other hand, neither were relations worsening, which was mildly encouraging.

Much of the difficulty experienced in enforcing economic measures against China concerned Hong Kong. In part this followed from the colony's exposed position and in part from reluctance on the part of the Colonial Office to cooperate wholeheartedly. A. A. E. Franklin minuted on 15 January that a powerful body of American opinion was highly critical of Hong Kong for sustaining the communist regime: many Americans felt that Hong Kong was propelled along by mercenary considerations. In order to prevent strategic materials reaching Hong Kong, the United States suspended almost all licences to Hong Kong and Macao in addition to China. The Americans were particularly anxious over such items as rubber, drugs, metals, trucks, steel plates and raw materials, especially cotton. Franklin commented that China was (in January 1951) treated precisely in the same way as the Soviet Union and Eastern Europe: the export of strategic materials was prohibited.[30] Oil, machine tools, defined chemicals, munitions and military supplies were all prohibited. In the first nine months of 1950 Hong Kong's exports to China and Macao amounted to £65.9 million and imports from China and Macao to £41.2 million.[31] The governor of Hong Kong, Sir Alexander Grantham, warned of the serious repercussions for the local economy and security of the colony through applying sanctions.[32] Grantham told the Colonial Office on 2 February that the American consul-general was allowed to examine all manifests of ships travelling between Hong Kong and China. Relevant figures were submitted to him. The purpose was for the American government to satisfy itself that goods of strategic importance originating in the United States were not reaching China. Grantham maintained that enough was being done and he was opposed to giving more detailed information to the Americans.[33] The Foreign Office was more inclined to be conciliatory; the Colonial Office shared Grantham's reservations. A meeting between officials from the two departments took place on 26 February. According to a minute by N. C. C. Trench, it became clear during discussion that neither the Colonial Office nor the authorities in Hong Kong had given any thought to alternative sources of supply or to a scheme for switching factories to different production. The Colonial Office resented suggestions that American criticism resulted from ineffectual controls over exports of strategic materials to China. Robert Scott reminded those present of the pressures from American public opinion encountered by the State Department.[34] At the same time the Foreign Office reminded the State Department that the perils of Hong Kong's predicament must be grasped: these could include communist occupation of the colony.[35] While this was unlikely to happen, it was apposite to underline the contingency to the Americans.

Christopher Steel of the embassy in Washington met Dean Rusk and State Department officials on 5 March. Steel explained the dilemmas caused by Hong Kong's exposed position. He was told that the State Department appreciated the problem but the Commerce Department was less sympathetic. Steel warned London of the embarrassments inherent in Britain's approach: if Britain pressed for special understanding over Hong Kong, the Americans might request a corresponding concession over sanctions when applied to China outside Hong Kong.[36] A meeting of interested government departments, held at the beginning of March, devised a list of items of fundamental importance strategically to China. This comprised metal-working machine tools for producing armaments; military vehicles and parts; electronic equipment; armour plate; non-ferrous metals and ferro-alloys used for armaments purposes, together with nickel, molybdenum, ferro-vanadium, ferro-tungsten, ferro-tetarium and ferro-niobium; special steels manufactured from metals or alloys; airfield and road-making machinery.[37] Chemicals were discussed and it was decided to add explosives to the list. The strategic criteria had been kept scrupulously in mind so as to forestall criticism from India or other quarters that Britain was hitting the civilian economy in China.

Further American pressure for a toughening in the British position occurred in the spring of 1951. This was fuelled by President Truman's removal of General MacArthur in April. MacArthur and his supporters were well aware of British criticism which had contributed to Truman's decision to dismiss the general.[38] They took their revenge by castigating British policy for weakness, evasion and duplicity. They pointed to the role of Hong Kong in reducing strategic and economic pressure on China. MacArthur gave added force to the criticisms in his statements during the joint Senate hearings into the circumstance of his removal.[39] Sir Alexander Grantham challenged MacArthur's observation that exports from Hong Kong, particularly petrol supplies, had

proved valuable to the communists in Korea. Grantham described the allegation as at least a huge distortion, and, so far as petrol and associated products
were concerned, was wholly erroneous.[40] Franks reported from Washington that
there was certain to be an increase in American criticism of Britain for helping
the Chinese. In order to counter-attack quickly, Franks requested up-to-date
figures for Japanese exports to China.[41] The point here was that MacArthur held
office as SCAP in Japan until his dismissal a month before: therefore, he bore
responsibility for Japanese exports to China at that time which would mean that
he, too, could be accused of encouraging Chinese resistance. The Foreign Office
immediately obtained the monthly values of Japanese exports for the first three
months of 1951. These read:

January	493,000 US dollars
February	827,000 US dollars
March	1,063,000 US dollars.

The chief items consisted of textiles, sewing machines and bicycles.[42] Franks
was asked to comment on a press report from Washington that the United States
'is going to permit Japan to continue trading in strategic goods with Communist
China'.[43] This report stated that nearly 15 million US dollars worth of total
Japanese exports of 16 million US dollars to China in 1950 comprised iron and
steel manufactured goods. Franks investigated the report and told the Foreign
Office that the United States was permitting Japan to pursue trading in non-
strategic goods with China. The authorities in Tokyo permitted the Japanese to
sell cotton fabrics, bicycles, tricycles, woven silk, imitation pearl necklaces,
sewing machines, cotton yarn, filament, writing and photo-printing paper. Raw
materials and semi-processed goods were stopped at the end of 1950. The State
Department, in a slight correction, indicated that approximately 15 million US
dollars worth of Japanese exports to China in 1950 comprised iron and steel
goods.[44]

Much of the argument generated by the controversy over MacArthur stimulated consideration of rubber exports from Hong Kong to China. Anthony
Rumbold minuted on 5 May that the president of the Board of Trade, Sir
Hartley Shawcross, intended raising orally the subject of exports to China when
he reported in cabinet on 7 May. A total embargo on rubber exports to China
was contemplated from British territories instead of the existing quota restriction permitting exports from Malaya up to 2,500 tons per month. In addition,
quantitative control applying to items currently on list 2 should be treated as if
on list 1 and accordingly added to a complete embargo. In the first three months
of 1951 rubber exports to China averaged 13,000 tons a month; as a result of
restrictions imposed since this figure had fallen to 2,500 tons a month. The
Colonial Office opposed an embargo on rubber shipments but Rumbold
described it as a weak response: he could see no valid reason for not acting rigorously. Rubber had become one of the most delicate features 'in our relations
with the United States and our representatives in the United States are finding
it increasingly difficult to meet hostile criticism'.[45]

Attention on this topic was further concentrated by a debate in the House
of Commons on 10 May. The leader of the opposition, Churchill, spoke at length
of the necessity for achieving close cooperation with the United States. Churchill

added that while he supported *de facto* recognition of communist China late in 1949 because this corresponded with reality, he had not favoured *de jure* recognition. The Attlee government implemented a policy which meant that it had recognised a government with which it was effectively at war in Korea.[46] The Additional Measures Committee proposed tougher action so as to embargo arms, ammunition, atomic energy materials, petroleum, transportation materials and to ensure effective cooperation between the members of the UN in enforcing sanctions.[47] The cabinet decided on 7 May that the president of the Board of Trade and the colonial secretary should devise proposals for a more restrictive policy regarding exports. A lengthy memorandum reviewing policy was drafted for a meeting of the Far Eastern (Official) Committee on 23 May. This recommended that all exports to China should come under formal licensing control under the supervision of the Security Exports Control Working Party; the aim should be to attain a complete embargo on goods declared to the UN and that others could be halted if desired; reports made to the Additional Measures Committee should deal only with embargoed goods. As regards the colonies, export licensing should be developed to include all goods to be defined as embargoed in fulfilling the UN resolution; a careful watch should be maintained on other exports and on transshipment so that further measures could be prepared if required. Full publicity should be given to the measures to be applied and the United States notified; NATO countries should be urged to work in unison with Britain.[48]

After further discussion agreement was reached and the American government was informed on 14 June that Britain was implementing the following decisions. Export licence control and embargo would be applied and would be observed in British colonies and overseas dependent territories. The prohibited list for export to China included all aircraft defence material and munitions; atomic energy materials and equipment; all ships and petroleum products; all other industrial goods of importance for waging war; other items of military or strategic significance; and other items including rubber. The authorities in Hong Kong were being told to control import of all items on the prohibited list and issue import licences only for use in the colony. Issues relating to transshipment were being considered further. Subsequently the cabinet rejected action on transshipment. The United States government should appreciate that the measures taken were a wide-ranging interpretation of Britain's obligations under the terms of the resolution of the UN General Assembly approved on 18 May.[49] Officials in the State Department expressed satisfaction but indicated that they regarded the UN resolution as clearly including transshipment and carriage of prohibited goods. The State Department urged that greater detail should be provided regarding the list of prohibited goods.[50] Britain felt that transshipment was not mandatory and it was decided not to fall into line with the United States for the present.[51]

The Truman administration was largely satisfied but right-wing Republicans continued to snipe away at Britain. The authorities in Hong Kong endeavoured to be more positive and to cooperate with visiting American representatives.[52] The Foreign Office assessed trade statistics carefully and it was noted late in October 1951 that pharmaceutical exports from Hong Kong to

China were increasing rapidly. F. S. Tomlinson commented, in a letter to John Shattock that interest in the topic of exports had declined in Washington but it might revive. He added that the impression in the United States was that Hong Kong was not adversely affected by economic sanctions and that the colony enjoyed reasonable prosperity.[53] Before Tomlinson's letter arrived in London, the Security Exports Control Working Party decided to submit a paper to ministers on British policy concerning pharmaceuticals exported to the Soviet bloc and China.[54] Early action was not seen as necessary but the position would be watched. The issue of policy relating to carriage of strategic goods in British vessels continued to rumble on during the latter part of 1951. The Far East (Official) Committee considered the position on 13 November and the Ministry of Transport could not concur in a recommendation to ministers to approve stronger action.[55] R. M. K. Slater commented that the subject had arisen in the context of considering action to be taken in the event of a breakdown in the Korean armistice talks.[56] The cabinet's Economic Policy Committee discussed the topic on 19 December 1951. The Foreign Office urged action to control carriage in British ships if the armistice talks failed. This view was opposed by the Ministry of Transport and by the secretary of state for Coordination of Transport and Power on the grounds that the administrative problems of issuing voyage licences were considerable and that action would most likely be ineffective. Unilateral moves would not be sensible and there were also considerations connected with non-interference in shipping.[57] At the beginning of 1952 Tomlinson wrote that while the United States would prefer British ships not to visit Chinese ports, they had never requested this. Shipping could be divided into two categories – reputable and disreputable. The latter consisted of smaller coastal vessels owned by British firms and registered in Hong Kong. Direct British interest was slight and ownership in each instance appeared to rest in the hands of Hong Kong Chinese whose true allegiance was uncertain. Roger Makins remarked that the cabinet had rejected a recommendation that transshipment control should be enforced in Britain with effect to all goods on the Chinese embargo list.[58] When General Bradley made a statement in November 1951 alleging that trade with China had increased, figures were produced to refute it. The numbers of British and Panamanian ships engaged in the China trade during 1951 progressively declined from a total of 158 in February to 64 in November. British exports varied but had dropped markedly in the last quarter of 1951; the principal items comprised machinery (mostly textile), chemicals and drugs. The value of Hong Kong's exports remained relatively high but declined slightly in the third quarter of 1951 compared with the same period in 1950.[59]

Paradoxically Britain endeavoured simultaneously to foster and to restrict trade with China. Traditional firms in the China trade – Jardine, Matheson and Butterfield and Swire, the British–American Tobacco Company and Shell – hoped that business would improve and that the Chinese authorities would adopt a more accommodating approach. They hoped in vain. In January 1951 John Swire visited the Foreign Office for advice before departing for Hong Kong. He spoke of the profound uncertainties of trade with China and of the reluctance of some employees of Butterfield and Swire to take up posts in Shanghai: 'He was told that although in the long run we felt that China would come to realise that economic links and trade with the West were to her advantage, present indications were that business conditions might become even more difficult than now and we would not want to encourage firms to sink further sums in China unless they thought that it was in their own interests to do so.'[60] In addition to Swire's call, J. L. S. Steel and S. P. Leigh of ICI visited the Foreign Office for a general discussion. They were advised that women and children should be withdrawn from Shanghai and that the trend in trade was to reduce exports to China, particularly for items of strategic value.[61] Friction between British managers and Chinese employees persisted and ugly incidents sometimes occurred. John Keswick visited the Foreign Office on 28 February 1951 to state that H. H. Lennox, Jardine's manager in Shanghai, had been arrested because of a dispute involving the Shanghai and Hongkew Wharf Company, a firm for which Jardine, Matheson acted as agents. Jardine's did not want publicity; the present nature of the charges against Lennox were unclear. The dispute resulted from the effective bankruptcy of the Wharf Company; its funds had declined and it could not afford to pay its labour force which was agitating for the customary New Year bonus.[62] The embassy in Peking investigated and discovered that Lennox had not been arrested and that negotiations might succeed in solving the problem provided there was no adverse publicity.[63] Lennox negotiated with the relevant union and managed to produce additional funds which he forwarded to the union; he had already been summoned to court and could be called again and ordered to realise the second half of the bonus. The consul-general in Shanghai reported that he had given up any idea of challenging the Chinese authorities and was manoeuvring in 'classic Jardine's manner'.[64] Lennox was trying to find a solution which would involve leaving the company's wharf properties.

More problems involving British firms developed and the China Association wrote to the Foreign Office on 26 April urging that representations be made in Peking against the harsh treatment meted out to British businessmen.[65] The Office responded that the difficulties were fully appreciated and the government's views had been conveyed in Peking. As regards *habeas corpus*, a generalised complaint could not be made against the constitutional or judicial system of another sovereign country. Retaliation against Chinese nationals for delaying business arrangements could encourage escalation.[66] Leo Lamb wrote privately to Robert Scott saying that conditions were deteriorating for foreigners and that a 'police state' was growing. A pervasive air of insecurity existed, accentuated by arbitrary police and judicial actions.[67] The British chambers of commerce in China urged the China Association to make renewed representations to the Foreign Office in May: contrary to pledges made by the Chinese communists in 1949, they had not respected foreigners and basic civil rights were denied.[68] In the second half of June Robert Scott chaired a meeting attended by British officials and a delegation from the China Association headed by its chairman, J. K. Swire. An exchange of views took place relating to China and the Japanese peace treaty. Scott believed that China would undermine foreign interests and felt it was unlikely that representations would deter the Peking government. Decisions on whether to stay in China or depart must be taken by the companies and individuals concerned and not by the British government.[69]

The embassy in Peking considered future steps and regarded joint action with other diplomats as possibly offering prospects for achieving something, as suggested by the China Association. Lamb thought that the participation of the Indian ambassador, K. M. Panikkar, would help. The diplomats in Peking consulted the Soviet ambassador, Roschin, in his capacity as doyen of the diplomatic body. Lamb spoke to Roschin of the unsatisfactory conduct of the Chinese authorities which included denying exit permits, imprisoning individuals incommunicado and failure of the Foreign Ministry to listen to foreign representations. Roschin spoke sympathetically in reply and offered to pursue the matter at a high level as soon as he could. Apparently a Soviet citizen had been arrested, too.[70] The Foreign Office approved of joint representations.[71] Reactions within the Commonwealth were mixed: Australia did not want to participate, Pakistan might do so but would not commit itself, India might but wanted the Korean negotiations completed first, and Canada had not responded as yet.[72]

Panikkar met Chou En-lai at the beginning of August. Chou alleged that Roman Catholic missionaries were challenging the communist government and this could not be tolerated. Protestant missionaries included worthy individuals motivated by the desire to improve education and health standards and they would be encouraged. Missionaries endeavouring to make converts were not wanted. Panikkar raised problems experienced by businessmen and referred to exit visa delays. Chou conceded that delays could have arisen but insisted that genuine businessmen were welcome. He desired more trade with the West: he added that trade with Western Europe and the United States was significantly greater than trade with Eastern Europe. Chou agreed to review treatment of foreign companies but said that Chinese law must be respected. Panikkar was encouraged by Chou's tone but Lamb saw little to be positive about.[73] It was agreed that Lamb should address a note of protest to the Foreign Ministry.[74] The Foreign Office amended Lamb's draft note and prepared a press statement for circulation in London.[75] The American embassy informed the Office that more than 20 American citizens were imprisoned in China and the majority had been under arrest for six months or more. One had died and others were believed to be suffering physical or economic distress. In addition, approximately 30 Americans were under 'house arrest'. Chinese officials had proved negative in approach and no help was given to those looking after American interests.[76] Lamb forwarded the British note of protest to Chang Han-fu, the vice-minister for foreign affairs, on 30 August.[77] The note elicited no positive response. The Soviet ambassador expressed sympathy when he met the Indian ambassador and the Swiss minister on 18 September and claimed that he experienced similar difficulties in protecting Soviet citizens.[78]

In September 1951 the Hongkong and Shanghai Bank and the Chartered Bank decided to close branches in Peking and Tientsin because of worsening business conditions.[79] The British–American Tobacco Company had tried for more than a year to transfer its assets to the Chinese government without success.[80]

In 1952 conflicting trends in trade prospects could be discerned. On the one hand, the familiar tale of woe continued. On the other hand, the gathering of the Moscow Economic Conference appeared to offer opportunities for left-wing British businessmen to open up contacts with Chinese officials. Let us pursue the established British firms first. Representatives from ICI visited the Foreign Office on 12 March and stated that the company had a foreign staff of six of whom four were in Shanghai; Chinese employees totalled 223. ICI properties in China were valued at £800,000. ICI wished to handle matters in a low-key way and wished to avoid any suggestion of coercion. If ICI decided to leave, this could be accomplished in stages.[81] Five days later the consul-general in Shanghai reported that Jardine's manager in Shanghai, Gordon, had been arrested. He was detained in his capacity as chairman of EWO Breweries, which had suffered extremely low sales recently and did not have the money to pay wages to its 240 workers. The company was warned by the labour unions and police that action would be taken against it.[82] Simultaneously Lamb reported that the Chinese authorities were acting more harshly. Lamb felt that efforts should be made to negotiate and it must be emphasised that British firms would have to leave China completely unless matters improved.[83] The British–American Tobacco Company was negotiating termination of its interests and was seeking exit permits for approximately 20 foreign employees, mostly British. Under Chinese law the company was compelled to continue employing a large labour force. Because of insufficient leaf supplies allocated to the company, its business had come to a halt and there was no money to pay staff.[84] Representatives from the China Association visited the Foreign Office on 18 March and stated that British firms wanted to leave China.[85] On a slightly more promising note, Gordon, of Jardine's, was released from prison on 20 March.[86]

The leading British banks had already decided to withdraw. Sir Arthur Morse wrote to the Foreign Office on 11 January to say that the Hongkong and Shanghai Bank would definitely leave China.[87] The Chartered Bank decided to close its Tientsin office and the Mercantile Bank was contemplating withdrawal from China. The Foreign Office anticipated that negotiations would be protracted and contentious.[88] One delicate issue involved US dollar assets held by British banks on behalf of the Bank of China and now frozen in the United States: this amounted to 4 million US dollars. The American Treasury proved obdurate over releasing funds because of the amount and would not release sums from blocked accounts to extract representatives of American banks from China.[89] In December Lamb reported that he had pursued matters with bank representatives and they concluded reluctantly that they could not terminate operations unless they settled prewar deposits and frozen US currency. The banks would have to be willing to trade assets together with considerable cash payments against all their obligations. It would be expensive but not as costly as continuing to trade at a loss.[90]

An inter-departmental meeting met in the Foreign Office on 2 April to discuss the plight of British firms. It was reported that Butterfield and Swire and Jardine, Matheson had decided not to send vessels to Chinese ports after Lamb had delivered the note to the Foreign Ministry. The British–American Tobacco Company was expected to sign the final transfer agreement with Chinese officials that day: this would affect their properties in Tientsin. As regards remittances to China the Treasury indicated that it would almost certainly be impossible for the Bank of England or Treasury to state that firms enjoyed official support in rejecting Chinese 'blackmail'; the problem was essentially one for the Hong Kong administration. The Colonial Office indicated that the governor of Hong Kong firmly opposed introduction of any kind of controls. The contingency of retaliatory action was considered: the sole suggestion was that all Hong Kong currency should be recalled so as to prevent the Chinese possessing appreciable Hong Kong currency known to be in south China. This was not viewed favourably by the Colonial Office. Preparations were made for ensuring that Lamb made representations in Peking as approved by Anthony Eden, the foreign secretary, and by R. A. Butler, the chancellor of the exchequer. Eden would meet a delegation from the China Association; firms would instruct their Chinese representatives to apply for closure and this would occur two days after Lamb's note had been communicated.[91] Sir William Strang suggested that Eden bring the matter before cabinet and Eden agreed.[92]

Eden met a delegation from the China Association on 7 April. He expressed sympathy for their predicament: 'He described it as a terrible chapter in our history.'[93] The businessmen explained their difficulties. They wanted the chargé d'affaires in Peking to hand a note to the Chinese authorities worded moderately and indicating the problems. They preferred an 'innocuous' approach so that there would be no unpleasant consequences for shipping controlled by those firms which had decided to close. Firms would forward individual applications around the end of April stating their intention to withdraw and requesting exit permits. The obvious dilemma in the second stage concerned actual withdrawal of staff; they feared that attempts would be made to blackmail them into remitting large amounts in foreign currency while the Chinese treated local managers as effective hostages. Those present wished to know whether the government could act to control remittances so that companies could notify the Chinese that applications to remit had been refused by the British government. The Hong Kong authorities did not want to see any control of remittances implemented. The assets to be handed over by Jardine, Matheson would amount to approximately £20 million in order to secure release of staff. Butterfield and Swire would be faced with handing over about half of this sum. The only alternative was to continue sending remittances as anticipated. The British–American Tobacco Company had negotiated for two years to end its activities in China and had just reached preliminary agreement with the Chinese for transferring their interests. The position of the banks would take longer to resolve. Pressure could be applied to China through moving against the Bank of China in London, Hong Kong and Singapore; by controlling remittances from overseas Chinese in Malaya to China; and perhaps by halting jute shipments from India and rubber shipments from Ceylon, providing the latter governments would cooperate (and this was doubtful).[94]

J. K. Drinkall of the Foreign Office wrote on 22 May that Eden would submit a paper to the Economic Policy Committee indicating possible action. The weapons in British hands were limited and double-edged. He suggested that counter-measures could include obligations not fulfilled by the communist government regarding railway loans; the position of employees of the Shanghai Municipal Council; control of remittances; freezing Chinese sterling assets; seizing Chinese assets and property; stopping trade with China; and withdrawing the British chargé d'affaires from Peking.[95] Following discussion with other government departments Drinkall gloomily concluded that each of the contemplated forms of retaliation was hazardous and such a drastic step as halting all trade would strangle Hong Kong or involve a Chinese attack on the colony. It did not seem sensible to instruct Lamb to leave China.[96]

Eden spoke in the House of Commons on 20 May and his statement was endorsed by the Labour spokesman, Herbert Morrison; it was clear that trade between Britain and China could not be developed satisfactorily in the circumstances.[97] Matters proceeded slowly and in early June the embassy in Peking reported that the Chinese were reacting more favourably. A less critical approach to British firms could be seen; it might be the case that the Chinese government realised that it should behave in a more friendly way in order to secure fulfilment of the agreement for exchange of goods reached at the Moscow Economic Conference (see below). British firms should hold out for better terms and not dispose of assets on poor terms.[98] As part of the overall endeavour to achieve a reduction in tension, a suggestion had emerged of sending a British trade group to Peking to meet the Ministry of Foreign Affairs. According to this report from Lamb, the Chinese reaction seemed positive. Robert Scott told members of the China Association on 9 July that the Chinese government should grasp that withdrawal did not denote unwillingness to trade. If China behaved in a more conciliatory manner, then it should be feasible to achieve more satisfactory terms.[99]

Differences between British firms rendered it more difficult for the Foreign Office to handle the situation. Robert Scott explained the frustrations within the Office clearly when he met Collar, the Hong Kong manager of ICI and chairman of the Hong Kong Chamber of Commerce: 'I put it to him quite bluntly that I thought there was a risk of differences in policy between British trading interests and British industrial interests in China and moreover that there was a risk of differences between British firms in Hong Kong and the China Association here.'[100] Collar agreed: there were divergent views between traders wishing to continue trading and industrial interests wishing to terminate their operations through transfer, lease, handing over and removal of their foreign staff. He believed that most of the Hong Kong firms wanted to pursue trade either via a group in Peking, through Hong Kong, East Berlin, or, in the longer term, through a Chinese trading agency to be established in London. Collar felt that the China Association in London conveyed the impression of being a governing body in charge of the activities of firms in Hong Kong. This was valid in some cases but not in others. In addition, differences of opinion seemed to exist within the China Association in London. Scott replied that the Foreign Office was anxious to assist but it must be made clear whether there was an agreed policy between firms. He summarised the Office's position as one of facilitating the departure of businessmen wishing to leave; inducing the Chinese to cooperate in disposing of assets where firms wanted to go; and helping those firms aiming to continue trading. Collar commented that he was proceeding to

Berlin later in the week to meet the Chinese trading agency established in East Berlin. He considered the Chinese as having acted shrewdly in setting up the agency. There were signs that China might be interested in establishing a trading agency in London; he gathered that the Board of Trade was sympathetic but the Foreign Office was not.[101] Scott said that no proposal had been made by China and that his personal opinion was that Britain should be in no hurry to see the establishment of a Chinese trade agency in London: progress should be made in resolving outstanding disputes first.[102]

Negotiations proceeded slowly between the Chinese authorities and firms wishing to withdraw. Jardine's reached provisional agreement at the beginning of November 1952 to surrender local assets against remission of liabilities. It was thought that assets would exceed liabilities by approximately £160,000. The Chinese wanted to follow the precedent set by British–American Tobacco of a direct exchange of assets against liabilities. Lamb described the Chinese terms as amounting to robbery.[103] The Foreign Office was critical of Jardine's for making it difficult for other firms to negotiate.[104] British companies in Tientsin were forced to recognise that all they could expect was a direct exchange of assets for liabilities on terms dictated by the Chinese.[105] On 20 November the Shanghai Municipal Military Control Commission took over the property of the Shanghai Electrical Construction Company, the Shanghai Waterworks, the Shanghai Gasworks and Mackenzie and Company; the property of the latter company in Tientsin had also been seized. This seemed to be in retaliation for the award to American claimants of aircraft in Hong Kong against strong claims by the Chinese government (this issue will be examined in the next chapter). Lamb urged that a protest should be made.[106] He was duly instructed to protest vigorously.[107] The protest included reference to previous seizure of property of several British firms, again in connection with the controversy over the aircraft in Hong Kong.[108]

The more hopeful indications for trade prospects arose from discussions at the Moscow Economic Conference in April 1952. A negotiating group of businessmen with left-wing political sympathies visited Moscow with the aim of opening talks with Chinese officials for exporting textiles, metals and chemicals in exchange for Chinese coal, egg products, bristles, soya beans and vegetable oils.[109] The known members of the group were W. D. Lorimer (a director of the North British Locomotive Company), Sydney Silverman (Labour MP for Nelson and Colne), plus King, Poulton and Perry. Silverman was representing textile manufacturers in his Lancashire constituency.[110] It was decided, in exchanges between Lorimer and a Chinese official that the intention should be to secure trade to the value of £10 million, to be completed by 31 December 1952. The British businessmen would endeavour to persuade the British government to approve their actions.[111] Sales by Britain would comprise 35 per cent textiles, 30 per cent chemicals and 35 per cent metals. Sales by China would comprise 25 per cent coal and bristles, 20 per cent frozen eggs and other egg products and 55 per cent certain agreed Chinese products.[112] However, doubts existed over how many exports would originate in Britain: it appeared that textiles would be the only ones to come from Britain with the rest coming from East Germany.[113] The Foreign Office was distinctly interested in the possibility that China would develop trade; the Peking embassy was reminded that goods of strategic significance must be excluded.[114] The Foreign Office implied that well-established British merchants in Shanghai and Hong Kong should be used and was dubious over the possible role of goods from East Germany; the Board of Trade did not wish to alienate the Chinese, however.[115]

The news of the initiative taken by rival businessmen annoyed established British firms in the China trade. John Keswick wrote to W. J. Keswick, 'It is particularly irksome that these ridiculous uninformed businessmen should go hobnobbing with the Chinese at a time when we are being squeezed to death by them. However, I suppose that is the way the world goes round.'[116] John Keswick felt that the Chinese might offer 'some attractive and succulent bait', which might induce some British merchants to stay on but he held that it was preferable to leave. Lorimer visited the Board of Trade on 19 April to report on his actions at the Moscow conference. His firm wished to send locomotives to China or the Soviet Union; he appreciated that these could not be exported now but it could be different once the Korean war ended. Lorimer had become chairman of the 'Businessmen's Group' and had signed the agreement in Moscow with the chairman of the Chinese delegation. Lorimer stated that the Chinese were adamant that they would not conduct business through the Shanghai or Hong Kong merchants. He regarded the agreement as flexible in that the Chinese might agree that metals could not be provided. Lorimer was vague over details.[117] Lamb talked to seven businessmen when they visited Peking. They professed belief that China genuinely desired trade and Lamb feared that they had succumbed to Chinese propaganda. They appeared ignorant of the situation in China. J. O. Lloyd suspected that they belonged to 'the Progressive Businessmen's Forum, which is a fellow travelling outfit'; if not, they were 'plain gullible'.[118]

On 10 June the *Manchester Guardian* reported that a further agreement had been signed for £6.5 million worth of textiles and chemicals to be sold to China.[119] The Board of Trade believed that China was sincere in wishing to encourage trade and expected the agreement to be implemented. The businessmen's group was viewed as 'scruffy' but the reputable China firms would probably become involved subsequently. The list of British goods to be provided comprised wool, wool tops, rayon, yarn, woollen and worsted piece goods and cotton; the total value was £3.5 million.[120] Two of the businessmen were King and Sternberg of the Propane Company; a member of the East–West Trade Branch of the British High Commission in Germany identified the Propane Company as the agent of the Chemical Branch of the East Zone Government Foreign Trade Department.[121] Not surprisingly, the Foreign Office regarded them suspiciously.[122] The Board of Trade was notified on 1 July by Perry, a businessman in the group dealing with textiles, that firm contracts were being produced following negotiations in East Berlin for the export of £1 million of textiles from Britain, mostly wool tops with some rayon yarn, and for £800,000 of chemicals. Perry indicated that Jardine, Matheson had been represented at the meeting and they were advancing rapidly towards signing contracts. The Chinese had sterling in London and were opening letters of credit. Perry said that he was visiting the Bradford Chamber of Commerce and would keep

Manchester informed.[123] It appeared that the Chinese no longer intended using the satellite states to sell Chinese produce; instead they could deal with it themselves.

H. J. Collar, the Hong Kong manager of ICI, met Robert Scott on 6 August to tell him of his recent visit to East Berlin. It had gone successfully and he met Liu Shu-chang, chief of the head office of the newly established China National Import-Export Corporation. Liu impressed Collar and emphasised China's genuine wish to foster trade. Collar stressed the problems faced by British firms but Liu attributed these to the consequences of the Korean war; when normality returned, the difficulties would diminish.[124] The Board of Trade estimated that the total value of goods exported to, or ordered by, China since the Moscow conference was slightly over £2 million, much less than the figure of £10 million claimed by Silverman.[125] Leo Lamb confirmed, on 15 August, that Jardine, Matheson had participated in the signature of the trade agreement. Charles Johnston of the Foreign Office found this diverting in the light of the confidential letter from John Keswick, supplied to the Office in April.[126] He wrote to Lamb describing recent developments as positive: the Chinese seemed to be responding positively and appeared disillusioned with the handling of trade by the Soviet Union and East Germany.[127] Johnston favoured the establishment of a trade office in London. He looked towards the attainment of full diplomatic relations. The continuance of the Korean war rendered this difficult to secure but the setting up of a trade mission would be a step towards the greater aim. Also the presence of Chinese diplomats in Britain would facilitate retaliation if the Chinese took action against British diplomats.[128] Johnston thought that the timing of British recognition of communist China had perhaps been wrong and Anthony Eden commented, 'I though so.'[129] Johnston rightly remarked on the delicacy of matters in the context of Anglo-American relations, not least with the imminence of the presidential election. It followed that a trade mission should not be approved before the end of 1952. F. S. Tomlinson of the embassy in Washington endorsed this advice given the volatility of American opinion over the Korean war.[130]

Rothschilds and Company approached the Foreign Office in the second half of October to obtain backing for a request to the Export Credits Guarantee Department to facilitate Chinese purchases in Britain. Rothschilds wanted cover for £450,000 of a £1 million credit. The Treasury and the Bank of England did not object; publicity would not be given but it would probably be known in financial circles. Anglo-Chinese trading figures for 1951 and the first half of 1952 were as follows:

		Imports from China	Exports to China
	1951	£7.7 million	£2.7 million
Jan–June	1952	£1.8 million	£0.7 million

The Bank of England was unaware of the use to which the £6 million trading balance had been put but pointed out that it could be used anywhere in the sterling area. It might have been deployed in purchasing Ceylon rubber or could have been used for purchasing other commodities via European agents. It was unsatisfactory to be unsure what had happened and the Foreign Office was fully conscious of the delicate state of Anglo-American relations where trade with China figured. It was best to be cautious.[131] Charles Johnston thought Rothschilds's request could be approved on the basis of observing carefully what transpired.[132] After consultation with Eden it was decided, on policy grounds, to urge the Treasury to refuse Rothschilds's approach.[133] Leo Lamb wrote to Johnston on 31 October regretting that the hopes of a more positive attitude from the Chinese authorities had not occurred. He attributed this to ideological and other handicaps.[134]

As 1952 drew to a close, so the enthusiasm of Jardine, Matheson declined once more. W. J. Keswick called to see Robert Scott on 12 December and expressed anxiety about signing large financial commitments for egg contracts because of uncertainty over future Chinese policy; he was also worried that the new Republican administration in Washington might pursue a tougher policy in Korea which could have repercussions on Anglo-Chinese relations. Excessive risk could not be incurred in the course of endeavouring to preserve the China market.[135]

At the start of 1953 government departments considered their reactions to the holding of an economic conference in Peking as an extension of the deliberations at the Moscow conference. Barnaby Drayson, Conservative MP for Skipton and a director of a textile company, Hill Brown Limited, was active in advocating increasing trade with China; his representations were not regarded favourably in the Foreign Office.[136] J. W. Nicolls assessed the problem lucidly in a minute for Sir William Strang. The subject was to be considered in cabinet and Nicolls explained that Perry, Berger and Buckman, three of the businessmen active in urging British firms to attend the Peking conference, were covert members of the Communist Party. The Moscow conference was organised as part of the 'Peace Campaign', although the connection between the 'Peace Campaign' and the Moscow conference had been concealed. Any success enjoyed by the Peking conference would be regarded as evidence of support for the 'peace movement'. The British government discouraged its nationals from participating in the Moscow conference: similar action was taken by the Brussels Treaty powers and by NATO. If the cabinet decided to change policy for the Peking conference, then it would be essential to inform the NATO Council of the reasons for the change in approach. It was highly desirable that the United States should be consulted so as to preserve a joint approach.[137] Strang minuted that he was not aware of any intention to encourage participation by British businessmen.[138]

The embassy in Washington arrived at the same conclusion as Nicholls:

'Red China' is popularly regarded as worse than the Soviet Union. It is a recognised aggressor and a country with which the United States and its Allies are in practice at war, even though this war is limited to certain areas.
British trade with China is one of the most telling points made by our enemies here ...[139]

Government departments differed in their views, the Board of Trade, in particular, leaning towards encouraging trade. J. M. Addis wrote on 4 February that the cabinet paper represented the agreed views of the Foreign Office, Board of Trade and Ministry of Transport that the government should not discourage British businessmen from attending the Peking conference on the understanding that the propaganda side of it should be brought to the attention of those desiring guidance. It had been decided Eden would say in cabinet that British participants would, simply by attending, be lending themselves to a communist campaign. The president of the Board of Trade insisted that a written reference in the latter sense should be removed from the draft cabinet paper but he accepted that Eden should refer to it orally.[140] The cabinet decided that suitable advice should be given to those requesting guidance; friendly governments were to be notified and urged to extend analogous advice.[141] The Peking conference met in June 1953; 18 British businessmen took part under the leadership of Roland Berger, director of the British Council for the Promotion of International Trade.[142]

Britain trod an invidious path in navigating the complexities caused by dealing with communist China in the midst of the Korean war. The Chinese were frequently negative in their attitudes and American suspicions caused serious problems. While General Eisenhower was a reassuring figure as the new president, he had to make some concessions to right-wing Republicans in operating his administration. Senators Taft and Knowland were vocal in their criticisms, not to mention Joe McCarthy.

Notes

1 See Evan Luard, *History of the United Nations*, 2 vols (London: Macmillan, 1982), vol. I, pp. 251–6 and Callum MacDonald, *Korea: The War before Vietnam* (London: Macmillan, 1986), pp. 70–84.
2 Meeting of Commonwealth prime ministers, 4 January 1951, PMM(51)1, Cab 133/90.
3 *Ibid.*
4 *Ibid.*, 4 January 1951, PMM(51)2.
5 *Ibid.*, 5 January 1951, PMM(51)3.
6 *Ibid.*, PMM(51)4.
7 *Ibid.*, 8 January 1951, PMM(51)5.
8 *Ibid.*, 9 January 1951, PMM(51)10.
9 *Ibid.*, 11 January 1951, PMM(51)10.
10 Joint Intelligence Committee, conclusions attached, *ibid.*
11 See chapter 11, dealing with Korea in January 1951.
12 Note, 'Effect on British Shipping of stoppage of trade with China', by W. P. S. Ormond, 16 January 1951, FO 371/92273/22G.
13 *Ibid.*
14 *Ibid.*
15 New York to FO, 16 February 1951, FO 371/92234/29.
16 FO to Washington, 17 February 1951, FO 371/92234/33.
17 *Ibid.*
18 FO to Washington, 17 February 1951, FO 371/92234/33.
19 *Ibid.*
20 Letter from R. H. Scott to Jebb, 17 February 1951, FO 371/92234/34.
21 New York to FO, 23 February 1951, FO 371/92234/43 and 44.
22 New York to FO, 23 February 1951, FO 371/92234/45.
23 Despatch from Hutchison to Bevin, 22 February 1951, FO 371/92220/1.

24 *Ibid.*
25 *Ibid.*
26 *Ibid.*
27 *Ibid.*
28 FO to Peking, 2 March 1951, FO 371/92235/58.
29 Peking to FO, 9 March 1951, FO 371/92235/66.
30 Minute by A. A. E. Franklin, 15 January 1951, FO 371/92274/37.
31 *Ibid.*
32 Grantham to CO, communicated to FO, 9 January 1951, FO 371/92272/15 and 30G,
    2 February 1951, FO 371/92275/71.
33 Grantham to CO, 2 February 1951, *ibid.*
34 Minute by N. C. C. Trench, 26 February 1951, FO 371/92276/111.
35 FO to Washington, 1 March 1951, *ibid.*
36 Washington to FO, 5 March 1951, FO 371/92276/123.
37 Minute by R. M. K. Slater, 7 March 1951, FO 371/92277/126.
38 See Peter Lowe, 'An Ally and a Recalcitrant General: Great Britain, Douglas MacArthur
    and the Korean War, 1950–1', *English Historical Review*, 105 (July 1990), pp. 624–53.
39 See *Hearings before the Committee on Armed Services and the Committee on Foreign Relations,
    United States Senate, 82nd Congress, First Session, To Conduct an Inquiry into the Military
    Situation in the Far East and the Facts Surrounding the Relief of General of the Army Douglas
    MacArthur from His Assignment in that Area*, 5 parts (Washington: Government Printing
    Office, 1951), part 1.
40 Grantham to CO, 6 May 1951, FO 371/92278/164.
41 Washington to FO, 7 May 1951, FO 371/92278/165.
42 FO to Washington, 16 May 1951, *ibid.*
43 *Ibid.*
44 Washington to FO, 18 May 1951, FO 371/92279/184.
45 Minute by A. Rumbold, 5 May 1951, FO 371/92278/175.
46 *Parliamentary Debates, Commons*, 10 May 1951, cols 2165–72, as included in FO
    371/92279/176.
47 FO to Shanghai, 19 May 1951, FO 371/92279/183.
48 Memorandum, 'Control of United Kingdom Exports to China', redrafted from meeting
    on 23 May 1951, FO 371/92279/196B.
49 FO to Washington, 14 June 1951, FO 371/92281/228.
50 Washington to FO, 16 June 1951, FO 37/92281/245.
51 See minute by M. J. M. Paton, no date, *ibid.*, and British high commissioner, Delhi, to
    Commonwealth Relations Office, 23 June 1951, FO 371/92282/271. The Indian govern-
    ment did not object to the decision regarding transshipment because articles on the
    controlled list were not exported from India.
52 Grantham to CO, 1 August 1951, FO 371/92284/313. Grantham reported on a recent
    visit to Hong Kong by Hanson, an official investigating trade matters on behalf of the
    US Senate. Grantham described Hanson as amiable and fair. It was likely that he would
    criticise some aspects, notably over the failure to control transit trade.
53 Letter from Tomlinson to Shattock, 29 October 1951, FO 371/92286/341.
54 Letter from Shattock to W. A. Morris (CO), 8 November 1951, *ibid.*
55 Minute by R. M. K. Slater, 14 November 1951, FO 371/92287/352.
56 Minute by Slater, 16 November 1951, *ibid.*
57 Brief for Lord Reading, for Economic Policy Committee, 18 December 1951, FO
    371/92287/366.
58 Minutes by F. S. Tomlinson and R. Makins, 6 January 1952, FO 371/92287/365/G.
59 Facts and figures to counter General Bradley's statement, no date, November 1951, FO
    371/92287/357.
60 FO to Peking, 21 January 1951, FO 371/92259/11.
61 *Ibid.*
62 Minute by R. H. Scott, 28 February 1951, FO 371/92260/24.
63 Peking to FO, 5 March 1951, FO 371/92260/26.
64 Shanghai to FO, 15 March 1951, FO 371/92260/34.

65 Letter from China Association to FO, 26 April 1951, FO 371/92261/54.
66 Letter from FO to China Association, 16 May 1951, *ibid.*
67 Letter from Lamb to R. H. Scott, 22 March 1951, FO 371/92261/57.
68 Shanghai to FO, 22 May 1951, FO 371/92262/65.
69 Letter from R. H. Scott to Lamb, 28 June 1951, FO 371/92262/74.
70 Peking to FO, 16 July 1951, FO 371/92263/93.
71 FO to Peking, 26 July 1951, *ibid.*
72 Minute by N. C. C. Trench, 23 July 1951, FO 371/92263/98.
73 Peking to FO, 4 August 1951, FO 371/92264/103.
74 Peking to FO, 11 August 1951, FO 371/92264/109.
75 FO to Peking, 21 and 29 August 1951, FO 371/92264/108 and 130.
76 Memorandum communicated by United States embassy, 30 August 1951, FO 371/92265/136.
77 Letter from Lamb to Chang Han-fu, 30 August 1951, FO 371/92266/182.
78 Peking to FO, 19 September 1951, FO 371/92266/161.
79 Letter, Chancery, Peking, to China and Korea Department, 24 September 1951, FO 371/92267/183.
80 Shanghai to FO, 17 December 1951, FO 371/92267/211.
81 Minute by Drinkall, 12 March 1952, FO 371/99283/45.
82 Shanghai to FO, 17 March 1952, FO 371/99283/47.
83 Peking to FO, 17 March 1952, FO 371/99283/60.
84 Minute by C. H. Johnston, 15 March 1952, FO 371/99283/53.
85 Minute by Drinkall, 18 March 1952, FO 371/99283/60.
86 Shanghai to FO, 20 March 1952, FO 371/99283/65.
87 Minute by Drinkall, 11 January 1952, FO 371/99304/3.
88 Letter from Johnson to Tomlinson, 13 February 1952, FO 371/99304/14.
89 Letter from Tomlinson to Addis, 6 November 1952, FO 371/99306/54.
90 Peking to FO, 18 December 1952, FO 371/99306/56.
91 Minute by Drinkall, 2 April 1952, FO 371/99285/104.
92 Minute by Strang, 3 April 1952 and Eden, 4 April 1952, *ibid.*
93 Record of meeting in Eden's room in the House of Commons, 7 April, 1952, FO 371/99285/14.
94 Minute by R. H. Scott, 9 April 1952, FO 371/99285/108.
95 Minute by Drinkall, 2 May 1952, FO 371/99287/153.
96 Minute by Drinkall, 6 May 1952, *ibid.*
97 *Parliamentary Debates, Commons*, 20 May 1952, cols 267–71, enclosed in FO 371/99288/192.
98 Peking to FO, 8 July 1952, FO 371/99290/250.
99 Record of meeting with the China Association, 9 July 1952, FO 371/99291/270.
100 Minute by R. H. Scott, 29 July 1952, FO 371/99292/298.
101 *Ibid.*
102 *Ibid.*
103 Peking to FO, 3 November 1952, FO 371/99296/400.
104 Minute by I. M. McKenzie, no date, *ibid.*
105 Minute by J. Snodgrass, 7 November 1952, FO 371/99296/403.
106 Minute by McKenzie, 3 December 1952, FO 371/99346/47.
107 FO to Peking, 10 December 1952, FO 371/99346/51.
108 Minute by Addis, 8 December 1952, FO 371/99346/66.
109 Moscow to FO, 8 April 1952, FO 371/99318/4.
110 Moscow to FO, 9 April 1952, FO 371/99318/5.
111 Moscow to FO, 10 April 1952, FO 371/99318/8.
112 Moscow to FO, 10 April 1952, FO 371/99318/10.
113 Moscow to FO, 10 April 1952, FO 371/99318/11.
114 FO to Peking, two telegrams, 17 April 1952, FO 371/99318/14.
115 Minute by Drinkall, 17 and 21 April 1952, FO 371/99318/20.
116 John Keswick to W. J. Keswick, 8 April 1952, sent to FO by W. J. Keswick, 16 April 1952, FO 371/99318/27.

117 Minute by S. H. Levine (Board of Trade), 19 April 1952, FO 371/99318/30.
118 Peking to FO, 23 April, with minute by J. O. Lloyd, 24 April 1952, FO 371/99318/32.
119 *Manchester Guardian*, 10 June 1952.
120 Minute by Levine, 16 June 1952, FO 371/99320/61.
121 Letter from S. W. Griffin to R. Arculus, 23 June 1952, FO 371/99320/67.
122 Minutes by Arculus, 13 and 18 June 1952, FO 371/99320/66.
123 Minute by Levine, 1 July 1952, FO 371/99320/71.
124 Minute by J. O. Lloyd, summarising discussion between Collar and Scott, 6 August 1952, FO 371/99320/80.
125 Minute by C. H. Johnston, 23 August 1952, FO 371/99320/84.
126 Minute by Johnston, 22 September 1952, FO 371/99320/89.
127 Letter from Johnston to Lamb, 26 September 1952, FO 371/99320/89.
128 Minute by Johnston, 4 September 1952, FO 371/99320/91.
129 Minute by Eden, 1 September 1952, *ibid.*
130 Letter from Tomlinson to Johnston, 7 October 1952, FO 371/99320/99.
131 Letter from Tomlinson to Johnston, 22 October 1952, FO 371/99321/102.
132 Minute by Johnston, 25 October 1952 (Addis signed on behalf of Johnston), FO 371/99321/105.
133 Minutes by Scott, J. E. Coulson, Strang, Eden, 27–29 October 1952, and letter from Addis to D. R. Serpell (Treasury), 11 November 1952, *ibid.*
134 Letter from Lamb to Johnston, 21 October 1952, FO 371/99321/111.
135 Minute by Scott, 12 December 1952, FO 371/99321/119.
136 Letter from P. F. D. Tennant to Dugald Malcolm, 2 January 1953, FO 371/105261/3/G.
137 Minute by Nicholls, 30 January 1953, FO 371/105261/16.
138 Minute by Strang, 30 January 1953, *ibid.*
139 Washington to FO, 7 February 1953, FO 371/105261/18.
140 Minute by Addis, 4 February 1953, FO 371/105261/21.
141 Minute by Shattock, 19 February 1953, FO 371/105261/23/G.
142 Grantham to CO, 17 June 1953, and Peking to FO, 23 June 1953, FO 371/105261/23/G. The embassy in Peking reported that 19 British businessmen were in Peking.

8

TAIWAN, AIRCRAFT AND FUTURE PROSPECTS

The outbreak of the Korean war sharpened friction between Britain and the United States over Taiwan. This applied in part because of the divergence predating the war and in part because of President Truman's public announcement in his statement on 27 June that neither side in the Chinese civil war would be allowed to attack the other. Taiwan was frozen politically in the sense that it would not be allowed to go communist: whether it could throw off the shackles of the KMT regime and remain anti-communist simultaneously remained to be seen. The question of Britain's relationship with the KMT, which the Attlee government believed it had resolved in January 1950, was stimulated into renewed life. The Foreign Office was compelled to address such aspects as the reorganisation of the KMT in Taiwan, the KMT harassment of shipping, covert intervention in the mainland by the KMT with American connivance and the role of Hong Kong in tackling disputes between the Peking government and the KMT regime, notably in the bitter argument regarding the ultimate fate of aircraft impounded in Hong Kong. Inevitably these matters interacted with American domestic politics because of the combination of the savage reactions to Chinese military intervention in Korea with the approach of a presidential campaign in the United States.

The British cabinet deeply deplored Truman's decision to link conflict in Korea with the fate of Taiwan.[1] As we saw in chapter 6, American policy towards Taiwan changed shortly before the start of the Korean war: Truman and Acheson accepted the views of the joint chiefs of staff and MacArthur that Taiwan was too valuable strategically to be permitted to fall into communist hands. However, this did not mean that the Truman administration was embracing Chiang Kai-shek's regime. Denying Taiwan to Mao Tse-tung's government was not synonymous with supporting the KMT. Truman, Acheson and Dulles were all completely disillusioned with Chiang and his circle and hoped an alternative form of government could emerge. This could be assisted by the UN but much depended on developments in Korea.[2] The arguments for acting more vigorously to help Taiwan repel the ambitions of the Peking government appealed to growing numbers of Americans from the start of the Korean war. Most obviously this applied to many in the Republican party, particularly in the party's right wing. Senators Robert A. Taft and William Knowland were vehement in expressing their opinions: in November 1950 they were joined in the Senate by Richard M. Nixon who ascended within Congress following his controversial defeat of Helen Gahagan Douglas in the California campaign.[3] Douglas MacArthur persuaded the joint chiefs to allow him to visit Taiwan in order to assess the position personally. He visited the island on 31 July and 1 August 1950. He met Chiang Kai-shek; no detailed account of the discussion apparently exists. MacArthur maintained afterwards that he was careful in all he said and did in Taiwan but this was not the impression derived by the State Department.[4] MacArthur ignored American diplomats and gave promises of air support for Taiwan exceeding his powers. What his true opinion of Chiang was is impossible to say: in public he praised Chiang generously as an outstandingly courageous opponent of communism. MacArthur could not have been blind to the failings of the KMT which he had observed at closer range than Taft or Knowland.

The British Foreign Office watched and waited with growing anxiety. Britain's position in relation to Taiwan was anomalous. When recognition was accorded to Peking in January 1950, it had been decided to retain communication with Taiwan, the fiction being conveniently observed that Britain was dealing solely with the provincial authorities in Taiwan and not with those claiming to constitute the government of China. The British were naturally influenced by the strength of American feeling, since the United States still recognised the KMT government. The British line convinced neither the communists nor the KMT and did not weigh particularly with the Americans. The British consul in Tamsui was placed in an invidious predicament. When the Korean war began, E. T. Biggs was in post in Tamsui. He was unhappy with the trend followed in British policy in the first two months of the Korean war. He informed the Foreign Office on 20 August of his anxiety concerning Britain's role in South-East Asia and in Taiwan. He believed the United States was correct on political and moral grounds in the policy pursued. In effect it was sensible to guarantee Taiwan from a communist invasion, since a successful communist invasion would be seriously detrimental to British interests in South-East Asia:

> If the United States is involved in hostilities in the island's defence and calls for assistance, it is in my opinion desirable even at the expense of our relations with Peking that we support her. Furthermore, I consider we should make our position clear now. Any impression that Britain would stand aloof and that the Formosan issue can be utilised to divide Britain and America as suggested in some sections of the British press will only encourage a Communist attack on Formosa and must at all costs be avoided.[5]

Biggs saw the best solution being achieved in a transfer of responsibility for the defence of Taiwan to the UN. He conceded that this was probably not feasible at this juncture. Biggs explained that the KMT government was virtually bankrupt and that if the Americans acted carefully they could assume responsibility in Taiwan themselves. This could lead to a general settlement under UN auspices. The indigenous Taiwanese would support this development because of resentment at KMT rule.

British representatives in Washington endeavoured to clarify American intentions during August. Dean Rusk, Philip Jessup and Sir Oliver Franks met on 10 August. Franks explained British concern in the light of reports that KMT aircraft were attacking the mainland, that jet aircraft had reached Taiwan, and over MacArthur's visit, closely followed by a visit from Averell Harriman. Rusk and Jessup denied that American policy had changed: 'The policy of putting Formosa on ice held firm without qualification.'[6] In return they enquired about British policy: would Britain accept a UN role in Taiwan; did Britain insist on the Cairo declaration, should the communists eventually obtain Taiwan? Franks replied that he would enquire in London.[7] Ernest Bevin minuted, 'Give me the papers with summary.'[8] Bernard Burrows of the embassy in Washington enclosed a note from John Miller, *The Times* correspondent in Washington, who told him of a conversation with Harriman. The latter was extremely emotional and said that the Soviet Union and China were involved in a joint conspiracy in Korea. Miller commented to Harriman about British awareness of Indian opinion and that India should not be alienated. Harriman said bluntly that Britain would have to decide whether to support the United States or India.[9] Officials in London were worried that Harriman would speak in such an emotional way, more reminiscent of a right-wing Republican than a Democrat.[10] John Shattock remarked: 'Perhaps we had better choose India. Her policy is at least saner & more balanced.'[11]

The State Department supplied a memorandum on 17 August outlining policy. There was no ulterior design over Taiwan nor was there any inclination to become caught up in general operations against the mainland. If the communist government refrained from intervening in Korea and Taiwan conflict could be avoided. The Truman administration desired a statement explaining British policy regarding Taiwan. John Paton Davies of the Policy Planning Staff told Burrows that the clarity of Bevin's views commanded genuine respect in the State Department but officials were 'even more acutely conscious of the intractability of public opinion here on this issue and no one had been optimistic about any early change in this factor'.[12] Burrows added, 'Please do not quote this paragraph to any American.'[13] Bevin was fully alert to the perils with the necessity to remind the Truman administration of its priorities:

> My first anxiety is to try to ensure that the United States do not, with their minds on their own public opinion, commit themselves to adopting an attitude on Formosa which will not command general support and from which they will subsequently find it impossible to recede.
>
> If this can be avoided, my aim would be to try to secure a basis of agreement on Formosa which would find a considerable measure of support and perhaps even the same degree of support as has been demonstrated over Korea. Our ideas ... are by no means final and we are quite willing to listen to what others have to say.[14]

In a personal telegram to Franks, Bevin stated that he wanted the ambassador to speak candidly to Acheson to see if there was common ground from which Bevin could take matters further when he met Acheson shortly for tripartite ministerial talks; he wondered whether France should be brought in and Britain would have to ponder consultation with the Commonwealth. Bevin stressed to Franks that he wished to avert a split with Washington.[15]

Oliver Franks explained British concern when he met Jessup, Matthews and Merchant of the State Department on 28 August. Britain feared that the

United States was 'out on a limb' regarding Taiwan: the island was significant because it was the one place in East Asia where the interests of the Soviet Union and China coincided. Franks warned of the danger of KMT agitation creating additional tension between communist China and the United States.[16] Bevin circulated a memorandum on Taiwan to cabinet colleagues on 31 August as part of a broad review of British policy in East Asia. He described the complex issues involved in Taiwan and added that it was potentially extremely dangerous. The conclusion pointed cautiously towards neutralisation of the island.[17] During the cabinet discussion on 4 September Bevin stated that he was endeavouring to persuade the United States to look at Asia as a whole. He did not feel that a lengthy American occupation of Taiwan would assist stability in East Asia. It was important to secure agreement over Taiwan because of the embarrassing consequences should war occur between China and the United States over Taiwan.[18]

In the middle of September tripartite discussions between the United States, Britain and France were held. Bevin spoke strongly on the repercussions of continued American recognition of the KMT: this was causing great harm to the West and could force China further into the embrace of the Soviet Union. Acheson claimed, not very convincingly, that the American position remained as defined in his notorious National Press Club speech in January 1950. The support expressed by China for North Korea made it extremely difficult to consider amending policy.[19] He agreed that full consultation with Britain was required. The State Department viewed the political situation in Taiwan as fluid but with Chiang Kai-shek possessing the upper hand. Chiang feared the Taiwanese and General Sun Li-jen and resented American interest in alternatives to his rule. Discontent existed within the KMT party because of the nature of Chiang's dominance and because of the emerging importance of Chiang's son, Chiang Ching-kuo. The latter was given considerable freedom by his father and this led to a reign of terror. Chiang Kai-shek was following his familiar 'divide and rule' tactics towards the Americans through his relationship with MacArthur. The KMT forces were thought to be in a worse state than several months earlier.[20] Within the State Department Acheson, Rusk and Dulles favoured moving ahead with a UN commission; this was greeted with predictable coolness by Wellington Koo, Chiang's ambassador in Washington.[21] British motives for supporting a UN commission were regarded doubtfully by some in the State Department. John Allison observed, at a meeting with Acheson and Dulles on 23 October, that a feeling prevailed among the Canadian and British delegations to the UN that the task of a commission would be to arrange the transfer of Taiwan to the Peking government. Dulles said that ultimately Taiwan should be restored as part of China but the timing was unclear. A UN commission should investigate the views of the people in Taiwan and, in particular, examine the extent to which Taiwan could be autonomous. Commercial relations between Japan and Taiwan required consideration. The UN might evaluate the permanent neutralisation of Taiwan. Acheson agreed with Dulles.[22] Dulles bluntly discounted any idea of American military power being deployed in China:

Mr. Dulles said that he considered this possibility presently out of the question as he understood that it was the clear judgment of our military authorities that the United States should not engage itself on mainland operations. We had done so exceptionally in the matter of Korea and had taken some serious risks … We were not, however, willing to engage in what would virtually be a war against those controlling the Chinese mainland.[23]

Acheson, Dulles and their officials had no faith in Chiang Kai-shek but they were faced with his obstinacy and the fact that he enjoyed support in right-wing circles in the United States. Chiang's power rested on 30 years' experience of factionalism in the KMT and he was not the kind of person to move aside voluntarily. Britain wanted to ensure that the United States did not become embroiled in deeper obligations to the KMT of the sort advocated by MacArthur. Developments in Korea in the second half of November 1950 transformed the situation. Ironically Mao Tse-tung's decision to commit enormous Chinese armies in Korea did more than anything else to help his old enemy sustain his tenuous hold in Taiwan.

Events in 1951 saw British policy moving towards acceptance of Taiwan's continued separation as a reaction to Chinese military intervention in Korea. The KMT itself made an attempt to convey a more positive image for the regime than before. Part of this propagandistic campaign is illustrated in a visit to Britain in February and March 1951 from Dr Han Li-wu. Han was an old friend of Robert Scott; he had been a research student in London in the later 1920s before continuing his education in Wisconsin. Han met Scott on 1 March and put the case for the KMT as persuasively as he could. He reminded Scott that the KMT had 640,000 troops in Taiwan of which around 400,000 comprised first-class, reliable soldiers. The Peking government was encountering more problems. It would be impossible to attain full normal relations with Mao's regime; Britain would not gain from the policy pursued. Han professed confidence in the ability of the KMT to regain power in the mainland. Scott enquired as to the number of Japanese advisers in Taiwan. Han replied that some had been used in the previous few years but only a very small number remained. Han stated his aim while in London was to establish relations between the KMT and Britain on an improved foundation. He came to Britain as a personal emissary of Chiang Kai-shek. Han was not so inept as to demand a reversal in British policy over recognition but instead he requested that no action should be taken which would weaken the KMT in Taiwan. Scott responded that Chiang had never been noted for his affection towards Britain. Han observed that Chiang now appreciated that British friendship was important. Scott defended British policy regarding recognition, adding that he would be most disappointed if this approach failed. Scott conceded that recognition had not achieved what had been anticipated. The principal defect in KMT strategy was that it desired international conflict and this could produce a third world war. Scott depicted British aims in a wider sense: recognition was linked with the growth of new Asian states such as India, Pakistan and Burma. Scott asked whether Han could point to any recent examples of British policy weakening Taiwan and Han replied in the negative.[24]

Scott forwarded Han's arguments to the consul in Tamsui who was now

Jacobs-Larkcom. The latter queried the figures on military strength. The effective KMT fighting force constituted 350,000 organised into 40 divisions. The total strength, including administrative and technical personnel, did not exceed 600,000. The navy totalled about 30,000 men and the air force about 35,000 men. Jacobs-Larkcom felt that criticism of Britain in Taiwan had diminished of late, which confirmed that Chiang was attempting to improve relations.[25] Leo Lamb gave Scott his appreciation of Han's statements. Lamb was more critical of Han but admitted that he, too, doubted 'whether the Peking regime has – and for that matter ever had – a sincere desire to establish proper friendly relations with us'. He added that he had entertained the same doubt about the KMT in the past.[26]

Great excitement in Taiwan was generated by the controversy surrounding MacArthur's removal by Truman. Jacobs-Larkcom reported to Herbert Morrison on 22 May that the KMT feared that American support might diminish. However, this was counter-balanced by the arrival of the Chase mission with the promise of more support from an American military mission. Britain was again censured in the KMT press for advocating appeasement policies for commercial gain and to protect Hong Kong.[27] KMT hopes for the future in part depended on the trend in American domestic politics, particularly the question as to who would be the Republican presidential candidate in 1952. Collectively the KMT must have prayed for MacArthur or Taft or, perhaps, a 'dream ticket' comprising both of these illustrious 'Asia-firsters'. Once the rumpus over MacArthur subsided in the summer of 1951, so KMT attention focused on the impending peace conference in San Francisco at which the Pacific war would be terminated formally by those states signing the treaties. The KMT was dissatisfied with its exclusion from the conference but was hopeful, justifiably, that a bilateral treaty between the KMT regime and Japan would be signed eventually.[28]

Jacobs-Larkcom wrote to Shattock on 2 November 1951, reflecting on the experience of the KMT during the preceding six months. American support strengthened the KMT significantly in 1951; the American aim was to create a self-sufficient economic unit in Taiwan which could render the island capable of conducting its own defence. The KMT contained some progressive elements but they were hindered by the powerful reactionaries dwelling in the inner circle of Chiang's followers including the 'Whampoa clique'. Chiang's elder son by his first marriage, Chiang Ching-kuo, was one of the leading reactionaries: he occupied a sinister position through his control of the Political Department of the Ministry of National Defence and the secret police. Chiang Kai-shek would accept change if convinced of its purpose; he was no longer seen by American diplomats as the main obstacle to advancement. Land reform, the biggest weakness of KMT policy in the past, was being implemented positively.[29] J. O. Drinkall minuted that Jacobs-Larkcom understated the totalitarian features of the KMT, commenting that the United States was preoccupied with achieving a competent administration and might accept a dictatorial approach as inherent in the price to be paid.[30] J. O. Lloyd commented that Taiwan was likely to prove far more challenging to resolve: 'All this makes it look as though Formosa will be one of the toughest nuts to crack, if not the toughest, in the Korean post-armistice phase when discussions take place on the future of Korea, with which the Chinese will undoubtedly link the question of Formosa.'[31]

The change of government in Britain in October 1951 with Churchill's return to office was greeted warmly in Taiwan. However, Jacobs-Larkcom pointed out that the KMT was hoist by its own petard in that while it wanted Churchill to win the election, it could not praise the Conservative Party openly, having previously condemned it as a party of 'imperialism' and 'colonialism'.[32] On 18 December he remarked, in his report for the previous month, that the KMT regime was disappointed that Churchill and Eden continued to recognise the Peking government.[33] During 1951 the Foreign Office moved towards greater acceptance of the KMT. Jacobs-Larkcom exhibited the familiar bias of the 'man on the spot' in arguing for a more accommodating approach. In May he argued that it would not be in Britain's interest for Taiwan to pass under Peking's control. Neither did the people of Taiwan wish to experience communist rule.[34] In partial acceptance of the latter point, G. G. Buzzard noted that when Herbert Morrison spoke in the House of Commons on 11 May, he had stated, in replying to a supplementary question, that the wishes of the Taiwanese people must be considered when a settlement of Chinese issues was finally attained.[35] On 30 May N. C. C. Trench commented that Britain could not recognise the KMT again as the government of China but it could recognise the KMT regime as the *de facto* government of Taiwan.[36] Trench's minute was provoked by a letter from Jacobs-Larkcom to Robert Scott conveying the good wishes of Dr George Yeh, the KMT foreign minister, with Yeh's regrets that a recent student demonstration in Tamsui resulted in the pulling-down of the Union Jack. Jacobs-Larkcom expounded his views more fully on 25 June. He argued that Britain should understand that the KMT would continue to occupy Taiwan and that existing policy antagonised Chiang Kai-shek's administration and, to some extent, the United States. Jacobs-Larkcom favoured a new policy of treating the KMT more amicably without announcing a formal change in approach. The dignity of the KMT should be respected and minor insults avoided. British views on Taiwan in the context of the impending Japanese peace treaty offended the KMT.[37] Robert Scott refuted his comments about worsening Anglo-American relations. The Japanese peace treaty had to be dealt with in the manner adopted owing to British recognition of the Peking government. Trade policy regarding Taiwan had been modified. Originally, in August 1950, it had been decided to place Taiwan on the same basis as the mainland. This had been changed so that the additional controls, announced on 18 June, would not be enforced against Taiwan. Current policy was that export to Taiwan of goods on the Munitions Lists and List I (goods of primary strategic significance) would still be prohibited, as would oil; supplies of rubber and other goods of secondary importance to the war effort would be rationed. Scott added that information obtained in Hong Kong indicated that some smuggling in items such as petrol and rubber was occurring between Taiwan and the mainland. Scott reminded Jacobs-Larkcom of past experience in dealing with the KMT: absence from the mainland did not make the British heart grow fonder.[38] The consul replied that there were some good elements in the regime but he did not like Chiang Kai-shek's dominance; smuggling was not significant.[39]

In December 1951 diplomatic relations resumed formally between the KMT regime and Japan after a period of more than 14 years. Japan established an agency in Taipei which was officially non-political, pending the end of the allied occupation, but this was clearly the prelude to resumption of full diplomatic relations. As 1951 drew to a close, Chiang repeated his ritualistic undertaking to reconquer the mainland. The KMT press criticised Britain for failing to defeat the insurgency in Malaya.[40] In his report for March 1952 Jacobs-Larkcom confirmed that American policy was one of 'acceptance of long-term responsibility for the economic rehabilitation of Formosa and its military defence'.[41] This was shown in increased aid, growing military and naval commitments, statements made by the American naval secretary on a recent visit, and transfer of responsibility for the defence of Taiwan from General Ridgway to Admiral Radford: this signified separating Taiwan from Korea. J. K. Drinkall minuted that the news was important and 'potentially very dangerous'.[42] On 28 April 1952 the KMT government signed a peace treaty with Japan as the latter regained sovereignty. This satisfied the KMT and compensated for exclusion from the San Francisco conference in September 1951. Full relations resumed in August 1952 following ratification of the treaty. Jacobs-Larkcom viewed the restoration of relations as desirable on overcoming various problems facing Taiwan.[43] Admiral Radford visited Taiwan in May 1952 for four days. He spoke favourably of the calibre of KMT forces, adding that he could not discuss political aspects. The size of the American military mission in Taiwan reached 550, all ranks.[44] Equipment included more artillery but not, so far as was known, tanks or aircraft.

In his report for June 1952 Jacobs-Larkcom commented explicitly on KMT views towards Britain. These had mellowed since Churchill's return to office and friction had decreased during 1952. As evidence he cited diminishing interference with shipping; a reduction in hostile propaganda in the press; and better relations between British subjects and senior Chinese officials. He added that anti-British feelings remained strong among the rank and file of KMT mainlanders.[45] Japanese military advice to the KMT regime was likely to diminish given the growing American role. General Nemoto Hiroshi, formerly commander of the Japanese army in north China, departed for Tokyo on 25 June. Nemoto was the most senior of Japanese personnel and had worked in the Advanced Combined Service Training College in Taipei.[46] In the wider political and economic spheres developing Japanese interest in Taiwan was visible in August 1952. Chiang Kai-shek cultivated Japan partly through fear of renewed Japanese might in future and partly as a reinsurance policy in the event of the United States changing direction.[47] Japan appointed a veteran diplomat, Yoshizawa Kenkichi, then 78 years of age, as its first ambassador. The size of the American military group attained a figure of almost 700 in September 1952.[48] On the negative side in KMT–British relations, attacks on British ships developed again in October 1952. It appeared that these represented deliberate KMT policy rather than sporadic guerrilla forays. However, vessels operated by the prestigious British firms, Jardine, Matheson and Butterfield and Swire, had not been attacked, although they traded with the mainland.[49] Admiral Radford paid a further visit to Taiwan for six days in October. He met Chiang twice. Radford indicated that he wished to assess the economic potential of Taiwan and to improve relations between his command and the military mission.[50]

In the spring and summer of 1952 considerable debate occurred in the Foreign Office on the future relationship including the possibility of extending diplomatic relations. This originated in the KMT's ardent desire to secure recognition. The indefatigable Dr Han Li-wu approached the Conservative MP, Julian Amery, making it clear that he wished to meet a member of the government before leaving London. Amery contacted Robert Scott on 4 February. Han repeated a request made to Scott in their earlier discussion that arrangements should be made for creating a system for transmitting messages from the KMT government to the British government. Scott told Amery that he had informed Han previously that this was not feasible and that avenues already existed informally whereby views could be transmitted via the consulate in Tamsui. Scott told Amery that it would not be possible to arrange a formal meeting between Han and a minister but an informal 'casual exchange' might be arranged.[51] The minister of state in the Foreign Office, Selwyn Lloyd, agreed, unenthusiastically, to meet Han at a party arranged by Amery on 5 February. Han came straight to the point and enquired whether Britain could recognise Chiang's government as the government of Taiwan. Lloyd referred to past official statements and criticised the presence of KMT troops in Burma, which was dangerous in itself and complicated Britain's relations with Burma and India.[52] Han sent a letter to the *Daily Telegraph* at the end of February in which he deplored lack of understanding for Taiwan; in particular, he castigated a reference by Attlee to Taiwan, in a recent political broadcast. The former prime minister described Chiang's regime as 'corrupt and reactionary'.[53] J. K. Drinkall minuted that it was rather too much to stomach Han's reference to Chiang as a 'staunch ally & friend of Britain'.[54] Jacobs-Larkcom reflected on Han's visit and on the response in London. He wrote to Charles Johnston on 14 March assessing the 'pros and cons' of amending policy over Taiwan. There were significant factors on both sides of the argument. In favour of a switch in policy were the likely benefits economically and the closer alignment with the United States. Clearly he favoured a change in policy; the Foreign Office did not.[55] Drinkall doubted whether the gains would be significant. Political differences could be pursued with the Americans. As for trade, Britain could not send military equipment to Taiwan; rubber was shipped in limited quantities. A relaxation in policy concerning export of strategic goods had been approved recently.[56] Johnston wrote to Jacobs-Larkcom on 7 May stating that the outcome of the review in the Office was that the arguments for not recognising Chiang's regime were perceived to be more cogent. The legal position was complex and meant that Britain could not recognise Chiang's administration as the *de jure* government of Taiwan; recognition could only be accorded to the KMT regime as the *de facto* government of Taiwan but this would not be very different to the existing policy of recognising the provincial government as the *de facto* government of Taiwan.[57]

Jacobs-Larkcom responded that he favoured *de facto* recognition. There was an important distinction between the central and provincial government: the former handled external and internal policy. Britain could not communicate with the real policy-makers. The KMT authorities would welcome *de facto* recognition. He understood the delicacy of relations with Peking when British subjects were effectively held as hostages.[58] Johnston replied that it was not practicable to change policy; if China committed a new act of aggression the position might be different.[59] Jacobs-Larkcom regarded the morale and capabilities of the KMT forces as having improved markedly but an invasion of the mainland was not feasible. The aim of the American military mission was to ensure that the island could be defended against invasion. He talked to the American minister, Karl Rankin, who said that the KMT forces were much better than in 1949 and that American public opinion was better disposed towards them.[60] The Foreign Office was again sceptical. According to information provided by the Americans in strict confidence, the strength of KMT forces comprised: ground-force, 375,000; air forces, 68,000 (with 111 piston fighters and 31 piston light bombers); naval forces, 60 small vessels, 7 destroyer escorts. This compared with a Chinese communist army of over three million with an additional militia of six million and an air force of over 1,000 jet fighters. The basic problem for the KMT remained motivation and firm commitment. If the communists invaded, the KMT would require American help.[61] J. M. Addis commented that morale was the key: no doubt the KMT had improved in Taiwan but it was hard to believe that the KMT forces could equal the resolution of communist troops.[62]

The Foreign Office requested the views of intelligence chiefs regarding KMT prowess (or lack of it). Major-General A. C. Shortt, the Director of Military Intelligence (DMI), commented on 28 November that one or two recent episodes, such as a raid on an island off the coast had stimulated rethinking but fundamentally the DMI believed that KMT forces still suffered from inept leadership. The KMT could launch an invasion of the mainland only with Western help.[63] Air Vice-Marshal F. J. Fressanges commented on air strength. The air force totalled 67,000 men with approximately 350 front line aircraft comprising fighter, close support reconnaissance and bomber types; the United States had recently supplied 24 additional fighters. It was thought that jet aircraft would be delivered subsequently. The KMT air force possessed early warning radar and a competent air defence system. Morale in the air force seemed to be good. If equipped with jet aircraft, the air force should prove as proficient, squadron for squadron, as the communist air force.[64] Rear-Admiral Sir A. Buzzard was more critical: KMT forces could not possibly succeed in an invasion of the mainland without powerful American support. KMT troops might desert if they landed. The KMT navy was capable of implementing small-scale amphibious operations against the mainland but it was improbable that they could do more.[65]

The American presidential campaign unfolded in the course of 1952 provoking speculation as to how rival candidates would react. Senator Robert A. Taft, the principal right-wing contender for the Republican nomination, advocated arming KMT troops and allowing them to invade the mainland, according to a statement made in February 1952.[66] John Foster Dulles was not a candidate but was determined to be secretary of state if the Republicans won. Therefore, he had to appear as all things to all men and women and he produced an ambiguous statement, leading some to deduce that he was not far removed from Taft's stance. Governor Earl Warren of California, the leading liberal

Republican contender for the nomination, opposed Taft's suggestion and regarded it as inherently dangerous; Senator Wayne Morse agreed with Warren.[67] General Eisenhower was a Europe-firster but had to pay heed to Republicans of a different outlook.[68] American policy under Truman was already moving towards a much greater commitment to support for Taiwan. Eisenhower favoured a tougher policy with China as part of his strategy for ending the Korean war within a relatively short time. Governor Adlai Stevenson of Illinois, the Democratic candidate, sought to establish a middle position, advocating domestic reform and a firm foreign policy of combating communism.[69] Eisenhower's smashing victory in November 1952 was welcomed in Taiwan. Although Chiang would have preferred a right-wing Republican as president, Eisenhower was preferable to Stevenson and the new vice-president, Richard Nixon of California, was noted for his hardline views on the Korean war.[70]

At the end of 1952 an increase in KMT attacks on communist-held islands raised anxiety over an escalation in tension. Anthony Eden minuted on 26 December, '... I don't like this at all' and added that Churchill should be notified before his forthcoming visit to Washington.[71] In a later minute Eden wrote that it was probably best that the matter not be raised by Churchill with the president-elect but that Churchill should be warned not to assent to escalation.[72] Addis commented on 16 January 1953 that accounts of Churchill's discussions in New York did not preclude raising again with the State Department the worrying situation existing in the Taiwan Strait.[73] Rumours circulated in January that Eisenhower intended lifting Truman's ban on KMT raids directly against the mainland. British anxiety was conveyed promptly to the State Department.[74] Advance notice was given on 30 January that Eisenhower would announce on 2 February, in his State of the Union message, that the 7th Fleet would no longer be employed as a shield for the mainland of China. The president did not regard this as aggressive in intent but as reflecting the changes which had occurred since Truman's statement of 27 June 1950.[75] Eden told the embassy in Washington to convey his alarm together with a warning of possible reactions in the UN. In Eden's view, it would not contribute towards settling the Korean conflict. The prime minister was informed and he phoned Charles Johnston to say that care must be exercised so as not to appear critical of a State of the Union message. The wording of the telegram was amended without Eden's knowledge, since he was asleep at the time.[76] The embassy reported that Eisenhower's message was well received; the right wing had desired something of a more sensational nature but moderates were satisfied that the president had gone no further in 'taking off the wraps'.[77]

Aneurin Bevan, the leader of the left wing of the Labour Party, speaking in Birkenhead, emphasised his profound doubts over Eisenhower's decision and underlined his suspicion of Dulles, the secretary of state.[78] Robert Scott sensibly recommended acquiescing in Eisenhower's statement and ensuring it was applied with minimal friction. Although Chiang Kai-shek claimed that it was the first major step in his triumphant return to the mainland, Scott discounted the likelihood of Eisenhower supporting Chiang in such an enterprise.[79] E. T. Biggs, now working in the Foreign Office, believed that developments in Korea would probably be more dangerous than Taiwan but he argued for obtaining assurances from Washington that the United States would not take part in KMT operations aimed at the mainland.[80] In addition, Britain must be consulted properly if the Americans contemplated larger-scale operations against the mainland. Meanwhile, Bevan, who was by then touring India, assailed American policy over Taiwan and Korea: if the Eisenhower administration wanted to restore Chiang Kai-shek to power, it would cause a third world war.[81] British diplomats in the American Midwest reported that there was strong resentment at British criticism over Taiwan and due care should be exercised.[82] Eden met Dulles on 6 February and conveyed the concern of the British chiefs of staff over the repercussions for Hong Kong of Eisenhower's message. He requested Dulles to discourage the KMT regime from interfering with British shipping. Dulles assured him that military aid to Taiwan would not extend beyond that agreed by the Truman administration.[83]

Anxiety resulted from KMT raids grew in the summer of 1953 and worried the government because of fears at the possible impact on the delicate situation in Korea where Syngman Rhee was behaving most obstinately over an armistice.[84] Fortunately an armistice agreement was signed on 27 July while the KMT forces stepped up raids on communist-held islands. A raid on Tungshan, north of Swatow, culminated in a serious reverse for the KMT with casualties of approximately 3,000, according to an American naval source. Lord Reading, the minister of state, minuted that it was probably as well that the raid failed. The information placed before Reading indicated that 'Western Enterprises' had helped in planning the raid. This alluded to covert American operations to assist the KMT. The American journalist, Joseph Alsop, discussed 'Western Enterprises Incorporated' in an article in the *New York Herald Tribune* published on 29 October. He amusingly described it as 'the most uncovered covert organization in the world with its own PX Commissary, two social clubs, and a housing development known as "Spook Center"'.[85] Robert Scott, writing from Washington to the acting foreign secretary, the Marquess of Salisbury, discussed the existence of a secret, informal understanding between the United States and the KMT government. This was confirmed in a press report from Marguerite Higgins, published in the *New York Herald Tribune* on 17 August. This showed that the KMT regime had agreed not to implement large-scale military operations against communist forces without consulting the American military authorities beforehand.[86] Jacobs-Larkcom advocated, in September 1953, that the United States and Britain should cooperate to secure joint recognition of communist China and Taiwan as separate states. He also proposed that the consulate in Tamsui should be raised in status to a consulate-general. Colin Crowe identified the weakness in Jacobs-Larkcom's strategy: the rival regimes opposed a two-state solution on the grounds that each constituted the official government of China. If anything, the KMT was more insistent than the communists because it constituted the *raison d'être* for the KMT regime.[87]

One of the intriguing minor controversies in Britain's relations with China and the United States concerned the fate of 71 aircraft impounded in Hong Kong at the beginning of 1950 while an acrimonious dispute over ownership proceeded between the Chinese communist government and American interests closely involved with the KMT, behind which stood the American government. American pressure groups working with the China Lobby played a significant part in escalating tension. This is illustrated in material found in the papers of Claire Chennault. The aircraft had been owned by the KMT government via a company owned by it: this transferred ownership to an American-owned company which represented cooperation between right-wing American interests, American intelligence and the KMT. The British authorities in Hong Kong wanted the aircraft removed from the colony before Britain recognised the communist government: this was not done, apparently for commercial reasons but also, very probably, because of a wish to embroil Britain and China in an argument over the issue. The Peking government demanded that the planes be handed to them: this was vehemently resisted by the Civil Air Transport Corporation. The chief justice in Hong Kong enquired as to the degree of recognition accorded by Britain to the two Chinese regimes in the period between 10 October 1949 and 5 January 1950. This was an embarrassing question which the Foreign Office preferred to evade if possible.[88] Sir E. Beckett, legal adviser to the Foreign Office, disliked evasion and urged a positive response that Britain recognised the communist regime as the *de facto* government in those parts of China controlled by it. The American embassy in London emphasised its desire for the Hong Kong court to be informed that *de facto* recognition had not been accorded. John Shattock commented that the broader implications must be appreciated: 'It is particularly important at this juncture, when the question of Marshall Aid is before Congress, to avoid any ... events of this kind.'[89]

The chief justice in Hong Kong gave judgment on 23 February 1950 and decided that the planes were owned by the communist government.[90] In March the governor of Hong Kong was notified that Ernest Bevin deemed the communist government to be the *de facto* government of those areas of China which it controlled after 1 October 1949.[91] Meanwhile the State Department had conveyed its view that at the time of the contract signed between the KMT government and Chennault and Willauer (representing the new owners of the aircraft) that Britain recognised the KMT as the government of China: the date referred to was in November 1949.[92] Britain found itself caught between attempting to foster better relations with Peking and offending the United States which could have serious consequences. The American embassy warned that President Truman was personally observing developments closely.[93] The best hope in the near future appeared to lie in the usual delays inherent in legal processes.

Truman and Acheson were experiencing severe criticism from many Republicans and some Democrats over the 'loss' of China and could not be seen as acting weakly. Claire Chennault played a key role in heightening pressure and in orchestrating publicity in the United States. He had long admired China and was to the fore in urging aid for China during the war against Japan from 1937. He became a fervent admirer of Chiang Kai-shek and was an arch-rival of 'Vinegar Joe' Stilwell whose views of Chiang (the 'Peanut') were diametrically opposed to those of Chennault. Chennault's private papers reveal the range of his activities and pursuit of zealous propaganda. In June and July 1949 he circulated a statement of his opinions to members of Congress in both parties. Letters of support arrived from Senators John Sparkman (Democrat, Alabama), Walter

F. George (Democrat, Georgia), J. William Fulbright (Democrat, Arkansas), Paul H. Douglas (Democrat, Illinois) and from Congressman John F. Kennedy (Democrat, Massachusetts).[94] Rather more circumspect replies came from Senators Hubert H. Humphrey (Democrat-Labour, Minnesota), Wayne Morse (Republican, Oregon) and Lyndon B. Johnson (Democrat, Texas).[95] Herbert Hoover, the former president, wrote to Senator William F. Knowland (Republican, California) at the end of 1949 stating that the American government must continue to support Chiang Kai-shek and under no circumstances recognise the Peking government.[96] Chennault worked closely with Knowland, one of the most outspoken advocates of support for KMT China and a man of considerable ambition within the Republican party: he became known as the 'Senator for Formosa'. Chennault wrote to him in February 1950 urging the appointment of a supreme commander to coordinate economic, political and military resistance to communism throughout the Far East: 'You also realize that there can be only one choice for this vital position and that is the man who has prominently qualified himself for this post by his outstanding record of loyal patriotic service and achievement since December 7, 1941 – MacArthur.'[97] No one would have concurred more than Douglas MacArthur. Chennault castigated the State Department's handling of China as 'a tragic history of incompetence, inconsistency, failure to protect the interests of the United States and its citizens and, worst of all, the betrayal of a trusting ally and hundreds of millions of people who looked to us for friendly aid and advice'.[98]

Chennault circulated letters addressed to 'My Dear Fellow American' attacking the British response to the aircraft controversy: 'The Hongkong British are protecting their own property in Shanghai and elsewhere in China, by paying "squeeze" to Chinese Communists out of American property.'[99] He believed that maximum pressure should be brought to bear on the British government. The State Department continued to make representations in London and Chennault's company pursued legal action, appealing against the decision of the Hong Kong court. The appeal, announced on 13 May 1950, upheld the chief justice's decision of 23 February in refusing to appoint a receiver for the assets of the two Chinese companies from which Chennault's company acquired the planes. As a result of American representations, an Order in Council, issued in London on 11 May, prepared the way for an appeal to be made to the Privy Council and instructed that the aircraft should remain in Hong Kong for the time being. Civil Air Transport Inc.'s legal counsel took steps to submit an appeal to the Privy Council.[100] The legal processes proved fully as protracted as anticipated. Despite Chennault's castigation of the State Department, he warmly commended their persistent representations to the Foreign Office which led to the issuing of the Order in Council; this was essential because without it, the Hong Kong authorities' inclination to defer to Peking might have prevailed. In a letter written in August 1952 Chennault applauded the 'tenacious interest and assistance' of Arthur Ringwalt and of the State Department. He also praised Karl Rankin, Walter McConaughay and Ralph Hunt in acting effectively in Hong Kong to prevent planes and equipment reaching 'Red China'. Further praise was lavished on Adrian Fisher, Livingston Merchant, Robert Barnett and Horace Aurine of the State Department.[101] It must have been one of the strangest communications received by Dean Acheson during his term of office.

The culmination to the controversy occurred in the summer of 1952 when the long awaited Privy Council hearing took place. Hartley Shawcross, the former attorney-general in the Labour government, acted on behalf of Chennault's company; the latter's chief legal representative was a prominent Washington lawyer, Thomas Corcoran. The Privy Council ruled that the planes belonged to Chennault's company and thus vindicated the prolonged struggle to determine their fate. Corcoran wrote to Chief Justice Fred M. Vinson that the decision was 'the first Cold War victory in the Far East'. He expressed warm appreciation for Vinson's keen interest which had 'contributed greatly to the result'.[102] He told Vinson that 'our people' desperately wished the air fleet to be removed intact from Hong Kong and overhauled for use by the French in Indo-China. Forty planes were transferred from Hong Kong to California in October 1952. A local judgment for the remaining 32 aircraft was made in the Hong Kong court in October, subject to a six-week delay, pending an appeal by the Peking government.[103] Chennault was immensely encouraged by his success and proceeded to draft memoranda proposing schemes for assisting Chiang Kai-shek's return to the mainland.[104] He exchanged letters with Senator Joseph McCarthy (Republican, Wisconsin) to whose reelection campaign he contributed.[105] McCarthy enthused at the thought of Chiang reconquering the mainland. Neither Chennault nor McCarthy could accept that the likelihood of Chiang's return could be seen positively only in the realms of fantasy.

What were the prospects for Anglo-Chinese relations as the Korean war ended in July 1953? On the commercial side the Churchill government wished to see trade flourish so as to assist the export drive and to help, in the longer term, in establishing relations on a more stable basis. However, relations with the United States overshadowed those with China. The Eisenhower administration was more committed to support for the KMT in Taiwan than its predecessor had been. Eisenhower and Dulles favoured a firm line in dealing with China. Vice-President Nixon and Senators Taft and Knowland looked to much tougher action. Churchill wished to modify the most dangerous manifestations of the Cold War in the summer of 1953 but he was preoccupied with the Soviet Union rather than China. Churchill was not very interested in China and derived no encouragement from Mao Tse-tung. Britain moved towards wider acceptance of Taiwan not with enthusiasm but through a feeling of inevitability. Communist China could not be allowed to take over Taiwan and the KMT was gradually restoring its fortunes on the island, if with heavy dependence on the United States. Appreciable problems could be discerned in future as a result of the coalescence of the American desire to retaliate against 'Red China', Chiang's wish for a more assertive policy (provided the Americans backed him), and the complications arising from the accident of occupation of the numerous small islands off the Chinese coast. As for the Chinese communists, they wished to encourage trade in the longer term and did not want to rely excessively on the Soviet Union. But they saw Britain as fulfilling American demands, a process likely to be continued given Britain's declining power. Therefore, the signs were not encouraging for any substantial improvement in Sino-British relations in the short to medium term.

Notes

1 See cabinet minutes, 27 June, CM39(50)4, Cab 128/17, 3 July, CM42(50)3, 6 July, CM43(50)2, Cab 128/18, all in 1950.

2 See Callum MacDonald, *Korea: The War before Vietnam* (London: Macmillan, 1986), pp. 25–6, 43–7, 52.

3 See Stephen Ambrose, *Nixon: The Education of a Politician, 1913–1962*, vol. I (London: Simon and Schuster, 1987), pp. 209–23. Ambrose shows the strength of Nixon's hard-line views on China and Korea where Nixon was an advocate of all-out victory. The nature of Nixon's campaign against Helen Gahagan Douglas is assessed clearly. The papers of Senator Robert A. Taft, Sr, held in the Library of Congress, Washington D.C., include a considerable quantity of correspondence relating to foreign issues, especially in Asia, and underline the degree of Taft's commitment to an 'Asia First' policy.

4 See MacArthur to Department of Army, 7 August 1950, RG9, box 43, JCS outgoing file, MacArthur papers, MacArthur Memorial, Norfolk, Virginia. For the views of the American representative in Taiwan, see Strong to Acheson, 3 August 1950, selected records relating to the Korean war, box 6, folder 1, Truman papers, Harry S. Truman Library, Independence, Missouri.

5 Tamsui to FO, 20 August 1950, FO 371/83298/58G.

6 Washington to FO, 10 August 1950, FO 371/83320/19.

7 *Ibid.*

8 Minute by Bevin, no date, *ibid.*

9 Letter from Burrows to R. H. Scott, 12 August 1950, FO 371/83320/23.

10 Minutes by C. F. Crowe, 15 August, F. S. Tomlinson, 18 August, K. M. Anderson, 28 August 1950, *ibid.*

11 Minute by Shattock, no date, *ibid.*

12 Letter from Burroughs to Shattock, 17 August 1950, FO 371/83320/26.

13 *Ibid.*

14 FO to Washington, 25 August 1950, *ibid.*

15 Personal telegram, Bevin to Franks, 25 August 1950, *ibid.*

16 *FRUS 1950*, vol. VI, p. 464, memorandum by Merchant, 28 August 1950.

17 Cabinet memorandum by Bevin, 31 August 1950, CP(50)194, Cab 129/41.

18 Cabinet minutes, 4 September 1950, 55(50)4, Cab 128/18.

19 *FRUS 1950*, vol. III, pp. 1224–5, US Delegation minutes, 4th meeting, 14 September 1950.

20 *FRUS 1950*, vol. VI, pp. 485–6, memorandum by Strong, 6 September 1950.

21 *Ibid.*, p. 512, memorandum by Clubb, 19 September 1950.

22 *Ibid.*, pp. 535–6, memorandum by Allison, 23 October 1950.

23 *Ibid.*, p. 543, memorandum by Dulles, 27 October 1950.

24 Minute by R. H. Scott, 2 March 1951, FO 371/92208/20/G.

25 Letter from Jacobs-Larkcom to Scott, 12 April 1951, FO 371/92208/36/G.

26 Letter from Lamb to Scott, 15 May 1951, FO 371/92209/49/G.

27 Despatch from Jacobs-Larkcom to Morrison, 22 May 1951, FO 371/92209/44.

28 Despatch from Jacobs-Larkcom to Morrison, summary of events for September 1951, 15 October 1951, FO 371/92210/84.

29 Letter from Jacobs-Larkcom to Shattock, 2 November 1951, FO 371/92210/88.

30 Minute by Drinkall, 16 November 1951, *ibid.*

31 Minute by Lloyd, 4 December 1951, *ibid.*

32 Despatch from Jacobs-Larkcom to Morrison, 15 October 1951, FO 371/92210/84.

33 Despatch from Jacobs-Larkcom to Eden, 18 December 1951, FO 371/92210/101.

34 Letter from Jacobs-Larkcom to Scott, 3 May 1951, FO 371/92225/23.

35 Minute by Buzzard, 29 May 1951, *ibid.*

36 Minute by Trench, 30 May 1951, on letter from Jacobs-Larkcom to Scott, 18 May 1951, FO 371/92225/24.

37 Letter from Jacobs-Larkcom to Scott, 25 June 1951, FO 371/92226/26.

38 Letter from Scott to Jacobs-Larkcom, 3 August 1951, *ibid.*

39 Letter from Jacobs-Larkcom to Shattock, 22 August 1951, FO 371/92226/31.

40 Despatch from Jacobs-Larkcom to Eden, summary of events for December 1951, 22 January 1952, FO 371/92239/10.
41 Jacobs-Larkcom to Eden, summary of events for March 1952, 16 April 1952, FO 371/99240/34.
42 Minute by Drinkall, 29 April 1952, *ibid.*
43 Despatch from Jacobs-Larkcom to Eden, report for April 1952, 14 May 1952, FO 371/99240/42A.
44 Despatch from Jacobs-Larkcom to Eden, summary of events for May 1952, 17 June 1952, FO 371/99240/44.
45 Despatch from Jacobs-Larkcom to Eden, summary of events for June 1952, 16 July 1952, FO 371/99240/47.
46 *Ibid.*
47 Despatch from Jacobs-Larkcom to Eden, summary of events for August 1952, 3 September 1952, FO 371/99240/54.
48 Despatch from Jacobs-Larkcom to Eden, summary of events for September 1952, 7 October 1952, FO 371/99241/61.
49 Despatch from Jacobs-Larkcom to Eden, summary of events for September 1952, 29 October 1952, FO 371/99241/67.
50 Despatch from Jacobs-Larkcom to Eden, summary of events for October 1952, 25 November 1952, FO 371/99241/72.
51 Minute by Scott, 4 February 1952, FO 371/99259/7.
52 Minute by Lloyd, 8 February 1952, and letter from C.H. Johnston to Jacobs-Larkcom, 25 February 1952, FO 371/99259/8 and 7.
53 *Daily Telegraph*, 29 February 1952, enclosed in FO 371/99259/9.
54 Minute by Drinkall, 4 March 1952, *ibid.*
55 Minutes by Drinkall, 3 and 30 April, Oakeshott, 8 April, and Lloyd, 10 April 1952; also minute by Fitzmaurice, 2 May 1952, *ibid.*
56 Minute by Drinkall, 3 April 1952, *ibid.*
57 Letter from Johnston to Jacobs-Larkcom, 7 May 1952, *ibid.*
58 Letter from Jacobs-Larkcom to Johnston, 21 May 1952, FO 371/99259/14.
59 Letter from Johnston to Jacobs-Larkcom, 18 June 1952, *ibid.*
60 Letter from Jacobs-Larkcom to Scott, 8 October 1952, FO 371/99259/21/G.
61 Minute by G. M. Toplas, 31 October 1952, *ibid.*
62 Minute by J. M. Addis, 31 October 1952, *ibid.*
63 Letter from Shortt to D. P. Reilly, 28 November 1952, FO 371/99259/23/G.
64 Letter from Fressanges to Reilly, 29 November 1952, FO 371/99259/25G.
65 Letter from Buzzard to Reilly, 4 December 1952, FO 371/99259/28G.
66 Washington to FO, 20 February 1952, FO 371/99268/13.
67 *Ibid.*
68 For further discussion of divisions and reactions in the Republican party, see Stephen Ambrose, *Eisenhower*, vol. I, *The Soldier, 1890–1952* (London: Allen and Unwin, 1983), pp. 522–69, and Ambrose, *Nixon*, vol. I, pp. 230–314.
69 Ambrose, *Nixon*, vol. I, pp. 296–9.
70 *Ibid.*, pp. 222, 269.
71 Minute by Eden, 26 December 1952, FO 371/105196/4/G.
72 Minute by Eden, no date, *ibid.*
73 Minute by Addis, 16 January 1953, *ibid.*
74 Washington to FO, 28 January 1953, FO 371/105196/5.
75 Washington to FO, 30 January 1953, FO 371/105196/6.
76 FO to Washington, 21 January 1953, with minute by Johnston, 31 January 1953, FO 371/105196/9.
77 Washington to FO, 3 February 1953, FO 371/105196/13.
78 *Manchester Guardian*, 2 February 1953, enclosed in FO 371/105196/30.
79 Minute by Scott, 4 February 1953, FO 371/105196/27.
80 Minute by Biggs, 31 January 1953, *ibid.*
81 High Commission, New Delhi, to Commonwealth Relations Office, 12 February 1953, FO 371/105197/51.

82 Letter from Sir Christopher Steel to Scott, 13 February 1953, enclosed in letter from Berkeley Gage to Steel, 20 February 1953, FO 371/105197/61.

83 Letter from Addis to Major-General W. H. A. Bishop (Commonwealth Relations Office), 2 March 1953, FO 371/105197/66. The Foreign Office was providing information for the Australian prime minister, Robert Menzies.

84 Minute by P. Wilkinson, 21 July 1953, FO 371/105198/95.

85 Hong Kong to Admiralty, for DNI, 4 August 1953, communicated by Admiralty to FO, FO 371/105198/105. See also *New York Herald Tribune*, 29 October 1953, enclosed in FO 371/105203/72.

86 Despatch from Scott to Lord Salisbury, 26 August 1953, FO 371/105198/112.

87 Letter from Jacobs-Larkcom to Shattock, 5 September 1953, FO 371/105203/64, with minutes by Wilkinson, 1 October, Biggs, 2 October, and Crowe, 4 October 1953. Biggs was more sympathetic to the proposed upgrading but as he had recently occupied the post of consul in Tamsui, this was scarcely surprising.

88 FO minutes, February 1950, FO 371/83302/7.

89 Minute by Shattock, 23 February 1950, FO 371/83302/7.

90 Governor of Hong Kong to CO, 23 February 1950, *ibid.*

91 CO to Hong Kong, 15 March 1950, *ibid.*

92 Letter from Ringwalt (US embassy, London) to Shattock, 22 February 1950, FO 371/83302/11.

93 Minute by Montagu-Pollock, 22 February 1950, FO 371/83302/12.

94 Letters from Sparkman to Chennault, 16 June 1949, George to Chennault, 23 June 1949, Fulbright to Chennault, 29 July 1949, Kennedy to Chennault, 20 June 1949, folder, correspondence with Congress, box 10, Chennault papers, Hoover Institution, Stanford, California. Kennedy wrote a PS in his own hand: 'You have certainly done an excellent job on your country's behalf.'

95 Letters from Humphrey to Chennault, 5 July 1949, Morse to Chennault, 8 July 1949, Johnson to Chennault, 28 July 1949, *ibid.*

96 Copy of letter from Hoover to Knowland, 31 December 1949, folder, correspondence with Knowland, box 10, Chennault papers, Hoover Institution.

97 Letter from Chennault to Knowland, 22 February 1950, *ibid.*

98 *Ibid.*

99 Circular letter, no date, enclosing article from *Time*, 6 March 1950, folder, Civil Air Transport Inc., box 11, Chennault papers, Hoover Institution.

100 Letter from McFall to Congressman Compton I. White, 26 May 1950, folder, Civil Air Transport Inc., box 11, Chennault papers.

101 Letter from Chennault to Acheson, 2 August 1952, folder, Civil Air Transport Inc., box 11, Chennault papers.

102 Letter from Corcoran to Vinson, 1 August 1952, *ibid.*

103 Letter from Corcoran to Senator Richard B. Russell (Democrat, Georgia), 8 October 1952, folder, Civil Air Transport Inc., 1952, box 11, Chennault papers.

104 Memorandum by Chennault, 22 November 1952, folder, proposed invasion of China, box 11, Chennault papers.

105 Letter from McCarthy to Chennault, 2 December 1952, *ibid.*

PART III

KOREA

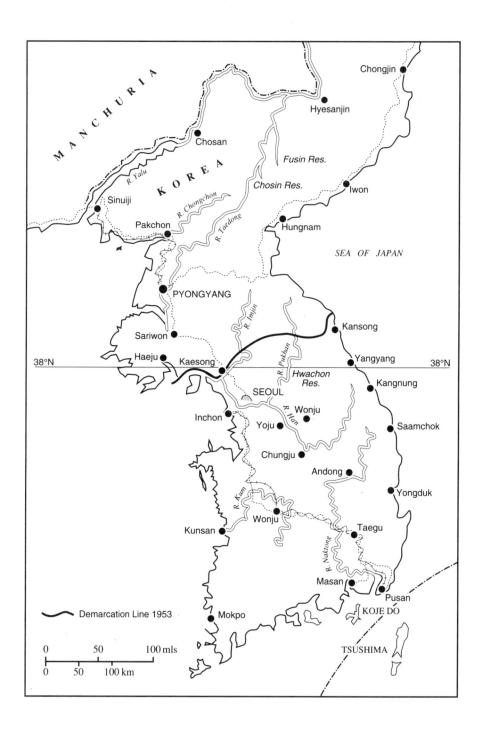

Map 3 **Korea**

9

BRITAIN AND THE EMERGENCE OF TWO KOREAS, 1945 TO JUNE 1950

Korea did not attract British political or economic interest to any significant extent in the second half of the nineteenth century: China and Japan were the principal recipients of British attention in East Asia. A treaty was concluded between representatives of the Korean monarch and Queen Victoria in 1883 but this was not followed by an intense commercial drive from Britain.[1] Concern over the future of Korea was prompted by rivalry between China, Japan and Tsarist Russia for dominance in the peninsula between the early 1880s and 1905. British policy in East Asia was directed particularly at preventing an expansion of Russian power, for this was associated with the whole question of a Russian threat to British interests in China and India. In this context Japan was perceived as assisting British aims and relations between London and Tokyo warmed accordingly. The closer relationship was symbolised in the signing of the Anglo-Japanese commercial treaty in 1894, providing for the relinquishment of extraterritoriality in Japan, and, more dramatically, by the signature of the first Anglo-Japanese alliance in 1902. The alliance quickly established itself as a cornerstone of British global strategy, a feature which endured until the end of the Great War in November 1918.[2] Part of the price Britain paid was acquiescence in Japanese control of Korea, which was implemented *de facto* in 1905, following the defeat of Russia in the war of 1904–5, and *de jure* in 1910 with Japan's formal annexation of Korea to its colonial empire. British firms protested at Japan's regaining tariff autonomy in 1911 but Sir Edward Grey, the foreign secretary, made clear that Korea was regarded as a legitimate Japanese possession.[3] Japanese rule was tough, repressive yet efficient. No sympathy was shown to Korean nationalism and considerable brutality was employed in suppressing dissident elements, especially in the first decade of Japanese rule. Korea's strategic importance meant that priority was assigned to consolidating Japanese control and with the exploitation of Korean resources for Japanese gain. An infrastructure was created with new roads and rail lines: the growth of industry was stimulated.[4] Korean anger at the loss of independence and resentment at the humiliation of treatment as a colony gave vent to the serious unrest in 1919; demonstrations were put down with extreme rigour and gave rise to strong criticism in Britain. Lord Curzon, the foreign secretary, rebuked Japan and a further impetus was given to diminishing faith in the Anglo-Japanese alliance.[5] The end of the alliance in 1923 was not accompanied by a more assertive approach to Korean issues. The Japanese administration was slightly more enlightened in the 1920s and more freedom was permitted to Korean cultural aspirations. Little attention was devoted to Korea by the British in the interwar years amidst the many pressing domestic and international problems but the implicit assumption was that Japanese control would continue for a long time to come.

In a memorandum prepared in the summer of 1945 the far eastern department of the Foreign Office observed that there was some British missionary involvement in Korea but that British economic interests were slight: 'in the years 1935–39 inclusive the average annual exports from the United Kingdom to Korea amounted to £156,000 and the imports from Korea to the United Kingdom to £9,000'.[6] On the political side a negative assessment of British views was arrived at:

> Korea is situated in an area in which British influence was steadily diminishing before the war, and it is unlikely that we shall be able to restore our position in the years immediately following the war. In view of the political consequences which may ensue from Russia's renaissance as a Far Eastern Power, it may not even be desirable to do so. The vital interests of the British Commonwealth in the Far East lie in the area south of the Tropic of Cancer and it is likely that all our available resources will be required for re-establishing and maintaining our influence there.
>
> The United Kingdom has little interest in the future of Korea except for the fact that she is a signatory of the Cairo Declaration.[7]

The Cairo declaration, issued by President Roosevelt, Prime Minister Churchill and Generalissimo Chiang Kai-shek in December 1943, pledged the allies to dismantling the Japanese empire and restoring freedom to its constituent parts. Departments of the American government produced lengthy appraisals of Korea in the latter part of the Pacific war but without achieving a clearcut policy. One of the most persistent visitors to the State Department and other offices of the American government was Dr Syngman Rhee. He possessed a Princeton doctorate and had long opposed Japanese dominance of his country. Rhee had participated originally in the Korean government-in-exile based in Shanghai but had broken with his colleagues and based himself in the United States. Rhee was imbued with fanatical zeal and belief in Korean unity, allied with equal confidence in his own abilities and leadership.[8] American officials tended to regard him cynically but Rhee developed valuable contacts in other circles including intelligence: the deputy head of the Office of Strategic Services (OSS), Colonel M. Preston Goodfellow, was particularly significant. Goodfellow did much to advance Rhee's political career and worked quite closely with him for a lengthy period extending through the Korean war, as shown in correspondence in Goodfellow's private papers.[9] John M. Allison of the State Department wrote to Sir John Sterndale Bennett of the Foreign Office at the end of February 1945 explaining that Rhee was urging recognition of the Korean provisional government and warning that unless the Americans acted promptly, the Soviet Union could absorb Korea easily at the close of the Pacific war. It had been decided not to recognise the provisional government for the time being.[10] Arthur de la Mare of the far eastern department welcomed this decision: 'These people cannot in any true sense be said to represent Korea and Anglo–U.S. recognition of them might well lead to those problems we have experienced over the "London Poles".[11]

The principal American objective in July and August 1945 was to obtain Japanese surrender, preferably without the Soviet Union playing a prominent role. It was known from intelligence sources and from Japanese approaches to Moscow that Japan was anxious to bring the war to an end provided that enough reassurance was forthcoming regarding the future of the monarchy. Once Truman knew that the atomic bomb had been tested successfully in July 1945, he was willing to sanction its use so as to save allied lives and obviate some of the difficulties consequent upon Soviet participation. At the same time Truman was interested in the fate of Korea and did not relish the prospect of Soviet occupation of much of the peninsula. Had Korea been made a priority, American forces could have occupied most of it before Soviet forces advanced. The Soviet army proceeded relatively slowly with the occupation. However, American military chiefs, and particularly General Douglas MacArthur, concentrated on securing Japanese surrender and the ensuing arrangements for allied occupation of Japan. Truman was not prepared to impose his views.[12] Instead agreement was reached swiftly by the American and Soviet governments, following a recommendation from the Pentagon for which Colonel Dean Rusk was partly responsible, that the 38th parallel should be adopted as the formal demarcation line between the Soviet and American zones of occupation in Korea. This meant that the Korean capital city, Seoul, would fall into the American zone. Since the United States was slow in deploying its forces in Korea, the Soviet army could have occupied the greater part of the country had it so chosen but Stalin adhered to the understanding agreed with Washington. Far bigger issues than Korea had to be decided in Europe and Stalin perhaps hoped that it might be feasible to establish a Soviet foothold within the allied occupation of Japan.

Britain was not consulted by the United States over Korean policy. The Foreign Office memorandum of 8 September, cited earlier, stated that 'so far as is known', Korea was not considered at any meeting attended by British representatives during the Potsdam conference in July 1945. The first indication received in London of the proposed division of Korea was contained in a copy of an order from MacArthur, conveyed by Truman to Attlee (now prime minister) on 15 August. This summarised the various suggestions put forward in the United States and Britain for determining the future administration of Korea during a 'period of tutelage'. These comprised: restoration of formal sovereignty to Korea with foreign advisers exercising effective control; Korea to be administered by a smaller power possessing colonial experience; the implementation of shared control between all the great powers; or Korea to be administered by one great power. The first and third of these proposals were deemed to be in the best interests of the Korean people before Korea could regain full independence. If the fourth proposal was applied, it was held that the majority of Koreans would prefer the United States to the Soviet Union or China. Having assessed the probable course of events, the memorandum concluded that joint control by the United States and the Soviet Union was most likely, possibly with nominal involvement of other powers including Britain:

This will be an uneasy partnership, but there may be some guarantee of security in the respect which either side will feel for the military strength of its partner. Since the Governments, both of the Soviet Union and the United States are, like His Majesty's Government, committed to the Cairo Declaration, this solution would not conflict with any British guarantee or undertaking. In view of our small commercial and strategic interest in this area any solution which did not contravene the terms of the Cairo Declaration would be acceptable to us, but we should leave it to the Americans to play the hand.[13]

Thus Korea was not seen as a priority in the Foreign Office and it was felt that the United States and the Soviet Union must be left to handle Korea as they saw fit. The Truman administration advocated trusteeship as the best method of governing Korea during an era of transition. The problem with this solution was that Korea was in ferment and the Korean people, left and right, rejected it. The secretary of state, James F. Byrnes, told Attlee in November 1945, when the prime minister visited Washington, that it was essential to determine future arrangements for Korea so as to avoid a *fait accompli* of Soviet control. Byrnes advocated a quadripartite trusteeship comprising the Soviet Union, the United States, Britain and China. Further enquiry in the State Department revealed that the draft scheme envisaged a neutral high commissioner, possibly Dutch or Swiss, functioning with an advisory council including representatives of the trusteeship powers. The actual administration would be in the hands of Koreans under the guidance of foreign advisers. Occupation troops would be removed and Korean police expanded in number. The Truman administration was reported to be anxious to withdraw troops because the existing situation was intolerable.[14] Arthur de la Mare minuted that the American attitude was defensive as if prepared to explain away or to forestall criticism. He reflected with a certain ironic satisfaction:

Both in Korea and in the Philippines the Americans are beginning to experience some of the difficulties of Pacific problems. This is no doubt the reason for the relatively sympathetic attitude which they have taken up towards our own problems in the N.E.I. [Netherlands East Indies] and in French Indo-China.[15]

The Americans had indeed advanced in a spirit of blithe optimism into a situation far more complex than they had imagined. Despite the preparation of numerous position papers on Korea, little thought had been given to the practical questions of administration. MacArthur was in overall command but was wholly preoccupied with the occupation of Japan and displayed little interest in Korea. The head of the American military government in Korea was General John Reed Hodge. He was a courageous fighting soldier with an admirable record in the Pacific war. However, he had no knowledge of Korea and was thrust into navigating challenges which would have taxed to the full the skills of someone acquainted in depth with the problems. Hodge was honest, blunt, direct and unsubtle. He detested communism and regarded unrest as the outcome of communist intrigue. While Washington was committed to trusteeship and cooperation with the Soviet Union, Hodge reached the conclusion that this was neither feasible nor desirable. Apart from the strength of his own convictions, Hodge was faced with a country in turmoil. The Korean right wing was largely discredited by past collaboration with the Japanese. Syngman Rhee had returned but required time to use his formidable political talent to out-manoeuvre his rivals and establish himself as the leader of anti-communist nationalism. Kim Ku was discredited by the failure of an attempted coup against the American military government at the end of December 1945. A spirit of spontaneous revolutionary zeal prevailed in much of south Korea but was grad-ually undermined through American discrimination in favour of the right and by the recovery of right-wing elements. Hodge became impatient with the approach of Washington and, like 'the man on the spot' in the nineteenth century, believed that he had to force the pace.[16]

At the Moscow conference of American, Russian and British foreign ministers in December 1945, a Soviet proposal providing for the creation of a joint commission comprising representatives from the American and Soviet mili-tary commands was approved with minor amendments. This body would prepare the ground for the formation of a provisional government for the whole of Korea. Thus the idea of a trusteeship was diminished: trusteeship would be reviewed after the creation of a Korean government. Hodge disapproved because he felt that trusteeship as a concept was dead: he was also sceptical as to what would emerge from a joint commission. Relations between the Americans and the Russians in Korea slowly deteriorated during the first half of 1946. The joint commission met in Seoul in March with five from each side present, the respec-tive delegations being led by Major-General Arnold and Colonel-General Shtyikov. Considerable argument occurred concerning which Korean groups should be contacted *vis-à-vis* forming a provisional government. The Soviet atti-tude was that those Koreans who had attacked the Moscow agreement should not be seen because they rejected the agreement reached between the powers. The Americans revealed that they intended to recognise the Representative Democratic Council (RDC), formed in February 1946 at the instigation of Rhee, Hodge and Goodfellow, as the principal consultative body. Therefore, the Americans showed that they had diverged significantly from trusteeship. Following further debate it was decided on 16 May that the joint commission should adjourn until the following year.[17]

British officials observed the worsening scene gloomily. D. F. McDermot reported to Ernest Bevin late in December 1945 that he had visited Korea and was alarmed at what he had seen. The arbitrary division of Korea at the 38th parallel was disastrous economically, for heavy industry was mostly situated north of the parallel with light industry and agriculture predominating south of the parallel. The calibre of the administration in the south was poor and the Koreans employed by the American military government were 'almost hope-lessly incompetent.'[18] McDermot stated that the Americans were fully aware of the problem and that there was no intention of pushing the Koreans into pre-mature independence. Arthur de la Mare reviewed developments at the end of June 1946. He recalled that it had been decided that Australia should constitute the fourth member of a trusteeship when established and that Britain should not participate directly. However, in the light of the most recent reports, it appeared doubtful whether the trusteeship would be set up. Without exaggeration the Korean situation could be defined as a serious threat to world peace. If relations between the Soviet Union and the United States deteriorated further, it would be difficult for Britain to keep out.[19] Esler Dening remarked that he had always felt that the Americans did not appreciate the complexity of the Korean question. It would be unfortunate if the United States retreated from the responsibilities it had assumed in Korea but the Americans had awoken belatedly to the perils of being in a Soviet-dominated area.[20] At the beginning of September 1946 de la Mare concluded that Hodge's administration was not adequate to the tasks facing it. The Americans were undermined by inexperience, changes in personnel resulting from demobilisation, corruption and the inertia of Koreans.[21]

Rhee was involved in growing acrimony with Hodge in 1946–47 as the venerable nationalist manoeuvred to consolidate his hold as the leading right-wing contender for power in Seoul. Rhee decided to send Byung Chic Limb to London for an exchange of views. The consul-general in Seoul, D. W. Kermode, believed, reluctantly, that Limb should be seen but de la Mare minuted that Limb should not be received because British policy was to support the Moscow agreement.[22] Kermode accurately assessed Rhee's position:

> Although Rhee poses plausibly as a champion of Corean [sic] independence, and he made a deep impression on sentimental audiences in United States, his admittedly genuine desire for the country's independence is really the desire of a megalomaniac. An extremist of the Right he is interested in the welfare of the people only in so far as some concession to their welfare is necessary to enable him to gain and retain dictatorial leadership.[23]

Kermode added that given Rhee's age – he was 72 – he would utilise any means of achieving his ambition of reunifying Korea including, if necessary, 'the blood of his deluded followers'.[24] Limb obtained a visa in Washington and duly arrived in London. He was received unenthusiastically in the Foreign Office and justified the apprehension entertained by his hosts. Limb gave a mendacious account of the position in Korea; he urged abandonment of trusteeship, removal of foreign troops and independence for Korea as a unified state including membership of the UN. Limb was told, with appropriate ambiguity, that Britain was observing developments with interest.[25]

In March 1947 Korea became a focal point for discussion in Washington during the Truman administration's exchange with Congress involving the issue of American commitments to Greece, Turkey and Korea. Consideration hinged on economic aid, which was envisaged as amounting to a grant-in-aid of 600 million US dollars, spread over three years. A committee of State and Treasury Department officials, together with General Arnold, was responsible for submitting proposals. The intention was to strengthen the viability of south Korea, since unification of the country might not occur for some years. Dean Acheson, under-secretary of state, was involved actively in dealing with proposals. He met the Senate Foreign Relations Committee on 24 March to discuss all three countries.[26] The British ambassador, Lord Inverchapel, observed sardonically in a telegram to Bevin, 'I draw your attention to Mr. Acheson's denial that the

programmes for aid to Greece, Turkey and Korea constitute an ideological
crusade and to his following remarks which show that that is precisely what they
are.'[27] Two days earlier the *Manchester Guardian* reflected that new thinking was
required on Korea because it had become one of the most dangerous regions of
Soviet–American confrontation:

> To-day Korea is one of the two parts of the world (Germany is the other) where
> the United States and the Soviet Union meet face to face in physical contact.
> The chances of a direct agreement are so remote and the dangers of a clash
> so serious that there is a strong case for broadening the discussion. Britain and
> China, as trustees-elect, clearly have a right to be consulted, but the best
> chance now would seem to be to scrap the Moscow agreement and for the
> United States to arrange for a simultaneous withdrawal and for the establish-
> ment of a united Korean Government. It might not be a very democratic or
> very efficient Government, but almost anything would be better than the
> present absurd and dangerous division.[28]

Leading members of the government and of the opposition entirely shared the
anxiety. R. A. Butler, a leading Conservative spokesman, stated in the House of
Commons on 27 February that he regarded the situation in Korea as 'perhaps
the greatest danger spot for peace in the Far East'.[29] Ernest Bevin told the
Labour Party conference in Margate in May 1947 that the confrontation in
Korea was extremely alarming, as much so as in Europe.[30]

The Japan and Pacific department of the Foreign Office produced a
substantial reassessment of Korea on 22 May 1947. The basic characteristics
were identified as: the inability of the Koreans to govern themselves; Soviet
determination to transform Korea into a puppet state; and American determination to resist this through a combination of 'political education and by
economic support'.[31] Soviet tactics in the joint commission would provide an
insight into their ultimate intentions. The Soviet Union had to pursue a resolute
policy in Korea because of its strategic importance in the defence of Soviet far
eastern territory. Korea possessed ice-free harbours which Soviet territory
lacked. It was too early to say what the Soviet reaction would be to the new
American policy. It appeared most likely that the Russians would take their time:

> They undoubtedly realise that the Truman doctrine, of which the policy of aid
> for Korea is one aspect is not universally popular in the United States, and
> may eventually have to be abandoned or drastically restricted. The Soviet
> Command might therefore accept an apparently unfavourable settlement in
> the Joint Commission and then wait for the Koreans to dissipate their
> American dollars, dissolve into warring factions, and lay themselves open to
> Communist domination at about the time the United States occupation forces
> leave Japan.[32]

Recent reports suggested that the Russians were reducing their forces in the
north. It was possible that they would advocate withdrawal of all allied forces
and rely on their Korean protégés to undermine the American aim of democratisation. The Soviet Union could afford to tolerate the present impasse,
confident that matters would unfold eventually in the way they desired.

As regards the United States, it was obvious that the same considerations that had inspired loans to Greece and Turkey obtained in the case of Korea. Logically American policy should be 'even firmer *vis-à-vis* Korea than Greece and Turkey, as one-half of Korea is already under Soviet occupation'.[33] The situation was depressing with the consolidation of communist power in the north and with an unstable political and economic outlook in the south. Many Koreans in the south were weary of the American administration and felt they were faring worse than under the Japanese. Since the Koreans lacked the capacity to govern themselves successfully, American withdrawal would be disastrous. General Hodge was described as not having demonstrated the qualities for leadership and could not equal MacArthur's 'qualities of statesmanship'.[34]

Attlee's personal representative in Tokyo, General Gairdner, paid a brief visit to Seoul and met MacArthur on 12 July when he returned. Gairdner explained to MacArthur that he had attended a meeting of the reconvened joint commission and that the outlook was negative. MacArthur then stated his personal views on Korea and China. He believed that the Truman administration erred in dealing with Korea 'on a low level'.[35] He had informed the secretary of state, General Marshall, that Korean issues should be handled as part of the total far eastern question. He thought deadlock would continue. While it was premature to say whether the joint commission would end, as before, in fundamental deadlock, MacArthur believed it was likely that the Soviet Union would urge withdrawal of occupation forces: 'The geographical propinquity of the Russians would thus enable them to dominate Korea whenever they wished to do so!'[36] MacArthur conveyed his own lack of confidence in American policy towards Korea and China.[37] Exchanges in the joint commission became more acrimonious as the Soviet delegates emphasised their dissatisfaction with American tactics. The *Soviet Monitor* for 25 July 1947, issued by the Tass agency, contained a full summary of Soviet views based on a press conference held by General Shtykov. It was recalled that the Americans had diverged from the decisions reached at the Moscow conference in December 1945. They were supporting those opposed to trusteeship in south Korea. The Americans had produced a list of organisations for consultation, many of which were of dubious credibility, if they existed at all. Shtykov emphasised the Soviet wish to accomplish 'a truly democratic Government in Korea'.[38] At the beginning of August the State Department notified the British embassy that matters had reached an explosive stage and it had been decided to take prompt measures. It would be proposed that the joint commission should be told to submit a report by 15 August and that concrete proposals should comprise holding of elections in north and south based on universal suffrage; that each legislature established should select representatives to meet representatives of the major powers to consider the provision of assistance; then a date should be agreed whereby foreign troops would be removed.[39] The British embassy in Moscow reported that Soviet spokesmen continued to reiterate that the United States was responsible for undercutting existing agreements. John Killick of the Japan and Pacific department minuted, 'There appears to be some justification for the Soviet attitude.'[40]

The political atmosphere in south Korea worsened as Syngman Rhee intensified the pressure so as to gain support for his leadership challenge. Having been built up by the American military in Seoul, Rhee proved an intransigent leader and followed an independent path with considerable skill to the profound ire of Hodge. Kermode, the British consul-general in Seoul, reported on 3 September that the attempt to bridge the Soviet–American rift would fail. All Koreans wanted occupation forces withdrawn even if civil war ensued: 'There is in fact amongst Koreans a growing resignation to the idea that only civil war can settle the issue.'[41] In late September Shtykov called for withdrawal of Soviet and American troops from Korea.[42] This caused right-wing leaders to reconsider their shrill rhetoric for, as Kermode reported, immediate withdrawal would be followed by a communist assumption of power.[43] The Truman administration decided that the aid of the UN should be invoked. The UN at this time was a relatively small body dominated by the United States.[44] Since there was considerable support in Western countries for taking contentious issues to the UN, such action would depict American policy in a reasonable light and could permit the Americans to extricate themselves from the more invidious features of their predicament in Korea. The State Department indicated that a UN resolution would stipulate the establishment of a commission charged with supervising elections in both zones and with facilitating the establishment of a provisional government: the commission should liaise with the occupying powers to decide procedure for withdrawal. John Killick observed soberly:

> I think the Americans realize that they are fighting a rearguard action, whose outcome is certain & can only be delayed as long as possible. Military & economic support cannot be given indefinitely, especially in view of the attitude of Congress to further large appropriations, & I should imagine that, if the attempt to reach a settlement in the Assembly fails, the Americans will be obliged to cut their losses & evacuate Korea.[45]

Confirmation for this interruption came in the form of a telegram from the embassy in Moscow reporting a conversation between the British and American ambassadors, Sir Maurice Petersen and General Walter Bedell Smith. The latter, who had just returned from Washington, described American proposals as little more than a face-saving device: 'United States Government regard Korea as certain to fall under Communist domination once their troops are withdrawn.'[46] The fundamental explanation was financial: with so many other demands on American resources they could not afford appreciable expenditure for Korea. Bedell Smith thought that the repercussions for the Kuomintang regime in China would be serious. Killick minuted that, 'This depressing statement has the merit of being frank & realistic.'[47] D. F. McDermot added, 'There is no disguising that it is a major American capitulation.'[48] Robin Hankey was concerned at the European implications: 'This will much encourage the Russians to dig their toes in in Europe, I am afraid, e.g. in the forthcoming discussions about Germany.'[49]

Therefore, Britain supported the American resolution in the UN General Assembly in October 1947 which marked the beginning of the traumatic UN involvement in Korean matters and which was to lead the UN in 1950 into the first occasion in its history – and sole occasion until the Gulf war in 1991 – when the UN was committed to participation in a full-scale war in defence (or alleged defence) of the UN charter. The original resolution, carried in November 1947, established the UN Temporary Commission on Korea (UNTCOK). This body was instructed to observe the process of fulfilling elections for the whole of Korea and was going to submit advice regarding the establishment of a unified Korea. Elections were to be held by the end of March 1948. American and Russian forces would be removed no later than three months after the creation of a Korean government. The Soviet Union and its allies predictably made clear categorical opposition to the setting up and functions of UNTCOK.[50] The members of UNTCOK came from India, Canada, Australia, France, China, El Salvador, the Philippines and Syria. The chairman was the Indian diplomat, Kumara P. S. Menon. UNTCOK was endeavouring to achieve the impossible. North Korea had no intention of holding elections; the Soviet Union was hostile; south Korean right-wing leaders wished to use the authority of the UN simply to legitimise the establishment of a state dominated by themselves; the United States similarly wanted to see the transition from the military government to an independent south Korea. The chances of UNTCOK achieving anything significant were slim. A minority of the body believed it should report back to UN headquarters that nothing could be accomplished. However, the majority believed UNTCOK should observe elections in the south, despite opposition from Australia, Canada and India. The interim committee of the UN General Assembly, which functioned when the assembly was not in session, decided in February 1948 that UNTCOK should fulfil what it could including supervision of elections in the south. The American military government announced that elections would take place on 9 May 1948. Canada and Australia were among the leading critics of the decisions reached but to no avail. Friction soon developed between certain of the members of UNTCOK and the American military. Joseph E. Jacobs, Hodge's political adviser, was particularly critical of those he described as constituting a 'British bloc' – Jackson (Australia), Patterson (Canada) and Menon (India).[51] Jackson was deemed the most objectionable and anti-American in his approach. Hodge reached the conclusion that the arrival of UNTCOK was a mixed blessing and that certain members of UNTCOK conceived of a longer-term UN role in Korea which conflicted with his own understanding. He felt that it might be necessary to discard UNTCOK and proceed with the formation of a government in south Korea.[52] The British Foreign Office held that whatever transpired would be unsatisfactory but that UNTCOK should do the best it could. The significant contribution made by members of the British Commonwealth naturally influenced thinking, for this was a period of importance in the evolution of the Commonwealth. The four dominions were moving towards complete independence but many of the old ties of kinship and friendship with Canada and Australia remained; New Zealand still looked towards Britain and relations between Britain and South Africa remained warm so long as Jan Smuts remained in office. India had just attained independence and this momentous event meant that emphasis was placed upon securing sufficient cooperation and coordination in policy formulation. The British consul-general in Seoul described Jackson as able, steady and responsible. According to Jackson, MacArthur told him, when they met in Tokyo, to assist American aims, since Jackson was an 'Anglo-Saxon' and not to be pushed into an early return to New York with admission of UNTCOK's failure.[53]

The British view in the middle of February 1948 was that if absolutely necessary separate elections should be held in south Korea but it had to be understood that such an eventuality would exacerbate divisions between north and south. It would be best not to take decisions hastily and some time should be allowed for possible consultations between leaders from the two halves of Korea, unlikely as this appeared as regards a positive outcome. The British delegate to the UN was instructed to remind the Americans of the danger that Russia could make propaganda with the allegation that the United States used UN machinery to impose policy upon Korea without consulting the Korean people. In addition, Britain must keep in mind the views of Canada, Australia and India: the Kashmir dispute between India and Pakistan meant that Britain would not wish to oppose, without convincing justification, any constructive proposals which might be made by Menon.[54] Meanwhile, Rhee was seeking to exploit matters with the deployment of the full range of his formidable talents. Kermode, the consul-general, believed that Rhee would manoeuvre his followers into power through a combination of ruthlessness, force and corruption:

> First of all, therefore, he will establish his group by rigged elections as the Government of the South, then by a simple arithmetical calculation he will claim the extension of its authority over the whole of Korea, and finally, through this authority, he will be recognized by the United Nations as the titular head of the whole Korean State. That is his plan. It is so transparent that people can be forgiven for thinking him crazed.[55]

Kermode added that American policy had been inept and that Hodge, while well intentioned, had made many mistakes:

> It is certainly true that General Hodge has poked his fingers, often imprudently, into the South Korean political pie. He talks much of democracy but he hates the Left, regarding in common with many Americans, anyone Left of Centre as a blood relation of the Communists.[56]

Hodge underestimated Rhee's ambitions and then endeavoured to switch support to the moderate Kim Kyu-sik. However, Kim lacked sufficient guile and Rhee was firmly in the ascendancy. Hodge's errors had been the concomitants of 'good will' and 'they illustrate the disastrous effect of good will without good judgment'.[57] The sad fact was that the blundering policy of the American military government had driven Korean youth into the arms of the communists, particularly in the first phase of the occupation. Genuinely patriotic people had allied themselves with the communists. The entire situation was most unstable and could be disturbed fatally by either an initiative from Rhee or from north Korea. This was an accurate anticipation of the political relationship between the two parts of Korea down to June 1950. The outcome of the struggle between the Kuomintang and the Chinese communists in Manchuria would affect Korea significantly. Kermode concluded with somewhat rueful reflections on the American impact in Korea:

Although American policy in Korea may have hastened the end, no policy for Korea alone could have permanently averted it. The question that remains to trouble the mind is whether America, when freed from her responsibilities here, will concentrate her thus released politico-military attentions on some other threatened country and, in her ignorance of the nature of non-American peoples, make the same disastrous blunders there as she has made in Korea.[58]

The elections were duly held in south Korea amidst purely nominal supervision by UNTCOK. The latter described the results as valid in those regions visited by members of the body. However, UNTCOK did not recognise the assembly elected as appropriate in leading to the establishment of a national government. Rhee and his supporters comprised the predominant forces. The Republic of Korea (ROK) was proclaimed formally in July 1948 and Rhee was elected president. The United States extended economic aid to the new state and subsequently set up a military mission (KMAG) to guide the development of the South Korean armed forces: this was originally the second largest mission (after the mission to Turkey) and was later the largest. In north Korea the communist regime sponsored by the Russians consisted of comrades from disparate backgrounds: exiles who had operated as guerrillas against the Japanese from Soviet or Chinese bases, exiles who had worked closely with the Chinese communists in Yenan, indigenous Koreans who had pursued clandestine activities in north or south Korea during Japanese occupation.[59] Kim Il Sung soon emerged as the principal personality. Kim's earlier career is opaque but it is accepted generally that he conducted guerrilla forays against the Japanese in the 1930s. It is likely that he collaborated with the Russians and the Chinese.[60] Kim was depicted frequently in the West as a front man for Soviet imperialism: as one American colonel remarked, the relationship between Stalin and Kim was analogous to that between Walt Disney and Donald Duck. It is understandable that such views were held when the Cold War was expanding at a frightening rate in Eastern Europe with local communist leaders, except Tito, perceived as Stalinist stooges. Kim Il Sung was a fervent nationalist equalling Syngman Rhee in his ardent desire for reunification of Korea. Just as Rhee used the Americans for his own purposes and looked forward to the day when he could dispense with their services, so Kim Il Sung used the Russians and, to a lesser extent at this time, the Chinese for his own reasons and similarly looked forward to the day when he could dispense with their services and dominate the whole of Korea. It took Kim an appreciable time to establish his power and in the early years he was compelled to manoeuvre against competing factions; he did not establish his base fully until after the Korean war when he purged various rivals. Revolutionary policies were implemented in north Korea between 1945 and 1948 and a harsh, repressive regime evolved under Kim's direction. Economic and military aid was forthcoming from the Soviet Union but, it would appear, not as extensively as was thought in the West.[61] At the beginning of 1948 the Soviet authorities took steps to lay the foundation for a north Korean government. In July 1948 a constitution was approved claiming, as did the constitution in the south, to represent all of Korea. Kim Il Sung addressed a conference of the North Korean People's Council and extolled the great achievements accomplished with Soviet help. Kim alleged that the south Korean state was phoney, the bastard product of American imperialism spearheaded by General Hodge and reactionary rightists led by Rhee. According to an analysis completed in the British Foreign Office, the constitution revealed the incorporation of familiar features from the Soviet constitution; there was evidence that the Meiji constitution in Japan had been consulted.[62] Thus the Democratic People's Republic of Korea (DPRK) emerged.

When the UN General Assembly resumed its deliberations in Paris, in October 1948, it was faced with the formal existence of two Korean states. Decisions would have to be reached by the General Assembly regarding the degree of recognition to be accorded. A British official in the Foreign Office, Edward Scott, drafted a minute on 13 October stating that the United States was contemplating a resolution on the basis that the ROK was entitled to full recognition as the government of the whole of Korea under the terms of the resolution carried on 14 November 1947. He commented that the British government would have preferred a resolution simply conveying approval of UNTCOK's report, which would have allowed member states to decide for themselves the extent of recognition to be granted. The American resolution was seen as unnecessarily controversial, since it referred to the ROK government as the government of all of Korea: 'It is the view of His Majesty's Government that the new Government cannot be recognised as the Government of all Korea since, owing to Soviet obstruction, it is based on elections held in South Korea only, and since it exercises no authority in the north.'[63] Naturally it was impossible to consider recognition of the DPRK because the Soviet Union displayed consistent defiance of the UN. At the same time and despite the apparent lack of realism involved, the British government believed that provision should be incorporated for the ultimate unification of Korea. One way of achieving this aim would be for the appointment of a UN representative instructed to observe withdrawal of the occupying forces, to endeavour to secure the removal of the barriers at the 38th parallel, and to observe the holding of elections in the north.[64]

UNTCOK's report to the General Assembly stated that the ROK met the basic criteria for a functioning government and that the possibility of reunification existed. Negotiations between Seoul and Pyongyang, before the departure of Soviet and American forces, were recommended. Under American pressure the General Assembly approved a resolution recognising the ROK and accepting the results of the election in May as legitimate. It was recommended that foreign troops should leave and a new UN body, the UN Commission on Korea (UNCOK) should replace UNTCOK, the aim being to improve the prospects for unification.[65] The resolution was unclear as to whether the ROK was regarded as 'South Korea' or as a government qualified to represent the whole of Korea. Any chance UNCOK might possess of reconciling the two Koreas was doomed by the vitriolic mutual hatred of the ROK and DPRK. The ROK was faced with extensive unrest, a continuation of the situation prevailing since the Japanese surrender. This was partly fuelled, as in Cheju island and in certain provinces, by long-standing grievances against centralised authority. Hatred of the police, who were associated with the repression of the colonial period, and resentment of corruption manifested in Rhee's regime, accentuated instability. Kim Il Sung and his colleagues appear to have felt that it was merely a question of time before a major rebellion erupted in the south. When the moment was ripe, North Korean forces would strike to liquidate the decadent Rhee regime and Korea would be united again. The position along the 38th parallel was chronically disturbed. Trigger-happy troops were present on each side and both were responsible for provoking minor and major incidents. Rhee and Kim indulged in extravagant rhetoric reiterating faith in unification being secured soon. The unrest along the 38th parallel gave rise to a further resolution, moved by the United States in 1949, calling upon UNCOK to watch developments along the border and report back to the UN.[66]

The first British minister to the ROK, Captain Vyvyan Holt, reported in November 1948 that President Rhee was embroiled in disputes with the assembly regarding the formation of a new cabinet; Rhee had been denounced for autocracy by his opponents.[67] Holt also referred to rebellion in the Otai mountains, near Seoul, and to serious problems in Chonju; in addition, the situation along the 38th parallel was alarming.[68] On 1 March 1949 Holt stated that only half of the rice required to supply rations until the next harvest had been collected and it was unlikely that the government could continue the daily grain ration for much longer. In a subsequent economic report, forwarded in July, Holt commented that while more severe rationing had not yet caused as much unrest as he had feared, the general trend of retail prices in Seoul was rising pointing to accelerating inflation: 'The economy of the country is completely dependent on the $150 million aid which President Truman has asked Congress to approve.'[69] Holt added that British firms were showing more interest in trade with Korea: there appeared to be encouraging signs for dealings in Korean minerals and good earnings in freight for shipping agents.

In December 1949 British thinking focused on the ability of the ROK to withstand an attack by DPRK forces. Holt discussed the subject with the American ambassador, John J. Muccio. Muccio was a capable career diplomat and worked vigorously to prop up the Rhee government while not hesitating to convey criticism of the numerous political and economic defects of the ROK administration. Holt pursued with Muccio the possibility of the ROK government withdrawing to the south in the event of a North Korean offensive threatening Seoul. Holt reported:

> He [Muccio] said that they might try but he could not believe that the present regime could survive for more than a few days if the Government abandoned the Capital. I agree with this view. I think that the President and the Cabinet would probably flee the country and try to persuade the American Government to support them in Hawaii or elsewhere as a Government in exile. Anyhow there is little that I could do for them or for H.M.G. by running after them ...
>
> My conclusion is that there are few British interests here to protect and little protection that we could give to anything if the Korean Republic collapsed either as the result of external or internal pressures. Nevertheless if you take a different view or if you think it a good thing to keep someone here to try to establish relations of some kind with whatever regime might follow the collapse of the Republic, I shall not in the least mind staying here to see what happens.[70]

The final paragraph was indeed prophetic for when the North Koreans attacked in June 1950, Holt remained, was captured and endured harsh treatment during which nothing was heard of him until the Foreign Office eventually used Russian good offices to secure his repatriation.

The Foreign Office requested an assessment from the War Office on the apposite topic of the ROK's ability to withstand an onslaught from the DPRK. Major Ferguson-Innes wrote to Edward Scott on 30 December stating that the bulk of intelligence on Korea came from American sources, although British intelligence contributed, too. Ferguson-Innes explained that the opinion had been held in the War Office for some time that the North Korean forces could advance south without difficulty. The Pentagon had arrived previously at a different conclusion, not surprisingly given the American role and activities of KMAG. Lately the Americans had swung around to the more critical British line. As regards DPRK ambitions:

> On the question of aggression by the North, there can be no doubt whatever that their ultimate objective is to overrun the South; and I think in the long term there is no doubt that they will do so in which case, as you so aptly remark, the Americans will have made a rather handsome contribution of equipment to the military strength of Asiatic Communism. As to their method of achieving their object, short of World War III beginning, I think they will adopt the well tried tactics of preparing the country from within rather than resort to open aggression although 'frontier incidents' will doubtless continue.[71]

He believed three divisions and one tank regiment had returned to Korea from Manchuria, although this could not be proved. The Russians were thought to be maintaining arms and equipment supplies to the DPRK and there was a Soviet military mission of approximately 3,000 in North Korea. He ended with an admission of ignorance concerning American aims:

> Regarding American policy, if in fact one exists towards South Korea, I can only say we know little, and of their future intentions even less. Their military advisory group consists, we believe, of 300 and the emphasis is on 'advisory'.[72]

It was clear what North Korean ambitions connoted but an invasion of the south was considered unlikely within the immediate future. Ferguson-Innes concluded:

> however, if it did take place, I think it improbable that the Americans would become involved. The possession of South Korea is not essential for Allied strategic plans, and though it would obviously be desirable to deny it to the enemy, it would not be of sufficient importance to make it the cause of World War III. Meanwhile, we must accept an uneasy status quo and hope for the best.[73]

As with China and Japan, Britain was not consulted or properly informed of American intentions in Korea. In the first few months of 1950 the signs indicated that the Truman administration did not regard Korea as a priority. Bruce Cumings had examined the complexity and speculation surrounding the erratic development of American policy towards East Asia in 1950 in exhaustive and fascinating detail in his second volume analysing the origins of the Korean war.[74] Cumings has explored the actual, probable or possible motives of different parts of the American government and of key individuals, some holding office and others in shadowy roles linked with intelligence or pressure groups. There were murky or mysterious features inherent in the development of American policies relating to China, Taiwan and Korea. The political atmosphere in the United States was highly charged as the Cold War gathered more rapid momentum and hysterical reactions to communism of an extreme nature exerted a baleful influence upon the Truman administration, Congress and pressure groups. One of the central and most controversial personalities in the formulation of American policy was Dean Acheson. He was a man of great ability and equal arrogance. Cumings sees Acheson as possessing a world view which was the product of deep reflection: fundamental to it was the construction of a strategy which would contain communist movements while exploiting divisions that might exist within communism, most obviously between the Soviet Union and communist China. Certain of these aspects were pursued in the section of this volume focusing primarily on China: here the emphasis is on the Korean dimension. On 12 January 1950 Acheson delivered his famous address in the National Press Club, Washington, D.C., surveying the foreign policy of the Truman administration. The speech was ostensibly delivered on the basis of notes but Cumings has shown that the speech was carefully prepared over a lengthy period.[75] At first sight Acheson seemed to have excluded Korea from his definition of essential American interests in East Asia and the western Pacific. In fact Acheson included a balanced, if opaque, reference to the potential of the UN in combating aggression. However, Acheson's speech could not be regarded as a ringing declaration of American determination to defend Korea.[76] Acheson's speech followed closely upon Truman's press statement of a week before disclaiming any intention of intervening in Taiwan to prevent the final defeat of the Kuomintang. On 19 January 1950 the House of Representatives voted narrowly to reject the administration's Korean aid bill. The defeat was something of a fluke caused by complacency on the part of administration officials, accentuated through dissatisfaction with policy regarding China and the absence through grave ill-health of Senator Arthur H. Vandenberg (Republican, Michigan) who could not exert his considerable influence upon fellow Republican legislators. Preston Goodfellow sought to reassure an irate Rhee, writing that no one in Congress was shooting at Korea: it was in the nature of a family dispute between Truman and Acheson on one side and their congressional critics on the other. Goodfellow believed the defeat would assist Korea through focusing more attention on it.[77] The ROK government was deeply upset and the South Korean ambassador protested to the State Department.

Just as the alarm was subsiding, Senator Tom Connally (Democrat, Texas), chairman of the Senate Foreign Relations Committee, spoke in unwise terms in an interview published in the *US News and World Report* for 5 May. Connally stated that Korea and probably Taiwan could be captured by the communists. He indicated that he did not regard Korea as of fundamental importance to American policy in East Asia.[78] Rhee protested with extreme vehemence and Ambassador Muccio emphasised to the State Department how serious was the damage done in statements made since January by Truman, Acheson and Connally: 'I should like to urge that those persons particularly charged with drafting speeches and statements on United States policy have this problem brought to their attention so that in any listing of Asiatic countries in whose freedom the United States maintains a continuing interest, Korea may always be included.'[79] Muccio's rebuke may have played a part in the decision that John Foster Dulles should visit Seoul in June, before proceeding to Japan to discuss the peace treaty, and in the stirring address Dulles delivered to the ROK assembly.

The state of the South Korean economy caused much anxiety in Washington, not least the growth of inflation. This problem was highly reminiscent of recent events in China, which had accelerated the fall of the Kuomintang in mainland China. Concern was also inspired by the acrimonious disputes between Rhee and the assembly and by fears that Rhee might seek to postpone the general election in May. Firm representations were made on both matters and the election was held as planned: Rhee lost support and a larger number of independent members was returned (but it should be noted that some of these were willing to support Rhee).[80] One obvious method for the ROK to seek to regain American support was to draw attention to the likelihood of North Korean aggression. Holt reported on 23 May that the minister of defence and acting prime minister had told newspaper reporters, on 10 May, that North Korean troops were being concentrated on the 38th parallel for a possible attack. A similar statement was made afterwards by the ROK chief of the general staff. A new infantry division of 5,000 men was allegedly being organised near Pyongyang but American military opinion did not regard the South Korean accusations as convincing evidence. The Americans inferred that the ROK agitation was designed to obtain more military equipment from America; Holt thought it was connected with the timing of the South Korean election.[81] A political campaign for reunification was launched from Pyongyang in the spring and summer of 1950 with appeals for support directed at those disillusioned with Rhee and his cronies; a reunified Korea was promised, to be accomplished in August. The policy of the Truman administration towards developments through East Asia hardened between April and June 1950 in consequence of the emphasis placed by General MacArthur and the Pentagon on the necessity of denying Taiwan to the communists: this was reinforced through approval of NSC-68. However, no blunt statement was forthcoming from Washington regarding a response to aggression in Korea, so that ambiguity persisted over what, if anything, the United States would do in the event of war erupting in Korea. No particular attention was devoted to Korea by the Foreign Office or chiefs of staff before the outbreak of war. Indeed much less attention was focused on Korea than had been the case in 1947. This was explicable in part through the dominance of the Cold War in Europe, especially following the Berlin blockade in 1948–49; British politicians and officials were less worried about Chinese communism than were their counterparts in the United States. They were wholly taken by surprise by the events of June 1950. Whether American policy-makers were as surprised is a subject of great controversy. The received picture is one of a somnolent Washington deeply shaken with Truman absent in Independence and Acheson away at his farm rather than at his desk. Bruce Cumings has suggested that there was knowledge of impending moves from North Korea on the part of certain intelligence operatives and perhaps of others involved in Korean intrigue. Cumings believes that Truman was not aware and reacted genuinely. He sees Acheson as not aware but prepared to utilise the situation in accordance with the global policy Acheson had evolved during the preceding year, vital features of which he revealed to no one: the secrets went with him to the grave.[82]

What did happen in Korea in June 1950? This has been the centre of intense speculation from June 1950 to the present. In the light of the partial opening of Soviet and Chinese archives since the end of the Cold War, more pieces of the jigsaw puzzle have emerged so that we now possess a clearer picture than before but important pieces of the puzzle are still missing. When the war began a common assumption in the West was that North Korea acted at the instigation of, or with the connivance of, the Soviet Union: Kim Il Sung's action was motivated by a Soviet initiative to test the resolution of the United States and its allies. If Kim succeeded in conquering South Korea, this would strengthen communism in Asia, counter-balance the American policy of rebuilding the Japanese economy, and diminish the prestige of the West in other parts of the world. Some commentators entertained reservations and underlined Kim's capacity for acting with a degree of independence in addition to keeping in mind provocation offered by Syngman Rhee's regime. However, the prevailing interpretation was that Stalin manoeuvred Kim into attacking but with no intention of the Soviet Union becoming *directly* involved. In the 1970s and 1980s this interpretation was assailed by a number of scholars emphasising that the Korean war must be seen as a civil war, dating at least from the end of the Pacific war in August 1945 and the roots of which reached back to the closing phase of the decadent Yi dynasty. Robert Simmons and Bruce Cumings stressed the significance of the profound rifts in Korean society, following on from the fascinating analysis put forward by the American diplomat-historian, Gregory Henderson.[83] Cumings is the most influential in his brilliant two volumes analysing the origins of the Korean conflict. In the first volume Cumings demonstrated, with abundant evidence, the deep alienation between left and right and the savagery lurking not far beneath the surface. Without doubt the Korean war was, to a large extent, a civil one. In his second massive volume Cumings produced a wide-ranging examination of the diverse trends, in terms of domestic and international developments, culminating in the events of June 1950. Cumings believed that China was more influential because of Mao Tse-tung's authorisation for Korean veterans from the Yenan era to return to the North Korean army in 1949–50 and because of Mao's determination to assert China's new importance as a major player in international relations.[84] Therefore, it was highly probable, if not inevitable, that China would intervene in the Korean war if it lasted for months rather than weeks. Cumings placed less emphasis on Stalin's contribution and brought out the provocation from the ROK together with the murky activities of those involved in the 'China Lobby' in the United States and those possessing links with intelligence bodies, such as the enigmatic M. Preston Goodfellow.[85]

Cumings's analysis was in part overtaken by revelations from Soviet and Chinese sources including information derived from individuals who participated personally at the time or who had received privileged access to party archives. As regards the Soviet Union, valuable evidence is to be found in the triple-authored volume by Sergei N. Goncharov, John W. Lewis and Xue Litai and in an analysis by Kathryn Weathersby.[86] Each of these scholars assesses the deep tensions and suspicions in the relationship between the Soviet Union and China. Stalin appreciated only too well what the CCP's triumph connoted for world communism: it was essential for him to work with Mao and yet to prevent Mao from becoming too powerful a figure on the world stage. Rapprochement between the United States and China must be prevented: here Stalin was helped by the intractable problem of Taiwan and by the hysteria engendered by the right wing of the Republican party (and by some Democrats). Goncharov, Lewis and Xue show that Stalin moved to a more adventurous policy over Korea in April 1950[87] but it is essential to note that the original impetus came from Kim Il Sung, not from Stalin. Kim was determined to unify Korea sooner rather than later and felt that the best opportunity would occur in 1950. There has been speculation as to when Kim visited Moscow to meet Stalin. Nikita Kruschev's 'reminiscences' refer vaguely to a visit by Kim in 1949 or 1950 in the course of which Stalin agreed that Kim could advance, provided that the military operations were completed swiftly and that a local episode in Korea did not escalate into an embarrassing international crisis. It now appears likely that Kim visited Moscow on two occasions, in March 1949 and in March/April 1950 and conveyed to Stalin his faith in a rapid victory to be accomplished by the military superiority of the North Korean army (provided that Stalin approved greater material assistance, including participation by the Soviet military advisers) linked with an uprising in South Korea against Rhee's regime.[88] In April 1950 Stalin moved away from his customary caution in the international sphere and encouraged Kim in his ambition. Stalin acted in the belief that the scenario depicted by Kim would materialise and that a relatively cheap victory for communism in Asia could be attained: Stalin wanted to preserve Soviet leadership in Asia *vis-à-vis* China.[89] Stalin was influenced by the fierce rhetoric of Syngman Rhee and by Rhee's professed aim of unifying Korea within the near future; it would be too dangerous to permit Rhee to launch an initiative. Kathryn Weathersby observes that Stalin's Korean policy resulted from Soviet weakness rather than strength, that is by Stalin's apprehension concerning China.[90]

Between April and June 1950 increased Soviet military aid arrived in the DPRK and new Soviet military advisers, possessing substantial battle experience, replaced men with limited experience.[91] The Soviet role in the approach of the war in June 1950 was very significant and Kim Il Sung could not have launched an offensive of such potency without Soviet aid. What of the Chinese contribution? Chen Jian has produced an excellent analysis of the Chinese position, although it has not been possible for him to research the Peking party archives which are closed; however, he has interviewed individuals granted privileged access to these records and he cites their evidence in his monograph.[92] Chen emphasises the relative ignorance of Mao and his colleagues over North Korean intentions. Kim visited Peking in May 1950 and told Mao that he intended to unite Korea in the near future: Chinese military aid would not be needed, since the DPRK was capable of achieving victory through its own armed forces, supported by a guerrilla uprising in the ROK.[93] However, neither Stalin nor Kim consulted Mao in June 1950 and there was no wish, *at that time*, for China to act. Chen qualifies Cumings's interpretation in observing that factionalism in the North Korean regime was a more potent factor than Cumings indicated in his second volume, although Cumings gave more weight to this in his first volume. The North Korean party was divided between factions looking respectively to Moscow and Peking, and factions associated with comrades in South Korea plus those loyal to Kim and those committed to no particular group. Kim had no desire to strengthen the pro-Chinese faction and this might occur if he moved too close to Peking. Rather, Kim aimed, with appreciable skill, to play on the mutual suspicions of Stalin and Mao to his own benefit.[94] The Korean veterans from the Chinese civil war were important but Kim did not wish to place too large an emphasis on their participation. Thus China was, in essence, fulfilling a passive role in June 1950. This was soon to change when the United States committed itself and the UN to military action in Korea, thereby eliminating the assumptions underpinning the earlier decisions of Kim and Stalin.

Finally, as regards British aspects, we should remind ourselves of the activities of Stalin's highly placed spies, Donald Maclean, Guy Burgess and Kim Philby. A great deal of confidential information concerning Western diplomacy and strategy went to Moscow: what we do not know is precisely what Stalin deduced from what he received, whether he feared that some might be 'disinformation' and ignored it, and how much he passed on to Peking and Pyongyang. From our knowledge of Stalin's character the answer to the last question is probably not a great deal. And then we should recall that the man in charge of British intelligence in Seoul was George Blake who was captured with Captain Holt and others in the North Korean advance, was interned, years later was arrested and found guilty of treachery after trial in Britain, and at last reached Moscow in a physical in addition to spiritual sense after a spectacular escape from gaol in Britain. Was Blake working for Stalin before the Korean war began?[95] All that can be said with conviction is that the British vessel was leaking dangerously, unknown to Clement Attlee and Ernest Bevin, as they surveyed this alarming crisis from the bridge.

Notes

1 See Ian Nish, 'The Anglo-Korean Treaty of 1883', in Ian Nish (ed.), *Aspects of Anglo-Korean Relations*, International Studies, 1984/1 (London: ICERD, London School of Economics, 1984), pp. 15–26. For an excellent, wide-ranging analysis of Korean society and Korea's role internationally, see Gregory Henderson, *Korea: The Politics of the Vortex* (Cambridge, MA: Harvard University Press, 1968).

2 For discussion of British policy towards Japan, see Ian Nish, *The Anglo-Japanese Alliance* (London: Athlone Press, 1966) and *Alliance in Decline: Anglo-Japanese Relations, 1908–1923* (London: Athlone Press, 1972). See also Peter Lowe, *Great Britain and Japan, 1911–15: A Study of British Far Eastern Policy* (London: Macmillan, 1969).

3 See Lowe, *Great Britain and Japan*, pp. 298–309.

4 For a useful general assessment of Korea, written during the era of Japanese control, see

A. J. Grajdanzev, *Modern Korea* (New York: Institute of Pacific Relations, distributed John Day, 1944). For discussion of Japanese colonial policy, including much on Korea, see R. H. Myers and M. R. Peattie (eds), *The Japanese Colonial Empire, 1895–1945* (Guildford: Princeton University Press, 1984).

5 Lowe, *Great Britain and Japan*, p. 309.

6 Memorandum, 'The Future of Korea', 8 September 1945, FO 371/46468/6733. This was the final draft of a paper prepared originally in July, see draft memorandum, 22 July 1945, FO 371/46468/4702.

7 *Ibid.*

8 See R. T. Oliver, *Syngman Rhee and American Involvement in Korea, 1942–1960* (Seoul: Panmun Books, 1978).

9 See letters from Rhee to Goodfellow, 29 November 1948, 23 December 1949, 19 January 1950, and Goodfellow to Rhee, 24 January 1950, folder, Rhee, box 1, M. Preston Goodfellow papers, Hoover Institution, Stanford, California. The main themes of the correspondence concern the importance of American economic and military assistance for South Korea: Goodfellow was involved in various activities involving business deals. It appears clear that he was fulfilling an intelligence role.

10 Letter from Allison to Sterndale Bennet, 28 February 1945, FO 371/46468/1394.

11 Minute by de la Mare, 13 March 1945, *ibid.*

12 For an illuminating account of American policy in 1945, see Michael Sandusky, *America's Parallel* (Alexandria, VA: University of Virginia Press, 1983).

13 Memorandum, 8 September 1945, FO 371/46468/6733.

14 Washington to FO, 16 November 1945, FO 371/46469/10145.

15 Minute by de la Mare, no date, *ibid.*

16 For a comprehensive, challenging examination of developments after the Pacific war, see Bruce Cumings, *The Origins of the Korean War*, 2 vols (Princeton: Princeton University Press, 1981–90). Note also Cumings (ed.), *Child of Conflict: The Korean–American Relationship, 1943–1953* (London: University of Washington Press, 1983). Cumings has produced the most lively and penetrating analyses of developments concerning Korea between 1945 and 1950. For a concise account, see Peter Lowe, *The Origins of the Korean War* (London: Longman, 1986).

17 Lowe, *Origins*, pp. 26–7.

18 Despatch from McDermot to Bevin, 29 December 1945, FO 371/54249/729.

19 Minute by de la Mare, 29 June 1946, FO 371/54250/9219.

20 Minute by Dening, 28 June 1946, *ibid.*

21 Minute by de la Mare, 5 September 1946, FO 371/54251/12585.

22 Seoul to FO, 8 February 1947, with minute by de la Mare, 11 February 1947, FO 371/63831/1712.

23 Seoul to FO, 8 February 1947, *ibid.*

24 *Ibid.*

25 FO to Seoul, 28 February 1947, FO 371/63831/2095.

26 Lowe, *Origins*, p. 31.

27 Washington to FO, 29 March 1947, FO 371/63832/4751.

28 *Manchester Guardian*, leading article, 22 March 1947.

29 FO to Seoul, 28 February 1947, FO 371/63831/2944.

30 Letter from Gascoigne to Wheeler, 6 June 1947, file, British Mission, Correspondence, August 1945–December 1947, RG9, box 107, MacArthur papers, MacArthur Memorial Norfolk, VA. For Bevin's views at the Margate conference in 1947, see Alan Bullock, *The Life and Times of Ernest Bevin*, vol. III, *Foreign Secretary, 1945–1951* (London: Heinemann, 1983), pp. 398–400.

31 Memorandum, 'Korea', 22 May 1947, FO 371/23835/7634.

32 *Ibid.*

33 *Ibid.*

34 *Ibid.*

35 Tokyo to FO, 13 July 1947, FO 371/63836/9362.

36 *Ibid.*

37 *Ibid.*

38 *Soviet Monitor*, 25 July 1947, enclosed in FO 371/63836/10318.

39 Washington to FO, 4 August 1947, FO 371/63836/10470.

40 Moscow to FO, 8 August 1947, with minute by Killick, 13 August 1947, FO 371/63836/10800.

41 Seoul to FO, 3 September 1947, FO 371/63837/12185.

42 Moscow to FO, 29 September 1947, FO 371/63838/13232.

43 Seoul to FO, 5 October 1947, FO 371/63839/13473.

44 For a lucid analysis of the evolution of the UN, see Evan Luard, *A History of the United Nations*, vol. I, *The Years of Western Domination, 1945–1955* (London: Macmillan, 1982).

45 Washington to New York (UK delegation to UN), 6 October 1947, with minute by Killick, 16 October 1947, FO 371/63839/13571.

46 Moscow to FO, 29 October 1947, FO 371/63840/14555.

47 Minute by Killick, 31 October 1947, *ibid.*

48 Minute by McDermot, 31 October 1947, *ibid.*

49 Minute by Hankey, 1 November 1947, *ibid.*

50 See Luard, *The Years of Western Domination*, pp. 232–6.

51 *FRUS 1948*, vol. VI, p. 1107, Jacobs to Marshall, 12 February 1948.

52 *Ibid.*, pp. 1110–13, Hodge to Marshall, 14 February 1948.

53 Seoul to FO, 13 January 1948, FO 371/69937/682.

54 FO to New York, 13 February 1948, FO 371/69937/2280.

55 Despatch, Kermode to Bevin, 17 January 1948, FO 371/69939/2829.

56 *Ibid.*

57 *Ibid.*

58 *Ibid.*

59 See R. A. Scalapino and Chong-sik Lee, *Communism in Korea*, 2 parts (Berkeley: University of California Press, 1972) and Dae-sook Suh, *The Korean Communist Movement, 1918–1948* (Princeton: Princeton University Press, 1967).

60 For a helpful biography of Kim, see Dae-sook Suh, *Kim Il Sung: The North Korean Leader* (New York: Columbia University Press, 1988).

61 See Cumings, *Origins*, vol. II, pp. 365, 445–8.

62 Memorandum by R. S. Milward, FO Research Department, 'The Constitution of North Korea', 10 October 1948, FO 371/69936/15019.

63 Minute by E. J. F. Scott, 13 October 1948, FO 371/69946/14369.

64 *Ibid.*

65 Luard, *The Years of Western Dominance*, pp. 237–8.

66 *Ibid.*, p. 238.

67 Despatch from Holt to Bevin, 19 November 1948, FO 371/69949/17775.

68 Despatch from Holt to Bevin, 19 November 1948, FO 371/69949/17774.

69 Seoul to FO, 'Korea: Economic Report No. 6', 16 July 1949, FO 371/76260/10554.

70 Letter from Holt to Peter Scarlett, 22 December 1949, FO 371/84078/1.

71 Letter from Ferguson-Innes to E. J. F. Scott, 30 December 1949, FO 371/84076/2.

72 *Ibid.*

73 *Ibid.*

74 Cumings, *Origins*, vol. II, pp. 379–438.

75 *Ibid*, pp. 420–1.

76 *Ibid.*, pp. 421–2. Cumings argues that 'South Korea was not pointedly excluded from the American defense perimeter, a common misconception' (p. 422) but Acheson's reference to the UN charter came across as vague rather than precise. For Acheson's explanation of his speech, see Dean Acheson, *Present at the Creation: My Years in the State Department* (London: Hamish Hamilton, 1970), pp. 354–8.

77 Letter from Goodfellow to Rhee, 24 January 1950, folder, Rhee, box 1, Goodfellow papers, Hoover Institution. See also *FRUS 1950*, vol. VII, p. 12, memorandum by John Z. Williams, 20 January 1950, and p. 42, memorandum by Niles W. Bond, 3 April 1950.

78 *FRUS 1950*, vol. VII, pp. 88–9, Muccio to Rusk, 25 May 1950.

79 *Ibid.*

80 See Lowe, *Origins*, pp. 56–65.

81 Letter from Holt to Tomlinson, 23 May 1950, FO 371/84078/5.

82 Cumings, *Origins*, vol. II, pp. 625–30.

83 See Henderson, *Korea*; R. R. Simmons, *The Strained Alliance: Peking, Pyongyang, Moscow and the Politics of the Korean Civil War* (London: Collier-Macmillan, 1975); and Cumings, 2 vols.

84 Cumings, *Origins*, vol. II, pp. 617, 651–3.

85 *Ibid.*, pp. 562–7, 618.

86 S. N. Goncharov, J. W. Lewis and Xue Litai, *Uncertain Partners: Stalin, Mao and the Korean War* (Stanford, CA: Stanford University Press, 1994) and Kathryn Weathersby, *Soviet Aims in Korea and the Origins of the Korean War, 1945–1950: New Evidence from Russian Archives*, Cold War International History Project (Washington, D.C.: Woodrow Wilson International Center for Scholars, 1993).

87 Goncharov, Lewis and Xue, *Uncertain Partners*, pp. 142, 148.

88 *Ibid.*, pp. 137–46 and Weathersby, *Soviet Aims*, pp. 23–4.

89 Goncharov, Lewis and Litai, *Uncertain Partners*, pp. 150–1 and Weathersby, *Soviet Aims*, p. 29.

90 Weathersby, *Soviet Aims*, pp. 31–2.

91 *Ibid.*, p. 25.

92 Chen Jian, *China's Road to the Korean War: The Making of the Sino-American Confrontation* (New York: Columbia University Press, 1994), p. 6.

93 *Ibid.*, pp. 112, 134.

94 *Ibid.*, p. 110 and Goncharov, Lewis and Xue, *Uncertain Partners*, p. 146.

95 For Blake's not particularly illuminating account, written in Moscow, see George Blake, *No Other Choice* (London: Jonathan Cape, 1990), pp. 110–49. Blake went to Seoul in October 1948. He states that before leaving London he read a small handbook entitled, 'Theory and Practice of Communism' by Carew Hunt, 'the senior SIS theoretician on Marxism'. This provided a succinct definition of the central features of Marxism. Blake comments that this had a deep impact: 'I was left with the feeling that the theory of Communism sounded convincing, that its explanation of history made sense and that its objectives seemed wholly desirable and did not differ all that much from Christian ideals even though the methods to attain them did. I began to ask myself whether Communism was really the terrible evil it was made out to be' (pp. 110–11).

10

BRITAIN AND ROLLBACK IN KOREA, JUNE TO NOVEMBER 1950

The outbreak of the Korean war came as a complete shock to the Labour government, to the Conservative and Liberal opposition parties, and to public opinion. Attlee's administration was worn down by the cumulative domestic and international strains of the problems with which it had wrestled since 1945. The government had been returned narrowly in the general election of February 1950 but had lost most of its original fire which had made it the greatest reforming administration since the Liberal government of 1905 to 1915. The Korean war was a major watershed for the Attlee government, for it marked the accentuation of serious political and economic dilemmas which led to the government's defeat in the general election of October 1951. The already onerous defence burden was exacerbated by a further large commitment to expand the British defence budget to wholly unwise levels – this is such an extent that the Churchill government was compelled to reduce defence spending. For the Labour Party itself the Korean conflict opened up rifts between the left, centre and right of the party which constituted the beginning of the bitter internal disputes that weakened Labour progressively down to the 1980s.[1]

It is important to understand reactions to the news of events in Korea in order to grasp the nature of the British response. The outlook of political leaders was conditioned by the fact that they had lived through two catastrophic world wars within a generation and they were grappling with many of the consequences. It was widely believed that the Second World War could have been averted had resolute steps been taken to combat Japanese, Italian and German aggression during the 1930s when this first emerged. The disastrous imcompetence of the prewar era was symbolised in the Munich conference and agreement of September 1938. Rather than cave in to brutal expansion it was far better to face up to painful decisions and oppose aggressors vigorously. This view was common across the political spectrum with the exception of some on the far left of the Labour Party who were pacifists or fellow travellers. For those in the Labour and Liberal Parties and for some in the Conservative Party, the position was rendered even more demanding because of the challenges confronting the UN. The League of Nations was believed to have failed because of the weakness of its principal members, which amounted to a betrayal of its principles. This must not be repeated for, if the UN collapsed in analogous fashion, the repercussions would be immense and could lead to a third world war. Now that the Soviet Union possessed the atomic bomb the dangers were intensified considerably. A third world war could mean the obliteration of much of Europe. Thus there was firm support in Britain for opposing perceived North Korean aggression but ambivalence could be discerned. The conflict in Korea could connote a diversion of attention and resources from Europe to East Asia with a concomitant diminution in American involvement in Europe. The war in Korea could help the 'Asia firsters' in the United States.

The cabinet met on 27 June and decided unanimously that Britain should react positively to the American appeal for support following the North Korean advance south of the 38th parallel on 25 June:

> The Cabinet at once agreed that the United Kingdom Government should support the substance of the resolution which was to be put to the Security Council urging all members of the United Nations to assist the Republic of Korea to repel this armed attack. It was the clear duty of the United Kingdom Government to do everything in their power, in concert with other members of the United Nations, to help the South Koreans to resist this aggression.[2]

The discussion concentrated largely upon the wisdom of referring, in the proposed resolution for the UN Security Council, to 'centrally-directed Communist imperialism', as the United States wished to do. There was no actual proof that North Korea had implemented orders from Moscow and it was argued by some in the cabinet that it would be sensible to act as though the DPRK was responsible, so as to afford the Soviet Union an opportunity to withdraw without loss of face. The suggested American wording would render it more invidious for the Russians to act constructively. Furthermore the American wish to include a reference to Taiwan presented considerable difficulties for the British government because of British recognition of the Peking government. Other members of the cabinet emphasised the urgency of the Korean crisis and that the primary American aim was to prevent South Korea being overrun. Ernest Bevin was recovering from an operation in a nursing home but he was consulted: his view was that the resolution to be placed before the UN Security Council should be restricted to developments in Korea. Western leaders were fully aware of communist threats in Malaya, Indo-China and in other areas but it would not be propitious to include such allusions in a resolution. The cabinet reminded itself of comparisons with events before 1939:

> In further discussion it was recognised that, by the terms of their proposed announcement, the United States Government were deliberately taking the major risk of making it clear to the Soviet Union that they were resolved to put a stop to armed aggression. In this they were doubtless influenced by the consideration that, as had been amply demonstrated by the events preceding the Second World War, it would be easier to make such a stand in the earlier rather than in the later, stages of imperialist expansion by a totalitarian State. Though major risks were involved, it was arguable that there would be ever greater risks in allowing the Soviet Government to conclude, as Hitler had done, that aggression would succeed if its victims could be over-powered sufficiently quickly.[3]

The cabinet concluded that the United States must be supported but that a reference to 'communist imperialism' should be omitted; the advice of the chiefs of staff must be obtained; it was essential to discuss matters with the Conservative opposition; and policy must be coordinated with the Commonwealth.[4]

On 28 June Attlee chaired a meeting of the cabinet defence committee. A recommendation from the chiefs of staff was received proposing that the units of the Royal Navy present in Japanese waters should immediately be placed under the authority of the United States naval commander to function in fulfilment of the Security Council's resolution of 27 June. This called the UN members to oppose North Korean aggression. The first sea lord, Admiral Lord Fraser of North Cape, stated that the chiefs of staff welcomed the American decision to act and believed that this would have salutary effects if successful. This would be beneficial to Hong Kong, Malaya and throughout the world. Admittedly there was a risk that the Soviet Union might precipitate a world war but this seemed unlikely. However, it was essential that British naval action should not arise in connection with Taiwan.[5] The United States appreciated the British offer of naval assistance, since it took some time for the American navy to make its presence felt. The British chiefs of staff viewed possible assistance from the army and the Royal Air Force in a different light. The North Korean advance made it more likely that the United States would press for ground troops to be sent. The chiefs reviewed matters on 30 June and concluded, predictably, that British troops were already deployed extensively throughout the globe and it was difficult to contemplate sending British ground forces to Korea.[6]

When the cabinet met on 4 July a full discussion took place on various implications of Korean developments. The North Korean advance was so successful that the Truman administration was preparing to commit American ground troops contrary to the initial recommendations of the American joint chiefs of staff.[7] The cabinet devoted the first part of its deliberations to deciding how to handle a debate in the House of Commons and agreed on the terms of a motion to be tabled in the names of Attlee and five colleagues. Some time was spent in determining how to handle criticism that the response of the American and British governments did not comply with the UN charter. This hinged on the intriguing absence of the Soviet Union from the Security Council on 27 June. It was pointed out that decisions had been taken in the absence of a permanent member and that the Soviet government had acquiesced. Forty members of the UN had stated support for the resolution carried in the Security Council on 27 June. Article 51 of the charter stipulated that the right of individual or collective self-defence as not qualified by any other section of the charter and that, although South Korea was not a member of the UN, the action taken was compatible with this article. The cabinet decided that Attlee should argue accordingly in the debate and should emphasise that the Security Council's decision was 'in fact the first significant demonstration of the principle of collective security against aggression'.[8] As regards the possible despatch of British troops, the cabinet minutes stated: 'No formal request for reinforcements had been received from the United States Government; and in all the circumstances the Government spokesmen in the debate would be well-advised to discount any expectation that the United Kingdom could make further forces available for operations in Korea.'[9] Further discussion centred on trade aspects involving China and Hong Kong: these will be considered separately in the context of relations with China.[10] Attlee told the cabinet on 6 July that the defence committee had considered the position again and, 'In view of the risks to which we were exposed elsewhere in the Far East and South-East Asia, it was not proposed that further United Kingdom forces should be sent to Korea.'[11] The House of Commons expressed valuable support as regards the resolution of the Security Council: doubts had not been expressed over the legal validity of action taken.

On 7 July the Security Council approved the establishment of a Unified Command under the UN to implement the UN's commitment to defeat North Korean aggression. To the surprise of no one General Douglas MacArthur, commander-in-chief of American land and air forces in the Far East and SCAP in Japan, was appointed to this office. In terms of length of service and outstanding achievement MacArthur was the obvious choice. As a military commander he possessed original insight, courage, boldness and zest. However, he was 70 years of age and had not fulfilled an active campaigning command for nearly five years. His proconsular lifestyle in Japan accentuated his natural arrogance and remoteness; this was compounded by his preference for surrounding himself with senior officers who had served in the Pacific campaigns and who were sycophantic in approach. In addition, MacArthur's interest in the possibility of moving from the Dai-Ichi building to the White House has to be kept in mind. A successful campaign in Korea might prove the final stepping-stone to the presidency and, given his age, the 1952 election would be the last opportunity for MacArthur to achieve his final ambition.[12] Those in the American government who had dealt with him at close quarters recognised the importance of reminding him of his deeper responsibilities and of curbing his inclination to act independently. Louis Johnson, secretary of defense, said at the first Blair House meeting on 25 June that instructions to MacArthur should be explicit 'so as not to give him too much discretion': there should 'not be a real delegation of Presidential authority to General MacArthur'.[13] John Foster Dulles wrote to Dean Acheson on 7 July:

> I suggest that the President might want to emphasize by personal message to General MacArthur the delicate nature of the responsibilities which he will now be carrying not only on behalf of the United States but on behalf of the United Nations, and the importance of instructing his staff to comply scrupulously with political and military limitations and instructions which may be sent, the reasons for which may not always be immediately apparent but which will often have behind them political considerations of gravity.[14]

These prophetic words were not heeded and instructions sent to MacArthur were couched usually in terms that were too broad. However, MacArthur's prestige was so great that it was not easy to control him. The British government supported MacArthur's appointment and the anxiety which became so conspicuous a few months later was not then apparent.

The urgency of the military situation in Korea compelled the sending of fervent appeals for support to those members of the UN committed to repelling aggression. The ROK and American forces were compelled to retreat towards the Pusan redout and the real possibility existed of the UN being pushed out of the Korean peninsula. Such an eventuality would be disastrous and the cabinet and chiefs of staff reconsidered reluctantly their previous decision. Attlee told the cabinet on 25 July that the ambassador in Washington, Sir Oliver Franks, had reported that an offer of British troops would improve Anglo-American relations. Attlee stated that the defence committee had discussed matters again in conjunction with the chiefs of staff:

> They adhered to the view that it would be unsound to divert to Korea troops required to meet other Communist threats in this area in Hong Kong and in Malaya. They also recognised the military disadvantages of operating in Korea a mixed force with separate supply lines. They had, however, come to the conclusion that the disadvantage was outweighed by the political advantages which would be secured by an announcement that some British land forces were to be sent to Korea. Such an announcement would have a valuable effect upon public opinion in the United States, and it would also give a useful lead to other members of the United Nations.[15]

The defence committee had arranged for a brigade group to be formed, subject to cabinet approval, without cutting the strength of the forces available in Hong Kong and Malaya; this should be sent as soon as possible to join Unified Command.

Subsequently the British response was coordinated with the Commonwealth to constitute the first Commonwealth division. The British contribution comprised two infantry brigades, one armoured regiment, one and a half artillery regiments, one and a half engineer regiments and supporting ground forces. In addition, Sunderland aircraft were provided. Australia contributed two infantry battalions, part of the first Commonwealth division, two destroyers or frigates, one aircraft carrier and a fighter squadron. Canada provided one reinforced infantry brigade, with tank and artillery forces, part of the first Commonwealth division, three destroyers and a squadron of transport aircraft. New Zealand contributed one regiment of artillery and part of the first Commonwealth division. The Union of South Africa contributed one fighter squadron. India provided an ambulance unit.[16] Even before the decision to send British troops it had been decided that a British defence representative should be appointed to liaise with MacArthur's staff in Tokyo. Sir Alvary Gascoigne favoured the appointment of General Gairdner who had served previously as Attlee's representative.[17] Gairdner had retired, however, and the chiefs of staff decided to appoint Air Vice-Marshal Cecil Bouchier.[18] Gascoigne was not enthused for Bouchier had served under MacArthur and might not show enough independence. Officials in the Foreign Office shared this reservation. On the credit side Bouchier worked extremely hard, typing his own lengthy reports to London since he had little assistance; he reported fully and conveyed much information but he reflected MacArthur's opinions excessively.

Before pursuing military developments further it is necessary for us to examine the British attempt to maintain diplomatic links with the Soviet Union in the initial phase of the war in an attempt to maintain diplomatic relations on a positive note. This well intentioned attempt gave rise to sharp Anglo-American exchanges and was the first real indication of the tensions generated by the war.

It is difficult to assess the role of the Soviet Union with accuracy. The Soviet delegate, Jacob Malik, was absent from the vital meeting of the UN Security Council when North Korea was condemned for aggression. Had he been present and used his veto then it would not have been possible for the UN to be committed to military action in Korea. Andrei Gromyko, in one of the few revealing passages in his memoirs, stated that the Soviet Foreign Ministry was astonished at Stalin's decision that Malik should not attend the Security Council.[19] A Soviet diplomat, interviewed for the Thames Television series dealing with the Korean war, commented that it was a grave blunder.[20] An alternative explanation proffered at the time by the Yugoslav delegate to the UN, Alex Bebler, was that Stalin did not want communist China represented in the UN and that he was pursuing a Machiavellian strategy designed to embroil the United States and China.[21] Bebler had his own reasons for levelling this accusation, given Yugoslavia's break with the Soviet Union in 1948, but it remains a possible explanation. Whatever the reason it was undoubtedly a fundamental error. According to information obtained from North Korean POWs, the Soviet Union ordered the withdrawal of Soviet military advisers and tank teams from North Korea shortly after the UN committed itself to military action. The order to withdraw was given apparently about the eighth day of the war. Intelligence sources revealed that the Russians had 15 military advisers attached to each North Korean division. It was believed that the Soviet advisers had indicated full approval of North Korean strategy and of the calibre of the DPRK offensive in the early weeks of the war. It was thought, in late August, that Soviet advisers might still remain with the North Korean army headquarters.[22] Ernest Bevin and his cabinet colleagues believed, in late June and early July, that whatever was the true role of the Soviet Union in the outbreak of the war, Soviet diplomatic contacts should be used to ascertain whether Moscow might cooperate in trying to end the war. *Pravda* placed the blame squarely on South Korea and the United States in a leading article published on 28 June – the 'Clique of Syngman Rhee entered on the road of military adventure' aided by 'their masters across the sea'.[23] Truman had linked the situation in Taiwan with events in Korea and thus was guilty of 'aggression against Korean Popular Democratic Republic and against the Chinese People's Republic'.[24]

Beneath the blasts of Cold War propaganda appreciable anxiety emerged in Moscow. Initially it proved extremely difficult for British or American diplomats to contact senior Soviet representatives.[25] Truman and Acheson were suspicious of the British desire for talks with the Russians and highly sceptical of what, if anything, would emerge from them. The British ambassador in Moscow, Sir David Kelly, was instructed to contact Gromyko: the Americans were kept fully informed. On 6 July Admiral Kirk, the American ambassador in Moscow, reported that Gromyko had invited Kelly to see him and had told him that the Soviet Union desired a peaceful solution in Korea. Kelly told Gromyko that the Soviet Union could use its influence in Pyongyang to dissuade the North Koreans from further bloodshed. Kelly stated that Britain wished to restore the *status quo ante* and to end the fighting. Gromyko nodded agreement. Kelly asked if Gromyko's reaction meant that, despite his recent statement that Soviet policy remained one of non-interference the Soviet government might be willing to act positively. Gromyko added simply that the ambassador was conversant with the Soviet position.[26] The Foreign Office believed that serious thought must be given to the next step and it was necessary to proceed with discretion. Attlee sent a personal message to Truman on 6 July proposing that British and American representatives should meet to consider the overall situation facing the West, including strategic implications in various regions. Attlee expressed the wish that Lord Tedder, the principal British defence liaison representative in Washington, should be consulted. Attlee emphasised the need for frank exchanges.[27] Acheson agreed to Kelly carefully sounding out Gromyko further.[28] Bevin sent a personal telegram to Oliver Franks which was handed by Franks to Acheson on 8 July. Bevin deduced that the Soviet government might be willing to cooperate in resolving the Korean crisis. If so, a bargaining position might be established and it was important to anticipate points that could be raised by Gromyko. It was probable that Taiwan would be pursued, since the United States did not enjoy the degree of support over this issue which obtained with Korea. Bevin recognised that the Russians might be playing a devious game linked with the Soviet world peace campaign launched earlier in the year, although he doubted it. He recognised further that restoration of the *status quo ante* could in itself lead to a situation similar to that seen in Czechoslovakia in 1948; the UN military campaign must be sustained.[29]

Bevin touched a raw nerve in referring so candidly to Taiwan. The whole question of American policy towards China was particularly sensitive, given the acrimony existing in American domestic politics. Nothing had done more harm to Acheson's reputation than the allegation that he had been responsible for the 'loss' of China. Acheson was not prepared to embark on bargaining with the Soviet Union over the future of Taiwan. He sent a lengthy message to Bevin on 10 July reiterating the lessons of the 1930s as the ghost of Munich walked again.[30] He was convinced that the Soviet Union was responsible for orchestrating aggression and there was some evidence that the Chinese communists might be involved in the Korean fighting. Soviet accusations that the United States had rendered it impossible for the Soviet Union to participate constructively in the UN were 'sheer unadulterated blackmail'.[31] Acheson felt that Anglo-American divergences in policy regarding China could not be bridged. In an accompanying personal message to Lewis Douglas, the ambassador, Acheson said bluntly that he felt very strongly about Bevin's message and his ire should be conveyed to him.[32] Bevin was convalescing and Kenneth Younger, the minister of state, dealt with daily business. Younger had become more critical of American policy because of its blundering nature and lack of subtlety. A middle line should be followed whereby the principles for which the UN stood, and which were being applied in Korea, were sustained but the door was also open for discussions with the Russians. The Americans were too emotional. It was important to work closely with the Commonwealth, especially Canada and Australia. Talks should be held with the Conservative opposition but Younger regarded Churchill as an obstacle:

> I am bound to say, however, that so far as Mr. Churchill personally is concerned, I would much prefer not to tell him anything until we have ascer-

tained that Canada and Australia were in broad agreement with us. He is likely to be unimpressed, if not actually antagonised, by our arguments regarding India, and he showed no disposition the other day to regard the Korean incident as anything more than an opportunity to win a few votes. The other Conservative leaders are, of course, on quite a different footing.[33]

Bevin regarded the Soviet attitude as not discouraging but it had to be treated with caution. Roderick Barclay, Bevin's private secretary, reported Bevin's opinion:

> The Secretary of State said he did not believe that Stalin wanted the situation in the Far East to develop in such a way as to cause the United States to build up tremendous forces there. It was possible that Mao Tse Tung [sic] wanted to try to involve Stalin in war with the United States, but he thought that Stalin would get out of this.[34]

Bevin was distressed at the tone of Acheson's message but attributed it to the emotionalism prevailing in the United States. On 18 July Attlee informed the cabinet that Gromyko had handed the British ambassador a message the previous evening, emphasising that the most positive way of working towards a Korean settlement was to convene the Security Council with the participation of representatives of the Peking government and that 'representatives of the Korean people should be heard by the Council'.[35] No suggestion of a halt to the North Korean offensive was contained in the Soviet communication and the Soviet Union had therefore made no concession. Nehru was deeply concerned and wished to explore further the possibility of compromise. The cabinet agreed that the Soviet response was not satisfactory: 'There was no necessary connection between the stopping of aggression in Korea and the admission of the People's Government of China to the Security Council, and the two issues should at this stage be kept distinct.'[36] Negotiations were impossible unless the North Korean forces pulled back. Issues relating to China and membership of the UN could be considered after North Korea had acted suitably. Nehru should be told that the United States was prepared to accept a majority vote with regard to admission of the Peking government to the UN. It was agreed that exchanges with the Soviet government should be continued. However, no further progress could be made with the Soviet Union and the talks lapsed. Stalin pursued a waiting game to see how the military campaign fared.

Much importance was attached by the cabinet to coordinating policy with the Commonwealth. This connoted particularly Canada, Australia and New Zealand and, in a discrete category, India. Relations with Canada were cordial: the prime minister, Louis St Laurent, was liked and respected and there was deep trust in the secretary for external affairs, Lester ('Mike') Pearson. Relations with Australia had been tempestuous on occasions and this was accentuated by the abrasive personalities of the two successive ministers for external affairs, Dr Herbert Evatt and Sir Percy Spender. Sir Robert Menzies was an old-fashioned adherent of links with London.[37] He acted as a restraining influence in areas that could cause friction in relations with London. Australia was preoccupied with security and looked towards the United States as the principal source of reassurance. New Zealand was closest to Britain but geostrategic considerations pushed New Zealand in the same direction as Australia. South Africa wished to maintain cooperation with Britain in defence matters, despite the isolationist tendencies present in the outlook of some members of Dr Malan's government.[38] India represented a very different factor for political and racial reasons. Attlee wanted to maintain good relations with India, appreciating the significance of the emerging Indian role in Asia.[39]

Nehru was in fact critical of the United States. He deemed Truman and Acheson too impulsive and lacking in patience. He explained his attitude in a frank letter to Attlee sent on 21 July. At the beginning he stated his acceptance of the initial response of the UN to events in Korea.

> I am quite clear that North Korea, probably with the connivance of the Soviet government and certainly after full preparation, deliberately committed aggression on South Korea. Because of this, the United Nations were fully justified in declaring North Korea as an aggressor and we supported them in this decision, even though all the available information at our disposal about South Korea is not to its advantage.[40]

Nehru observed that the aim should be to confine hostilities to the Korean peninsula. He remarked on the immense process of change in East and South-East Asia since the Pacific war and the inability of the Western powers properly to come to terms with the consequences. There was a profound desire for fundamental social change and agrarian reform, which meant that people did not see communism as a menace. Naive castigation of communism achieved nothing. The Soviet Union and its allies revealed a shrewder grasp of realities in Asia. Nehru had no false illusions over Soviet aims: 'I know very well that the Soviet Government is probably playing its own expansionist game and that it would be a disaster if it succeeded in that.'[41] He feared that prolongation of the war in Korea could lead to a world war. Nehru described his opinions as 'trite' but reiterated:

> But I do feel that we are drifting fast in a wrong direction which can only lead to evil results. There is too facile an impression that military strength and economic resources will solve the problem in the end to our advantage. But it seems to me perfectly clear, in Asia at least, that something more is required than military and economic strength. That something at the present moment is lacking in the approach of the Western Powers ...[42]

The Americans were not persuaded and felt that Nehru was far too sympathetic to the Peking government. While there was excessive idealism in Nehru's opinions, the United States showed little skill or sagacity in its dealings with India during the Korean war.

The dominating issue in the latter part of the summer of 1950 concerned policy towards North Korea once the DPRK forces had been compelled to retreat to the 38th parallel. Kim Il Sung's troops performed well in forcing the ROK army to retreat to the south-eastern part of the peninsula but they could not administer a swift knock-out blow. The ROK army would clearly have been defeated had it not been for the intervention of the UN. General MacArthur had faced daunting challenges in the past, notably in the Philippines in 1942, and was confident that he would succeed in reversing the fortunes of war decisively. He implemented a bold stroke in the landing in Inchon, the last major successful initiative in his military career. The joint chiefs were dubious of the wisdom of the landing but MacArthur's judgement was vindicated in the triumphant landing in Inchon on 15 September.[43] Now it was the turn of the DPRK army to retreat rapidly: the political questions present from the beginning of the war assumed urgency. Should the UN forces halt at the 38th parallel? To stop here might appear timid and as inviting renewed warfare subsequently; in addition, the UN had been pledged to secure the reunification of Korea since 1947. Against this it could be argued that the original aim of the UN had been to achieve reunification by persuasion, not force, and that if the North Koreans were hurled back to the 38th parallel, this could be deemed an important success. Furthermore to advance north of the parallel would be to invite Chinese intervention and thus to produce a conflict of a wholly different nature.

Within the State Department divergent views existed from the start of the war. John M. Allison, director of the Office of North-East Asian affairs, was a hardliner who always advocated crushing North Korea. On 1 July he wrote to Dean Rusk, the assistant secretary of state for far eastern affairs, and said that he had heard a suggestion that President Truman should state in a forthcoming speech that UN troops would not cross the 38th parallel. He rejected this totally: the opportunity to unite Korea must be seized and UN forces should continue to the Manchurian and Siberian borders if possible.[44] Rusk signified approval.[45] The opposing view was advanced from within the policy planning staff by Paul Nitze and Herbert Feis. They argued that the principal aims of the UN operations would be satisfied by halting at the 38th parallel and that to advance further north would incur undue risk.[46] Truman, Acheson and the joint chiefs were influenced deeply by the analysis of policy arrived at a few months previously, notably in NSC 68 with its heavy emphasis on meeting and repelling aggression. The Truman administration adopted a policy of 'rollback', of not simply forcing an aggressor to evacuate territory conquered but of occupying the aggressor's own territory. If successful this would be the first occasion when a communist state had been liquidated.[47] This would transform the political fortunes of the administration. MacArthur's master stroke at Inchon offered the seductive prospect of turning this vision into reality. As for MacArthur he had no qualms over proceeding north. He despised the North Koreans almost as much as he hated the Chinese communists; he knew that this was the final military campaign of his career and he wanted it to end on a resounding note. Thus MacArthur's aim in driving north coincided with those of Truman, Acheson and the joint chiefs: the difference was that MacArthur was prepared to go further in risking Chinese intervention.

Within the British bureaucracy differences of view existed, too, but here it was not a matter of divergences within the Foreign Office but of a sharp distinction between the chiefs of staff, who opposed advancing further north, and the cabinet and the Foreign Office who supported proceeding north. It is best to consider the latter aspect first, for the assessments of the chiefs of staff require more extensive discussion. The Foreign Office, as represented by the far eastern specialists, believed that while there was a risk of Chinese intervention if UN forces advanced north of the 38th parallel, it was not likely that China would commit itself to military operations of a hazardous and unpredictable character. China had not intervened in July and August and the gist of early Chinese statements focused mainly upon criticism of American policy relating to Taiwan. Since it was virtually impossible for British diplomats in Peking to report fully, information supplied by the Indian ambassador in Peking, K. M. Panikkar, was especially significant.[48] Before the last ten days of September Panikkar deduced that China was unlikely to act in Korea but his reports changed markedly following MacArthur's success at Inchon. He reported warnings from Chou En-lai that China would intervene if UN forces moved beyond the 38th parallel. However, the seductive impact of Inchon had more impact than Panikkar's warnings as relayed to London from New Delhi. The cabinet discussed the situation on 26 September. Attlee began by stating that the UN General Assembly would have to determine shortly the course of actions to be followed in the light of the destruction of the North Korean army:

> It would be the duty of the United Nations to restore peace and order in the country as a whole, and to establish an independent Democratic Government for all Korea. It might well be necessary for United Nations forces to enter North Korea for the purpose of achieving these objectives.[49]

A draft resolution prepared by Bevin was handed around the table. During the subsequent debate it was pointed out that the Soviet Union might reoccupy North Korea if the UN forces stopped at the 38th parallel or anarchy might occur. It would be impossible to create a stable administration in South Korea in either of these eventualities: 'It would, however, be necessary to present clearly to public opinion the reasons justifying the military occupation of the whole of Korea, its temporary character and its limited objectives.'[50] It was expected that the Indian government would experience difficulty in endorsing a resolution providing for an advance north of the 38th parallel. The Canadian government had adopted a legalistic view that the elections held in South Korea applied to the entire country but it might be possible to persuade Canada to cooperate. The other members of the Commonwealth would probably support the action advocated by Bevin. It was noted that the resolution should stipulate the creation of a UN civil administration between the initial phase of military administration and the attainment of a wholly democratic Korean government. Since some time might elapse before free elections could take place, it was imperative that a functioning civil administration should be established. Britain should be represented in any body established to consider economic aid required by Korea so as to ensure that the burden was distributed fairly. If UN forces advanced north of the 38th parallel, British troops would have to participate. A British commitment in the north should be limited in scope: guerrilla warfare could prove prolonged and, given British responsibilities in Malaya and in other areas, British forces should not be involved in an extended role during pacification.[51]

On 28 September the cabinet was informed of a report from Panikkar indicating growing Chinese hostility towards the United States. The cabinet was evidently uneasy but decided to confirm existing policy:

> There was general agreement that the policy of the United Kingdom

Government towards the Korean problem should stand. At the same time it was desirable to allay Chinese fears to take part in discussions in the United Nations on some of the outstanding questions, such as Formosa and should also endeavour to placate the Chinese Government in regard to the flights of United States aircraft over Manchuria and the alleged bombing of places in Manchuria.[52]

The latter observation related to incidents in which American planes had bombed Chinese and Soviet territory. Some may have been accidental but others were openly provocative. On 10 October, Stratemeyer, commanding general of the far eastern air force, issued a rebuke following a Soviet protest and a border violation. Stratemeyer stated that he and MacArthur were extremely unhappy over recent incidents and to be 100 miles off target was inexcusable.[53] On 11 October the joint chiefs of staff told MacArthur that it was essential that suitable action was taken to ensure that subordinates compiled with orders.[54] Attlee and Bevin decided to adhere to the cabinet's conclusion that Britain should support an advance north of the 38th parallel. Sir Roger Makins informed Bevin on 5 October that the far eastern experts in the Office believed that it was unlikely that full-scale Chinese intervention would occur, although small-scale action was possible.[55] On 7 October Britain sponsored a resolution carried in the UN General Assembly which provided for the establishment of UNCURK (Australia, Chile, the Netherlands, Pakistan, the Philippines, Thailand and Turkey); this commission would take over the functions of UNCOK, fulfil UN aims of accomplishing a unified, independent and democratic government for the whole of Korea, deal with matters concerning relief and rehabilitation, make interim arrangements pending the arrival of the new commission in Korea, and call for regular reports to be submitted to the General Assembly and any relevant special sessions.[56]

The British chiefs of staff arrived at a radically different assessment than that of the Foreign Office and one that proved far more accurate. The background is explained by the original reluctance of the chiefs of staff to see military and air forces committed to the Korean theatre because of the numerous other claims on resources. They did not wish to see the troops despatched, reluctantly through American pressure, committed indefinitely to Korean operations. In particular they were alarmed at the danger of large-scale Chinese intervention, which would render operations in Korea infinitely more hazardous. The three individual chiefs varied somewhat in their views. Field Marshal Sir William Slim, the chief of the imperial general staff, vacillated in early October before coming down decisively against proceeding north. Admiral of the Fleet Lord Fraser of North Cape, the first sea lord, consistently opposed going north. The greatest intellectual contribution in arguing the case for caution came from Marshal of the Royal Air Force Sir John Slessor. Slessor was the ablest of the chiefs and pursued his arguments with courage, conviction and skill. He became one of the most vigorous and effective critics of American policy in Korea and played an important role in endeavouring to steady American decision-making during the most dangerous phase of the war in January 1951. Slessor began reflecting on the aims of the UN early in July and communicated his opinions to his colleagues in a meeting held on 17 July. He understood the purpose of UN action as intended to force the North Korean troops back to the 38th parallel and to restore the *status quo ante*.[57] Lord Tedder told the chiefs on 2 August that the North Korean attack had come as a shock to the American government because of inadequate intelligence and complacency and to the American public through the depth of the trauma: Tedder thought the impact on American public opinion was salutary, 'comparable in some ways to Pearl Harbour in the recent war'.[58] He said that the Americans 'had not yet made up their minds as to what action they would take when the forces of North Korea had been thrown back to the 38° parallel'.[59]

On 14 September Slessor prepared a memorandum for his colleagues in which he stated that recent information from Bouchier in Tokyo had strengthened his suspicion that the Americans were unclear as to their aims in Korea and that, unless considerable care was exercised, victory in South Korea could lead to new and onerous commitments which, to put it at its worst, could involve grave risks of a clash between the West and Russia and China. Slessor felt that the Americans would agree with the British that there was no real strategic interest in Korea at all. While based upon free elections under UN supervision, it was doubtful whether any Korean regime would ever be democratic in the Western sense and equally dubious as to how independent it could be with China and the Soviet Union on the other side of the Yalu. It was definitely not in the allied interest to have an extensive, prolonged commitment to keep forces in Korea. It was highly desirable, because of pressure in other parts of the globe, to reduce the forces in Korea so that they could be deployed more constructively against other communist threats. He recognised that some forces would have to be maintained in Korea so as to deter future aggression and the basic objective should be to ensure that the position was no worse than before the North Korean attack:

> That being so, what is the object of our sending any forces – except perhaps S. Korean forces – north of the 38th parallel at all? If we assume the N.K. army is destroyed south of the 38th parallel as the result of present operations, what is the military advantage to be gained by occupying North Korea? True, it would ensure more certainly that [sic] anything else could that North Korea does not repeat her invasion of South Korea in a few months or years time. But after having had her army destroyed and all her industries knocked flat, I find it difficult to envisage North Korea, even with Russian assistance, becoming a menace again for a long time to come.[60]

To advance north of the 38th parallel would be to antagonise India and other Asiatic states, risk a huge increase in UN forces required for security purposes and run the danger of conflict with China and the Soviet Union: 'I'd have thought from that point of view there was a lot to be said for having a couple of hundred miles between the American/British troops and the Yalu.'[61] An attempt should be made to persuade North Korea to accept reunification to be achieved through free elections for all of Korea but, if the North Korean government declined, then it should be left as a Russian satellite. UN efforts should focus upon making South Korea a better run state in political and economic terms. Slessor made clear his distaste for Rhee and his cronies: 'Rhee and co. must not have a free hand to misgovern the place as they did before; land reforms etc. should be enforced and the UN. Commission will have to remain in S. Korea for a long time.'[62]

This observation underlined the growing dissatisfaction in Britain as a result of press reports concerning the brutality and corruption associated with Rhee's administration. The reports appearing in the *Daily Worker* were not very influential, since this newspaper's persistent attacks on the Attlee government as lackeys of the White House and Pentagon diminished the effects of Alan Winnington's reports. It was a different matter where reporters like Louis Heren of *The Times* and James Cameron of *Picture Post* were involved (a dispute with the paper's proprietor over Korea caused Cameron's departure). Alarm over the savage conduct of the Rhee government mounted steadily between September and November. Slessor weighed up the considerations involved at the end of his memorandum. He conceded that it would be disappointing to see the restoration of the *status quo ante* and the Americans, in particular, would demur at it. He then explained the positive features:

> From a political point of view it would not be so good as to get a Unified Korea under U.N. auspices; but it would be much better than it was before in rela- tion to U.S. and British and U.N. prestige in Asia – we shall have inflicted a great defeat on aggressive Communism and re-establish the legal U.N. posi- tion, and that will serve as a warning to others. It would have some added advantage that the free countries could not be accused of achieving any gains at the expense of the Communist Powers.
>
> From a military point of view it would mean a much less onerous commit- ment than any occupation of North Korea.[63]

In the discussion of Slessor's paper, Slim stated that the problem was mainly a political one. In military terms Korea was not important for Western strategy against communism: if world war occurred, Korea would be abandoned. Slim was opposed to UN forces moving into North Korea; he believed that South Korean troops, supported by a small UN force, could defend the 38th parallel effectively. There was general support for the opinions expressed in Slessor's memorandum. The chiefs of staff concluded that unless appropriate instructions were issued to General MacArthur there was a serious danger of UN forces advancing into North Korea without full awareness of the perils.[64] On 3 October Robert Scott of the Foreign Office attended a meeting with the chiefs of staff for a candid exchange. He began by revealing that Chou En-lai had notified Panikkar that if American troops moved north of the 38th parallel, China would send troops into Korea to assist the North Koreans: it appeared to be the case that China would not act if ROK forces alone crossed the paral- lel. Scott remarked that this could be bluff, but equally it could not be ignored. Clarification of American intentions was being sought urgently from the State Department. The view of the Foreign Office was that the Korean war should not be extended in scope and should be brought to an end as soon as possible, preferably through political rather than military means. Scott stated that his personal opinion was that the Chinese would not be deterred from sending forces to Korea by fear of the damage which the Americans could wreak on Chinese cities.[65] Slim made somewhat muddled observations. Either UN forces should stop at the 38th parallel or advance to the Yalu. From a military perspec- tive a subsequent military commitment would be greater if UN forces stayed south of the parallel because occupation of the whole of Korea would mean that the Unified Command would need to keep sufficient forces to combat guerrilla operations throughout Korea. If UN forces halted at the parallel, sizeable forces would be required to prevent incursions from the north.[66] Lord Fraser said that UN forces should go only as far north as was essential to prevent the North Koreans from preparing a major attack.[67] Slessor cogently reiterated the line he had pursued before:

> He found it hard to understand the view that if we stopped at the 38th. Parallel and left North Korea as an entity Russia would virtually have triumphed and the whole United Nations effort would have been in vain. The complete defeat of this obviously Soviet-inspired Communist aggression represented a triumph for the United Nations on any count. The one essential was that the United Nations position in Korea must be no worse than if the invasion had never happened.[68]

He rejected Slim's statement that it would be preferable, in military terms, to occupy North Korea.

The chiefs of staff met again on 4 and 5 October. On the first occasion Fraser stated bluntly that the 38th parallel should not be crossed. Slim rather confusingly observed that while there was no desire to frighten the Chinese and push them into intervention, neither should the UN accept intimidation via Chinese threats; there was no military necessity for advancing north of the parallel. It was desirable that MacArthur should be instructed to pause before crossing the parallel.[69] On 5 October Fraser emphasised that the risks entailed in moving north were too great and at best would result in only minor gains. Bevin's anxiety not to jeopardise Anglo-American relations was conveyed to the committee.[70] The debate within the British bureaucracy had already become academic. South Korean troops crossed the 38th parallel on 1 October. UN forces moved north of the parallel on 7 October following passage in the General Assembly of the resolution sponsored by Britain. MacArthur was imbued with supreme confidence and contempt for the Chinese and he favoured proceeding north as rapidly as possible. At Truman's request he flew to Wake island in the Pacific for a summit conference with the president on 15 October. Truman's motives were probably a blend of wishing to draw MacArthur on his strategy for the rest of the campaign, including the possibility of Chinese intervention, and utilising the occasion to boost the chances of Democrats in the forthcoming congressional elections. MacArthur felt that the meeting was a waste of time and he agreed with reluctance to meet Truman. Their encounter at Wake island was regarded contemporaneously as satisfactory by both men, if for different reasons. MacArthur assured the president that he had no fears over the culmination of the campaign and that he did not believe that China would intervene: if China did act it would not have a significant effect because the war was effectively won.[71] Truman had secured part of what he wanted: later, when matters went tragically wrong, he authorised the leaking of the record to a journalist, Anthony Leviero.[72] As for the election campaign in November, this was disappointing with the Republicans making significant gains. MacArthur deemed the meeting to be encouraging since his discussion with Truman had been amicable and a further medal had been pinned on the general's chest by the president for the benefit of press photographers.

Meanwhile ominous decisions had been made in Peking. Mao Tse-tung and Chou En-lai determined to act, confirming that they meant what they had said. The trend in interpretation is to regard Chinese intervention as inevitable from the beginning of the Korean war, as underlined by Bruce Cumings. Mao's close links with his Korean comrades who had fought with him during the Chinese civil war and his resentment at American actions in East Asia inclined him to feel that it was imperative to intervene. Analyses of China's approach to intervention, based on Western sources, have tended to emphasise the serious errors made by American and, to a lesser extent, British policy-makers in accepting an advance north of the 38th parallel, aimed at securing Korean unification on an anti-communist (or non-communist) basis. China was forced to intervene in order to defend the security of its borders through the implementation of rollback. Accounts arising from the examination of material now available in Chinese and Russian archives agree that China was not directly involved in the discussions preceding the North Korean advance in June 1950. Mao Tse-tung was affronted by his exclusion from the planning and this was accentuated by Kim Il Sung's initial statement to the PRC government that he hoped to complete unification of Korea without Chinese involvement.[73] Mao was already suspicious of Stalin's intentions and almost certainly interpreted exclusion as an attempt to strengthen Soviet dominance in East Asia through cementing the relationship between Moscow and Pyongyang.[74] Mao resented the discourtesy shown to the PRC and himself. He had recently brought the CCP to power in an amazingly brief period against powerful odds. China under Mao's direction was a force to be reckoned with and Mao did not envisage that a Korean conflict would proceed for long without Chinese involvement. Thus the issue in July–August 1950 was not whether but *when* China would act.

This is not to imply that the Chinese leadership was united on this subject because it was not. Certain of Mao's colleagues, notably Lin Piao, opposed intervention on the grounds of the superior technological and economic resources of the United States. In all, a majority of the Politburo and senior military commanders expressed doubts. China was recovering from decades of civil war and war against Japan: it was not sensible to take on the United States. Mao listened to the views expressed in top meetings and made clear his own opinion that China had no choice but to intervene. He was strengthened in this view by American policy regarding Taiwan. Mao felt passionately over completing the civil war through capturing the various islands held by KMT forces off the China coast.[75] As Chen Jian has shown, Mao was irate at the inability of the PLA to capture three islands late in 1949 and he warned military and naval chiefs not to underestimate the enemy.[76] Mao's ardent wish to invade Taiwan was frustrated permanently by President Truman's decision to deny Taiwan to the PRC, as stated baldly in Truman's first formal reaction to events in Korea. The United States, as Mao saw matters, was behaving in a most provocative way: it was scarcely surprising that the slogan in China soon became, 'Defeat American arrogance'.[77]

Lin Piao declined to lead Chinese 'volunteers' into Korea.[78] He did so on health grounds and, indeed, he visited Moscow for medical treatment in 1950. However, Lin conveyed unmistakably his lack of approval for the action contemplated. Peng Teh-huai, another prominent and able general, offered to lead the 'volunteers' and Mao accepted.[79] Detailed planning took place early in October, following a frantic appeal for assistance from Kim Il Sung in consequence of the serious reverses experienced after the Inchon landing.[80] Mao must have savoured the irony of the approach in the light of Kim's dismissive attitude three months before. According to Chen Jian, some evidence exists pointing towards dissidents in the North Korean regime having appealed to Mao for assistance in removing Kim in the second half of September.[81] Mao rejected the approach, concluding that Kim had to be supported in the current situation.[82] Stalin urged Mao to act: it was essential to prevent a collapse of the DPRK and Chinese military action was the only means of achieving this objective. The Soviet Union would provide substantial military aid including air support but would not intervene directly: to do so would be to risk a third world war.[83] Stalin was moving towards the position that World War Three could begin in the mid-1950s, hence his concern in fostering swift progress in the development of a hydrogen bomb.[84] But Soviet military action in Korea could not occur overtly. Mao had decided between July and September that China should act, so the Soviet entreaties were a secondary consideration. For Stalin, Chinese intervention would spell the end of any prospect of Sino-American *rapprochement* for a long time to come. The hatred of China found in much of the Republican party and in parts of the Democratic party would expand to embrace most Americans when the forces of the two countries were locked in mortal combat in the harsh terrain of Korea. A total of 255,000 Chinese troops was transferred to the vicinity of the Korean border by the end of July 1950. Mao told Stalin that the Chinese troops must be described as 'volunteers': it was impossible for China to become involved formally in war against the UN.[85]

American intelligence appears to have underestimated seriously the numbers of Chinese moving into Korea. It was clear that there was a major build-up of Chinese forces and supplies in Manchuria but this could be regarded as bluff. MacArthur and his principal advisers regarded the Chinese scornfully and maintained their belief that victory was almost complete. This atmosphere was conveyed vividly in telegrams from Bouchier (in Tokyo) to London. Bouchier did not meet MacArthur with any frequency and relied on information from others in the general's office. On 27 October Bouchier emphasised that there was no likelihood of significant Chinese action:

> There is no (repeat no) evidence whatever that any Chinese Communist troops have crossed over South of Yalu River and are in conflict with our forces advancing Northwards to Manchurian border. I make this positive and authoritative statement to negative any exaggeration and alarmist reports which may appear at any time now in your home press as a result of irresponsible reports made here by some newspaper men. Such reports are generally based upon a single unconfirmed statement made by a single enemy prisoner of war who does not know what he is talking about.[86]

He added that Koreans who had fought with the Chinese communist armies during the Chinese civil war had returned to Korea within the previous year. Informed opinion reckoned it was most improbable that the Chinese would intervene on a large scale; the North Korean army was effectively routed and if the Chinese intervened, they would be fighting almost alone. The view that the North Korean army was eliminated as a serious force was widely held, but Bruce Cumings has demonstrated that it remained as an important body and continued to resist tenaciously.[87]

Unfortunately for Bouchier, just as he was delivering his sanguine analysis the first major action by Chinese troops occurred. ROK forces were defeated in an engagement with the Chinese on 28 October and American troops had to move in to halt the reverse. Bouchier reported on 30 October that some Chinese were captured following the battle at Unsan but he did not regard this as really significant.[88] On the following day he stated that two Chinese divisions had evidently crossed the Yalu: this would explain the new determination displayed by the enemy. Chinese action was not official since shoulder straps had been removed. The Chinese government pretended that its soldiers were 'volunteers' as part of its policy of avoiding too formal a commitment: this was arguably equivalent to Truman's description of the UN action in Korea as 'police action' rather than war. On 2 November Bouchier at last conceded that the Chinese were definitely taking part in the war, although he still tried to play down its full importance.[89]

The Foreign Office and the cabinet now showed considerable alarm and were converted to the approach of the chiefs of staff. On 6 November the cabinet agreed that policy should be directed towards averting a major conflict in East Asia; it was held that part of the problem resulted from exclusion of the Peking government from the UN since this might have restrained impulsive action.[90] On 9 November Bevin told his colleagues that the extent of Chinese action was uncertain and involved appreciable difficulty in conducting relations with Peking: 'The situation was an ugly one and the results of the Congressional elections might unfavourably affect its handling by the United States Government, but he did not feel that either China or Russia was at present working deliberately to spread the conflict.'[91] The cabinet met again on 13 November with the chief of the air staff, Slessor, present to speak on behalf of the chiefs of staff committee. Bevin said he had done his best to obviate Chinese intervention because this would increase greatly the danger of general war in the Far East. Chinese intervention had been reported to the UN Security Council and the aim should be to prevent further exacerbation. The situation was critical and could be determined by the handling of exchanges over coming days. He 'had no confidence in India's influence as a mediator with the Communist Government of China'.[92] Slessor stated that while there were large Chinese forces in Manchuria they had not, as yet, been deployed in substantial numbers in Korea. The American intelligence sources estimated that about 35,000 Chinese troops were present in Korea. Russian types of fighter aircraft were being encountered in larger numbers but were probably piloted by Chinese or North Koreans: UN superiority in the air should be maintained unless Soviet pilots were used. Slessor then summarised the essence of the opinions of the chiefs of staff:

> it was no longer practicable, without risking a major war, to attain the original objective of occupying the whole of North Korea and placing it under a

United Nations regime. They were doubtful whether the United Nations forces could reach the northern frontier without making air attacks on targets in Manchuria; and even if the frontier could be reached, it would be a difficult task to hold it along a line of about 450 miles in mountainous country. Korea was of no strategic importance to the democratic Powers; and further operations there should now be conducted with a view to preventing any extension of the conflict and avoiding any lasting commitment in this area.[93]

He explained that in order to attain this objective, the chiefs of staff advocated withdrawal of UN forces to a shorter line across the 'neck' of Korea extending from Chongju to Tokchon, approximately along the 40th parallel. It would be more defensible and it might be feasible to declare the buffer area to be a demilitarised zone. A cease-fire might be agreed on the basis of this line pending the outcome of talks in the Security Council.[94]

Bevin commented that this proposal was compatible with political aims: he was trying to persuade the United States government from being led by their military advisers into policies inviting extended Chinese intervention. He recognised that legitimate Chinese apprehension existed and it should be made clear that the UN did not pose a threat to China. The time had come to propose an all-embracing solution to the Korean crisis and a buffer zone, as urged by Slessor, offered a partial answer. General support was forthcoming from the cabinet. The contemplated policy would 'enable both the Americans and the Chinese to modify their present attitude without loss of prestige and also held the promise that a larger proportion of the further expenditure of the United Nations in Korea might be directed towards reconstruction rather than hostilities'.[95] At the chiefs of staff committee meeting on 20 November, Slim spoke trenchantly of his profound anxiety over Korea. It appeared that the war was largely regarded in the United States as a domestic matter and that its handling by the Truman administration was coloured by the internal acrimony of American politics. Slim reiterated the concern expressed earlier by Slessor that MacArthur should be restrained, at least temporarily, from pressing ahead with the offensive towards the Yalu.[96] MacArthur's attitude remained the same: there was no alternative to advancing to the Yalu and he repudiated British criticism as redolent of Munich-type appeasement.[97] Truman went out of his way, in a statement made at a press conference held on 16 November, to be conciliatory and to emphasise that there was no desire for conflict with China. Truman's statement was welcomed by Bevin in a message to Dean Acheson. Bevin had urged compromise on Washington for the previous ten days. He informed Acheson on 17 November:

> I am proposing to make a statement in the House of Commons to secure publicity in China. In it I would try to convince the Chinese that the objectives of the United Nations in Korea are those publicly stated, that we have not ulterior designs and no intentions to violate Chinese territorial integrity, that the implications of Chinese action in Korea are extremely grave and that while it is our earnest desire to prevent any extension of the conflict, the decision and the responsibility will lie with them.[98]

Despite the problems in communicating with the most senior members of the Chinese government, Bevin intended instructing John Hutchison, the chargé d'affaires in Peking, to see Chou En-lai or, if not, the next highest official to convey a statement of British views. Bevin did not intend formally to convey the British proposal for a demilitarised zone but instead Hutchison would utilise a convenient opening to put forward the suggestion of a demilitarised zone as his own idea. Given the extent of Indian concern, Bevin would inform Nehru. Suitable instructions were sent to Hutchison.[99]

Acheson had thus far noted British unease which, to some extent, he shared. Now that British policy was fast hardening in urging a demilitarised zone, he felt that he should no longer acquiesce in British attempts to promote conciliation but that he should state that a demilitarised zone was not acceptable to the Truman administration. On 21 November Acheson informed the British embassy that he did not want the British to put forward a proposal for a demilitarised zone because it would confuse MacArthur and the Unified Command. Chinese communist emissaries were due to arrive in New York for talks and it would be wise to await their arrival. When he met Sir Oliver Franks on 18 November he had not meant to indicate acceptance of the proposal now being made or the specific terms envisaged, but rather to express a receptive attitude to some method of separating the opposing forces after MacArthur's operations had shown what could safely be done and how.[100] A reply was sent repeating that a demilitarised zone offered the best chance of reaching a solution.[101] On 22 November Hutchison met Chang Han-fu, the vice foreign minister; he handed Chang the message and expressed the hope that Chou En-lai would consider it quickly. He then spoke in a personal capacity in outlining the proposal for a demilitarised zone on the Korean side of the frontier. He invited Chinese reactions. Chang was accompanied by the head of the West European and African department. Chang appeared to listen most carefully and asked whether this was an official suggestion from the British government. Hutchison repeated that it was a personal suggestion. Chang asked him to define the nature of a zone further. Hutchison responded that he contemplated 'a sort of cushion on the Korean side of the border in which fighting would cease and from which military units would be withdrawn'.[102] Hutchison assumed that local North Korean authorities would maintain law and order in the zone. Hutchison thought that his proposal had been anticipated by Chang: the latter made no alternative suggestion as to how Chinese interests might be safeguarded. Chang promised to inform Chou En-lai of his conversation with Hutchison.[103] The Foreign Office was thinking along similar lines to Hutchison regarding administration of a zone but it was decided not to pursue this aspect further for the time being.[104]

Meanwhile Bevin decided to speak candidly to the American chargé d'affaires in London. Holmes was accompanied by Arthur Ringwalt when they visited Bevin on the morning of 22 November: they stated American anxiety at the proposal for a zone being discussed in New York at the UN. Bevin asked if Acheson 'was going back on the whole idea or not'.[105] Holmes replied in the negative but added that the military features of the proposal required study. Holmes urged that the British should take no action in the UN for the time being. Bevin said he would reflect on it. Bevin remarked that MacArthur himself, in a conversation with Esler Dening, had emphasised the urgency of securing a political settlement. Bevin warned that the UN should not 'drift into a position where control of the situation was in the hands of the military commander, General MacArthur'.[106] Bevin referred to rumours that a demilitarised zone might include Manchurian territory: he was firmly opposed to this because it would indicate that China was participating in the war. Holmes enquired about administration of a zone. Bevin replied that a local police force and a local administration under the UN commission should deal with this, utilising some of the local inhabitants.[107]

It was obvious that the British and American governments diverged in approach. Truman and Acheson were still attracted by rollback, despite their fears regarding Chinese intervention. To adopt a demilitarised zone would mean a public row with MacArthur and with those Republicans and Democrats advocating an advance to the Yalu. For an administration already experiencing heavy pressure and having suffered setbacks in the mid-term elections, this was asking too much. In any case it was too late. MacArthur launched his final offensive on 25 November, one prong of his dual advance having previously reached the Yalu. It was then that the Chinese struck with devastating effect. On 13 November Bouchier told the chiefs of staff that an estimated 90,000 Chinese troops were present in Korea of which approximately 50,000 had advanced to the two fronts.[108] Reflecting the attitude of MacArthur's 'court', Bouchier blithely remarked, 'Over all I consider the military picture here is a confident and much more hopeful one than is probably presented in other parts of the world.'[109] On 25 November Bouchier described MacArthur's visit to Korea the previous day, which included an observation trip to the Yalu. While MacArthur's reference to American troops going home for Christmas was perhaps too optimistic, 'there can be little doubt now that the war here will be decisively won in the next few weeks'.[110] UN forces would be along the whole of the Manchurian border by January. He thought that the Chinese position in such a confined area in northern Korea would be hopeless and that UN air superiority would be vital.[111]

On 29 November Bouchier stated that the massive Chinese attack on the previous day had transformed the war. The past confident predictions had literally been exploded:

> From last night, however, all doubts of her intentions have been expelled and China now stands in the open. From yesterday it is known and accepted that there are 6 Chinese Armies or Corps comprising of 18 divisions actually committed in Northern Korea with the possibility of 2 more armies crossing over Tumen River in the North-East.[112]

The Chinese forces totalled approximately 250,000.[113] After the sanguine predictions of September and October 1950 the first phase of the Korean war ended in catastrophe for the UN and was to seal the fate of the Truman administration.

Notes

1 For an excellent account of the Attlee government, see K. O. Morgan, *Labour in Power, 1945–1951* (Oxford: Oxford University Press, 1984).
2 Cabinet minutes, CM(50)39(4), Cab 128/17.

3 *Ibid.*

4 *Ibid.*

5 Cabinet defence committee, DO(50)11, 28 June 1950, FO 371/84062/139G.

6 Chiefs of staff committee, COS(50)100(1), Defe 4/32.

7 For the development of American reactions in late June and early July, see *FRUS 1950*, vol. VII, pp. 125–345.

8 Cabinet minutes, CM(50)42(3), 4 July 1950, Cab 128/18.

9 *Ibid.*

10 For an assessment of trade problems in Anglo-Chinese relations resulting from the Korean war, see chapter 7.

11 Cabinet minutes, CM(50)43(2), 6 July 1950, Cab 128/18.

12 For a lucid account of MacArthur's role in the Korean war, see D. Clayton James, *The Years of MacArthur*, vol. III, *Triumph and Disaster, 1945–1964* (Boston, MA: Houghton Mifflin, 1985), pp. 387–604.

13 *FRUS 1950*, vol. VII, p. 160, memorandum by Jessup, 25 June 1950.

14 *Ibid.*, p. 328, Dulles to Acheson, 7 July 1950.

15 Cabinet minutes, CM(50)50(3), 25 July 1950, Cab 128/18.

16 This summary is based on Robert O'Neill, *Australia in the Korean War*, vol. I (Canberra: The Australian War Memorial and the Australian Government Publishing Service, 1981), p. 462.

17 Tokyo to FO, 14 July 1950, FO 371/84158/2G.

18 Gascoigne thought that Lt. General Sir Horace Robertson, the Australian officer who headed the Commonwealth forces in Japan, would resent Gairdner's appointment; see Tokyo to FO, 14 July 1950, FO 371/84158/3G. British officers were generally critical of Robertson for being difficult to cooperate with. For a more favourable view of Robertson, see Jeffrey Grey, *Australian Brass: The Career of Lieutenant General Sir Horace Robertson* (Cambridge: Cambridge University Press, 1992).

19 A. Gromyko, *Memories* (London: Hutchinson, 1989), pp. 101–2.

20 Interview in Thames Television series dealing with the Korean war, executive producer, Phillip Whitehead, shown on British Television in July and August 1988.

21 Washington to FO, 29 June 1950, FO 371/84080/24. This was based on information given by Perkins of the State Department to Hoyer Millar of the British embassy in Washington.

22 BBC Monitoring, 24 August 1950, based on Central News from Korea, with minute by R. S. Milward, 29 August 1950, FO 371/84130/5. See also Tokyo to FO, 23 August 1950, with comments from the military adviser to the British liaison mission concerning the interrogation of the POWs, FO 371/84156/3.

23 Moscow to FO, 28 June 1950, enclosing translation of front page article from Pravda, 28 June 1950, FO 371/84057/52.

24 *FRUS 1950*, vol. VII, p. 204, Kirk to Acheson, 27 June 1950, where the American ambassador to Moscow reported that he had endeavoured to contact Gromyko five times without success. Vyshinski was said to be away from Moscow.

25 *Ibid.*, pp. 312–13, Kirk to Acheson, 6 July 1950.

26 *Ibid.*, pp. 313–14, British embassy to State Department, 6 July 1950.

27 *Ibid.*, pp. 314–15, Attlee to Truman, 6 July 1950.

28 *Ibid.*, pp. 327–8, Acheson to embassy in London, 7 July 1950.

29 *Ibid.*, pp. 329–30, British embassy to State Department, 8 July 1950, enclosing message from Bevin to Franks, 7 July 1950.

30 *Ibid.*, p. 347, Acheson to embassy in London, 10 July 1950.

31 *Ibid.*, p. 348.

32 *Ibid.*, pp. 351–2, Acheson to Douglas, 10 July 1950.

33 Memorandum by Younger, 11 July 1950, FO 371/84091/215/G.

34 Minute by Barclay, 12 July 1950, FO 371/84085/96/G.

35 Cabinet minutes, CM(50)47(1), 18 July 1950, Cab 128/18.

36 *Ibid.*

37 Kenneth Younger diary, entry for 29 October 1950, where Younger referred critically to Evatt and Spender, particularly the latter. The diary was in the possession of Professor

Geoffrey Warner when I consulted it. I am most grateful to Lady Younger and Professor Warner for permission to refer to the diary.

38 For a valuable examination of the role of the Commonwealth after 1945, see Ritchie Ovendale, *The English-Speaking Alliance: Britain, the United States, the Dominions and the Cold War, 1945–1951* (London: Allen and Unwin, 1985). For a helpful account of Commonwealth relations during the Korean war, see O'Neill, *Australia in the Korean War*, vol. I.

39 For a discussion of Nehru's views on foreign affairs, see S. Gopal, *Jawaharlal Nehru: A Biography*, vol. II, *1947–1956* (London: Jonathan Cape, 1979).

40 Letter from Nehru to Attlee, 21 July 1950, FO 371/84095/281/G.

41 *Ibid.*

42 *Ibid.*

43 For a discussion of the planning and implementation of the Inchon landing, see Clayton James, *Years of MacArthur*, vol. III, pp. 426, 443–4, 464–78.

44 *FRUS 1950*, vol. VII, p. 272, memorandum from Allison to Rusk, 1 July 1950.

45 *Ibid.*, p. 272.

46 *Ibid.*

47 Cumings points out that rollback united Americans of diverse outlook in other respects ranging from rabid anti-communists on the right to liberal officials in the State Department such as John Vincent and Edmund Clubb; see Bruce Cumings, *The Origins of the Korean War*, vol. II, *The Roaring of the Cataract, 1947–1950* (Princeton, NJ: Princeton University Press, 1990), p. 709. Cumings provides an illuminating discussion of the evolution of rollback in this volume. See also C. A. MacDonald, *Korea: The War before Vietnam* (London: Macmillan, 1986), pp. 18–72.

48 See Peter Lowe, *The Origins of the Korean War* (London: Longman, 1986), pp. 186, 189, 192, for brief references to Panikkar.

49 Cabinet minutes, 26 September 1950, CM(50)61(2), Cab 128/18.

50 *Ibid.*

51 *Ibid.*

52 Cabinet minutes, 28 September 1950, CM(50)62(5), Cab 128/18.

53 Stratemeyer to Patridge, 10 October 1950, RG9, box 112, MacArthur papers, MacArthur Memorial, Norfolk, VA.

54 Joint chiefs of staff to MacArthur, 11 October 1950, RG9, box 43, MacArthur papers.

55 Minute by Makins for Bevin, 5 October 1950, FO 371/84100/416/G.

56 *FRUS 1950*, vol. VII, pp. 904–6, resolution 376 (v), adopted by General Assembly, 7 October 1950.

57 Chiefs of staff minutes, confidential annex, COS(50)112(1), 17 July 1950, Defe 4/33. At this stage Slessor was focusing on the possibility that UN forces might be compelled to withdraw from Korea.

58 Chiefs of staff minutes, confidential annex, COS(50)122(1), 2 August 1950, Defe 4/34.

59 *Ibid.*

60 Appendix, 'Policy Following on Enemy Defeat in S. Korea. Note by the Chief of the Air Staff', 14 September 1950, to COS minutes, confidential annex, COS(50)152(8), 20 September 1950, Defe 4/36.

61 *Ibid.*

62 *Ibid.*

63 *Ibid.*

64 Chiefs of staff minutes, confidential annex, COS(50)152(8), 20 September 1950, Defe 4/36.

65 Chiefs of staff minutes, COS(50)160(2), 3 October 1950, Defe 4/36.

66 *Ibid.*

67 *Ibid.*

68 *Ibid.*

69 Chiefs of staff minutes, COS(50)161(1), 4 October 1950, Defe 4/36.

70 Chiefs of staff minutes, COS(50)162(1), 5 October 1950, Defe 4/36.

71 For a concise record of the Wake island conference, based on notes taken by General Omar Bradley, see *FRUS 1950*, vol. VII, pp. 948–60. For the declassified record of the talks, as

preserved in Truman's papers, see memorandum compiled by Bradley, folder, October 1950, box 65, Acheson papers, Harry S. Truman Library, Independence, Missouri.

72 R. J. Donovan, *Tumultuous Years: The Presidency of Harry S. Truman, 1949–1953* (London: Norton, 1982), p. 369.

73 Chen Jian, *China's Road to the Korean War: The Making of the Sino-American Confrontation* (New York: Columbia Unversity Press, 1994), pp. 112, 134.

74 S. N. Goncharov, J. W. Lewis and Xue Litai, *Uncertain Partners: Stalin, Mao and the Korean War* (Stanford, CA: Stanford University Press, 1994), p. 154.

75 *Ibid.*, p. 180.

76 Chen Jian, *China's Road to the Korean War*, p. 99.

77 *Ibid.*, p. 140.

78 Goncharov, Lewis and Xue, *Uncertain Partners*, p. 180.

79 *Ibid.*, p. 183. See also Peng Teh-huai, *Memoirs of a Chinese Marshal: A Cultural Revolution 'Confession' by Marshal Peng Dehuai (1898–1974)* (Beijing: Foreign Languages Press, 1984), pp. 472–5.

80 Goncharov, Lewis and Litai, *Uncertain Partners*, p. 172.

81 Chen Jian, *China's Road to the Korean War*, p. 162.

82 *Ibid.*

83 Goncharov, Lewis and Xue, *Uncertain Partners*, pp. 189, 199–200.

84 *Ibid.*, pp. 212–13.

85 *Ibid.*, p. 178.

86 Bouchier to Chiefs of Staff, 27 October 1950, FO 371/84070/267/G.

87 Cumings, *Origins*, vol. II, pp. 740, 744.

88 Bouchier to Chiefs of Staff, 30 October 1950, FO 371/84070/267/G.

89 Bouchier to Chiefs of Staff, 31 October 1950, *ibid.*

90 Cabinet minutes, CM(50)71(4), 6 November 1950, Cab 128/18.

91 Cabinet minutes, CM(50)72(5), 9 November 1950, Cab 128/18.

92 Cabinet minutes, CM(50)73(2), 13 November 1950, Cab 128/18.

93 *Ibid.*

94 *Ibid.*

95 *Ibid.*

96 Chiefs of Staff committee minutes, confidential annex, COS(50)182(1), Defe 4/36.

97 *FRUS 1950*, vol. VII, pp. 1107–10, MacArthur to Joint Chiefs of Staff, 9 November 1950.

98 FO to Washington, 17 November 1950, FO 371/84114/109/G.

99 FO to Peking, 18 November 1950, FO 371/84116/139.

100 Washington to FO, 21 November 1950, FO 371/84116/149/G.

101 FO to Washington, 22 November 1950, *ibid.*

102 Peking to FO, 23 November 1950, FO 371/84117/150.

103 *Ibid.*

104 FO to Peking, 25 November 1950, *ibid.*

105 Despatch from Bevin to Franks, 22 November 1950, FO 371/84118/167/G.

106 *Ibid.*

107 *Ibid.*

108 Bouchier to Chiefs of Staff, 13 November 1950, FO 371/84072/296/G.

109 *Ibid.*

110 Bouchier to Chiefs of Staff, 25 November 1950, FO 371/84073/313/G.

111 *Ibid.*

112 Bouchier to Chiefs of Staff, 29 November 1950, *ibid.*

113 *Ibid.*

11

THE REPERCUSSIONS OF CHINESE INTERVENTION AND THE DISMISSAL OF GENERAL MACARTHUR, NOVEMBER 1950 TO JULY 1951

China's dramatic intervention in Korea in November 1950 raised huge questions as to the future direction and course of the war. The possibilities included a swift military defeat for the Unified Command with the consequent expulsion of the UN from Korea; establishment of a fortified line by the Unified Command followed by military stalemate; use of the atomic weapon and of economic sanctions to coerce China; and escalation of the conflict into a third world war with the direct participation of the Soviet Union. For almost two months, until late January 1951, great uncertainty existed regarding the nature of military strategy in Korea; developments were extremely fluid and it was a period of hectic, urgent consultations between governments and among UN delegates in New York. The most profound cause of anxiety concerned the atomic bomb. Just after the war began, in late June 1950, the British chiefs of staff considered that the United States might wish to deploy the atomic weapon.[1] This stimulated Pierson Dixon of the Foreign Office to observe, on 1 July, that he had a nasty suspicion that if matters deteriorated the American joint chiefs of staff might recommend use of the atomic bomb and that it was essential to ensure that full consultation occurred with Britain before decisions were reached.[2] The abruptness of the transformation of the war in November had a traumatic effect on public opinion in Britain as elsewhere. The worsening of the Cold War during the preceding three years focused attention on the prospect of a third catastrophic war to hit Europe within a generation and, on this occasion, a war that was likely to be terminal. American policy-making possessed erratic qualities and a beleaguered administration might succumb to the atomic temptation. Such fears were accentuated by remarks made by President Truman at a press conference held at the end of November. In reality serious thought had been devoted within the administration to the atomic option since the war started. The principal restraining factor, whenever the policy-makers in Washington discussed the issue, under the Truman and Eisenhower administrations, was always the repercussions on America's allies and the great apprehension in Europe that arose from fear that the continent could become an atomic battleground.[3]

Within the British Labour Party latent unease was transformed into vocal criticism of the United States. A circular letter containing approximately 80 signatures from Labour MPs was sent to Attlee on 30 November drawing attention to Truman's remarks and stating that if the atomic weapon was used, British forces should be withdrawn from Korea. The first signatory was a leading left-winger, Ian Mikardo, but other signatories included representatives of the centre and right-wing of the party in addition to the left – George Thomas, Fred Messer, Gordon Lang, A. J. Irvine, Fred Mulley, Michael Foot, Elizabeth Braddock, Barbara Castle, Alice Bacon, Eirene White, Jean Mann, Roy Jenkins, Richard Acland, Harold Lever and R. T. Paget (Jean Mann wrote subsequently to Attlee withdrawing her support for the petition).[4] Hugh Gaitskell, the chancellor of the exchequer and a leading figure on the right, strongly urged Attlee to fly to Washington to see Truman: 'The latest events so full of the gravest possibilities – including Truman's statement today on the atomic bomb – have convinced me that *you ought to fly out to Washington* at once – to confer with Truman.'[5] Gaitskell added that Bevin's health was so bad as to preclude his flying and it was wise to handle the matter at the highest level. Furthermore this would reassure the party, 'who are again full of gloom & distress at the latest developments'.[6] The small group of Liberal MPs informed Attlee that the atomic bomb should not be deployed except with the 'prior approval of United Nations'.[7]

At a cabinet meeting held on 29 November Bevin told his colleagues that he had communicated urgently with the United States government because of concern that General MacArthur might seek to implement air attacks on military targets beyond the Manchurian border. He had received some reassurance from Dean Acheson who had stated that the crisis would continue to be handled through the UN.[8] Attlee emphasised that, 'it was of the first importance that the United Nations should not be trapped into diverting a disproportionate effort to the Far East'.[9] The Korean campaign was important as denoting symbolic opposition to aggression but Korea itself was of lesser importance than Europe and the Middle East. In the ensuing discussion comments were made on the unhappiness of Labour backbenchers and references were included to distrust of MacArthur. The latter was seen as an independent agent over whom no adequate control was exerted. Some cabinet members referred to MacArthur's achievements earlier in the fighting.[10] It was observed correctly that Britain bore substantial responsibility for the course of events, having sponsored the UN resolution of 7 October. The cabinet was disturbed at the Truman administration's wish to submit a resolution to the UN Security Council condemning Chinese aggression in Korea. However, the familiar dilemma of not wanting to risk antagonising the United States because of the consequences for Europe surfaced in the closing stages of the debate. The gravity of the situation was such that Attlee determined to fly to Washington as soon as possible. Cynics might argue that he reached the decision so as to demonstrate to his Labour followers that he was doing something, and it would be fair to conclude that this played a part in his move. But Attlee had wanted to meet Truman for a considerable time: the president had been reluctant to see him.[11] Now, given the magnitude of the crisis, Truman could not refuse.

Attlee was accompanied by the minister of state in the Foreign Office, Kenneth Younger, and by the two chief British representatives in Washington, Sir Oliver Franks and Lord Tedder. Truman was accompanied by Acheson and the joint chiefs. The talks centred on broad strategic and political problems and not solely on far eastern issues. The discussions began on a tense, if not bleak, note but improved somewhat afterwards. It was an embarrassing occasion and neither of the principals was suited ideally to engendering a more relaxed atmosphere. Attlee was dry, meticulous, precise and had no hestitation in conveying the extent of British disquiet. Truman favoured blunt language and took pride in a midwesterner's reluctance to indulge in diplomatic verbiage. The meeting occurred at the gravest point in the history of the Truman presidency and Truman was disinclined to receive too many criticisms of his policies. Franks could claim justly much of the credit for the more satisfactory evolution of the deliberations, for he deployed his extensive conciliatory gifts to positive effect. Attlee emphasised the British view that the best prospect of reaching a solution in Korea was to link the other major issues involving China and Korea. This denoted the entry of the Peking government into the UN in place of the Kuomintang regime and a settlement of Taiwan. Since American acceptance of these issues would necessitate fundamental concessions by the United States at a time of grave embarrassment, it was extremely difficult to pursue. At the first formal meeting, held on 4 December, Truman stated that very important military decisions must be taken shortly and significant decisions would be required regarding procedure in the UN. Attlee commented that opinion in the UN, Europe, America and Asia had to be assessed and policies formulated in the light of all relevant considerations. One basic problem was that communist China did not belong to the UN and the reactions of the Peking government resulted partly from fear: they felt strongly about Taiwan and, to a lesser degree, about Hong Kong. Chinese aims in Korea were unclear. He reiterated that Western defence strategy must continue to rest on recognition of Europe as the priority:

> According to his view, we must not get so involved in the East as to lay ourselves open to attack in the West. The West is, after all, the vital part in our line against communism. We cannot take action that will weaken it. We must strengthen our hands in the West as much as possible.

Dean Acheson stated the administration's opinion that the Peking government was dominated by the Soviet Union: 'All they do is based on the Moscow pattern and they are better pupils even than the Eastern European satellites.'[13] Acheson added that Attlee had raised very serious matters and the implications could be profound elsewhere, as for example in Indo-China. Truman crisply defined his attitude to China. He believed:

> that they are satellites of Russia and will be satellites so long as the present Peiping [Peking] regime is in power. He thought they were complete satellites. The only way to meet communism is to eliminate it. After Korea it would be Indochina, then Hong Kong, then Malaya. There was no chance to approach a solution without seeing clearly the course we should follow. He does not want war with China or anyone else but the situation looks very dark to him.[14]

Truman summarised the key points as he saw them: that a cease-fire was desirable militarily; the UN could then concentrate on stabilising the ROK; if China moved appreciable forces south of the 38th parallel, then the UN forces might have to leave Korea. Since the consequences of evacuation would be grave, this should occur only for military reasons.

Acheson considered the first session to be too rigid and believed that a more relaxed atmosphere should be created with the avoidance of raising issues in too blunt a way.[15] He conveyed this view to Franks who endeavoured to secure what was desired by Acheson, since he held the same opinion.[16] At the same time Franks believed that the division in approach to China was such that it could not be evaded: the British should state their assessment and the Americans should respond. At the second formal meeting on 5 December, Truman began by stating that a cease-fire was most desirable and that UN commitments in Korea must be fulfilled. He was influenced particularly by the need to protect those in the ROK who would otherwise be murdered or tortured. The military situation was alarming but the Unified Command must adhere to its task: 'He wanted to make it perfectly plain here that we do not desert our friends when the going is rough. He thought that the Prime Minister felt the same way in his heart.'[17] Attlee concurred and deemed a balanced response to be best: aggression must be deterred but the limits to UN action must be recognised. He observed that previous British policy towards China was based on the premiss that it should be possible to drive a wedge between Moscow and Peking. Acheson commented that this depended on China making concessions.[18]

On 6 December, after dinner in the British ambassador's residence, the most candid exchanges so far occurred. Truman, Acheson, Marshall and Bradley were present in addition to Attlee, Slim and Franks. Acheson reminded the British of the fundamental repercussions of the talks for future Anglo-American relations, a familiar tactic when under pressure:

> The Secretary told them that there was a feeling in Washington that the British were not doing all they could do. He said that if the President and General Marshall were convinced that the British were doing all they could, this would help a great deal in meeting the feeling in this country to the contrary.[19]

Progress could be made in NATO only if America and Britain took the lead. Attlee then raised the thorny issue of General MacArthur. The British record of the talks is more explicit than the American record regarding statements made by Truman and Acheson.[20] Attlee emphasised the anxiety in Europe and the UN that MacArthur possessed too much power. Truman conceded that MacArthur had made regrettable public pronouncements. Marshall said that MacArthur had acted in accordance with UN directives. Marshall maintained that the allies were always consulted over military strategy and gave as an example the question of 'hot pursuit' in Manchuria: this was advocated by MacArthur but was dropped because of allied objections. Acheson's ire at MacArthur was evident from his frank rhetorical question as to 'whether any Government had any control over General MacArthur, a point on which he desired to express no view'.[21] Attlee commented that consultation would be vital if evacuation of Korea became an urgent matter. Truman thought it futile to consider this, since the UN must stay in Korea.[22]

Differences between the United States and Britain over China were marked and could not be surmounted. No surprise was occasioned by this, since the divergence on China extended back to the latter part of 1949. The British realised that it would be impossible for the Truman administration to contemplate recognition of the Peking government, but they wondered whether the United States should continue to recognise Chiang Kai-shek's regime. Franks referred to this in a meeting with Acheson: the latter appeared to have some sympathy with the question but said that it was dangerous to pursue it, given the political climate in the United States.[23] At the final session on 7 December a further review of policy was conducted and the talks ended with Truman reiterating the importance of the two countries working closely.[24]

The Truman–Attlee talks did some good in clarifying the differences in approach and led to a better personal understanding between the two leaders. Truman stated in private on 12 December that he was satisfied with the discussions.[25] Attlee told the cabinet on his return that the talks were pursued 'in an atmosphere of frankness and candour'.[26] The military situation was very alarming in Korea but when he left Washington there appeared to be likelihood of UN forces establishing a line below the 38th parallel. The American government believed that Chinese policy was controlled by the Soviet Union and 'they had been considering the idea of a limited war against China by way of an economic blockade and stirring up internal trouble in China'.[27] He had sought to persuade Truman and Acheson of the merits of the British approach to China and that it would be unwise to force China into a closer relationship with the Soviet Union. Truman agreed that a cease-fire should be achieved and that it should not involve prolonged exchanges over the terms. He had conveyed doubts over MacArthur's intervention in the political sphere but his earlier military successes in Korea must be remembered. It had been agreed that Taiwan was not an immediate issue and Attlee had suggested a compromise whereby Taiwan might be neutralised under nominal Chinese sovereignty. As regards the atomic bomb Truman assured him that it would not be used without full consultation unless America itself came under sudden attack. Kenneth Younger wrote in his diary that he was present at the second day of the Washington talks and that Attlee handled them skilfully; he added that Attlee was always effective on Asian issues.[28] Younger was extremely critical of American policy-making: 'I find their whole conception, military and political, half-baked and disastrous.'[29] The basic problem was the negative American approach to China and its impact on Peking:

> If neither of these things is done [American recognition of communist China and a solution to Taiwan] I do not see how the communists can be expected to believe that the Korean operation is anything but a part of a US plan for preventing the fulfilment of the Chinese revolution. If that is the true US intention (and I myself believe that at the moment it is), then I can see no peaceful way out of the Korean affair.[30]

Younger remarked that the strength of American feeling regarding China almost precipitated a row at the start of the talks but Attlee's visit was highly successful. The most worrying feature was that the United States was gripped with a war psychosis accentuated by press agitation. While Labour MPs were to some extent reassured by Attlee's visit, Hugh Dalton recorded a conversation with James Callaghan in his diary on 21 December in which the latter was reported as stating that many Labour MPs were alarmed at the international situation and the danger of conflict with Russia: it was felt that Attlee had not been tough enough in his dealings with the Americans.[31]

India made strenuous efforts to foster negotiations between the Americans and the Chinese: the United States regarded these endeavours critically. From the Chinese viewpoint the situation was encouraging and the possibility existed of extorting major concessions from the Americans. Chou En-lai made it clear to K. M. Panikkar that progress was dependent on admission of China to the UN and a solution to Taiwan. A Chinese emissary, General Wu Hsiu-chuan, was sent to New York to participate in discussions. The British delegate to the UN, Sir Gladwyn Jebb, contributed with characteristic vigour to the hectic exchanges. Wu, while congenial to deal with, told the UN secretary-general, Trygve Lie, that a cease-fire could be achieved only on the terms indicated by the Soviet delegate, Jacob Malik, in a speech made on the previous day. Foreign troops must be withdrawn from Korea and Anglo-American aggression in the Far East must end.[32] On 18 December Jebb reported attending a meeting of the UN Cease-fire Committee together with the American delegate, Ernest Gross. The latter was preoccupied with avoiding anything suggestive of American submission to Chinese aggression. Gross and Jebb were involved in a sharp exchange concerning the consequences of failure to make progress in New York. Gross said that if the UN failed to counter Chinese aggression, it would have unfortunate effects on American public opinion, stimulate isolationism and, conceivably, lead to the collapse of the UN. Jebb was never slow to respond to a challenge and replied that:

> While we could not altogether dispute the possibilities indicated by Gross an even quicker way of breaking-up the United Nations would be for the United States to embark on what was in fact a war with China while other members of the United Nations did not do so. It might be that the People's Government would force a general war; but if we were to get the United Nations to face such a war together it was essential to demonstrate that every possible step had been taken to meet all legitimate Chinese grievances.[33]

Thus deadlock prevailed in the UN, although intense efforts continued for the rest of December and throughout January 1951 to achieve progress. The dilemma was that neither the United States nor China wished to be depicted as softening significantly in approach and each felt that time was on its side. In the sense of securing a Korean settlement and a solution to Chinese demands both sides were wrong.

The military strategy of the Unified Command caused ceaseless debate from the end of November 1950 until the removal of MacArthur in April 1951. Winston Churchill admired MacArthur's prowess as a commander and sent him copies of each volume of his history of the Second World War.[34] He was not impressed with MacArthur's strategy in Korea, however. Lord Selborne talked at length with Churchill at an 'Other Club' dinner on 7 December:

> I tried to draw Winston about Korea and future developments, but he was very cagey. When I said to him: 'What do you think is going to happen?', he replied: 'I don't think there is going to be an election' which wasn't at all what I was thinking of.

He quite clearly did not think much of General MacArthur's tactics. He borrowed my pen and drew on the back of the menu a map illustrating what he would have done if he had been General MacArthur. That is to say that in his view the Americans, when they got to the neck of Korea, should have made a fortified line before they went on to the Chinese frontier. It was MacArthur's failure to do this that had caused the American's severe set-back.[35]

Instead of establishing a fortified line MacArthur authorised the longest military retreat in American history. Since the Chinese forces were not exerting stong pressure at this time, MacArthur's motives gave rise to much speculation. Perhaps he wished to withdraw from Korea and to use a combination of atomic and economic weapons to coerce China. The British chiefs of staff, their advisers, the cabinet and diplomats in the Foreign Office anxiously contemplated the future direction of an erratic American policy. The military adviser to the British liaison mission in Tokyo, Brigadier Ferguson, sent a telegram to the director of military intelligence in London on 31 December expressing deep misgivings at the repeated statements emanating from MacArthur's headquarters, describing the size and formidable character of the Chinese forces. The impact on UN and ROK morale was lamentable because they were, in effect, being told that they could not make a firm stand against the enemy. Ferguson was uncertain whether the statistics issued by MacArthur's command assessing Chinese strength were justified or were fictitious. It was claimed that 150,000 Chinese were available immediately to be used against the eighth army, reinforced with an additional 100,000 to 150,000 in the Hungnam area plus a further 100,000 to 150,000 'whose entry into Korea has not yet been confirmed'.[36] The UN forces were thrown into jitters by such reports. Even if the quoted figures were correct, Ferguson commented that the disparity in strength was not remarkable. The figures published for assigned strength of all ground forces under the command of the US eighth army in Korea amounted to approximately 360,000 with sufficient arms and equipment; UN forces possessed air and naval supremacy.[37] Air Vice-Marshal Bouchier informed the chiefs of staff on 4 January that MacArthur's policy aimed at preserving the integrity of the Unified Command. He foresaw a continuous retreat until this culminated in another Pusan bridgehead area.[38]

The Foreign Office and the chiefs of staff concluded early in January that representations must be made in Washington. This was accentuated by the anxiety felt in the Commonwealth and which was conveyed vigorously when the Commonwealth prime ministers met in London in January. Franks was told on 6 January to make urgent representations with the request that these be brought to Truman's attention; it was imperative to clarify American intentions. Franks was informed, for his personal information, that it was feared that MacArthur's political sympathies were determining his military strategy.[39] Each of the Commonwealth prime ministers attended the conference with the exception of the Union of South Africa which was represented by a senior cabinet minister. Robert Menzies of Australia and Sidney Holland of New Zealand were particularly concerned over questions involving Korea, Japan and the future of Pacific security. Louis St Laurent of Canada was worried about Korea in the context of the UN, keeping in mind Pearson's strenuous endeavours to promote compromise in New York. Nehru was by far the most critical of American policy, his natural concern exacerbated by the blows to his vanity resulting from brusque American reactions to his initiatives. The leaders of Pakistan and Ceylon were concerned at threats to Asian stability. At the beginning of the conference Attlee discussed the grave tensions in the Far East with the deteriorating crises in Korea and Indo-China and the danger of trouble spreading in Burma, Malaya and Indonesia. Legitimate national aspirations must be recognised and in the case of China it was necessary to recall the depredations of foreign imperialism in the past. He explained the deductions drawn from his visit to Washington. The Americans did not want a major conflict with China but they had shown some inclination to contemplate a limited war. This was worrying because a limited war could escalate into a far more serious conflict. He did not believe that China would be content to act as a Soviet satellite but the American attitude was different. Nehru broadly agreed: realism was essential and many existing problems were the consequence of not facing facts. India was alarmed at the trend of American policy towards China. The best defence against communism in Asia was to improve living standards. He did not believe that the Soviet Union or China wanted major war.[40]

Menzies underlined the great importance of the United States for the defence of the free world. America had borne the brunt of UN operations in Korea and this must be kept in mind. There could be no solution in Korea without compromising with China but the UN was already in armed conflict with China: it was necessary to think of methods of inducing the United States to be positive in arriving at a solution. One of the dilemmas lay in reconciling necessary opposition to subversive or aggressive movements with the broad tolerance of all kinds of thought including the most radical.[41] Ernest Bevin told the conference that in the ordinary sense China could be defined as an aggressor in Korea but when it came to branding China formally as an aggressor, he was opposed to doing so, since it would be counter-productive. He pointed out correctly that China had not advanced its own case by its negative policies following British recognition of the Peking government.[42]

The chiefs of staff produced a memorandum on the future situation in Korea on 6 January. They estimated that there were 350,000 Chinese troops deployed in 12 armies with 170,000 North Korean troops in eight corps. The British estimate of Chinese troop strength was markedly lower than the American. It was estimated that 400,000 Chinese troops organised in 13 armies were present in Manchuria and these could be transferred to Korea without difficulty. It was thought unlikely that existing enemy strength in Korea and Manchuria would increase significantly. The Chinese army was believed to be occupied wholly in combating anti-communist guerrilla activity in south China. UN troop strength comprised 350,000 including 130,000 ROK troops. It was estimated that approximately 210,000 were front-line fighting troops. These consisted of ten ROK divisions 'of doubtful reliability', of which nine were in the line with the remaining divisions further south.[43] There were seven American divisions, two British brigades, a Turkish brigade and a number of independent battalions provided by other UN members. As regards air power the Chinese were believed to possess only about 400 front-line aircraft and the North

Koreans 40. It was probable that Russian pilots had been used in the region of the Manchurian frontier, possibly using aircraft from two Soviet air regiments based in the Mukden-Antung area. UN air strength consisted of 86 medium bombers, 93 light bombers, 219 fighter bombers, 228 transport aircraft, 101 reconnaisance aircraft and 282 fighters. UN naval forces were far superior to the Chinese and North Korean forces.[44]

The chiefs of staff (COS) also produced a succinct assessment of a contingency of war against China based on an appraisal prepared by the Joint Intelligence Committee (JIC). The JIC assumed that the Soviet Union would assist China extensively short of direct participation. The COS diverged from the JIC in contending that war against China could connote open involvement by the Soviet Union. The essence of the JIC appraisal was that China was not vulnerable to any significant extent: 'A war between the United States and China would be the old story of the fight between the whale and the elephant – neither can directly do the other … real harm.'[45] However, it was the case that, indirectly, China could cause much more damage to the United States and the UN. Should full-scale war against China occur, it was probably the position that most Chinese cities could be destroyed if the United States decided to devote sufficient resources. But the Chinese people had always been used to suffering and devastation for a combination of natural and man-made reasons. The Chinese economy would obviously be harmed by intensive bombing of cities but they would presumably receive heavy armaments from the Soviet Union. 'So it is hardly an exaggeration to say that, while they would suffer inconvenience and hardship, to which they are inured by their national characteristics based on generations of tradition, they are virtually invulnerable to Western attack.'[46] The West would have to divert resources required urgently in the decisive theatre (the West) to the Far East. Clearly, this would be to Soviet benefit. The COS held that an open struggle against China would probably spread to become a world war. But even if this did not happen, China could inflict more damage on the Western powers than *vice versa*. The Americans would still prevent the capture of Taiwan but overt Chinese intervention in Indo-China would defeat the French. The COS then foresaw a domino effect: Thailand and Burma would collapse, India and East Pakistan would be threatened, the rice bowl of Asia would be controlled by the communists 'with all that would involve in India, Ceylon, Malaya and last but not least Japan'.[47] Hong Kong would be conquered, since it was impossible to defend it against overwhelming attack. The COS's conclusion was that war must be avoided:

> Finally, a war with China would throw her irretrievably into the Soviet camp – an eventuality which in the long term we do not now believe is by any means inevitable and which should be avoided at almost any cost. It should surely be one of the main preoccupations of Western policy not to solidify against us the 700 millions of combined Russia and China, backed by Russia's enormous military industrial capacity.[48]

The only conclusion to be drawn by Commonwealth leaders was that they should encourage negotiations in New York. This was underlined when Field Marshal Slim attended a session of the conference on 8 January. Bevin reported that the United States wanted China condemned formally in the UN for aggression with the pursuance of a 'limited war' against China which in his view would be most dangerous. Nehru stated that China would not accept the principles produced by the Cease-fire group on 4 January: the Chinese government was not willing to contemplate a settlement of Korean issues which excluded Taiwan.[49] On 9 January Bevin informed the conference that the American government favoured an initiative from Commonwealth prime ministers. The first objective should be to induce the United States and China to participate in a conference convened to resolve far eastern problems. The second aim should be to obviate a significant split in policy between the United States and Britain. Nehru and Liaquat Ali Khan of Pakistan concurred.[50] The conference approved proposals which were then sent to Franks in Washington. It was agreed that a resolution should be secured in the UN General Assembly comprising in essence a firm request to the governments of the United States, Britain, the Soviet Union and the People's Government of China to meet to discuss outstanding issues in the Far East in accordance with international responsibilities and the provisions of the UN Charter. The terms of the resolution could refer to Korea and the overall situation in the Far East. The Commonwealth leaders had not devised a suitable wording and felt this could be handled by the representatives in New York. It was imperative to ascertain whether the United States would cooperate. They recalled that Truman and Attlee had declared their willingness to find a peaceful solution. If the American government responded positively, it should be feasible for the Cease-fire group to produce a draft resolution within the immediate future. Another body could be used if necessary but it was preferable to proceed through the Cease-fire committee.[51]

At their tenth session on 11 January the prime ministers resumed consideration of the matter. They agreed to support the revised principles of the Cease-fire committee with an amendment to the fifth point, so that as soon as a cease-fire had been arranged, the General Assembly would set up a suitable body to include the British, American, Soviet and Chinese governments with the aim of securing a settlement 'in conformity with existing international obligations and the provisions of the United Nations Charter, of Far Eastern problems including among others those of Formosa and of representation of China in the United Nations'.[52] The phrase 'international obligations', was meant to connote a reference to the Cairo declaration. The 'appropriate body' should be compact, not large. With reference to a cease-fire, it was not contemplated that talks would proceed while fighting continued. If a cease-fire and appointment of a committee were both referred to in the 'principles', then there was no reason for insisting that a cease-fire should come before the appointment of a committee.[53] At the concluding meeting, held on 12 January, Nehru said he was unhappy at press reports of Gladwyn Jebb's speech in the UN Political Committee: it seemed patronising towards the Peking government – in such a delicate situation it was essential to proceed carefully.[54]

While the Commonwealth leaders deliberated, the COS met on several occasions to consider Korean developments. They were notified from Tokyo on 8 January of MacArthur's opinion that the only alternative to withdrawal from Korea was war with China. It was noted that the Commonwealth prime ministers had decided that a military presence must be retained in Korea even if reduced to a bridgehead around Pusan. Grave concern was voiced regarding American intentions: there were 20,000 British troops in the peninsula and there was every right to expect close consultation. The repercussions of withdrawal would be immense and could affect Europe.[55] In a confidential annex to the record of a further meeting on 8 January it was noted that the COS believed that MacArthur had been instructed to hold a line in Korea but it was feared that he might disregard such an order so as to promote complete withdrawal from Korea.[56] On 9 January they considered a telegram from Tedder in Washington. Slessor stated that decisions were required on various points. Was it possible to hold a bridgehead in Korea? Slim commented that the JCS appeared unsure over MacArthur's intentions. Slessor saw the position in stark terms:

> It appeared to him possible that General MacArthur now intended to with-draw from Korea and having done so, to attack China by sea and air, making use of Chinese Nationalists to attack China on land. According to the latest United States estimates, the disparity between China and the United Nations forces in Korea was comparatively small and with the United Nations over-whelming superiority in fire power and complete air supremacy it should by normal military standards be perfectly feasible to hold a bridgehead. It seemed, however, that the United States troops had no longer the will to fight and were so intent on evacuation that even if General MacArthur were now definitely ordered to hold a bridgehead it seemed doubtful whether he would in fact be able to do so.[57]

Lord Fraser alluded to the effects of withdrawal upon events in Indo-China, Hong Kong and Malaya. Fraser thought China wanted to gain all it could without commencing overt global war. Slim observed that the American aim of submitting a resolution to the UN, condemning China for aggression, would render the situation far more invidious to handle.[58]

It was decided after discussion between Attlee and the COS that Sir John Slessor should visit Washington in order to hold frank talks with the JCS. The existing uncertainties were too extensive and disturbing to continue. When Slessor met his COS colleagues on 12 January, Slessor told them that he wished to adopt a line of total candour in Washington and to reiterate the alarm felt in Britain and the Commonwealth. There was growing reluctance to 'tag along' behind the United States. Divergent reports had been received concerning future American policy from highly placed Americans including General Bradley. It was essential to ascertain what MacArthur's position really was and what the JCS proposed to do. Consultation over policy formulation must be improved.[59] Slessor's general approach was approved, subject to a qualification that the COS did not doubt MacArthur's military expertise but that his politi-cal insight and calibre of his intelligence service gave rise to concern. A telegram from Tedder was reported on 12 January suggesting that American forces might leave Korea, although American policy was extremely confused. Slim commented that evacuation was possible and that MacArthur might envisage utilising Chiang Kai-shek's forces to invade the mainland. Fraser agreed with Slim that the Americans were devising excuses for leaving Korea. Slessor referred contemptuously to the Kuomintang troops: '... he had little confidence that if put into China they would not fight – they would probably just go off home – the Chinese Communists no doubt also realised this'.[60]

Slessor flew to Washington and took the lead in important exchanges in meetings held on 15 and 16 January 1951. On 15 January he was accompanied by Lord Tedder and other senior British officers at a meeting held in the Pentagon with an American delegation headed by General Omar N. Bradley and Admiral Forrest P. Sherman. Slessor made a lengthy, courageous and effective statement at the beginning. He defined the purpose of his visit as being to secure information concerning prospects in Korea. He would speak with entire frankness and knew the same would apply to Bradley. He would begin with an assessment of British and Commonwealth opinion. The problems confronting policy-makers in Washington were understood fully including the pressures exerted by American public opinion. Equally, the impact on British public opinion must be considered. In general there was profound doubt as to the course American policy was taking and where it would lead:

> There was in England, and the Commonwealth, a very real concern about the possibility that present tension might lead to general war before we were ready. There was also an intense dislike in England and in the Commonwealth as a whole for the idea of a war with China. There was finally among Ministers, the Chiefs of Staff, in the Press and in all sections of the public a general feeling of puzzlement about the conduct of the campaign in Korea and concern about where it was leading us to. The Chiefs of Staff were frequently asked for their appreciation of the situation and found it very difficult to give a sound reply in view of the somewhat scanty and often conflicting information we received. There was also a feeling in England that General MacArthur, whom we all recognised as being a great soldier, was nevertheless inclined to be too political and too independent of Washington control.[61]

Slessor underlined Commonwealth fears and the need to retain the support of the Asiatic dominions. Britain was the centre of a huge Commonwealth which included 'the two greatest Asiatic nations outside China (one of whom is also the biggest Moslem Power)'.[62] In addition, British political and economic interests in the Far East were enormous.

It would be futile to indulge in recriminations. Britain had accepted the position of the United States as the principal agent of the UN despite misgivings on occasions. No attempt had been made to communicate directly with MacArthur and the liaison representative in Tokyo, Bouchier, had been used only as a source of strategic information MacArthur chose to supply. It was essential to discuss clearly future policy in Korea. There was increasing disinclination in Britain (and, Slessor believed, in the Commonwealth) to 'tag along' behind the United States without consultation. What was needed was information on MacArthur's orders and assessment of the likelihood of being able to remain in Korea. Consultation should be much strengthened so as to achieve a joint military policy which could be recommended to both governments. The British COS wished to defend a substantial line in Korea. It was agreed that it would not be wise to put large reinforcements of UN troops into Korea and that the basic Western global strategy must not be affected. The COS understood the political dilemmas in the United States including a possible stimulus to isolationism. However, it was stongly held in Britain that a resolution condemning China for aggression should not be moved in the UN at this time.

General Bradley responded and began by recalling the original aims of the UN in Korea – to halt aggression and achieve a free, unified Korea. There had been no desire for conflict with China and this had occurred because of Chinese action. The UN was engaged effectively in war against China. Bradley did not want to commit additional resources to Korea: too many men and resources were already committed to Korea, and the Far East as a whole, 'was no place to fight a major war'.[63] It was impossible to stabilise the present line because of the disparity in strength and repeated infiltration via the excessively extended front. The best he anticipated was to establish a perimeter of approximately 40–50 miles around Pusan. He was sceptical of the military merits of so doing, although such a perimeter included two airfields. No change had been made, however, in American policy since Attlee's visit. The aim was to stay in Korea for as long as possible. He felt that evacuation would occur eventually and this might be preferable to keeping forces in a small part of Korea. Withdrawal should be relatively straightforward to implement. As regards MacArthur, Bradley felt that criticism had gone too far. MacArthur was compelled to take political decisions on various matters relating to the ROK government. The JCS did not relish all of MacArthur's decisions but held that rigid direction at a distance of 7,000 miles was not practicable. Bradley concurred with Slessor that Anglo-American relations had experienced too much strain. American opinion was moving in a more isolationist direction and it was felt that the UN was finished. The JCS were definitely opposed to war with China but this came into the political, rather than the military, sphere. Admiral Sherman stated that there was a tendency to underestimate Chinese vulnerability and China's capacity for further aggression. Sherman supported proceeding with a UN resolution condemning China and doubted whether it would wreck the UN: even if an aggressor could not be defeated through 'material action', the UN would retain value for discussion and mediation.[64] He believed that an economic blockade of China would accomplish more than the British maintained: it should be possible to prevent Hong Kong experiencing excessive pressure.

This was followed by a general discussion concerning economic sanctions, North Korean POWs, the ROK forces, Soviet troops in Manchuria, Taiwan, French Indo-China and air action against China. Bradley made one point which he requested should not be minuted. This pointed to recent intelligence reports indicating that the Chinese were equipping an additional 27 North Korean divisions so that the DPRK forces would total approximately half a million. Against this were approximately 120,000 South Koreans, amounting nominally to nine divisions but in his opinion constituting two divisions following their recent setbacks. This problem had to be considered in relation to the five-point resolution urging withdrawal of all non-Korean forces, referring here to the proposal from the Cease-fire committee. Bradley's observation was recorded in a confidential annex.[65]

On 16 January a second meeting was held in Bradley's office. Slessor was accompanied by Sir Oliver Franks and Lord Tedder plus two other officers;

Bradley was accompanied by Sherman, Dean Rusk and one officer. Franks made the initial statement: the British government hoped that progress would be made with the five-point resolution but it was unlikely this would occur. Therefore, discussion should be based on the assumption that UN forces would stay in Korea. Franks identified three problems: public opinion in Britain and the United States; the prestige and power of the UN as an organisation; and the repercussions for the entire far eastern situation. Unless progress was made soon in negotiations, Franks believed it would be difficult for the UN not to accept a resolution condemning China. In contemplating economic measures it was important to avoid action that was either ineffective or so potent as to risk a major war.[66] Rusk spoke next and agreed with Franks's broad approach: the American view was that a cease-fire line must be based on the 38th parallel. The challenge was to combat what appeared to be a programme of Chinese expansion which could affect Indo-China, Taiwan and possibly Hong Kong. The Western powers should apply pressure to stop the Chinese by non-military means. The drawbacks to applying economic sanctions were understood but did not invalidate resort to sanctions.[67] Bradley then reiterated his earlier question as to whether it was wise for UN forces to remain in Korea indefinitely. He recognised the divergence between public opinion in the United States and in Britain. Franks thought that selective sanctions would meet with greater approval in the UN. Rusk enquired how the British government would react as regards diplomatic recognition of China and membership of the UN. Franks replied that there would be no thought of withdrawing diplomatic representatives because it would be an empty gesture; the aim should be to curb further expansion. Franks doubted whether the Chinese possessed a precise programme of expansion as Rusk seemed to think. Franks advocated the attainment of a stabilised line because it would increase the likelihood of reaching a negotiated agreement with the Chinese. Bradley asked if Britain would consider the use of Kuomintang troops in Korea but Franks stated that there had been no change in Britain's position.[68]

Slessor reported to the cabinet on his return. He deduced that the JCS would like to extricate UN forces from Korea if possible. However, since his departure from Washington there appeared to be some improvement in the military situation. Morale among UN forces had been improved by recent changes in command. The Americans were very keen to see a condemnatory resolution carried in the UN and American pressure might subside once it was carried. Slessor added that it was unlikely that the JCS would approve an air attack on the Chinese mainland except in a critical phase in which UN forces were attacked powerfully from the air.[69] Slessor's mission was valuable since it gave rise to the most candid exchange on strategy in Korea so far. Slessor conducted the talks capably and had spoken with necessary bluntness. Franks proved a suitable foil, once more bringing his diplomatic gifts to bear.

The cabinet was preoccupied with developments relating to the endeavours of the Cease-fire committee in New York. The latter had put forward its five proposals in mid-January: these included aspects unpalatable to the United States. Dean Acheson decided to accept them in a calculated gamble that the Chinese would hold out for further American concessions. Given the Chinese attitude since the end of November, this was a reasonable assumption. It proved accurate, for China rejected the five points. Acheson then resumed the more congenial task of twisting arms so as to secure sufficient support for a resolution in the UN General Assembly. This caused an acrimonious exchange between the American and British governments, for Attlee and the cabinet were unhappy about the resolution in itself and about the tactics employed by the Americans. Since Bevin's health had deteriorated, Kenneth Younger was carrying the greater part of the burden in dealing with day-to-day business. Younger noted in his diary for 21 January that he favoured a more resolute approach in dealing with the Americans despite the risks entailed. They would react initially with rage but would then act in accordance with their preception of their true interests. It would be salutary in its effect on the Russians, too, and would show that Europeans could stand up to the Americans if necessary.[70] A personal telegram from Bevin to Franks had been sent on the previous day, initialled by Bevin, expressing grave anxiety at the dangers implicit in American policy and instructing Franks to communicate his views to Acheson. A recent statement by Ernest Gross about bombing policy was 'profoundly disquieting'.[71] If a decision was reached to extend bombing outside Korea, it should not be taken without UN authority. On 23 January a trenchantly worded telegram was sent to Washington. The cabinet believed that the latest Chinese reply, for clarification of China's attitude, included a 'slight opening'; which should be pursued further.[72] It was important to pursue every avenue before adopting a condemnatory resolution. If the Americans were obdurate, the time would come for 'plain speaking' with regard to the tactics used by Acheson and his officials. American tactics could almost have been invented in Moscow in the sense of driving a wedge between the United States and the other Western democracies.[73] Parliament was reassembling and it would be difficult to carry opinion on the basis of support for American policy. The defect with current American policy was that it was too subservient to its own public opinion while ignoring public opinion in other countries.[74] He objected to a statement by MacArthur on 21 January describing Chinese action in Korea as 'a sneak attack far more infamous than Japan's at Pearl Harbour'. Ernest Gross had similarly made a provocative statement on Taiwan. Bevin stated, 'It must be brought home to the United States that it is not the rest of the world which is out of step with them but their own public opinion which is out on a limb by itself.'[75] It was foolish of the United States to exert extreme pressure.

When the cabinet met on 25 January it was decided that Britain should be prepared, if necessary, to vote against a UN-sponsored resolution despite the risks involved for future Anglo-American relations.[76] The cabinet was divided between those very sympathetic to the United States, those who adopted a centrist, if more critical, view, and those who were hostile. Kenneth Younger was usually in a centrist role but had become more critical. According to Hugh Dalton's diary, Aneurin Bevan, James Griffiths, Chuter Ede and Dalton himself took the lead in opposing the American resolution. Their chief opponent was Hugh Gaitskell, the chancellor of the exchequer.[77] Gaitskell was the most sympathetic to the United States and was additionally acutely aware of Britain's difficult economic circumstances with the concomitant deduction that the

Americans should not be alienated.[78] When the cabinet met again on the following day, Attlee reported on the latest developments and said the Americans were prepared to moderate the wording of the resolution. Younger, attending for this item, said that in his opinion he did not think it mattered greatly how Britain voted but his advisers in the Foreign Office took a different view. Attlee summed up at the end in characteristic style that the balance of argument pointed to urging the United States to accept amendments to paragraphs 2 and 8 of the resolution.[79] On 29 January Younger told the cabinet that further concessions were being made to the British position and the trend pointed towards Britain now being able to support the resolution. Attention was drawn to another regrettable public pronouncement by MacArthur.[80] The concessions made were deemed acceptable and Britain voted for the resolution in the General Assembly on 1 February.

It is fitting to move next to a problem where the views of the British and American governments eventually converged – the future of General Douglas MacArthur. Doubts about MacArthur's conduct had grown since October 1950 and were accentuated by MacArthur's penchant for making public statements of controversial character in which he seemed to be assuming certain of the powers belonging to the president. It was appreciated that MacArthur had preserved links with some of the influential figures on the right wing of the Republican party and that he was – or saw himself – as a possible candidate for the Republican presidential nomination in 1952.[81] The events of late November and early December 1950 dealt a serious blow to MacArthur's reputation. To a man of MacArthur's character and past accomplishments it was a bitter blow. His resentment induced a growing inclination to act independently in public statements regardless of the consequences. This evolved into a constitutional and personal confrontation with Truman. It is possible that MacArthur's judgement was so affected that he believed that he could treat Truman with contempt indefinitely. Equally, perhaps, he felt that a confrontation with the president might assist his political ambitions. MacArthur became extremely irate with the British because of criticism in the press and Parliament of his strategy and statements. His annoyance manifested itself in reluctance to meet the head of the British liaison mission in Tokyo, Sir Alvary Gascoigne. He had to see Gascoigne on 6 February before the latter departed to take up a new appointment as ambassador to Moscow. MacArthur vehemently defended his strategy and emphasised his resentment at British criticism: he excluded Attlee and Bevin from his strictures. If the British COS entertained doubts these had not been communicated to him by the JCS or by Bouchier.[82] His anger was shown in his deliberate snubbing of Gascoigne when he departed from Haneda airport by not attending and refraining from appointing anyone to represent him.

In reality MacArthur's power was not as great as it had been since General Ridgway's appointment to head the eighth army in succession to General Walker. The JCS communicated directly with Ridgway and were less in awe of MacArthur than previously. As the UN forces hit back at the enemy so the familiar issue arose of whether or not to cross the 38th parallel. The British COS opposed an advance significantly north of the parallel and believed the dangers were too great.[83] Limited operations beyond the parallel might be needed. Slim told the COS on 21 March that there was no reason to change opinions expressed before: no major attempt should be made to occupy much of North Korea.[84] Bouchier reported on 4 March that MacArthur had told him that he did not intend crossing the parallel: he aimed to establish a line as near the 38th parallel as possible.[85] In London it was feared that MacArthur would embark upon an adventurous policy again and that he would advocate bombing Manchuria to hinder Chinese efforts to send reinforcements. Distrust of MacArthur's motives and conduct were profound throughout Westminster, Whitehall and public opinion. The position was rendered more delicate by the fact that the American and British governments were contemplating a new initiative to secure negotiations with the Chinese. Truman informed MacArthur confidentially of his intention of issuing a suitably worded statement. Without consultation MacArthur then issued a public statement of his own in which he professed willingness to meet the enemy commander-in-chief to discuss an armistice, yet reiterating his opinion that a convincing military victory connoted the only satisfactory outcome. Clearly it was a direct challenge to Truman and it gave rise to consternation in Washington and among the allied powers. Bouchier reported that MacArthur wanted to avoid a stalemate in the vicinity of the 38th parallel because this would entail a higher casualty rate; MacArthur's offer to meet the enemy commander had been dropped from planes onto the Chinese forces. Bouchier naively commented that MacArthur always intended doing this at the correct 'psychological moment which he thinks has now arrived and which forms part of his psychological warfare programme'.[86] The Attlee cabinet decided before MacArthur's statement was known that serious thought should be given to launching an initiative to secure a negotiated settlement; this might include a statement of UN aims in Korea. The cabinet wanted the Truman administration to understand the strength of feeling in Britain against moving north of the 38th parallel on political and military grounds. It was recommended that a clear directive should be issued to MacArthur.[87] Dean Rusk indicated that a major crisis had resulted from MacArthur's action: he observed sardonically that the lesson to be drawn was that the Japanese peace treaty should be concluded rapidly, thus denoting an end to MacArthur's role as SCAP.[88]

Ernest Bevin at last resigned as foreign secretary in March. His health had worsened steadily for the preceding 12 months and he was not fit enough to discharge the basic responsibilities of the post. Younger's diary contains irritable observations on Bevin's refusal to resign. On 7 January Younger noted that Bevin's health meant that he wished to avoid arguments and that he was afraid of upsetting relations with Washington: 'I think the weakness is partly physical and that he simply hasn't the stamina for taking difficult decisions.'[89] There was no obvious successor to Bevin. Younger spoke warmly of Nye Bevan's ability: Bevan possessed vision and leadership qualities, although Younger doubted whether one would want Nye as a close personal friend. All the other senior members of the cabinet, he noted mordantly, were extinct volcanoes or had never been volcanoes at all.[90] He commented gloomily in his diary on 28 March that Bevin had resigned under pressure from Attlee but that Herbert Morrison had been appointed as his successor. He remarked again that he would have favoured Nye's appointment but this was impossible because of Nye's poor relations with Bevin and Morrison and, to a lesser extent, with Attlee. Younger described Morrison as more ignorant of foreign affairs than any other member of the cabinet: 'Basically he is a Little Englander who suspects everyone who is foreign. If he had the power he would like to be a Palmerston.'[91] In terms of seniority and service Morrison was an obvious choice but, as Younger observed, he knew little of foreign policy and accepted the Foreign Office because it would advance his ambition to be the next leader of the Labour Party and prime minister.[92] Not surprisingly he was repelled by MacArthur's adventurism and attracted at the prospect of achieving progress in an attempt to open negotiations in Korea. He was influenced by the growing vocal discontent in the Labour Party at grassroots level with MacArthur.[93] A telegram was sent to Washington on 30 March emphasising Morrison's desire for a new endeavour to obtain a settlement in Korea: it was necessary to clarify UN objectives in Korea.[94] Oliver Franks responded that he had at once talked to Dean Rusk who was sympathetic but warned that the evidence pointed to a new Chinese military offensive. It seemed unlikely that negotiations would commence within the near future.[95]

Within the first ten days of April the crisis concerning MacArthur reached a climax. Truman was faced with a challenge from the insolent general which could no longer be avoided. Not that Truman was the kind of personality to flinch from a showdown but his political antennae warned that a decisive clash with MacArthur should occur only if absolutely necessary. The removal of MacArthur would require delicate handling, given MacArthur's stature as an American hero and given the considerable support for him within the Republican party. MacArthur now acted in such a manner as to insult Truman still further. The Republican minority leader in the House of Representatives, Joseph W. Martin, published letters exchanged between MacArthur and himself in which the general made abundantly clear his contempt for the far eastern policy of the Truman administration.[96] On 5 April the *Daily Telegraph* in London published an extremely frank interview granted by MacArthur to its military correspondent, Lt. General H. G. Martin. MacArthur attacked the politicians for not providing a lucid definition of aims in Korea. With reference to perennial arguments over the 38th parallel, it was therefore the fault of politicians who had encroached on the military sphere. In any war the only objective should be to liquidate the enemy but this did not apply to Korea for political reasons. If only the politicians would 'take the wraps off', the Chinese would be defeated with relative ease. The Chinese economy lacked industrial potential, rubber, had little oil and inadequate food. Chinese leaders were, he stated optimistically, confronted by a developing guerrilla campaign against communism. UN forces should blockade the Chinese coast and destroy the weak railway system so as to bring about collapse. MacArthur dismissed the likelihood of Russian intervention. The Chinese were preparing a new offensive and this would probably occur in May. The calibre of Chinese troops was good but not, he thought, as formidable as the original North Korean forces at the beginning of the war. MacArthur ended by speaking warmly of the contributions made by British and Commonwealth forces in Korea.[97]

The COS committee met on 6 April and discussed MacArthur's position. Slim was ill and Major-General McLeod reported that Slim believed that

MacArthur was aiming to commit the UN to full-scale war against China. MacArthur exaggerated the Chinese build-up, although it was large, and Slim doubted if there was much prospect of a 'massive' air attack. The Chinese would very likely implement an air attack by a small number of bombers but the American air forces should be capable of disposing of this effectively. If UN forces stayed near the 38th parallel, this would be around the limit of the MIGs operating from Manchuria, and Chinese bombers would be ineffective without appropriate escort. Slim felt that 'we should be very careful not to give General MacArthur a "blank cheque" which enabled him to carry out unrestricted retaliation in China or Manchuria without specific authority from Washington'.[98] Slessor agreed with Slim 'that General MacArthur was probably trying to involve the United Nations in a real war with China'.[99] It was unlikely that the enemy was capable of launching 'massive' air attacks as stated by MacArthur. Such attacks would occur only if the Soviet Union intervened, a contingency admittedly rendered more likely by the courses of action advocated by MacArthur. Slessor suspected that MacArthur deliberately exaggerated Chinese strength in order to justify operations against China and to excuse in advance any reverses suffered by UN forces. In communicating with Lord Tedder in Washington, 'we should conclude by taking a strong line as regards the apparent inability of the authorities in Washington to exercise any control over General MacArthur'.[100] MacArthur should be told not to implement any operations outside Korea including counter-attacks aimed at enemy airfields without explicit instructions.

In Washington Truman reached the momentous decision that MacArthur must be removed. Truman's patience was exhausted and he was embarrassed by constant foreign enquiries about MacArthur's latest statements which contained the implication that the American government was not master in its own house. He consulted the JCS, Marshall, Acheson and Averell Harriman who all concurred that the time had come for MacArthur's dismissal. Truman braced himself for the inevitable backlash and set the wheels in motion to replace MacArthur with General Ridgway. Unfortunately the mechanics of notifying MacArthur were bungled owing to fears of press leaks. Instead of being informed personally ahead of a public announcement, MacArthur learned of his removal from the radio. At the same time, given MacArthur's indulgence in independent announcements, there was something ironically fitting about the outcome. The Attlee government was delighted to hear that MacArthur had been removed. Regret was felt, however, that such an illustrious career should end in such a way. Herbert Morrison reflected these sentiments in a statement to the House of Commons on 11 April. Excessive attention should not be devoted to recent events which had been unfortunate. MacArthur's past military service, particularly in the Pacific war, had been most distinguished. In addition: 'He has displayed qualities of the highest order in his conduct of the occupation in Japan. These are achievements which will be remembered long after the immediate controversy has been forgotten.'[101] Churchill, as leader of the opposition, endorsed Morrison's observations. MacArthur received a tumultuous welcome on his return to the United States which he had last visited in 1938. At first, fears among Democrats that the crisis would undermine Truman's administration seemed to be borne out but then it became clear that many Americans regarded applause as a gesture of thanks for MacArthur's long service rather than a wish that he should assume the leadership of the nation in 1953. MacArthur's farewell address to Congress was more accurate than he realised when he stated at the end that he would 'fade away', like the proverbial old soldier.[102] The protracted Senate hearings into the reasons for his removal became bogged down in repetitive and verbose exchanges and public interest waned. When he met the senators MacArthur made clear his detestation for British policy towards China but in total the hearings did far less harm to Anglo-American relations than was feared in London before they began.[103]

While happy to see MacArthur depart, Dean Acheson had no intention of permitting the British to entertain the fond illusion that the differences in approach between the American and British governments had now ended. In a telegram to the American embassy in London sent on 17 April, Acheson stated that it was essential that the British should not interpret the removal of an irritant (MacArthur) as denoting a change in policy. Rather, Acheson wished to utilise the situation to pressure the Attlee government towards objectives favoured by the Truman administration:

> Stated another way now is time for us to 'cash in' on new situation arising because of removal of MacArthur from scene. In this connection it is most important for Brit[ish] to understand this does not mean change in our position vis-à-vis Chi[nese] Commies which if changed in any way will be in direction of increased firmness.[104]

The British must be persuaded to support American initiatives on economic sanctions against China. He added that his comments were partly stimulated by criticism of Britain from MacArthur's supporters. However, the telegram revealed that the gulf between British and American policies over China was considerable and had been exacerbated but not caused by MacArthur's conduct.

American and British intelligence believed that the next Chinese offensive would begin in May but it commenced in late April. This represented the last major attempt to resolve the Korean war by military means. The Chinese lines of communication were too extended, their supply problems were considerable, they possessed inferior equipment and they lacked air strength. As their commander, Peng Teh-huai, ruefully conceded in his cultural revolution 'confession', the Chinese offensives of April and May 1951 ran out of vigour; the remarkable military campaign waged by the Chinese since November 1950 now reached the close of its offensive stage.[105] The question of the Chinese attacking UN forces from air bases in China had been discussed previously, since it involved the issue of retaliatory bombing. Morrison told the cabinet on 3 May that Acheson advocated retaliation should such attacks occur. Morrison thought this would have to be accepted if the situation became serious enough. The cabinet agreed but inserted the qualification that the United States should not be left to take a decision on its own. Since MacArthur's removal, American policy appeared less rash but risks could not be accepted. The cabinet decided that retaliatory bombing against bases in Manchuria could be accepted but the British must be consulted beforehand.[106] This secret decision aligned the Attlee government more closely to American policy than would have been desired or accepted by a significant number of Labour MPs. As will be seen in the next chapter, this decision became highly controversial the following year when Churchill, as prime minister, made public the Labour government's commitment to support bombing to the embarrassment of Attlee and Morrison. For the present the issue of bombing did not become urgent as the tide of battle turned. Bouchier told the COS on 24 May that the eighth army had taken the offensive and was advancing north in every sector. The Chinese were retreating and the eighth army was advancing towards the 38th parallel with great determination. He added that the enemy might contemplate a cease-fire before long.[107] A week later, Bouchier had a lengthy, amicable conversation with Ridgway. He commented that Ridgway was a good listener but that the latter held that there was no evidence indicating that the Chinese wanted a cease-fire. Ridgway felt that much depended on Russian reactions and how far they were willing to step up assistance to the Chinese. While the Chinese could afford manpower losses, the point had been reached where further casualties would inhibit the campaign. Bouchier concluded that Anglo-American relations and the Unified Command had improved under Ridgway.[108]

A general feeling that the Korean war could not be won militarily, at least without incurring risks of a third world war, developed among the states principally involved in late May and June 1951. As Ridgway observed, the Soviet attitude was the vital ingredient in deciding whether or not armistice talks should begin.[109] The State Department reached this conclusion in May and George Kennan was invited to pursue confidential discussions with the Soviet delegate to the UN, Jacob Malik. Kennan left the State Department at the end of August 1950 to follow an academic career but his prestige, while not as potent as in 1947–48, was still such that he was regarded as an admirable choice for this role. Kennan quickly deduced that the Russians wanted a cease-fire, although Malik kept referring to the problems existing in Sino-American relations. When he met Malik again on 5 June Malik was more open and emphasised the Soviet wish for a peaceful settlement in Korea. While the obstacles were appreciable, Kennan believed progress could be made and that American policy should be constructed accordingly.[110]

The first public indication of the new trend occurred on 23 June when Malik made a radio broadcast in a series organised for the UN. After a ritualistic denunciation of post-1945 American foreign policy, Malik said that, in the context of the war in Korea, the Soviet Union believed in peaceful coexistence between communism and capitalism. Talks should begin to achieve a cease-fire and an armistice providing for mutual withdrawal of troops from the 38th parallel. The State Department promptly issued a statement to the effect that if the communist powers would cease aggression in Korea, then the United States would act positively in working to end hostilities. President Truman confirmed this in a speech delivered in Tennessee on 25 June.[111] Therefore, the Soviet Union took the lead in trying to escape from the carnage of Korea. The motivation for Stalin's decision remains a matter for speculation: most likely the war had become more of an embarrassment, since it was clear that it would drag on interminably unless armistice talks were started. The Soviet Union bore the brunt of the burden in supplying arms to the Chinese and North Koreans: it appears to have been the case that Soviet pilots participated in air battles.[112] If peace could be concluded on terms not disadvantageous to China and North Korea, it would be sensible to assist in bringing the war to an end.

The British reaction to Malik's broadcast was initially cautious: Morrison informed the cabinet on 25 June that it would be welcomed, although the sincerity of Malik's observations remained to be tested.[113] Three days later he told his colleagues that a conversation between the American ambassador in Moscow and Gromyko seemed promising.[114] It was noted that Syngman Rhee reacted negatively to the possibility of talks beginning which was entirely to be expected, given Rhee's fanatical hatred of communism and equally fanatical determination to reunify his country under his own leadership. Morrison optimistically commented that he would see what could be done to prevent Rhee from making critical statements.[115] The most difficult period of Anglo-American relations during the Korean struggle now terminated but many disputes lay ahead before the war finally ended in July 1953.

Notes

1 Chiefs of staff minutes, COS(50)97(1), 28 June 1950, Defe 4/32. Sir William Elliot stated that the Americans might wish to drop an atomic bomb on North Korea: 'There was general agreement that from a military point of view the dropping of an Atom Bomb in North Korea would be unsound. The effects of such action would be world wide and might well be very damaging. Moreover it would probably provoke a global war. Although it did not appear that the military situation in Korea could be restored unless American Ground Forces were deployed against the North Korean forces it would be unwise to advise the dropping of an Atom Bomb in order to restore the situation.'

2 Minute by Dixon, 1 July 1950, FO 371/84091/208G.

3 See R. Foot, *The Wrong War: American Policy and the Dimensions of the Korean Conflict, 1950–1953* (Ithaca and London: Cornell University Press, 1985), pp. 114–17 and C. A. MacDonald, *Korea: The War before Vietnam* (London: Macmillan, 1986), pp. 71, 74, 131–3.

4 Circular letter from Labour MPs to Attlee, 30 November 1950, fols 154–7, box 144, Attlee papers, Bodleian Library, Oxford. It is interesting to note the views of Dulles before China intervened massively, as expressed in a letter to Ferdinand Lathrop Mayer: 'My guess is that if we try by military means to get control of *all* of Korea we shall become bogged down in an interminable and costly operation like the Japanese "China Incident"' 9 November 1950, Dulles papers, box 48, Seely G. Mudd Library, Princeton.

5 Letter from Gaitskell to Attlee, 30 November 1950, fol. 158, box 144, Attlee papers.

6 *Ibid.*

7 Note from Emrys Roberts, Liberal MP for Merioneth, to Attlee's private secretary, fol. 161, box 144, Attlee papers.

8 Cabinet minutes, 29 November 1950, CM(50)78(1), Cab 128/18.

9 *Ibid.*

10 *Ibid.*

11 Memorandum by Acheson, 5 September 1950, folder of conversations, September 1950, box 65, Acheson papers, Harry S. Truman Library. Truman told Acheson he did not wish to see Attlee at this time: if necessary, Attlee could visit him in November.

12 *FRUS 1950*, vol. VII, p. 1366, US delegation minutes of first meeting between Truman and Attlee, 4 December 1950.

13 *Ibid.*, p. 1367.

14 *Ibid.*, p. 1368.

15 *Ibid.*, p. 1382, memorandum by McWilliams, 5 December 1950.

16 *Ibid.*, p. 1391, memorandum by Jessup, 5 December 1950.

17 *Ibid.*, p. 1395, US delegation minutes of second meeting, 5 December 1950.

18 *Ibid.*, pp. 1398–9.

19 *Ibid.*, p. 1430, memorandum by Battle, meeting held on 6 December 1950.

20 Attlee's visit to Washington, December 1950, Prem 8/1200.

21 *Ibid.*

22 *Ibid.*

23 *FRUS 1950*, vol. VII, pp. 1436–7, memorandum by Jessup, 7 December 1950.

24 *Ibid.*, pp. 1449–61, US delegation, minutes of fifth meeting, 7 December 1950.

25 Memorandum for the president, 12 December 1950, folder, memoranda (1950), box 220, PSF Subject Files, Truman papers, Truman Library.

26 Cabinet minutes, 12 December 1950, CM85(50)3, Cab 128/18.

27 *Ibid.*

28 Kenneth Younger diary, 11 December 1950.

29 *Ibid.*

30 *Ibid.*

31 Hugh Dalton diary, 21 December 1950, vol. 38, Dalton papers, British Library of Political and Economic Science.

32 New York to FO, 14 December 1950, FO 371/84136/2/G.

33 New York to FO, 18 December 1950, FO 371/84136/5.

34 Complimentary note from Churchill to MacArthur, accompanying volumes of *The Second World War*, 'With all good wishes from Winston S. Churchill', folder 88, box 1, RG 10, VIP files, MacArthur papers, MacArthur Memorial, Norfolk, Virginia.

35 Menu from 'Other Club' dinner, 7 December 1950, with sketch map by Churchill on reverse side, with memorandum by Selborne, 7 December 1950, MS Eng Hist d. 450, ff. 90–1, Selborne papers, Bodleian Library, Oxford. I am grateful to Dr Colin Buckley for kindly supplying this reference.

36 Tokyo to FO, personal, Ferguson to Johnstone, 31 December 1950, FO 371/92724/2/G.

37 *Ibid.*

38 Bouchier to COS, 4 January 1951, FO 371/92724/8/G.

39 FO to Washington, 6 January 1951, FO 371/92725/15/G.

40 Commonwealth prime ministers conference, 4 January 1951, PMM(51)1, Cab 133/90.

41 *Ibid.*, PMM(51)2.

42 *Ibid.*, 5 January 1951, PMM(51)3.

43 Memorandum by UK COS, 6 January 1951, PMM(51)12, Cab 133/90.

44 *Ibid.*

45 *Ibid.*, appendix, memorandum by COS.

46 *Ibid.*

47 *Ibid.*

48 *Ibid.*

49 *Ibid.*, 8 January 1951, PMM(51)5.

50 *Ibid.*, 9 January 1951, PMM(51)7.

51 Note by the secretariat, 'Korea and the Far East: Proposals for a Settlement', 9 January 1951, PMM(51)15, Cab 133/90.

52 Note by the secretariat, 'Korea and the Far East: Proposals for a Settlement', 11 January 1951, PMM(51)7, Cab 133/90.

53 *Ibid.*

54 *Ibid.*, 12 January 1951, PMM(51)12.

55 8 January 1951, COS51(51), Defe 4/39.

56 *Ibid.*, confidential annex.

57 COS8(51)5, 9 January 1951, confidential annex, Defe 4/39.

58 *Ibid.*

59 COS10(51)1, 12 January 1951, confidential annex, Defe 4/39.

60 COS10(51)5, *ibid.*

61 Washington discussions, January 1951, minutes of meeting held in Pentagon, 15 January 1951, COS(51)34, Defe 5/27.

62 *Ibid.*

63 *Ibid.*
64 *Ibid.*
65 *Ibid.*, confidential annex to meeting held, 15 January 1951.
66 Washington discussions, January 1951, minutes of meeting held in Bradley's room, 16 January 1951, COS(51)34, Defe 5/27.
67 *Ibid.*
68 *Ibid.*
69 CM5(51)3, 22 January 1951, Cab 128/19.
70 Kenneth Younger diary, 21 January 1951.
71 FO to Washington, personal for Franks, 20 January 1951, FO 371/92769/137/G.
72 FO to Washington, 23 January 1951, FO 371/92770/169/G.
73 *Ibid.*
74 *Ibid.*
75 *Ibid.*
76 CM8(51)1, 25 January 1951, Cab 128/19.
77 Dalton diary, 4 February 1951. For an account of Dalton's ministerial career after 1945, see Ben Pimlott, *Hugh Dalton*, paperback edition (London: Macmillan, 1986), pp. 423–606.
78 For discussion of Gaitskell's ministerial career, see Philip Williams, *Hugh Gaitskell* (London: Jonathan Cape, 1979), pp. 131–288.
79 CM9(51), 26 January 1951, Cab 128/19.
80 CM10(51)3, 29 January 1951, Cab 128/19.
81 For a lucid account of MacArthur's career during the Korean war, see D. Clayton James, *The Years of MacArthur*, vol. III, *Triumph and Disaster, 1945–1964* (Boston: Houghton Mifflin, 1985), pp. 387–604.
82 Despatch from Gascoigne to Bevin, 6 February 1951, FO 371/92808/22.
83 COS51(24)1, 5 February 1951, Defe 4/40.
84 COS51(51)2, 21 March 1951, Defe 4/41.
85 Bouchier to COS, 4 March 1951, FO 371/92731/76/G.
86 Bouchier to COS, 27 March 1951, FO 371/92732/84/G.
87 FO to Washington, 24 March 1951, FO 371/92813/8.
88 Washington to FO, 24 March 1951, FO 371/92813/9.
89 Kenneth Younger diary, 7 January 1951.
90 *Ibid.*, 4 February 1951.
91 *Ibid.*, 28 March 1951.
92 For an account of Morrison's career between 1945 and 1951, see Bernard Donoughue and G. W. Jones, *Herbert Morrison: Portrait of a Politician* (London: Weidenfeld and Nicolson, 1973).
93 See various letters from Labour Party branches to Morrison, March–April 1951, FO 371/92735/108. As specific examples, see South Hendon Labour Party to Morrison, 30 March 1951 and Ealing South Labour Party to Morrison, 1 April 1951. In the Princeton seminars, recorded in July 1953 not long after he left office, Dean Acheson stated that he had not been impressed by Herbert Morrison. He was an irritable person and made statements in the most annoying way possible. Another participant, Perkins, said that often Morrison did not know what he was talking about, for example in Ottawa in September 1951, Princeton seminars, Acheson papers, box 75, Truman Library.
94 FO to Washington, 30 March 1951, FO 371/92778/385.
95 Washington to FO, 30 March 1951, FO 371/92778/387.
96 See Clayton James, *Years of MacArthur*, vol. III, pp. 589–90, and Douglas MacArthur, *Reminiscences*, (London: Heinemann 1965) pp. 385–9, 439–43.
97 *Daily Telegraph*, 5 April 1951.
98 COS51(59)1, confidential annex, 6 April 1951, Defe 4/41.
99 *Ibid.*
100 *Ibid.*
101 Extract from *Parliamentary Debates*, Commons, 5th series, 486, col. 1030, 11 April 1951.
102 MacArthur, *Reminiscences*, pp. 454–60, for the text of the farewell address to Congress.
103 For the record of the hearings, see *Military Situation in the Far East: Hearings before the*

Committee on Armed Services and the Committee on Foreign Relations, 5 parts (Washington, D.C.: Government Printing Office, 1951).

104 *FRUS 1951,* vol. VII. part 1, p. 352, Acheson to embassy in Britain, 17 April 1951.

105 Peng Teh-huai, *Memoirs of a Chinese Marshal* (Beijing: Foreign Languages Press, 1984), p. 480.

106 CM33(51)2, 3 May 1951, Cab 128/19.

107 Bouchier to COS, 24 May 1951, FO 371/92737/142/G.

108 Bouchier to COS, 2 June 1951, *ibid.*

109 *FRUS 1951,* vol. VII, part 1, pp. 483–6, memorandum from Kennan to Matthews, 31 May 1951.

110 *Ibid.,* pp. 507–11, Kennan to Matthews, 5 June 1951.

111 *Ibid.,* pp. 546–7, editorial note.

112 Interview with Soviet official who referred to Russian pilots who had been killed in Korea being buried in Soviet territory adjacent to the Korean border, transmitted in Thames Television documentary series on Korea, shown on British television, June–July 1988.

113 CM46(51)2, 25 June 1951, Cab 128/19.

114 CM47(51)2, 28 June 1951, Cab 128/19.

115 *Ibid.*

12

NEGOTIATIONS TO END THE KOREAN WAR, 1951 TO 1953

The negotiations to terminate the Korean war occupied exactly two years, from July 1951 to July 1953. Both sides wearied of attempts to win the conflict by military means yet neither was sufficiently disillusioned to contemplate concessions extensive enough to induce the other to reciprocate. Thus the negotiations, held initially in Kaesong and soon transferred to Panmunjom, were prolonged, repetitive, acrimonious and negative. Each indulged in tedious crude propaganda claims for its own superiority and denigrated the other. The military was in the ascendant in both teams of negotiators and skilful diplomacy designed to reduce mutual suspicions and contribute to more meaningful exchanges was conspicuous by its absence. China was emboldened by its impact on the fighting into pursuing a truculent attitude with a belief that the Americans were more likely to tire first; North Korea concurred. The United States was deeply affected by virulent anti-communism and was determined not to expose itself to accusations of weakness. Therefore, each was the prisoner of its prejudices and was prepared to allow the talks to meander along in the hope that its opponents would crack first. From the British viewpoint the negotiations conducted by the United Nations Command (UNC) were completely dominated by the United States: the heavy American control of military operations was accompanied by an even more emphatic direction of the UNC's negotiations in Panmunjom. The relative decline in Great Britain's importance was made even more conspicuous in its treatment by the Truman and Eisenhower administrations in the course of the talks. British ministers and officials could only observe matters and pen mordant minutes while awaiting a suitable opportunity to make observations and to push the Americans towards a more realistic approach where feasible.[1]

The British chiefs of staff assessed the position between July and September 1951. On 11 July they agreed with the Foreign Office that it was highly desirable to prevent bombing operations on targets other than strictly military ones.[2] The Americans were concerned to establish how the UN would react in the event of the talks breaking down. Just before his sudden death Admiral Sherman visited London and suggested that a naval blockade of China should be established while recognising the particular claims of Hong Kong and Japan; in addition 'hot pursuit' in Korea should be contemplated to extend as far as the border or beyond it but without implementing bombing operations in China. In the event of a world war beginning Sherman agreed that evacuation of UN forces from Korea would occur.[3] Marshal of the Royal Air Force Sir John

Slessor submitted a minute to his colleagues on 1 August in which he raised the question as to whether Britain should participate in the negotiations. Slessor's deputy, Air Marshal Sir Arthur Sanders, attended a meeting that day and emphasised the great significance for Britain and France of current developments in the Far East: 'it was no less than the future of the Far East which was at stake in the negotiations now in progress, not merely the future of Korea'.[4]

In a confidential annex to the chiefs of staff conclusions for 29 August the results of the COS's consideration of possible action following a breakdown in the talks were recorded. The joint planning staff (JPS) had produced a report. Slessor suggested that a reference to 'hot pursuit' within Korea as far as the border or even beyond it should be incorporated. Robert Scott of the Foreign Office pointed out that political concomitants must be assessed; it was decided that the amended report should allude to the contingency of 'hot pursuit' but on the understanding that the states participating in the military operations must express approval. Similarly, Scott proposed that any question of a military advance northwards to the 'Northern waist' in response to a possible Chinese offensive, must be endorsed by all the countries involved. It was recognised that the matters involved should be discussed further after consultation with the Foreign Office, the UK liaison staffs for the Commonwealth and the defence committee.[5] The chiefs of staff returned to the issue of policy in the event of negotiations failing. General concurrence with a draft submitted by the Foreign Office was expressed. The COS were opposed to an advance to the Korean 'waist' unless Chinese forces appeared disorganised or demoralised and General Ridgway deemed the time propitious to act: in such circumstances a military advance to the 'waist' but certainly not beyond might be pursued. If the bombing of Chinese bases in Manchuria or 'hot pursuit' were contemplated, prior consultation was axiomatic.[6]

Herbert Morrison sent a message to Dean Acheson on 11 July stating that he was cautiously optimistic that the fighting in Korea could be ended. He felt that the Russians and North Koreans desired this, although he was less convinced about the Chinese. Looking ahead to the problems of achieving a political settlement in Korea under the auspices of the UN, Morrison was less sanguine. He anticipated a lengthy stalemate lasting perhaps for several years with Korea still divided. After the war China would be immersed in internal reconstruction and in building up military power. Morrison thought it unlikely that China would commit itself to military operations elsewhere, for example in Indo-China or Burma; China would no doubt encourage dissension in South-East Asia. As regards Korea the situation would remain potentially explosive.[7] John Addis perceptively remarked that, 'If we get to the stage of discussions for a Korean settlement after a ceasefire, one of our difficulties will be how to ensure that the peace is not broken by the South Koreans.'[8] John J. Muccio, the American ambassador in the ROK, was less apprehensive as regards Syngman Rhee creating difficulties but described him as a 'wily old bastard' who knew how to exploit his nuisance value.[9] The accuracy of this observation was ruefully appreciated in Washington and London in June–July 1953, as will be seen. The Foreign Office believed it was essential to look ahead to future political exchanges with the Chinese and North Koreans. A message was sent to

Washington on 3 August indicating alternative methods of moving into the first phase of political discussions: a five-power conference, a seven-power conference, resort to a mediator (as proposed by Trygve Lie) or establishment of a UN commission.[10]

Dean Rusk conveyed the views of the State Department in the latter part of August: the chief immediate priority was the signing of a Japanese peace treaty, closely followed by a cease-fire in Korea, and other outstanding issues in the Far East. The Western powers should assume the initiative in considering steps towards securing a general far eastern settlement following the signing of a Korean armistice. There must then be appropriate willingness to discuss matters raised by China or the Soviet Union. In a dig at the British, French and Indians, Rusk mentioned possible embarrassment should the Chinese wish to pursue the future of Hong Kong, Indo-China or Tibet but the American government would not exclude any issue. As regards Korea the State Department thought that the UN General Assembly might arrange for a small UN delegation, perhaps comprising three to five representatives of nations having forces in Korea, to pursue concrete negotiations with the communist states. Rusk was prepared to accept Lie's suggestion of a single UN mediator but he was firmly opposed to the British proposal for a five-power conference because this would imply that the five powers concerned had an exclusive right to deal with far eastern questions – Australia would definitely object. Indian and Japanese views would have to be taken into account. The State Department believed that the most suitable forum for discussing other far eastern matters would be a broad consultative conference which all countries possessing serious interest in the Far East should be eligible to attend. Rusk felt it made little difference whether a broad conference met under UN auspices or not. He said that in his personal view the Russians would not rush to discuss general political questions of the Pacific region and might be willing to permit matters to drift after a Korean armistice was signed.[11] The British reaction was that the General Assembly should approve a resolution providing for consultation between interested governments regarding an agreed solution to the Korean problem. It was desirable that North Korea and South Korea should be involved in consultations; a UN representative should be appointed to assist in the overall discussions. It was inferred that American objections to a five-power conference resulted from the third stage, concerning broader assessment of major problems in the Far East rather than the second stage, a Korean settlement. On the whole, the Foreign Office held that the smaller the number of powers concerned directly, the easier discussion would be. Once Britain and the United States, had agreed on their approach, an attempt should be made to ascertain the views of the Soviet Union. This would draw the Soviets into the central discussion which would assist in the deliberations.[12]

The State Department replied promptly agreeing that political discussions following a cease-fire should initially be restricted solely to Korea. The American government would be willing, after a cease-fire had been concluded, to hold political discussions including China and North Korea. Despite the fact that the United States did not recognise them, it would be willing to permit them to take part in exchanges regarding a Korean settlement. The State Department concurred with the British in anticipating that the communist states would not accept a UN mediator. Past experience indicated that direct discussions with the communists constituted the best and perhaps the only hope of solution. The Americans did not like the alternatives suggested by the British: a five-power or seven-power conference would not give adequate scope for a UN role to be fulfilled or for other interested countries, such as Australia, New Zealand or the Philippines, to do so. Predictably it was emphasised that the United States could not assent to any arrangement for a conference conveying the impression that the Peking government was the government of China.[13] Sir Gladwyn Jebb reported from New York that the chief advantage of the Americn proposal was that it rendered it easier to resolve the thorny issue of choosing which countries should participate in the discussions. A possible compromise could be reached for a General Assembly resolution initiating consultation to be framed in a generalised form which would, as far as possible, avoid defining status or the position of states which participated in discussions. It then followed that it would not be necessary to 'pick a United Nations team', but it would logically ensue that countries which had contributed significantly to military operations in Korea should be selected. Other vital participants would compromise the Soviet Union, China and the two Korean states. India could be included on the grounds that it had provided an ambulance unit.[14]

The truce talks did not start on a particularly encouraging note, although no one could have forecast that they would continue for as long as they did. It was thought either that the negotiations would lead to agreement within a relatively short period or that they would be broken off definitively. At first the Americans were more optimistic. Ridgway unwisely agreed that the talks should begin in Kaesong but this proved a bad decision because it was easy for the communists to devise an intimidatory atmosphere and to depict the UNC in a negative manner. Subsequently the talks were transferred to Panmunjom, which was preferable but by no means satisfactory as regards the harsh background to the exchanges.[15] From an early point British ministers and officials were perturbed at what they regarded as the erratic American approach to the talks. On occasions the Americans appeared too tough and on others insufficiently aware of dangers in their decisions. This is reflected in the discussions and minutes recorded in the British archive. Morrison sent a message to Washington on 29 July stating that negotiators should not be too rigid now that progress had been made in obtaining deferral of a substantive decision on withdrawal of foreign troops from Korea subsequent to political discussions. It was important that there should not be a collapse in negotiations provoked by this question. Morrison recommended that a more forthcoming attitude be adopted by the UNC and that the willingness of the latter to consider a political settlement should be conveyed.[16] The communists complained that American planes deliberately flew over the neutrality zone and thus exacerbated tension. A telegram was sent to Washington on 21 September conveying British belief that the concept of a neutrality zone assumed that neutrality should include the airspace over it. Morrison told Sir Oliver Franks that he should communicate with the State Department and suggest that Ridgway should issue instructions, without publicity, for stopping flights over the zone.[17] British anxiety was more candidly expressed in a letter from Robert Scott to F. S. Tomlinson (in Washington) sent on 29 September. Scott remarked that there was a danger that public opinion in Britain might conclude that the UNC was not seriously endeavouring to secure an armistice: he cited articles in *The Times* for 27 and 28 September as illustrating developing scepticism. Clearly Ridgway favoured a firm attitude but much depended on how precisely this was interpreted. Whether China and North Korea genuinely desired an armistice was a subject for speculation. Scott held that there was evidence suggesting that they did want an armistice and he reiterated the conclusions reached in London:

> The purpose of this letter is merely to repeat what I am sure you already know, i.e. that we attach very great importance to securing an armistice in Korea, that we are less pessimistic than the Americans about the chances, that we attach importance also to the way the talks are conducted and to the impression left on world opinion as regards responsibility for the outcome.[18]

Attlee decided to hold a general election in Britain in October 1951. The Labour government had declined in energy and vigour since 1949, the Korean conflict having contributed much to this process through the political and economic problems caused by it. Leading members of the cabinet were in ill-health: Bevin died in April 1951 and this was a serious blow since he had been a pillar behind Attlee's premiership and possessed vast influence within the wider Labour movement. Aneurin Bevan and Harold Wilson resigned in March 1951 partly because of the decision taken by Hugh Gaitskell, the chancellor of the exchequer, to impose prescription charges, which was held as undermining the principles guiding the establishment of the National Health Service. It was difficult to escape the conclusion that the government was suffering from the usual fate of Liberal and Labour governments during the past century (except for the Liberal government of 1905–14) and was exhausted by the demands of office.[19]

During the election campaign Morrison was irritated at reports from Alan Winnington published in the *Daily Worker* on 13 October that UNC planes had bombed the neutrality zone. John Shattock minuted on 16 Ocober that Ridgway admitted UNC responsibility but the planes acted contrary to orders and Ridgway had accordingly apologised.[20] Morrison minuted on 17 October that the 'U.S. has a long record of inaccurate bombing, etc', which was bad for the image of the UN.[21] The Americans should be urged to exercise more care; it was particularly regrettable in this case that two children had been killed in the attack. The result of the election was that Labour polled well but lost office through the vagaries of the electoral system and because of the smaller number of Liberal candidates standing compared with the general election in 1950. Winston Churchill and the Conservative Party returned to office with a small but manageable majority. Churchill lacked the sparkle of former years and was in gradual decline. However, his judgement was as shrewd as ever and, despite the developing handicaps of old age, Churchill dominated his cabinet successfully until the final phase in 1954–55.[22] Anthony Eden returned yet again to the Foreign Office in a spirit of frustration at Churchill's decision to continue leading the party to which Eden had been heir-apparent since the end of 1940.

Eden showed frequent petulance with Churchill but applied himself industriously to the numerous issues facing him in the Foreign Office.[23] Eden's health
was poor, the full extent of which emerges starkly from the published diaries of
his private secretary, Evelyn Shuckburgh.[24] Eden was noted for his not infrequent tantrums but the consolation for his staff was that his ire was usually
evanescent. In 1953 he was gravely ill for a lengthy period[25]; the repercussions
will be discussed below.

Soon after resuming office Churchill and Eden reviewed the situation in
Korea. The prime minister addressed one of his famous personal minutes to
Eden on 16 November:

> No one knows what is going on in Korea or which side is benefiting in strength
> from the humbug and grimaces at Panmunjom. We must try to penetrate the
> American mind and purpose. We may find this out when we are in Washington.
> Nobody knows it now. The other side clearly do not want an agreement. It is
> important to think out how prolonging the deadlock can benefit them.
> Obviously it diverts United Nations resources. But what do they hope for?
>
> Meanwhile a war is being carried on and the British troops are engaged
> with sharp losses.[26]

Eden requested observations from his officials, noting on 16 November that in
his opinion the UNC should pursue no new conditions beyond POW supervision.[27] Shattock prepared a minute for Eden stating that Britain had conveyed
its views to the Americans on various aspects of the armistic negotiations. He
provided a list – the air interdiction programme of UNC airforce, the proposal
to transfer the venue of the talks from Kaesong to another place, the importance
of exercising restraint in statements from UNC headquarters in the event of
negotiations breaking down to ensure that the blame was put on China and
recent enquiries as to why the talks had again become bogged down in matters
surrounding a demarcation line. For the present Shattock believed that there
was no need to make representations to Washington: Eden could mention to
Acheson, when they met in Paris the following week, that unease had been
voiced in some circles over the protracted nature of the talks. Eden could express
hopes for progress to be achieved as soon as practicable and perhaps add that
if the communists accepted the current UNC proposals then the latter should
not require too tight an inspection procedure for supervision of an armistice.[28]
In his reply to Churchill Eden stated that it had not been easy following the
course of the talks but it was beginning to become clearer. On 17 November the
UNC proposed that the demarcation line should be the present line of contact
with arrangements for a new line to be established if agreement was not reached
on the rest of the agenda within 30 days. In the previous ten days the UNC
negotiators were apprehensive that if the communists obtained agreement on a
demarcation line they would delay progress on other items, since a check would
have been implemented over military operations. The proposal made on 17
November was intended to obviate the dilemma.[29]

Churchill decided to request the COS to advise on the present military
position in Korea. He observed that before the armistice talks commenced the
UNC seemed to possess the upper hand, but several months had elapsed now

during which the Chinese had increased their resources and strengthened their artillery and airforce. Churchill wished to know whether American or other UN forces had been reinforced similarly; in addition, he enquired whether the Chinese were preparing a new offensive. If serious fighting occurred Churchill asked which were the vital targets in Manchuria that the Americans would want to attack. Churchill reflected, at the end of his minute for the COS on 26 November, that the principal responsibility for conducting the Korean war did not rest with the British but it was essential that the British government understood what was happening.[30]

On 29 November General McLean drafted a paper based on COS deliberations. Every effort should be made to attain an armistice and there was greater optimism in official British circles than in corresponding American circles over the chances of securing an armistice. Supervision raised obvious difficulties but the COS thought that the communists might accept supervision via teams headed by neutrals. If this did not materialise the alternatives consisted of the following: an armistice without satisfactory supervision and without threat of drastic action against China, an armistice without adequate supervision but with a threat of tough measures, or no armistice at all. The first possibility had nothing to commend it. If the second possibility arose, the problem would occur of having UNC bluff called or of risking global war. Canada, Australia and New Zealand were averse to this contingency; however, the Russians might restrain the Chinese from bellicosity and it might be feasible to reduce the number of British troops in Korea. Failure to conclude an armistice was preferable to the first possibility but the difficulties were manifest. The COS did not relish the prospect of keeping British troops in Korea for some time to come but the Anglo-American relationship required continued deployment in Korea. A prolonged stalemate would be detrimental to morale; additional forces would be needed to terminate the war successfully in military terms. Summing up, the COS concluded that the Americans must be reminded of the necessity for satisfactory supervision even if the talks broke down in consequence; they felt that the Americans wanted to secure an armistice so as to reassure American public opinion and did not wish to resume the war in the sense of pursuing a large offensive. On balance the COS favoured the second possibility – concluding without adequate supervision but with a threat of implementing drastic action against China: if a threat was devised, it should be in very general terms. The Americans put forward two specific suggestions for coercing China – a naval blockade or the bombing of airfields and bases in Manchuria. The COS believed that a blockade of China would take a long time to achieve full impact, would require massive resources, and to be wholly effective would have to incorporate Russian ports: this would risk a global war. A bombing campaign in Manchuria would not necessarily handicap Chinese offensive capacity seriously. In the opinion of the COS the only action which UNC air forces could constructively pursue in Manchuria would be the interdiction of communications and destruction of bases and power stations. Neither of these courses constituted a grave menace to the Chinese and it was not worth risking a world war in resorting to them. Furthermore such action would pose appreciable difficulties in Hong Kong. Undoubtedly the communists had gained from the negotiations in strengthening their forces and the UNC had not benefited to the same extent.[31]

On 30 November Churchill chaired a meeting attended by the COS, Eden and McLean. A difference of opinion regarding the probability of an armistice being observed by the communists existed between the British and the Americans. The British felt that an agreement would most likely be respected but the Americans were doubtful. The Americans were determined that an armistice agreement must be followed by a warning statement to the Chinese as regards the consequences of not honouring an agreement. The British attitude was that a warning declaration should be couched in general terms as in the case of Berlin: it would be unwise to be precise. It was imperative that the nature of a warning statement be discussed with the British beforehand. The meeting was in agreement that a naval blockade was more likely to provoke a third world war then a bombing campaign beyond the Yalu. If a naval blockade was enforced, Soviet ports must be excluded from its application even though this would largely nullify the blockade. In the longer term bombing of Chinese ports and communication centres would be far more efficacious than a blockade and was less likely to precipitate a world war. Churchill expressed scepticism that the Soviet Union would want a global conflict:

> The PRIME MINISTER, however, considered that Russia would start World War III when she wanted to: she certainly would not do so merely to honour her pledge to China. He was, therefore, not unduly worried about bombing targets in Manchuria. As regards a war with China, he considered that China was not a country against which one declared war; rather a country against which war was waged.[32]

Lord Ismay, the secretary of state for Commonwealth Relations, enquired about consultations with the Commonwealth. Churchill replied that Canada, Australia and New Zealand should be informed that a statement of British views would be sent to the State Department because of the urgency of the position. Churchill added that the Americans were showing a more positive attitude towards consultation than previously and this must be exploited:

> This was the first time since the Korean war began that the Americans had seen fit to consult us on any matter of major policy – this might even mark the beginning of a closer relationship between us. That was why it had not been possible to consult the Dominions earlier. India, on the other hand, should be told nothing at this stage.[33]

On 4 December the cabinet received a report from Eden based on discussions with the COS and an exchange of views between Eden and Dean Acheson during a foreign ministers' meeting in Rome. Eden stated that it appeared unlikely that effective supervision could be achieved and that communist forces had been strengthened while the armistice talks took place. Eden had been informed by Acheson that Ridgway should, in his view, be authorised to conclude an armistice even if it was not feasible to secure supervision that was wholly satisfactory. Doubts over supervision should be conveyed publicly to the UN and a trenchant warning transmitted to the communists over the grave repercussions of violating an armistice. Eden said that he had discussed the situation with Churchill and the COS and had given his reactions to the American government. He had suggested that a warning statement should be issued by the United States, Britain and as many of the countries participating in UN military operations as possible. The statement should be generalised and should state that in the circumstances contemplated, it might be impossible to localise conflict in Korea. It would not be possible for Britain to support a suggested naval blockade of China and it would be better, should the situation demand it, to approve the bombing of Chinese airfields, bases and junctions north of the Yalu river. There would be no question of launching a general attack on Chinese towns. The cabinet accepted Eden's statement and agreed that he should communicate the essential points to Attlee on a confidential basis.[34]

On 10 December the COS considered a letter from the Foreign Office summarising developments. It was agreed that a draft warning statement was needed in the absence of comprehensive supervisory arrangements. If it was possible to establish a supervisory body, then it must enjoy the right of unrestricted travel. As regards action following a breach of the armistice, the COS accepted Churchill's opinion that the Soviet Union would begin a world war only if it suited them. The importance of full consultation should be emphasised to the Americans. Some concern was voiced that the United States did not want information on the most recent exchanges forwarded to the 'Old Commonwealth'. A report from the joint intelligence committee was received. Lt. General Sir Nevile Brownjohn said that while he was in general agreement with the report, he believed that a future enemy air threat to ground forces had been understated.[35] Three days later the COS reviewed communist intentions during the coming six months. It was held that the communists would aim for a positive agreement and that in the effort to achieve this, they would be willing to spin out the talks indefinitely while simultaneously strengthening their forces in Korea. It was believed that the communists would respect an agreement once signed. The prospect of China intervening overtly in Indo-China was deemed unlikely but the Vietminh could attack with covert Chinese aid.[36] When the COS met on 18 December a telegram from Air Vice-Marshal Bouchier was considered in which Bouchier stated that the communist forces of Korea would be incapable again of achieving large-scale success or breakthrough with ground forces and they would be unable to use North Korean airfields. Field Marshal Slim described this as too sanguine: he was convinced that in certain circumstances the communists would be able to use North Korean airfields and they could mount an offensive with ground forces which could cause considerable trouble before it was contained. His colleagues concurred and the joint intelligence committee was asked to investigate as a matter of urgency.[37]

By the beginning of January 1952 the position was that progress had been made at Panmunjom in dealing with achievement of a demarcation line and inspection arrangements, although the latter continued to involve considerable difficulties concerning supervision. On 16 February it was proposed by the communists that Poland, Czechoslovakia and the Soviet Union should be nominated as members of the neutral inspection teams but the UNC opposed the Soviet nomination. Three days later agreement was reached that a political conference charged with securing a Korean settlement should be assembled within three months of an armistice being signed.

The most intractable issue turned out to be that involving the prisoners of war (POWs). The UNC proposed on 2 January that repatriation of POWs should be applied on a voluntary basis. The complication was that the Geneva convention of 1949 envisaged that POWs would be sent back to the states for which they fought when captured. In one sense this was a straightforward assumption. However, it was inappropriate for the situation obtaining in relation to Korea because large numbers of POWs did not wish to return to North Korea or China. The legal position was that the United States had approved but not ratified the Geneva convention while the Chinese communists had not participated in the preparation of the Geneva convention. North Korea had not originally accepted the application of the convention but had done so in July 1950 after the UNC confirmed its acceptance. The whole subject of the position of POWs was extremely complex and contentious: it took some months for the full range of problems to emerge. Once they had done so all concerned became familiar with the monotonous proclamation of the central dilemmas in the seemingly endless period until the armistice was finally signed. John Addis of the Foreign Office reviewed the position in a minute dated 24 January 1952. At this point he saw the deadlock as encompassing rehabilitation of airfields and voluntary repatriation of POWs. The UNC wanted an armistice agreement to prohibit extension of existing runways so as to facilitate use by jet aircraft, and the building of new airfields. The communists opposed prohibition as an unjustified intervention in their internal administration. As regards POWs the UNC argued that POWs on both sides should be able to choose repatriation or release so as to go elsewhere. Both of these issues had emerged quite recently: neither had been prominent in the principal problems identified when the talks began. The principle of restricting airfield construction had first been advanced at Panmunjom on 12 December. The principle of voluntary repatriation of POWs was first put forward on 2 January. In neither case had Britain been consulted before the principles were enunciated. It had been thought that inspection of airfields would be difficult to pursue but the communists conceded the principle of inspection on 3 December 1951 and advocated inspection by neutral teams. The UNC agreed to this proposal on 11 December. The communists accepted that they could not bring in more aircraft or arms and that if airfields were extended, they would be unable to move in new aircraft to be placed in them. Addis criticised the handling of negotiations by the UNC:

> The manner in which the United Nations Command have conducted the negotiations – rapid and unexplained changes of front on the main questions, and a policy of sometimes stepping up demands after concessions had been offered by the other side – has not contributed to removing the suspicion which undoubtedly exists on the Communist side that the Americans do not sincerely want an armistice. An offer is now necessary from our side to convince the Communists that the negotiations are genuine and to make progress possible.[38]

As regards airfields the concessions already made by the communists plus the warning statement to be conveyed afforded reasonable security for UN forces following the signing of an armistice. The progress made over airfields exceeded what had been expected at the time of the Rome conference at the end of November. Addis underestimated the potential of the POW question and commented rather naively that the armistice talks must not founder on this matter. He thought it curious that the Americans should be willing to risk the fate of American POWs in communist hands through pressing the principle of voluntary repatriation. Addis remarked that in Britain emotions were not so confused and it was doubtful whether the same attitude would emerge. In making this remark Addis underestimated the response of his political masters. Addis concluded that continuance of the existing deadlock would impose undue strain on East–West relations.[39]

Charles Johnston, head of the relevant department, examined the same issues four days afterwards. In essence he concurred in Addis's appraisal. The POW dispute was serious and involved genuine humanitarian considerations. He noted that the Americans, with the assistance of Kuomintang agents, had experienced some success in reindoctrinating Chinese POWs. He appeared to think that it should not be difficult for such Chinese to transfer to Chiang Kai-shek's army in Taiwan; this would be a boon for Chiang, since he had received no reinforcements since leaving the mainland and it would partially rejuvenate an ageing army. The Americans would not look forward to the convening of a political conference to decide the future of Korea, especially in an election year, but they would have to accept it. Johnston felt that a possible mutual agreement could be achieved through the communists compromising over repatriation in return for the Americans compromising over airfields. A great deal of progress had been made since negotiations began and it would be unfortunate if this was jeopardised through deadlock over the outstanding issues. He felt that the Americans did not show the same sense of urgency as the British: delicate as the position was, the time had come to pursue discussions with them. The assistance of neutral states could be invoked in achieving a solution to the dispute over POWs. He recommended approaching the American embassy in London.[40] Robert Scott agreed, observing that the Americans had not handled the questions of airfield inspection or POWs very competently.[41] Anthony Eden congratulated officials on the scope of the reviews and agreed that the Americans should be approached.[42]

President Truman determined for moral and practical political reasons to adopt an unyielding line over the POWs. It was repugnant for him to consider returning men to China or North Korea who hated the regimes in power and who would be tortured or murdered by their unforgiving states. Significant political dimensions were involved, too. Truman had been bitterly assailed by domestic opponents for the 'loss' of China and then for the reverses in Korea inflicted by Mao Tse-tung's armies. Now an opportunity occurred for demonstrating the attractions of the free world to those who had unwillingly served in communist armies. This was, of course, precisely the reason why the POW question was so objectionable to the communists. Having trumpeted the supposed superiority of communism to capitalism and having reiterated at tedious length the virtues of their states, they could scarcely acquiesce tamely in the refusal of many of their former soldiers to return to the delights of Chinese or North Korean society. In 1945 the American and British governments assented to the

forcible return of many Russians opposed to the communist government but
Truman refused to accept that this was a binding precedent. Churchill reacted
similarly and felt that Truman must be supported. What complicated matters
further was that much pressure had been exerted on some POWs, by American
administrations in prison camps and by Kuomintang or South Korea agents, to
refuse repatriation to their states. This became clear in the summer of 1952 with
revelations of alarming conditions prevailing in camps. Before this, Churchill
expressed exasperation at failure to make more headway in Korea. He addressed
Eden thus on 3 March: 'As you know, I have for some time past held that the
position in Korea had greatly deteriorated owing to the recovery the communists have made, not only of "face" by negotiating on equal terms but by
improving their Air Force and Artillery.' He alluded to a telegram sent by
Bouchier two days before reporting that the communists had constructed
powerful fortified lines: this presented a more disturbing picture than that
conveyed by General Omar Bradley previously.[43] Eden agreed but commented
that the UNC had also devised fortified lines; however, the calibre of the troops
in them was not as good as in the tried divisions. Eden added that he was puzzled
at the latest Soviet intervention, 'insisting upon themselves as one of the supervising neutrals'.[44] It looked less likely that the communists desired a settlement.
When he met Acheson in Lisbon recently, the latter was still professing optimism.

The Foreign Office investigated legal aspects relating to POWs and
concluded that it was impossible to sustain the argument for voluntary repatriation on the basis of the Geneva convention. Sir William Strang informed Eden
that the matter must be determined at ministerial level. Eden minuted on 21
March, 'I did not know that our legal grounds were so poor but this doesn't
make me like the idea of sending these poor devils back to death or worse.'[45]
F. S. Tomlinson wrote to Robert Scott on 2 April that he had spoken to Alexis
Johnson of the State Department to ascertain how the position in the
Panmunjom talks was viewed. Tomlinson pointed out that the British government had understood that when only one or two issues were outstanding, a
package deal would be negotiated. In Tomlinson's opinion three major items
remained to be resolved: whether the Soviet Union could act as a neutral inspec-
tor; rehabilitation of airfields; and the fate of POWs. Johnson replied that
Ridgway would not accept the Soviet Union as a member of an inspection team
but would accept Czechoslovakia and Poland. Johnson was cautiously sanguine
over the POW problem. Tomlinson emphasised that Britain must be consulted
before a final decision was reached in Washington on the POW issue. Johnson
was embarrassed at the stress placed on consultation: according to Tomlinson's
account, Johnson examined his fingernails for several seconds and said that it
was difficult to say when Britain would be consulted. Tomlinson repeated the
strength of opinion in Britain and added that a compromise must be reached.
Otherwise it might be necessary to consider abandoning the voluntary principle
or, alternatively, abandon the prospect of securing an armistice.[46] John Lloyd of
the Foreign Office minuted in acerbic tone that the State Department appeared
oblivious to the fate of UNC POWs and what was to happen: 'A little more solic-
itude for our own morale would be a good thing on their part.'[47]

Attention increasingly focused in Britain, in the summer of 1952, on the methods of screening POWs so as to ascertain their wishes regarding repatriation. Reassuring messages reached the Foreign Office from Washington to the effect that all was going smoothly. Eden conveyed this information to opposition politicians and to Parliament. For example, on 1 May he sent a joint letter to Clement Attlee and Clement Davies, leaders of the Labour and Liberal parties, and to Herbert Morrison stating that all POWs were understood to be fairly treated and had been told what the position was concerning repatriation. No pressure had been brought to bear on them and Kuomintang agents had not functioned as interpreters. The process of interrogation had been handled objectively. In the circumstances Eden felt that the UNC had no choice but to resist forced repatriation of POWs definitely wishing to say in the free world. Eden added that he was not ignoring the plight of British and Commonwealth POWs in communist hands and the natural concern of relatives and friends.[48] Clement Davies at once replied, agreeing that it would be unthinkable to compel 60,000 men to return against their will; he shared Eden's concern for worried relatives.[49] Attlee and Morrison sent brief acknowledgements.[50] Then in the second half of May, serious riots broke out in POW camps situated on Koje island, off the southern coast of Korea. This proved to be the ugly tip of a singularly ugly iceberg. The impression hitherto transmitted, of an orderly process of discovering the wishes of POWs, placed under no duress whatever, was abruptly shattered. What emerged was a sad and alarming picture of incompetent prison administration, of groups of POWs either of pro- or anti-communist persuasion, dominating particular camps and applying odious brutality, extending to torture and murder, to ensure that POWs opted for whatever response was desired by the prevailing hierarchy. The specific incidents in Koje included the capture of the American commandant by pro-communist POWs with the aim of forcing him to admit that unfair pressure had been applied to POWs with the use of much coercion. The deputy commandant agreed to issue a public statement admitting the communist allegations. Both senior officers were subsequently removed and demoted but the damage had been done. Details gradually reached the Foreign Office and created dissatisfaction. Eden sent a telegram to Washington on 21 May expressing profound anxiety. Evidence from the committee of the International Red Cross and press reports of events in Koje would raise fundamental doubts over the efficacy of the screening process. If pro-communist elements had possessed control of entire compounds into which American guards had been unable to advance, British public opinion would experience cynicism in grasping how, within ten days, 170,000 men were interrogated satisfactorily, 'individually and in reasonable privacy'.[51] Eden recommended that a second screening should be implemented to verify the results announced earlier.

On 23 May officials prepared a brief for Eden in which surprise was recorded at the latest revelation from Washington that the figure of 70,000 willing to accept repatriation was merely an estimate and that more than 40,000 POWs had still to be interrogated.[52] Charles Johnston minuted that this had not been appreciated and that the whole situation 'gets worse & worse'.[53] It was clear that the whole controversy over the POWs was not diminishing in intensity and that prospects for resolving the divergence between UNC and communist positions were as bleak as before. At this point additional controversy was injected by the UNC decision to implement bombing raids on power stations on the Yalu river on 23 June. Predictably this was regarded critically by many in Britain on the grounds that it would render concluding an armistice agreement still more difficult. The bombing was embarrassing because there had been no prior consultation and because the minister of defence, Viscount Alexander, and the minister of state in the Foreign Office, Selwyn Lloyd, were visiting Washington at the time and were neither consulted nor notified. Bradley told Alexander and Lloyd, when they met him on 24 June, that the targets were purely military. Alexander already had an appointment with Truman to tell him of the impression he had derived of the situation in Korea, which he had just visited. Alexander told Truman that he regarded the overall position as encouraging and that morale was satisfactory. Truman responded that he had approved the bombing raids on the power stations. Alexander remarked that the government could face invidious criticism in consequence. Bradley commented to Alexander, after they had left the White House, that responsibility for the failure to notify the British rested with the State Department.[54] This was confirmed shortly afterwards by the State Department. Freeman Matthews apologised and Selwyn Lloyd responded vigorously:

> Air bombing in the Yalu area was associated in the public mind with a new and significant extension of the war. The Yalu dams and power stations had long been a matter of public speculation and controversy and it was inevitable that any action in regard to them would arouse intense interest. His dilemma and that of the Minister of Defence was that although their visit was supposed to aim at closer cooperation and liaison and though they were on the spot, they had not been consulted upon what was generally taken to be an important change of policy. State Department maintained their line that they had not considered this a sufficiently large departure to require consultation. As we could not well challenge this admission of an error of judgement without directly imputing bad faith we left the matter there.[55]

General Mark Clark sent his apologies to Alexander for not telling him of the raids when they met in Korea: he said he had been unaware of the intended operation.[56]

The government faced critical questions in the House of Commons on 25 June and 2 July when a debate took place: the Labour opposition moved a motion regretting the failure of the government to obtain satisfactory consultation. The motion was defeated by 300 votes to 270 with the small band of Liberal MPs supporting the government.[57] The occasion was interesting for Churchill's revelation that the Labour government had assented in principle to the contemplated bombing in September 1951 but on the understanding that bombing of the Yalu plants would be in response to a renewed Chinese offensive. Churchill was dissuaded by Acheson from going too far in his information on grounds of not divulging confidential military details but Labour leaders were embarrassed.[58]

Certain officials in the Foreign Office had felt for some months that it was not wise to adhere to a rigid approach over repatriation. Churchill reiterated in a personal minute dictated on 12 July that:

> In my view there can be no question of forcing any Chinese prisoners-of-war
> to go back to Communist China against their will. These are the ones above
> all others who carry with them the moral significance as the ones who have
> opted for us would certainly be put to death or otherwise maltreated.[59]

John Addis added that the view in the department was that North Koreans
forcibly returned would more likely be victimised than the Chinese and it was
not certain that Chinese returned forcibly would be killed or otherwise
maltreated.[60] His superior, Charles Johnston, sharply observed that he would
not like to contemplate repatriation if he was a Chinese POW.[61] Churchill was
reluctant – in contrast to his approach in 1953 – to go too far by way of rebuk-
ing the Americans. He dictated a minute for Selwyn Lloyd on 26 August
stating that the United States was carrying almost all the burden of the Korean
war:

> It is very easy to talk about 'causing a general war in China' like the Socialists
> told us we would have a world war if we had fired the necessary volley at
> Abadan [a reference to the crisis in Iran in 1951]. I do not regard Communist
> China as a formidable adversary. Anyhow you can take it that for the next four
> or five years 400 million Chinese will be living just where they are now. They
> cannot swim, they are not much good at flying, and the Trans-Siberian railway
> is already overloaded. I do not see how they can get at us except in South-East
> Asia and Hong Kong.[62]

Churchill was prepared to consider measures being applied against China
provided they did not go too far. He expressed scepticism as to China's potential: 'I doubt whether Communist China is going to be the monster some people
imagine.'[63] His minute was provoked by a minute from Lloyd on 21 August
expressing anxiety that the Americans aimed to adopt too tough a line over
Korea in the UN General Assembly.[64]

In the autumn of 1952 attention focused on endeavouring, through diplomacy surrounding the meetings of the UN General Assembly, to reach a
compromise regarding the POW issue. It is as well to remind ourselves of the
number of POWs and of the revised thinking on numbers which had occurred
during 1952. At the start of the year it was thought that a minimum of 10 per
cent and a maximum of 25 per cent would refuse repatriation. The Truman
administration anticipated that approximately 116,000 out of a total of 132,000
prisoners and 18,000 out of 38,000 civilians would return; it was envisaged that
approximately 28,000 POWs and 30,000 civilians would decline to return and
that around 16,000 POWs and 20,000 civilians would oppose repatriation
forcibly. According to the results of the screening process in April 1952, approximately 70,000 wanted to return. After later rescreening it was reported that
those willing to accept repatriation totalled around 82,000; the eventual figure
of those accepting repatriation was 82,500, meaning that approximately 50,000
opted not to return.[65] The Americans advocated in August 1952 increased
economic pressure on China to be enforced through the Additional Measures
Committee of the UN General Assembly. Eden wrote to Churchill on 1
September that there were grave dangers in the American proposals. A thorough
embargo on trade with China would adversely affect Britain's economic posi-

tion and could entail the ruin of Hong Kong. A rigorous blockade would include the Soviet-controlled ports of Port Arthur, Dairen and Vladivostok in addition to Soviet and satellite shipping. A severance in diplomatic relations with China would do little to damage the communists and would remove a Western listening-post in Peking. The draft UN resolution devised by the Americans was too restrictive and limited the UNC negotiators in Panmunjom and, in any case, would give excessive publicity to the POW problem whereas quiet diplomacy was needed to tackle it. Eden forecast widespread opposition in the General Assembly to the American proposal. The Australian and South African governments held similar views to those of the Foreign Office. Eden concluded, 'We certainly should not be in the forefront of the opposition to the Americans but the essential thing is to avoid an open Anglo-American disagreement while the Assembly is sitting as happened over the resolution naming China an aggressor in February 1951.'[66] Churchill responded, 'Proceed as you propose: but don't lets fall out with US for the sake of Communist China.'[67]

Discussion in the UN between October and December 1952 centred around the Indian initiative to persuade each side to accept the establishment of a neutral commission which would be assigned responsibility for handling arrangements for POWs refusing repatriation. Nehru had long criticised American policy for truculence and absence of subtlety while equally deprecating communist intransigence. Nehru believed that Indian efforts in the UN and Peking could surmount the deadlock. His representative in the UN was the egregious Krishna Menon who combined nervous energy and persistence, with a not infrequent capacity for irritating those with whom he dealt because of the unpredictability of his initiatives. British ministers considered Menon to be well intentioned but tedious to deal with. The United States disliked Indian activity, feeling that the Indian aim was to weaken seriously the defence of principles regarded as basic in Washington. Eden, Selwyn Lloyd and Dean Acheson were the principal figures on the Western side in the hectic exchanges which occurred in the corridors of power occupied or haunted by the UN delegations. Appreciable strain was entailed for all concerned. Eden was in poor health, Acheson had endured prolonged pressure and savage personal attack from embittered opponents. Neither Eden nor Acheson particularly liked one another: Acheson was extremely arrogant and found certain of Eden's mannerisms annoying while Eden resented being lectured by his American colleague.[68] The looming presidential election in the United States complicated matters. A significant contribution was made by Lester ('Mike') Pearson, the Canadian external affairs minister who was the current president of the General Assembly.[69] Pearson was also a target for Acheson's acrid remarks. The British viewed the existing form of the draft Indian resolution as too woolly and imprecise. Menon contemplated release and repatriation as stipulated in the Geneva convention; establishment of a repatriation commission to attend to classification of POWs based on nationality and domicile; force should not be employed in deciding the fate of POWs who should possess the right of putting their cases to the repatriation commission.[70] British policy envisaged releasing POWs with provision for prompt repatriation; repudiation by both sides of use of force to return POWs following an armistice: appointment of neutral nations, to be assisted by joint teams from respective Red Cross societies with responsibility for seeing that the approved terms were implemented.[71]

Acheson wanted the terms to be as specific as possible. He wished to avoid arguments with the Pentagon. The presidential election resulted in the victory of the Republican candidate, General Dwight D. Eisenhower, over the Democrat, Governor Adlai Stevenson in a decisive personal vote of confidence in him, which also reflected a desire for change after a sustained period of Democratic dominance in the White House. Acheson was understandably sour at the Republican victory, not so much because of Eisenhower himself, who was a moderate Republican, as because of the influence some right-wing Republicans might achieve within the new administration when it assumed office in January 1953. Acheson warned that the Pentagon might encourage the president-elect into pursuing a harder line. The Americans did not like to think of Soviet satellites belonging to a commission but this could not be prevented if a solution was to be achieved. Progress was made in consultations between Eden and Menon and the latter produced a draft deemed acceptable by Eden. Acheson remained recalcitrant, arguing that Menon's amended version contained ambiguity over the disposal of POWs and that this could allow the communists to argue subsequently that the UN was not fulfilling the agreement correctly. During Eden's absence in London Selwyn Lloyd headed the British delegation in New York. Lloyd and Pearson tried to induce Acheson to become more cooperative but without success. At a meeting called by Acheson on 17 November, attended by representatives of 21 states, Lloyd argued in favour of the amended Indian proposal. Acheson spoke vehemently in the opposite direction but was supported only by the Australian and Greek delegates.[72] Acheson showed no signs of modifying his position and instead made additional efforts to convince the British to change sides.

When Eden returned he discovered that the atmosphere had deteriorated rather than improved. Eden rejected the speculation that Acheson's attitude was the consequence of Pentagon pressure: 'Acheson himself could not have been more rigid, legalistic and difficult.'[73] Eden added that he and others derived the impression that the 'United States Government were afraid of agreement at this time'.[74] Relations between the American and British delegates worsened and each resorted to selected press leaks to strengthen its position.[75] At this awkward moment an improbable agent of conciliation materialised in the person of Andrei Vyshinsky, the Soviet foreign minister. Vyshinsky proved negative in most of his contributions in New York and he suddenly produced a bitter onslaught on the Indian resolution during a debate in the First Committee of the UN. Acheson was presented with a magnificent opportunity to change course and he acted with speed and skill. He now praised Menon's efforts which he had castigated a short time before. He believed that the intention of the resolution needed sharpening but held that this should not be too difficult to accomplish. The Soviet Union and China confirmed their previous line that a cease-fire must precede determination of the POW issue. The United States voted in favour of the Indian resolution and this was carried against the opposition of the Soviet Union and its satellites.[76] No tangible progress had been made in resolving the gulf between the UNC and communist positions which remained as great as ever. However, the United States had been persuaded to act more constructively.

Eden reflected on the arduous discussions in which he and Lloyd had participated in a memorandum for the cabinet. Acheson had been difficult and on occasions most discourteous, as when he made derogatory remarks about Lloyd and Pearson when arriving for a meeting.[77] Eden described Acheson as having become more difficult to deal with than the American military, 'more royalist than the royalists'. Eden's personal animus was clear but there was no doubt that Acheson had been very intransigent.[78] While he was in New York Eden devoted appreciable effort to contacting General Eisenhower (who was in New York for part of the period) and to fostering cordial relations with him. Churchill and Eden knew him well from the Second World War and through his inauguration of NATO's military command. They thought well of him and welcomed his nomination as Republican candidate in 1952. Their doubts centred not on Eisenhower but on others who would occupy prominent roles in the new administration, not least the appointment of a secretary of state. Eden convinced an initially sceptical Eisenhower that much was to be said in favour of the Indian resolution; the result was that Eisenhower expressed gratitude for Indian endeavours and asked Eden to convey this to Nehru.[79] Churchill and Eden disliked the prospect of John Foster Dulles becoming the new secretary of state and Eden rather unwisely tried to prevent this. They thought that a better choice would be Governor Thomas E. Dewey of New York, twice unsuccessful Republican candidate for the presidency. When Eden met Eisenhower on 20 November the latter talked about his choice for the State Department:

> He began by saying he wished to explain to me that after all he had found it necessary to appoint Mr. Foster Dulles who would be his Secretary of State at least for a year. Eisenhower was almost apologetic about it. He explained that in view of Mr. Dulles's long training in foreign affairs and of the fact that he had been representative of the bipartisan foreign policy there had really been no choice in the matter. He had not asked Mr. Dulles to lunch that day because he thought we could talk more freely alone. Further, he wished me to know that if at any time I wanted to communicate with him I was not to hesitate to do so ...[80]

Eisenhower was determined that his administration would not be dominated and worn down by the Korean problem as the Truman administration had been.[81] He aimed to apply pressure to the Chinese reasonably soon so as to make evident that if they did not respond positively, the situation would become more painful for them as a result of economic and, conceivably, atomic action. The impression given in the records of meetings of the National Security Council (NSC) presided over by Eisenhower was that the new president was more assertive in foreign and defence questions than his predecessor and was more concerned to make an impact.[82] Eisenhower was unusual among American presidents in possessing greater experience in the foreign than the domestic sphere. He was excitable in some of his remarks and on occasions blew his top but in the main he showed a balanced, sensible approach and normally concluded his assessments by rejecting dangerous courses of action. Consideration was given to the possibility of conducting a limited military offensive to occupy the 'waist' of Korea, which would connote the capture of significant industrial areas within North Korea and concomitant improvements in UNC morale. Dulles told Eden on 5 March that while this was under discussion he could not guess what the military cost would be. The possibility of using the atomic weapon in Korea was discussed in the NSC. This was in no sense innovative, since periodic assessments of the possible deployment of atomic weapons had been pursued at various times during the war. It is likely that the United States was closer to using the bomb in November–December 1950 than in 1953. On 13 May Eisenhower revealed interest in using atomic weapons to remove the Chinese from their existing positions in Korea during a discussion in the NSC, but the military members present were doubtful of the effectiveness of such weapons in Korea.[83] The most serious aspect concerned the repercussions on America's allies of resorting to atomic retaliation. Eisenhower was well aware of European fears of a third world war from his recent service in Europe:

> there was simply nothing worse than global war for the reason that it would amount to the obliteration of European civilization ... We were already in considerable difficulties with these allies and, it seemed to the President, our relations with Great Britain had become worse in the last few weeks than at any time since the end of the war.[84]

Churchill took effective command of direction of British policy between April and June 1953 during Eden's prolonged absence for recuperation from a major operation. The prime minister was determined to seize every opportunity to advance the cause of *détente* with the Soviet Union. For some time Churchill had wished to reduce the harsh rigidities of the Cold War. Stalin's death in March 1953 appeared to offer the opportunity he sought. Churchill's decision to urge *détente* was courageous, since it was viewed dubiously by some of his colleagues inside and outside the government and it could be forecast that Eisenhower and Dulles would not view it with enthusiasm. Part of the explanation for Churchill's zeal probably lies in an elderly politician wishing to close his career on a note of triumph in addition to offering further justification for his continuance in office (as with Gladstone's emphasis on the importance of resolving Irish Home Rule from 1886). Churchill aimed to encourage faster progress in Korea and believed that an armistice should be attainable if the Russians exerted pressure in Peking and Pyongyang. In April 1953 agreement was reached at Panmunjom for an exchange of some sick and wounded POWs. Churchill was sceptical, as he had been for nearly a year, as to the wisdom of issuing a warning statement to the Chinese immediately after signature of an armistice agreement. He had long felt that this would strike a jarring note after 'kissing and making up'.[85] The State Department and the Pentagon were alarmed for they attached such importance to the 'Greater Sanctions Statement', which would convey to the Chinese in unambiguous terms the consequences of violating an armistice agreement.[86] On 4 May Churchill expressed, in the Commons, coded criticism of the direction of UNC negotiations at Panmunjom by General William Harrison, the head of the UNC team. Dissatisfaction had existed within the Foreign Office for an appreciable time with the talks in Panmunjom. Churchill stated that it should be possible to advance with the formulation of appropriate arrangements for dealing with POWs unwilling to be repatriated.[87] At the same time he rejected a Labour suggestion advanced by Barbara Castle (Labour, Blackburn) that it might be preferable for Britain to be directly involved in the negotiating team in Panmunjom. Showing his old debating skills, Churchill responded that General Harrison stood more chance of achieving agreement than would Mrs Castle if she went to Panmunjom.[88]

Churchill worked to encourage a positive Soviet contribution through developing links with Molotov who had again become foreign minister. Churchill sent a message to Molotov on 2 June in which he referred to wartime cooperation from 1941 to 1945 in the hope that future cooperation would reduce world tension. Churchill stated that it would be most beneficial 'if this Panmunjom prisoners-of-war business were got out of the way'.[89] Molotov replied immediately in cordial vein welcoming the prospect of exchanges. With reference to Panmunjom the outcome would not depend on the Soviet Union but 'we can state with satisfaction that the path to a successful conclusion of the negotiations has already been marked out'.[90] Thus Churchill was doing all he could to push both sides towards agreement. At this point Syngman Rhee moved again to the centre of the stage with impeccable timing. Rhee had always disliked negotiations at Panmunjom, since he was totally committed to Korean unification on his terms. Rhee was an astute politician and appreciated that he could hardly stop the United States from concluding an armistice if Eisenhower and Dulles decided to sign it. He could test American resolution and if the United States was adamant, he could obtain concessions in return for his reluctant acquiescence; such concessions would include a mutual security treaty and economic aid. Eisenhower and Dulles fully recognised Rhee's capacity for causing trouble. Churchill sympathised with the invidious position facing General Mark Clark, the head of UNC, and he incorporated praise for Clark in remarks made in the Commons on 9 June. Clark was most grateful and told the British ambassador in Tokyo, Sir Esler Dening, of his problems in controlling the POW camps properly because many prison guards were South Koreans. Clark told Dening that Rhee could procure a breakout of POWs if he wished and it would be impossible to stop him.[91]

On 4 June agreement was reached at Panmunjom that POWs would be handed over to the Neutral Nations Repatriation Commission (NNRC): the latter comprised Czechoslovakia, Poland, Sweden, Switzerland and India, with Indian troops functioning as guards. POWs accepting repatriation should be returned home within 60 days of an armistice. Those refusing repatriation would be held for a further period of between 90 and 120 days and it would be possible for the countries in whose forces they had fought to put arguments to them as to why they should accept repatriation. Non-repatriates would ultimately be freed or decisions on their future would be made by the UN General Assembly. On 18 June Rhee moved to undermine the agreement through releasing 25,000 North Korean POWs; this was fiercely denounced by the communists and threatened the signing of the armistice. Churchill reacted vehemently and sent a message to Molotov on 20 June to defuse the tension: 'I am sure the United

States Government are deeply angered by Syngman Rhee's outrage and so are we. We must not let our thoughts on dangerous issues be unduly disturbed by this sinister event.'[92] Three days later Churchill suffered a stroke and the Marquess of Salisbury took over day-to-day supervision of the Foreign Office. Churchill began to recover some days later and steps were taken to conceal the seriousness of the stroke. However, Churchill dealt with some business and communicated his ire in a personal minute dictated on 2 July, commenting on the contingency of the Americans deciding to allow Rhee to be removed by the communists:

> The first question is whether the United States can afford to leave Rhee to his fate and accept a Communist subjugation of Korea. It is purely a question of American sentimental pride ... Myself, I think the United States are so powerful that they can afford to be indifferent to a local Communist success. They could afford to let Rhee be squelched and Korea communised and spend the money saved on increasing their armaments ... If I were an American, as I might have been, I would vote for Rhee going to hell and taking Korea with him and would talk to the Americans direct on a heavily armed basis.[93]

Lord Salisbury replied on 3 July and pointed to the absurdity of the UNC possibly fighting both Rhee and the communists. The situation was alarming in its implications and would astonish those whose sons were serving in the armed forces and, equally, those who supported the ideals of the UN.[94] Consideration had been given in Washington to organising a coup in order to depose Rhee but there were obviously grave risks entailed plus implications for the UN itself and it was decided to keep this in reserve as an absolutely last resort. An assistant secretary of state for far eastern affairs, Walter Robertson, was despatched to Korea to negotiate with Rhee. Robertson experienced predictable problems but his mission was ironically helped in that the communists implemented new military offensives in June and July. Under the combined pressures facing him, Rhee reluctantly undertook not to obstruct conclusion of an armistice agreement, although he firmly refused to sign for the ROK. At long last, and amidst speculation to the end, an armistice was signed at Panmunjom on 27 July 1953. This took effect 12 hours afterwards and the military engagements of the Korean war were terminated. The British government was unhappy about issuing a warning statement, directed at China. However, Eisenhower considered it imperative to issue it and the statement appeared in the joint policy declarations by the allies on 7 August.[95]

The Korean war ended because the UNC and the communists were weary of it and felt that the law of diminishing returns applied to each side. Both sides could derive limited solace from the outcome. From the viewpoint of the UNC, North Korean aggression was repulsed and the ROK sustained. For the communist states the prowess of the Chinese army had been demonstrated and China was viewed far more seriously than before the war. Kim Il Sung survived the tergiversations of the conflict and possessed the means to establish his own power on an enduring basis. Syngman Rhee similarly survived and secured important guarantees from the United States; however, his personal power base was vulnerable so he did not resemble Kim Il Sung in this respect. For Great Britain the war involved sacrifice for limited rewards. Huge strains were imposed on Britain's fragile economic revival and the political and economic strains helped to finish the Labour government. Churchill and the Conservatives found the war as exasperating as their predecessors. The principle of combating perceived aggression through the UN was sustained but Anglo-American relations experienced great tensions. At the end of July 1953 there was still more than enough by way of Korean controversy to occupy those involved in deciding the final fate of POWs and in endeavouring to convene the political conference, provided for in the armistice agreement to ascertain if a reunified Korea could somehow be achieved. The omens were not encouraging.

On 8 August 1953 a mutual defence treaty was signed between the United States and the ROK, a step which the Truman administration had failed to provide before the Korean war but which was now inevitable as part of the process of inducing Rhee to acquiesce in the armistice. Appreciable financial aid was extended to the ROK. The British position regarding a political settlement was defined by Robert Scott when he met Walter Robertson in the State Department on 24 September. The objective should be to create a unified, neutralised Korea; this could be realised in three stages – free elections in the whole of Korea, unification and neutralisation including withdrawal of forces.[96] Implacable opposition to compromise came from Rhee. Dulles told Scott, when they met on 9 October, that the fundamental American aim in Korea was to prevent resumption of fighting. If war resumed, it could spread into a conflict involving China fully. One of the difficulties Dulles alluded to was a familiar theme extending back to 1949: that Rhee and Chiang Kai-shek shared a common interest in war occurring and cared little for the consequences. Chiang was easier to control, since he was isolated in Taiwan and the United States denied him enough ships to permit an invasion of the mainland. Rhee was more challenging to handle, since he was 'a wily and shrewd gambler'.[97] Rhee was persisting in a gamble to compel American action. There was a risk that if a political conference did not take place, Rhee could argue that the armistice terms had not been met and that he was, therefore, no longer obliged to observe them. Dulles intimated that the British should grasp that his purpose was to outmaneouvre Rhee. Vice-President Richard Nixon visited Seoul during a tour of Asian capitals. He was given specific guidance by President Eisenhower and was told to exercise great caution in discussions with Rhee. Nixon acted accordingly. He described Rhee as possessing a conspiratorial approach, 'not unlike that of a Communist'.[98] Nixon made clear to Rhee that he would not receive American support if he took rash action.

Political talks proceeded at Panmunjom to see if sufficient preliminary exchanges could pave the way for a political conference. The American delegate, Arthur Dean, was a capable Wall Street lawyer described by Gladwyn Jebb as 'a truly remarkable Republican Representative'.[99] Dean's personal views on how to deal with Peking 'appear to be slightly to the left of Her Majesty's Opposition' but he had to act toughly so as to impress right-wing Republicans.[100] This explained Dean's decision to walk out of the talks in Panmunjom following acrid Chinese observations concerning American policy. Dean was pessimistic over prospects for success in a political conference but nevertheless recommended proceeding.

One of the most delicate problems following conclusion of the armistice centred on the fate of POWs. The NNRC faced thorny issues. The honest wishes of POWs were to be met if possible but the ultimate fate of Chinese and North Korean POWs refusing to return to the states in whose armies they had fought was uncertain. Because of the adamant line pursued by the communist states, POWs in this category would be held pending later decisions. The role of chairing the NNRC was bound to be extremely demanding. Churchill pressed Nehru to accept 'this thankless task' and Nehru agreed.[111] The Indian contribution was most valuable and was fulfilled effectively amidst condemnation by China and both Korean states. The NNRC (comprising India, Sweden, Switzerland, Poland and Czechoslovakia) commenced work on 9 September 1953 and its members pursued their task industriously. On 20 January 1954, according to figures provided by India, a total of 14,227 Chinese and 7,582 North Koreans were handed to the UNC. The Chinese released sailed to Taiwan on 21 January: 104 POWs remained in camp and they wanted to go to a neutral country.[102] The work of the NNRC ended formally on 21 January. Anthony Eden paid a well-deserved tribute to the Indian forces when he spoke in the House of Commons on 22 February.[103]

Korea was a focal point for international discussion at the Berlin conference in January 1954. The British government's policy regarding a political settlement comprised eventual attainment of a unified, neutralised Korea to be accomplished in five stages embracing free elections in the whole of Korea under international supervision, creation of a government for all of Korea, based on the elections, unification of Korea, steps towards neutralisation, and departure of foreign forces on both sides. If it proved impossible to obtain a unified Korea, alternatives should be considered, such as continuance of a divided Korea with suitable guarantees, possibly including a buffer zone in the centre. Britain advocated convening a five-power conference to discuss Korea. The Soviet Union agreed, in the Berlin conference, that a further conference be convened in Geneva in April 1954. However, the priority in Asia now shifted from Korea to Indo-China. The Geneva conference was preoccupied with the latter. John Addis reflected philosophically, 'If we have in effect sacrificed our poor little Korean baby to attain a settlement in Indo-China, it will have been worthwhile.'[104]

The failure of the Geneva conference to achieve a political solution in Korea was entirely predictable but was nevertheless disappointing. The British approach was one of dogged persistence in striving to reduce differences. Eden worked most strenuously to secure progress over Korea and Indo-China. The reluctance of Eisenhower and Dulles to challenge right-wing Republicans compounded the dilemmas: American policy was imprisoned within the harsh rigours of the Cold War. The one consolation for the British was a slight thaw in Anglo-Chinese relations. At a private dinner between four British and Chinese diplomats during the Geneva conference, one of the Chinese proposed a toast, 'To the one great achievement of the Geneva Conference, the improvement of relations between our two countries.'[105]

Notes

1 For an examination of the armistice negotiations, see B. J. Bernstein, 'The Struggle over the Korean Armistice: Prisoners of Repatriation', in B. Cumings (ed.), *Child of Conflict: The Korean–American Relationship, 1943–1953* (London: University of Washington Press, 1983), pp. 261–307, Peter Lowe, 'The Settlement of the Korean War', in J. W. Young (ed.), *The Foreign Policy of Churchill's Peacetime Administration, 1951–1955* (Leicester: Leicester University Press, 1988), pp. 207–31, and Rosemary Foot, *A Substitute for Victory: The Politics of Peacemaking at the Korean Armistice Talks* (London: Cornell University Press, 1990).
2 Chiefs of staff conclusions, 11 July 1951, COS(51)114, Defe 4/45.
3 COS(51)120, 23 July 1951, Defe 4/45.
4 COS(51)124, 1 August 1951, Defe 4/45.
5 COS(51)137, 29 August 1951, Defe 4/46.
6 COS(51)147, 19 September 1951, Defe 4/47.
7 FO to Washington, 11 July 1951, FO 371/92788/660.
8 Minute by Addis, 11 July 1951, FO 371/92787/633.
9 Korea to FO, 10 July 1951, FO 371/92788/652.
10 FO to Washington, 3 August 1951, FO 371/92788/674.
11 Washington to FO, 23 August 1951, FO 371/92792/773.
12 FO to Washington, 30 August 1951, *ibid.*
13 Washington to FO, 31 August 1951, FO 371/92793/795.
14 New York to FO, 11 September 1951, FO 371/92793/814.
15 See Foot, *A Substitute for Victory*, pp. 42–73.
16 FO to Washington, 29 July 1951, FO 371/92790/718.
17 FO to Washington, 21 September 1951, FO 371/92793/816.
18 Letter from R. H. Scott to Tomlinson, 29 September 1951, FO 371/92795/841.
19 For a discussion of the concluding phase of the Labour government in 1950–1, see K. O. Morgan, *Labour in Power, 1945–1951* (Oxford: Clarendon Press, 1984).
20 Minute by Shattock, 16 October 1951, FO 371/92795/867.
21 Minute by Morrison, 17 October 1951, *ibid.*
22 For an account of Churchill's final years, see Martin Gilbert, *Winston S. Churchill*, vol. VIII, *Never Despair, 1945–1965* (London: Heinemann, 1988): part 3 deals with his second premiership, 1951–55.
23 For a discussion of Eden's career, see Robert Rhodes James, *Anthony Eden* (London: Weidenfeld and Nicolson, 1986).
24 See Evelyn Shuckburgh, *Descent to Suez* (London: Weidenfeld and Nicolson, 1986).
25 See Rhodes James, *Anthony Eden*, pp. 362–5.
26 Minute by Churchill, 16 November 1951, Prem 11/112.
27 Minute by Eden, 16 November 1951, FO 371/92797/912.
28 Minute by Shattock, 20 November 1951, *ibid.*
29 Eden to Churchill, 21 November 1951, Prem 11/112.
30 Minute by Churchill, 26 November 1951, *ibid.*
31 Paper signed by McLean, 29 November 1951, Prem 11/112. General Sir Kenneth McLean was chief of staff to the minister of defence.
32 COS(51)3, 30 November 1951, Prem 11/112.
33 *Ibid.*
34 Cabinet conclusions, CC14(51)2, 4 December 1951, Cab 128/23.
35 COS(51)200, 10 December 1951, Defe 4/50.
36 COS(51)764, memorandum, 13 December 1951, Defe 5/35.
37 COS(51)206, confidential annex, 18 December 1951, Defe 4/50.
38 Minute by Addis, 24 January 1952, FO 371/99564/34.
39 *Ibid.*
40 Minute by Johnston, 28 January 1952, FO 371/99565/52.
41 Minute by R. H. Scott, 29 January 1952, *ibid.*
42 Minute by Eden, 31 January 1952, *ibid.*
43 Minute by Churchill, 3 March 1952, FO 371/99568/122/G.

44 Minute by Eden, 3 March 1952, *ibid.*
45 Minutes by Strang and Eden, 20 and 21 March 1952, FO 371/99569/151.
46 Letter from Tomlinson to R. H. Scott, 2 April 1952, FO 371/99570/171.
47 Minute by J. O. Lloyd, 14 April 1952, *ibid.*
48 Letter from Eden to Attlee, Davies, and Morrison, 1 May 1952, FO 371/99572/215A.
49 Letter from Davies to Eden, 1 May 1952, *ibid.*
50 Acknowledgements from Attlee and Morrison to Eden, 1 May 1952, *ibid.*
51 FO to Washington, 21 May 1952, FO 371/99573/254.
52 Brief for Eden's meeting with Acheson, 3 May 1952, FO 371/99573/268.
53 Minute by Johnston, no date, *ibid.*
54 Washington to FO, 24 June 1952, FO 371/99598/15.
55 Washington to FO, 24 June 1952, FO 371/99598/16.
56 Tokyo to FO, 27 June 1952, FO 371/99599/25.
57 See *Parliamentary Debates, Commons,* fifth series, vol. 502, col. 2247ff. and vol. 503, col. 269ff.
58 For discussion of the bombing of the power plants, see Foot, *A Substitute for Victory,* pp. 136–7. General Bradley said that the attacks were implemented in order to 'ginger up' the peace process (Foot, p. 137).
59 Minute by Churchill, 12 July 1952, FO 371/99581/409.
60 Minute by Addis, 22 July 1952, *ibid.*
61 Minute by Johnston, 23 July 1952, *ibid.*
62 Minute by Churchill, 26 August 1952, Prem 11/301.
63 *Ibid.*
64 Minutes by Selwyn Lloyd, 21 August 1952, *ibid.*
65 See Bernstein 'Struggle over the Korean Armistice', in Cumings (ed.), *Child of Conflict,* pp. 284–6, 307.
66 Minute by Eden for Churchill, 1 September 1952, Prem 11/301.
67 Minute by Churchill, 3 September 1952, *ibid.*
68 Shuckburgh, *Descent to Suez,* p. 56, diary entry for 20 November 1952.
69 For Pearson's views as recorded in his diaries, see Lester Pearson, *Mike: The Memoirs of the Right Honourable Lester B. Pearson* ed. J. A. Munro and A. I. Inglis, vol. II, *1948–1957* (Toronto: University of Toronto Press, 1973), pp. 316–30.
70 New York to FO, 6 November 1952, FO 371/99589/621.
71 Commonwealth Relations Office to high commissioners in Commonwealth capitals, 6 November 1952, FO 371/99589/622.
72 New York to FO, 17 November 1952, FO 371/99589/646.
73 New York to FO, 23 November 1952, FO 371/99590/665.
74 *Ibid.*
75 Shuckburgh, *Descent to Suez,* p. 53, diary entry for 19 November 1952.
76 FO to Singapore (for commissioner-general, South-East Asia), 5 December 1952, FO 371/99592/732.
77 For Acheson's comments on Pearson, see Shuckburgh, *Descent to Suez,* pp. 53–4.
78 Cabinet conclusions, C(52)441, Cab 129/57.
79 Record of telephone conversation between Eden and Eisenhower, 18 November 1952, FO 371/99591/706 and text of personal message from Eden to Nehru, 25 November 1952, FO 371/99591/694G.
80 Despatch from Eden to Steel (Washington), 4 December 1952, Prem 11/323.
81 For discussion of Eisenhower's views, see Stephen Ambrose, *Eisenhower,* 2 vols (London: Allen & Unwin, 1983–4).
82 See NSC minutes in *FRUS 1952–1954,* vol. XV.
83 *FRUS 1952–1954,* vol. XV, p. 806.
84 *Ibid.,* p. 1016.
85 Lowe, 'Settlement of the Korean War', in Young (ed.), *Foreign Policy of Churchill's Administration,* pp. 223–4.
86 *FRUS 1952–4,* vol. XV, pp. 968–9.
87 Minute by Addis, 5 May 1953, FO 371/105489/196.
88 Statement in House of Commons, 4 May 1953, enclosed in FO 371/105489/196.

89 FO to Moscow, enclosing personal message from Churchill to Molotov, 2 June 1953, Prem 11/406.
90 FO to Moscow, 3 June 1953, *ibid.* This message was delivered by Malik in London.
91 Tokyo to FO, 10 June 1953, FO 371/105499/416.
92 Message to Churchill to Molotov, 20 June 1953, delivered to Malik at the Soviet embassy, Prem 11/406.
93 Minute by Churchill for Salisbury, 2 July 1953, FO 371/105508/626.
94 *Ibid.*
95 Peter Lowe, 'The Korean War in Anglo-U.S. Relations, 1950–53', in M. Dockrill and J. W. Young (eds), *British Foreign Policy, 1945–56* (London: Macmillan, 1989), p. 145.
96 Letter from R. Scott to D. Allen, 24 September 1953, FO 371/105531/341.
97 Washington to FO, 9 October 1953, FO 371/105532/385.
98 *FRUS 1952–1954*, vol. XV, pp. 1660–2, memorandum of NSC meeting, 15 December 1953.
99 Letter from Jebb to Kirkpatrick, 25 December 1953, FO 371/105538/589.
100 *Ibid.*
101 Minute by Selwyn Lloyd for Churchill, 22 January 1954, FO 371/110619/97.
102 Washington to FO, 22 January 1954, FO 371/110622/113.
103 *Parliamentary Debates, Commons*, 22 February 1954, enclosed in FO 371/110626/201. See also O. Lidin, 'Armistice in Korea, 1953–1955 – Private Recollections', in Ian Nish (ed.), *Aspects of the Korean War*, International Studies, 1987/1 (London: LSE, 1987), pp. 23–36. Note the full statistics cited in Foot, *A Substitute for Victory*, p. 191.
104 Draft letter from Addis to Peking, 23 June 1954, FO 371/110565/547.
105 Minute by Addis, 17 June 1954, FO 371/110565/545.

CONCLUSION

This study has examined the part played by British ministers and officials in the evolution of East Asia between 1948 and 1953. The era was crucial in the development of the region since it encompassed the victory of the communists in China, led by Mao Tse-tung; the conclusion of the allied occupation of Japan with the restoration of sovereignty to the Japanese state; and a savagely fought civil and international war in Korea which ensured the viability of South Korea and confirmed the political division of the Korean peninsula. Great Britain did not determine Western policies in East Asia but it did exert moderating influence on the United States on significant occasions. The Cold War necessitated cooperation between the two powers: Britain considered an American commitment to defend Western Europe to be funamental and this meant that a serious rift in Anglo-American relations must be avoided.

In 1948 British policy-makers experienced growing unease in contemplating the courses of action pursued (or not pursued) by the United States in East Asia. In China the Truman administration was tied to an incompetent, corrupt regime incapable of solving the problems of Chinese society and which appeared ever more likely to be hurled into the 'dustbin of history'. President Truman and Secretary of State Dean Acheson possessed no faith in Generalissimo Chiang Kai-shek but the consequences of the Cold War, linked with domestic political realities in the United States, rendered it impossible to envisage recognition of a government controlled by the CCP within the foreseeable future. The American reaction was fortified by the ingredient of moral approval when it came to granting recognition to a new government. This feature was absent from British policy. Clement Attlee, Ernest Bevin and their cabinet colleagues reacted in a spirit of vigorous British common sense: by the autumn of 1949 the CCP controlled most of mainland China and had declared itself formally to be the government of China. In such circumstances, and bearing in mind the exposed position of Hong Kong, pressure from India, and the aspirations entertained for British trade in China, recognition of the PRC was imperative. Attlee and Bevin wished to avoid divergence from the United States and for this reason devoted much time to diplomatic exchanges between London and Washington in the second half of 1949. The Truman administration was made fully aware of British thinking and determination to reach a decision reasonably soon. British leaders were influenced by the comforting but erroneous opinion that the United States would have to come to terms with the inevitability of communist victory in China as the year 1950 unfolded. Instead of this attractive scenario the last five weeks of 1950 saw UN forces locked in deadly conflict with the PRC's armed forces in Korea. Rather than the United States moving towards the PRC, the danger existed of the Truman administration becoming involved in all-out war against China and of Britain and the UN being dragged into war, too.

In Japan, American policy concentrated upon integrating a revived economy and state within the Western defence structure aimed at the containment of the Soviet Union and China and, additionally, at the containment of communist movements in South-East Asia. This trend emerged with increasing clarity between 1948 and 1950 and was stimulated powerfully by the impact of the Korean war. Britain contributed little to the formulation of allied policy in Japan: ministers and officials were unhappy with several of the distinguishing features of American policy. A spirit of excessive magnanimity marked the approaches of the 'Japan lobby' in Washington and of General MacArthur's administration in Tokyo, notwithstanding the sharp differences between the two. Despite reservations over MacArthur's generous treatment of the Japanese, the Foreign Office was more impressed by MacArthur than by his critics. The latter seemed to favour a swifter revival of the Japanese economy regardless of the danger of stimulating militarism. British reactions were governed by fears of renewed competition threatening British industries and exports and of a future military–naval threat materialising, as apprehended by Australia and New Zealand. The British deemed American policy towards Japan to be much more solid (if with potential danger in Japan, too) than American policies towards China and Korea prior to June 1950 but this was more of a comment on the latter than the former. A basic criticism in Whitehall between 1948 and 1950 was the failure to conclude a peace treaty with Japan. This was soon resolved through the great skill and devious manoeuvres of John Foster Dulles. He succeeded brilliantly in handling daunting challenges, internationally and domestically. It was, of course, ironical that the principal success for American policies in East Asia in the later 1940s and early 1950s resulted from the industry and zealous commitment of a Republican politician, serving temporarily a Democratic administration and motivated by the ardent desire to secure a Republican administration in Washington in January 1953 with himself as secretary of state. It was equally ironical that the man sharing the credit with Dulles for American success was also a Republican, if with loyalties lying elsewhere in the Republican party – Douglas MacArthur. British ministers and officials respected the achievements of both men in Japan but felt that Dulles was sometimes too adroit and unduly motivated by ulterior considerations. However, whatever the doubts, the peace treaty signed in San Francisco in September 1951 was a great achievement, although the signing of the ANZUS treaty underlined American dominance in the Pacific.

Korea was an obvious focal point for serious trouble on a par with Berlin for the same reason: the frontier of the Cold War was particularly dangerous given the confrontation between the Soviet Union and the United States and the nature of the rival regimes promoted by the two powers between 1945 and 1948. In British eyes American policy in Korea comprised a fusion between adventurism and vacillation with the latter gaining the upper hand down to June 1950. The involvement of the UN in Korea from 1947 onwards was a cause for regret rather than rejoicing. The United States expected the UN to endorse American policy and resented criticisms coming from the independently minded members of UN commissions. British officials were worried that the Truman administration could not sustain South Korea and would leave the problem for the UN to resolve, which would culminate in tarnishing the prestige of the UN as an organisation. Korea would probably become a communist peninsula. Syngman Rhee was no more attractive than Chiang Kai-shek, as perceived in London. He was imbued with similarly vacuous rhetoric which provided a wafer-thin veneer for a regime characterised by brutality, oppression and economic mismanagement. It was Rhee's luck to be in the right place at the right time in that a communist challenge in Korea had to be resisted by the United States when the challenge was thrown down in accordance with the philosophy driving NSC-68. When the crunch occurred mainland China was expendable, although Taiwan was defined as essential to deny to the PRC on the eve of the Korean war. The ROK was worthy of support because the prestige of the 'free world' would suffer gravely, possibly producing a 'domino effect' in various parts of the globe if communism triumphed in Korea. Soviet ineptitude allowed the United States to seize the initiative in the UN Security Council and to commit the UN to opposing the DPRK and, subsequently, China in the Korean struggle. UN policy was usually controlled or dominated by the United States throughout the Korean war. Britain committed itself to military participation in Korea because it had no alternative once President Truman decided to oppose North Korea militarily. The 'special relationship' necessitated joint action. The key to understanding Britain's role during the Korean conflict is to appreciate that British leaders – Attlee, Bevin, Churchill and Eden – saw themselves as stabilising influences, aiming to dissuade the Truman administration from impulsive or foolish decisions. This connoted no resort to atomic weapons, staying in the Korean peninsula instead of evacuating it in January 1951, not pressing condemnation of China too far in the UN, and not implementing excessively harsh economic measures against China, and then of demonstrating a greater preparedness to compromise during the later stages of the interminable armistice talks in Panmunjom in 1952–53. The Attlee and Churchill governments achieved some success in influencing the Truman and Eisenhower administrations in the directions favoured because each administration needed to secure continued cooperation, politically and militarily, with its allies. In addition, Truman, Acheson, Eisenhower and Dulles fully concurred that Europe was the priority: disagreements over Asia must not undermine the commitment to Europe. Naturally this priority worked both ways and explained why Britain could not allow friction in Anglo-American relations to go too far.

After the Korean war ended in July 1953, the Churchill government hoped for a definitive political settlement in Korea. The hopes were too sanguine and the first Geneva conference, in the spring of 1954, saw the effective burying of any prospect of a settlement until at least the demise of the 'Great Leader', Kim Il Sung. In 1954 China was stronger than before, defiant if largely isolated in terms of its relations with the West. Japan was recovering economically at a rapid rate, attributable in part to the repercussions in Japan of the demands arising from the Korean war. A question-mark surrounded the future direction of politics in Japan but the likelihood was that the right-wing forces would succeed in consolidating control further. Japan was incorporated within the Western defence structure in Asia; Australia and New Zealand were satisfied with the protection afforded by the ANZUS treaty. British power declined gradually while American might expanded powerfully in the 1950s. Britain concentrated on the challenges of decolonisation, departing from Malaya and Singapore in the later 1950s but still fulfilling an important defence role in defending Malaysia against Indonesia with the help of Australia and New Zealand, and then of focusing gradually upon the delicate and complex issues of departing from its last important colony, Hong Kong.

In the light of the savage blows dealt by Japan in 1941–42, Britain achieved more than might have been expected in returning actively to Asia in 1945 and after. Certainly Britain was more successful than the Netherlands and France in coping with colonial rule or, rather, terminating colonial rule. Britain also avoided the horrors of the Vietnam war, experienced so traumatically by the United States. The nearest equivalent for Britain was the Suez débâcle in 1956 but this belonged to the sphere of declining British power in the Middle East. The watersheds in East Asia were profound between 1948 and 1954 and the concomitants determined the character of international relations in East Asia for many years and, in a number of respects, to the present.

SELECT BIBLIOGRAPHY

Official papers

Public Record Office, Kew

Air 8	Chief of Air Staff, selected files
Cab 128	Cabinet minutes, 1948–54
Cab 129	Cabinet memoranda, 1948–54
Cab 130	Selected files relating to Economic Relations with Japan and visit of Australian Prime Minister, 1950
Cab 131	Defence Committee
Cab 133	Commonwealth Meetings, 1948–54
Cab 134	Far Eastern (Official) Committee; China and South-East Asia Committee
Defe 4	Ministry of Defence, Chiefs of Staff minutes, 1947–54
Defe 5	Chiefs of Staff memoranda, 1947–54
Defe 6	Joint Planning Staff papers, 1947–54
DO 35	Commonwealth Relations Office, selected files
DO 121	Commonwealth Relations Office, selected files
FO 371	Foreign Office, General Political Correspondence, files relating to China, Japan, Korea, 1948–54; Czechoslovakia, 1948; Germany (Berlin blockade), 1948–9; Soviet Union, 1948–53; United Nations, 1948–54; United States, 1948–54
FO 800	Papers of Ernest Bevin
Prem 8	Prime Minister's Office, selected files
Prem 11	Prime Minister's Office, selected files

National Archives, Washington, D.C.

Record Group 59, State Department, Decimal Files, 795, 1950, Korea; Record Group 218, Joint Chiefs of Staff files, Decimal files 091, 092, relating to Soviet Union and Eastern Europe, UN Command Operations in Korea, Wake island conference, Asia, Australia, Formosa, Korea, Omar Bradley papers, North Atlantic Treaty, China, Indo-China, MacArthur Hearings; Record Group 319, Army Operations, General, 1950–51, Decimal Files 091, Korea, 1950–51

Private papers

Great Britain

Cambridge:
Churchill College, Cambridge

Clement Attlee (1st Earl Attlee) papers
Philip Noel-Baker Papers
William Slim (1st Viscount Slim) papers

Durham:
University of Durham Library
Malcolm MacDonald papers (previously in temporary possession of the Royal
    Commonwealth Society, London)

London:
British Library of Political and Economic Science
Hugh Dalton (Baron Dalton) papers and diaries
Liddell Hart Centre for Military Archives, King's College
Sir Patrick Brind papers
Sir William Elliot papers
Private possession
Kenneth Younger diaries (Lady Younger, in temporary possession of Professor
    Geoffrey Warner)

Manchester:
John Rylands University Library of Manchester
Raymond Streat diaries (previously in temporary possession of Sir George Kenyon)

Oxford:
Western Manuscripts Department, Bodleian Library
Clement Attlee (1st Earl Attlee) papers

United States

Abilene, Kansas:
Dwight D. Eisenhower Library
John Foster Dulles papers
Dwight D. Eisenhower papers: Pre-Presidential files, 1916–1952, Ann Whitman
    Files, White House Central Files

Independence, Missouri
Harry S. Truman Library
Dean Acheson papers
George M. Elsey papers
Edgar A. J. Johnson papers
Thayer papers
Harry S. Truman papers: Foreign Affairs files, Official files: Selected Records relat-
    ing to Korean War, Department of Defense, Department of State; President's
    Secretary's files: CIA memoranda and reports and papers dealing with Korean
    War; General files; Post-Presidential files
James E. Webb papers

Norfolk, Virginia
Douglas MacArthur Memorial
Douglas MacArthur papers
Charles A. Willoughby papers

Princeton, New Jersey
Seeley G. Mudd Library, Princeton University
John Foster Dulles papers
George F. Kennan papers

Stanford, California
Hoover Institution on War, Revolution and Peace, Stanford University
David Dean Barratt papers
Hyden L. Boatner papers
Forrest Caraway papers
Claire Lee Chennault papers
M. Preston Goodfellow papers
Joseph E. Jacobs papers
Charles Turner Joy papers
Walter H. Judd papers
George H. Kerr papers
Roger Dearborn Lapham papers
George Fox Mott papers
John Leighton Stuart papers
Freda Utley papers

Washington, D.C.
Library of Congress
Loy Henderson papers
Robert A. Taft, Sr papers

Oral histories

Vernice Anderson
Niles W. Bond
Sir Ashley Clarke
Matthew J. Connelly
George M. Elsey
Lord Franks
Walter H. Judd (two separate interviews)
Robert A. Lovett
Sir Roger Makins (Lord Sherfield) (two separate interviews)
Livingston Merchant
John J. Muccio (two separate interviews)
Charles S. Murphy
Robert G. Nixon
Arthur D. Ringwalt
Earl Warren
Copies of the above are located in the Harry S. Truman Library, Independence, Missouri.

Published documentary series

Documents on British Policy Overseas, 1945–1955, series II, selected volumes. Note particularly vol. IV, Korea, 1950–1951. This volume was published after the research for this study was completed. It constitutes a most valuable selection of British documents, including many cited here from the original PRO files.

Documents on New Zealand External Relations, 3 vols (Wellington, 1972–85)

Foreign Relations of the United States, selected volumes, 1948–54 (Washington, D.C.)

Military Situation in the Far East. Hearings before the Committee on Armed Services and the Committee on Foreign Relations, United States Senate, 82nd Congress, First Session, To Conduct an Inquiry into the Military Situation in the Far East and the Facts Surrounding the Relief of General of the Army Douglas MacArthur from his Assignment in that Area. 5 parts (Washington, D.C.: Government Printing Office, 1951)

Dae-sook Suh, *Documents of Korean Communism, 1918–1948* (Princeton, NJ, 1970)

United Nations, Security Council Official Records. Fifth year, 1950 (New York, 1950)

United Nations, *Report of the United Nations Commission on Korea: Covering the Period from 15 December 1949 to 4 September 1950* (New York, 1950)

Newspapers

The British Labour Party's Foreign Press Cuttings Collection, John Rylands University Library of Manchester. This comprises a broad range of cuttings, taken largely from the British press. This was consulted for the period between 1945 and 1955.

Trade reports

Manchester Chamber of Commerce, Annual Reports and Monthly Record, 1948–54.

Memoirs and diaries (published)

Acheson, Dean, *Present at the Creation: My Years in the State Department* (London: Hamish Hamilton, 1970)

Allison, John M., *Ambassador from the Prairie* (Tokyo; Charles E. Tuttle, 1975)

Eden, Anthony, *Full Circle* (London: Cassell, 1960)

Eisenhower, Dwight D., *Mandate for Change* (New York: Doubleday & Co., 1963)

Waging Peace (New York: Doubleday & Co, 1965)

The Eisenhower Diaries, ed. Robert H. Ferrell (London: Norton, 1981)

Gaitskell, Hugh, *The Diary of Hugh Gaitskell, 1945–1956*, ed. Philip M. Williams (London: Jonathan Cape, 1983)

Gromyko, Andrei, *Memories* (London: Hutchinson, 1989)

Kennan, George F., *Memoirs, 1925–1950* (London: Hutchinson, 1968)

Memoirs, 1950–1963 (Boston: Little, Brown, 1972)

Khruschev, Nikita, S., *Khruschev Remembers* (London: Andre Deutsch, 1971)

MacArthur, Douglas, *Reminiscences* (London: Heinemann, 1965)

McGibbon, Ian (ed.), *Undiplomatic Dialogue: Letters between Carl Berendsen and Alister McIntosh, 1943–52* (Auckland: Auckland University Press, in association with the Ministry of Foreign Affairs and Trade and the Historical Branch, Department of Internal Affairs, 1993)

Pearson, Lester, *Mike: The Memoirs of the Right Honourable Lester B. Pearson*, vol. II *1948–1957*, ed. John A. Munro and Alex. I. Inglis (Toronto: University of Toronto Press, 1973)

Peng Teh-huai, *Memoirs of a Chinese Marshal: A Cultural Revolution 'Confession' by Marshal Peng Dehuai (1898–1974)* (Beijing: Foreign Languages Press, 1984)

Ridgway, Matthew B., *The War in Korea* (London: Barrie & Rockcliffe/The Cresset Press, 1967)

Sebald, William J., with Russell Brines, *With MacArthur in Japan: A Personal History of the Occupation* (London: Cresset Press, 1967)

Shuckburgh, Evelyn, *Descent to Suez: Diaries, 1951–56*, selected for publication by John Charmley (London: Weidenfeld & Nicolson, 1986)

Truman, Harry S., *Memoirs: Year of Decisions, 1945 and Years of Trial and Hope, 1946–52*, paperback edition (New York: Signet Books, 1965)

Secondary sources

Adamthwaite, Anthony, 'Britain and the World, 1945–9: The View from the Foreign Office', *International Affairs*, 61, no. 2 (1985), pp. 223–35.

Ambrose, Stephen, *Eisenhower*, 2 vols (London: Allen & Unwin, 1983–84)

———*Nixon*, vol. I, *The Education of a Politician, 1913–1962* (London: Simon and Schuster, 1987)

Anderson, Terry H., *The United States, Great Britain and the Cold War, 1944–1947* (London: University of Missouri Press, 1981)

Bachrack, Stanley, D., *The Committee of One Million: 'China Lobby' Politics, 1953–1971* (New York: Columbia University Press, 1976)

Bell, Roger J., *Unequal Allies: Australian–American Relations and the Pacific War* (Melbourne: Melbourne University Press, 1977)

Beloff, Max, *Soviet Policy in the Far East, 1944–1951* (London: Oxford University Press, 1953)

Bernstein, Barton J., 'New Light on the Korean War', *The International History Review*, 3, no. 2 (April 1981)

Blum, Robert M., *Drawing the Line: The Origin of American Containment Policy in East Asia* (London: Norton, 1982)

Borg, Dorothy and Waldo Heinrichs (eds), *Uncertain Years: Chinese–American Relations* (New York: Columbia University Press, 1980)

Buckley, Roger D., *Occupation Diplomacy: Britain, the United States and Japan, 1945–1952* (Cambridge: Cambridge University Press, 1982)

———*US–Japan Alliance Diplomacy, 1945–1990* (Cambridge: Cambridge University Press, 1992)

Buhite, R. D., "Major Interests": American Policy towards China, Taiwan, and Korea, 1945–1950', *Pacific Historical Review*, 47 (1978) pp. 425–51

Bullock, Alan, *The Life and Times of Ernest Bevin*, vol. III, *Foreign Secretary, 1945–1951* (London: Heinemann, 1983)

Burkman, Thomas W. (ed.), *The Occupation of Japan: The International Context* (Norfolk, VA: MacArthur Memorial, 1984)

Cable, James, *The Geneva Conference of 1954 on Indochina* (London: Macmillan, 1986)

Cairncross, Alec, *Years of Recovery: British Economic Policy 1945–1951* (London: Methuen, 1985)

Caridi, Ronald, *The Korean War and American Politics: The Republican Party as a Case Study* (Philadelphia: University of Pennsylvania Press, 1968)

Carlton, David, *Anthony Eden: A Biography* (London: Allen Lane, 1981)

Chang, Gordon H., *Friends and Enemies: The United States, China and the Soviet Union, 1948–1972* (Stanford, CA: Stanford University Press, Stanford, 1990)

Chen, Jian, *China's Road to the Korean War: The Making of the Sino-American Confrontation* (New York: Columbia University Press, 1994)

Clough, Ralph N., *Embattled Korea: The Rivalry for International Support* (London: Westview Press, 1987)

Cohen, Warren I. (ed.), *New Frontiers in American–East Asian Relations: Essays presented to Dorothy Borg* (New York: Columbia University Press, 1983)

Cohen, Warren I. and Akira Iriye (eds), *The Great Powers in East Asia, 1953–1960* (New York: Columbia University Press, 1990)

Cotton, James and Ian Neary (eds), *The Korean War in History* (Manchester: Manchester University Press, 1989)

Cumings, Bruce, *The Origins of the Korean War*, 2 vols (Princeton: Princeton University Press, 1981–90)

——(ed.), *Child of Conflict: The Korean–American Relationship, 1943–1953* (London: University of Washington Press, 1983)

Deighton, Anne (ed.), *Britain and the First Cold War* (London: Macmillan, in association with the Graduate School of European and International Studies, University of Reading, 1990)

Dingman, Roger, 'Atomic Diplomacy during the Korean War', *International Security*, 13, no. 3 (1988–89), pp. 50–91.

Divine, Robert A., *Eisenhower and the Cold War* (Oxford: Oxford University Press, 1981)

Dockrill, Michael, 'The Foreign Office, Anglo-American Relations and the Korean War, June 1950–June 1951', *International Affairs* 62 (1986), pp. 459–76.

Dockrill, Michael and J. W. Young (eds), *British Foreign Policy, 1945–56* (London: Macmillan, 1989)

Dockrill, Saki (ed.), *From Pearl Harbour to Hiroshima: The Second World War in Asia and the Pacific, 1941–45* (London: Macmillan, 1994)

Donovan, Robert J., *Tumultuous Years: The Presidency of Harry S. Truman, 1949–1953* (London: Norton, 1982)

Douglas, Roy, *From War to Cold War, 1942–1948* (London: Macmillan, 1983)

Dower, John W., *Empire and Aftermath: Yoshida Shigeru and the Japanese Experience, 1878–1954* (Cambridge, MA: Harvard University Press, 1979)

Drifte, Reinhard, *The Security Factor in Japan's Foreign Policy, 1945–1952* (East Sussex: Saltire Press, 1983)

Duus, Peter (ed.), *The Cambridge History of Japan*, vol. VI, *The Twentieth Century* (Cambridge: Cambridge University Press, 1989)

Eastman, Lloyd E., *Seeds of Destruction: North China in War and Revolution, 1937–1949* (Stanford, CA: Stanford University Press, 1984)

Fairbank, J. K. and Albert Feuerwerker (eds), *The Cambridge History of China*, vol. XIII, *Republican China, 1912–1949* (Cambridge: Cambridge University Pres, 1986)

Farrar, Peter N., 'Britain's Proposal for a Buffer Zone south of Yalu in November 1950', *Journal of Contemporary History*, 18, no. 2 (1983), pp. 327–51.

Farrar-Hockley, Anthony, *Official History: The British Part in the Korean War*, 2 vols (London: HMSO, 1990–95)

Feng, Zhong-ping, *The British Government's China Policy, 1945–1950* (Keele: Keele University Press, 1994)

Finn, Richard B., *Winners in Peace: MacArthur, Yoshida and Postwar Japan* (Oxford: University of California Press, 1992)

Foot, Rosemary, *The Wrong War: American Policy and the Dimensions of the Korean Conflict, 1950–1953* (Ithaca and London: Cornell University Press, 1985)

A Substitute for Victory: The Politics of Peacemaking at the Korean Armistice Talks

(London: Cornell University Press, 1990)

Franks, Sir Oliver, *American Impressions*, oration delivered at the London School of Economics, 11 December 1953 (London: LSE, 1954)

Fraser, T. G. and Peter Lowe (eds), *Conflict and Amity in East Asia: Essays in Honour of Ian Nish* (London: Macmillan, 1992)

——with Keith Jeffery (eds), *Men, Women and War: Historical Studies*, vol. XVIII, *Papers read before the XXth Irish Conference of Historians* (Dublin: Lilliput Press, 1993)

Gaddis, John, *Strategies of Containment* (Oxford: Oxford University Press, 1982)

——*The Long Peace: Inquiries into the History of the Cold War* (Oxford: Oxford University Press, 1987)

Gilbert, Martin, *Winston S. Churchill*, vols VI and VII, (London: Heinemann, 1986–8)

Gillin, D. G. and Charles Etter, 'Staying On: Japanese Soldiers and Civilians in China, 1945–1949', *Journal of Asian Studies*, 42, no. 3 (1983), pp. 497–518

Gimbel, John, *The Origins of the Marshall Plan* (Stanford, CA: Stanford University Press, 1976)

Goncharov, Sergei N., John W. Lewis and Xue Litai, *Uncertain Partners: Stalin, Mao and the Korean War* (Stanford, CA: Stanford University Press, 1994)

Gopal, Sarvepalli, *Jawaharlal Nehru: A Biography*, vol. II, *1947–1956* (London: Jonathan Cape, 1979)

Gordenker, Leon, *The United Nations and the Peaceful Unification of Korea: The Politics of Field Operations, 1947–1950* (The Hague: Martinus Nijhoff, 1959)

Grajdanzev, Andrew J., *Modern Korea* (New York: Institute of Pacific Relations, distributed by the John Day Company, 1944)

Grey, Jeffrey, *A Military History of Australia* (Cambridge: Cambridge University Press, 1990)

——*Australian Brass: The Career of Lieutenant-General Sir Horace Robertson* (Cambridge: Cambridge University Press, 1992)

Halliday, Jon, and Bruce Cumings, *Korea: The Unknown War* (London: Viking, 1988)

Harries, Meirion and Susie, *Sheathing the Sword: The Demilitarisation of Japan*, paperback edition (London: Heinemann, 1987)

Harris, Kenneth, *Attlee* (London: Weidenfeld & Nicolson, 1982)

Heller, F. and J. Gillingham (eds), *NATO: The Forming of the Atlantic Alliance and the Integration of Europe* (London: Macmillan, 1992)

Henderson, Gregory, *Korea: The Politics of the Vortex* (Cambridge, MA: Harvard University Press, 1968)

Henderson, Nicholas, *The Birth of NATO* (London: Weidenfeld & Nicolson, 1982)

Higgins, Rosalyn, *United Nations Peacekeeping, 1946–1967: Documents and Commentary*, vol. II, *Asia* (Royal Institute of International Affairs/Oxford University Press, 1970)

Higgins, Trumbull, *Korea and the Fall of MacArthur: A Precis in Limited War* (New York: Oxford University Press, 1960)

Hogan, Michael J., *The Marshall Plan: America, Britain and the Reconstruction of Western Europe, 1947–1952* (Cambridge: Cambridge University Press, 1987)

Holloway, David, *Stalin and the Bomb: The Soviet Union and Atomic Energy, 1939–1956* (London: Yale University Press, 1994)

Immerman, Richard H. (ed.), *John Foster Dulles and the Diplomacy of the Cold War* (Princeton: Princeton University Press, 1990)

James, D. Clayton, *The Years of MacArthur*, vol. III, *Triumph and Disaster, 1945–1964* (Boston, MA: Houghton Mifflin, 1985)

James, Robert Rhodes, *Anthony Eden* (London: Weidenfeld & Nicolson, 1986)

Kim, Joungwon A., *Divided Korea: The Politics of Development, 1945–1972* (Cambridge, MA: Harvard University Press, 1976)

Kimball, Warren F., *The Juggler: Franklin Roosevelt as Wartime Statesman* (Princeton: Princeton University Press, 1991)

Koen, Ross Y., *The China Lobby in American Politics*, ed. Richard C. Kagan, paperback edition (London: Harper & Row, 1974)

Kolko, Joyce and Gabriel, *The Limits of Power: The World and United States Foreign Policy, 1945–1954* (London: Harper & Row, 1972)

Lane, Anne and Howard Temperley (eds), *The Rise and Fall of the Grand Alliance* (London: Macmillan, 1995)

Large, Stephen, *Emperor Hirohito and Showa Japan* (London: Routledge, 1992)

Levine, Steve I., *Anvil of Victory: The Communist Revolution in Manchuria, 1945–1948* (New York: Columbia University Press, 1987)

Long, Edward W., 'Earl Warren and the Politics of Anti-Communism', *Pacific Historical Review*, 51 (1982), pp. 51–70

Louis, Wm. Roger and Hedley Bull (eds), *The Special Relationship: Anglo-American Relations since 1945*, paperback edition (Oxford: Oxford University Press, 1989)

Lowe, Peter, *The Origins of the Korean War* (London: Longman, 1986)

——with Herman Moeshart (eds), *Western Interactions with Japan: Expansion, the Armed Forces and Readjustment, 1859–1956* (Folkestone: The Japan Library, 1990)

——'Great Britain, the United Nations, and the Korean War, 1950–3', in Ian Nish (ed.), *Aspects of the Korean War, International Studies* 1987/1 (London: Suntory Toyota International Centre for Economics and Related Disciplines, London School of Economics, 1987), pp. 1–22

——'An Ally and a Recalcitrant General: Great Britain, Douglas MacArthur, and the Korean War, 1950–1', *English Historical Review* 105, no. 416 (1990), pp. 624–53

——'Herbert Morrison, the Labour Government, and the Japanese Peace Treaty, 1951', *International Studies*, IS/93/258 (STICERD, London School of Economics, 1993), pp. 1–27

——'The British Liaison Mission and SCAP, 1948–52: Exchanges during the Latter Part of the Occupation', *Japan Forum*, 5, no. 2 (1993), pp. 245–56

——'Sir Alvary Gascoigne in Japan, 1946–1951', in Ian Nish (ed.), *Britain and Japan: Biographical Portraits* (Folkestone: The Japan Library, 1994), pp. 279–94, 340–2

Luard, Evan, *A History of the United Nations*, vol. I, *The Years of Western Domination, 1945–1955* (London: Macmillan, 1982)

MacDonald, Callum, *Korea: The War before Vietnam* (London: Macmillan, 1986)

MacFarquhar, Roderick and J. K. Fairbank (eds), *The Cambridge History of China*, vol. XIV (Cambridge: Cambridge University Press, 1987)

McCormack, Gavan, 'The Reunification of Korea: Problems and Prospects', *Pacific Affairs*, 55, no. 1 (1982), pp. 5–31

McGibbon, Ian, *New Zealand and the Korean War*, vol. I *Politics and Diplomacy* (Auckland: Oxford University Press, in association with the Historical Branch, Department of Internal Affairs, Auckland, New Zealand, 1993)

McGlothlen, Ronald, *Controlling the Waves: Dean Acheson and U.S. Foreign Policy in Asia* (London: Norton, 1993)

McIntyre, W. David, *Background to the Anzus Pact: Policy-Making, Strategy and Diplomacy, 1945–55* (London: Macmillan, 1995)

Merrill, John, *Korea: The Peninsular Origins of the War* (London: Associated University Presses, 1989)

Messer, Robert L., *The End of an Alliance: James F. Byrnes, Roosevelt, Truman, and the*

Origins of the Cold War (Chapel Hill, NC: University of North Carolina Press, 1982)

Milward, Alan S., *The Reconstruction of Western Europe, 1945–51* (London: Methuen, 1984)

Morgan, Kenneth O., *Labour in Power, 1945–1951* (Oxford: Clarendon Press, 1984)

Murfett, Malcolm H., *Hostage of the Yangtze: Britain, China and the Amethyst Crisis of 1949* (Annapolis, MD: Naval Institute Press, 1991)

——*In Jeopardy: The Royal Navy and British Far Eastern Defence Policy, 1945–1951* (Kuala Lumpur: Oxford University Press, 1995)

Myant, Martin, *Socialism and Democracy in Czechoslovakia, 1945–1948* (Cambridge: Cambridge University Press, 1981)

Myers, Ramon H. and Mark R. Peattie (eds), *The Japanese Colonial Empire, 1895–1945* (Guildford: Princeton University Press, 1984)

Nagai, Yonnosuke and Akira Iriye (eds), *The Origins of the Cold War in Asia* (Tokyo: Univeristy of Tokyo Press, 1977)

Newman, Robert P., *Owen Lattimore and the 'Loss' of China* (Oxford: University of California Press, 1992)

Nish, Ian (ed.), *Anglo-Japanese Alienation, 1919–1952: Papers of the Anglo-Japanese Conference on the History of the Second World War* (Cambridge: Cambridge University Press, 1982)

——(ed.), *The East Asian Crisis, 1945–1951: The Problem of China, Korea and Japan*, International Studies 1982/1 (ICERD, London School of Economics, 1982)

——(ed.) *Aspects of the Allied Occupation of Japan*, International Studies, 1986/4 (London: ICERD, London School of Economics, 1986)

O'Neill, Robert, *Australia in the Korean War, 1950–53*, vol. I, *Strategy and Diplomacy* (Canberra: The Australian War Memorial and the Australian Government Publishing Service, 1981)

Ovendale, Ritchie, *The English-Speaking Alliance: Britain, the United States, the Dominions and the Cold War, 1945–1951* (London: Allen & Unwin, 1985)

——(ed.), *The Foreign Policy of the British Labour Governments, 1945–51* (Leicester: Leicester University Press, 1984)

Paige, Glenn, D., *The Korean Decision* (London: Collier-Macmillan, 1968)

Porter, Brian, *Britain and the Rise of Communist China: A Study of British Attitudes, 1945–1954* (London: Oxford University Press, 1967)

Reardon-Anderson, James, *Yenan and the Great Powers: The Origins of Chinese Communist Policy, 1944–46* (New York: Columbia University Press, 1980)

Reeves, Thomas, C., *The Life and Times of Joe McCarthy: A Biography* (London: Blond & Briggs, 1982)

Rothwell, Victor, *Britain and the Cold War, 1941–1947* (London: Jonathan Cape, 1982)

Scalapino, Robert A., and Chong-sik Lee, *Communism in Korea*, 2 parts (Berkeley: University of California Press, 1972)

Schaller, Michael, *The American Occupation of Japan: The Origins of the Cold War in Asia* (New York: Oxford University Press, 1985)

——*Douglas MacArthur: The Far Eastern General* (New York: Oxford University Press, 1989)

Schnabel, James F. and Robert J. Watson, *The History of the Joint Chiefs of Staff*, vol. III, 2 parts, *The Korean War* (Wilmington, DE: Michael Glazier, Inc., 1979)

Schonberger, Howard, *Aftermath of War: Americans and the Remaking of Japan, 1945–1952* (London: Kent State University Press, 1989)

Schram, Stuart R., *Mao Zedong: A Preliminary Reassessment* (Hong Kong: Chinese University Press, 1983)

Shao, Wenguang, *China, Britain and Businessmen: Political and Commercial Relations, 1949–57* (London and Oxford: Macmillan/St Antony's College, 1991)

Shlaim, Avi, *The United States and the Berlin Blockade, 1948–1949: A Study in Crisis Decision-Making* (London: University of California Press, 1983)

Short, Anthony, *The Communist Insurrection in Malaya, 1948–1960* (London: Frederick Muller, 1975)

——*The Origins of the Vietnam War* (London: Longman, 1989)

Simmons, Robert R., *The Strained Alliance: Peking, Pyongyang, Moscow and the Politics of the Korean Civil War* (London: Collier-Macmillan, 1975)

Singh, Anita Inder, *The Limits of British Influence: South Asia and the Anglo-American Relationship, 1947–56* (London: Pinter, 1993)

Smith, R. B., *An International History of the Vietnam War*, vol. I, *Revolution vs Containment 1955–61* (London: Macmillan, 1983)

Stueck, William W. Jr., *The Road to Confrontation: American Policy towards China and Korea, 1947–1950* (Chapel Hill, NC: University of North Carolina Press, 1981)

Suh, Dae-sook, *Kim Il Sung: the North Korean Leader* (New York: Columbia University Press, 1988)

Takeda, Kiyoko, *The Dual Image of the Japanese Emperor* (London: Macmillan, 1988)

Tang, James Tuck-Hong, *Britain's Encounter with Revolutionary China, 1949–54* (London: Macmillan, 1992)

Thorne, Christopher, *Allies of a Kind: The United States, Britain, and the War against Japan, 1941–45* (London: Hamish Hamilton, 1978)

Tsang, Steve (ed.), *In the Shadow of China: Political Developments in Taiwan since 1949* (London: Hurst, 1993)

Trotter, Ann, *New Zealand and Japan, 1945–1952: The Occupation and the Peace Treaty* (London: Athlone Press, 1990)

Tucker, Nancy B., *Patterns in the Dust: Chinese–American Relations and the Recognition Controversy, 1949–1950* (New York: Columbia University Press, 1983)

Van Ree, Erik, *Socialism in One Zone: Stalin's Policy in Korea, 1945–1947* (Oxford: Berg, 1989)

Watt, D. Cameron, *Succeeding John Bull: America in Britain's Place, 1900–1975* (Cambridge: Cambridge University Press, 1984)

Weathersby, Kathryn, *Soviet Aims in Korea and the Origins of the Korean War, 1945–1950: New Evidence from Russian Archives*, Cold War International History Project (Washington, D.C.: Woodrow Wilson International Center for Scholars, 1993)

Weiler, Peter, *British Labour and the Cold War* (Stanford, CA: Stanford University Press, 1988)

Whiting, Allen S., *China Crosses the Yalu: The Decision to Enter the Korean War* (London: Macmillan, 1960)

Wilson, Dick, *Chou: The Story of Zhou Enlai, 1898–1976* (London: Hutchinson, 1984)

Wolf, David, C., "To Secure a Convenience": Britain Recognises China – 1950', *Journal of Contemporary History*, 18, no. 2 (1983), pp. 299–326

Yoshitsu, Michael M., *Japan and the San Francisco Peace Settlement* (New York: Columbia University Press, 1983)

Young, John W., *Cold War Europe, 1945–89: A Political History* (London: Edward Arnold, 1991)

——*The Longman Companion to Cold War and Detente, 1941–91* (London: Longman, 1993)

——(ed.), *The Foreign Policy of Churchill's Peacetime Administration, 1951–1955* (Leicester: Leicester University Press, 1988)

INDEX